To: Lil —

" To change and change for the
better are two different things
                        German

Anneliese

A Child of War

Margot Palmgren

*Margot Palmgren
AKA Wright
neé Rester*

PublishAmerica
Baltimore

First printing

All events in this autobiography are true as seen through the eyes of the author. Some names have been changed to protect privacy.

At the specific preference of the author, PublishAmerica allowed this work to remain exactly as the author intended, verbatim, without editorial input.

ISBN: 1-4241-0575-7
PUBLISHED BY PUBLISHAMERICA, LLLP
www.publishamerica.com
Baltimore

Printed in the United States of America

Dedicated in memory of James Kerrigan, Fullerton College English instructor, who encouraged me to write in my second language.

Acknowledgements

The author wishes to thank:

Barbara Benedict of RWA who was the first to inspire me to write my story.

Marilys Wills and the people in my critique group who helped me Anglicize my Germanic language.

Barbara French, creative writing, and the critique group.

Margot J. Wright, my daughter, for typing the manuscript.

Table of Contents

CHAPTER ONE—The Night of the Broken Glass—Kristallnacht 9

CHAPTER TWO—Aryans—Winter 1938 18

CHAPTER THREE—The Assault—January 1939 30

CHAPTER FOUR—The Yarn—Spring 1939 39

CHAPTER FIVE Lina—Summer—1939 45

CHAPTER SIX—War—September 1939 53

CHAPTER SEVEN—Victory—Spring 1940 60

CHAPTER EIGHT—Hannelore—May—1940 65

CHAPTER NINE—Surprise Assault 1940 72

CHAPTER TEN—Summer 1940 80

CHAPTER ELEVEN—The Axis Cracks—1941 90

CHAPTER TWELVE—Winter 1941 98

CHAPTER THIRTEEN—Day Attack 1942 101

CHAPTER FOURTEEN—Russia—Winter 1942 111

CHAPTER FIFTEEN—Evacuation—Early Spring 1943 116

CHAPTER SIXTEEN—Austria—Spring 1943 120

CHAPTER SEVENTEEN—The Erlkoenig—Late Spring 1943 130

CHAPTER EIGHTEEN—Recovery—Summer 1943 137

CHAPTER NINETEEN—Heilbronn—Late Summer 1943 144

CHAPTER TWENTY—School—Fall 1943 152

CHAPTER TWENTY-ONE—Trains—Fall 1943 159

CHAPTER TWENTY-TWO—Trapped—Spring 1944 167

CHAPTER TWENTY-THREE—Invasion 1944......................................174

CHAPTER TWENTY-FOUR—Brackenheim—Summer 1944 180

CHAPTER TWENTY-FIVE—Olga—Winter 1944 190

CHAPTER TWENTY-SIX—Sonja's Story—December 1944 197

CHAPTER TWENTY-SEVEN—Wally's Story—December 1944 204

CHAPTER TWENTY-EIGHT—Beginning of 1945 212

CHAPTER TWENTY-NINE—Good Friday 219

CHAPTER THIRTY—Confirmation—Easter Sunday 1945 227

CHAPTER THIRTY-ONE—Looting—Easter Monday 1945.................233

CHAPTER THIRTY-TWO—Angst—Wednesday after Easter 241

CHAPTER THIRTY-THREE—Defeat—April 1945 250

CHAPTER THIRTY-FOUR—Capitulation—May 1945 257

CHAPTER THIRTY-FIVE—Shelters—Summer 1945 265

CHAPTER THIRTY-SIX—Return—October 1945 273

CHAPTER THIRTY-SEVEN—Frankfurt—Fall 1945 279

CHAPTER THIRTY-EIGHT—Coping—Early November 1945 286

CHAPTER THIRTY-NINE—Winter—November 1945 293

CHAPTER FORTY—Shame—November 1945 299

CHAPTER FORTY-ONE—Needs—Mid 1946 304

CHAPTER FORTY-TWO—Growing Up—Fall 1946..........................312

CHAPTER FORTY-THREE—Acceptance—March 1947 319

FAMILY PHOTOGRAPHS 330

CHAPTER ONE—The Night of the Broken Glass—Kristallnacht

Frankfurt, November 9, 1938. I stared in seven-year-old terror as flames surged toward heaven, each leap higher than the last. Through the inferno, I caught glimpses of the synagogue, its timbers licked by hot tongues of red. Pungent black smoke billowed over the crowd, darkening the horizon. Day turned into night.

Stepping out of the hushed crowd watching the inferno, a frumpy woman shook a fist and shouted, "For this, some day all of us will be punished by God."

What have we done? Her words filled me with terror.

"Shut your mouth, woman!" snarled a burly bystander.

Still shouting, the angry woman stabbed a finger at the burning building. "That's God's house."

Horrified, I watched as brown-shirted men danced to the drums of falling timber. Was this hell? Were they the devils?

A husky blond man, his arm banded by a swastika, grabbed the woman by the hair and dragged her toward the fire. "Stop screaming," he hissed, "or we'll roast you, too."

I froze in fear. The smoke's acrid smell invaded my nostrils as wind whipped the fire toward the onlookers. I rubbed my stinging eyes. Slowly backing away, I wondered, Would I be next?

"Run home little girl," said an urgent voice next to me.

In panic, I tightened my grip on the straps of my school backpack and ran. I didn't pause at any of the storefront windows, places I normally lingered to gaze at dresses, hats, and furniture. Not even shops with toys and books slowed my legs as I sprinted along Zeil Strasse, the main street in downtown Frankfurt.

Blinded by fear, I crashed into something, somebody.

"Watch where you're going, Kind! You almost knocked me over."

9

The old woman, gray-haired and thin, tightened the woolen scarf under her chin as she stooped to retrieve some of the items that had fallen from her shopping net.

Out of breath, I apologized. "Entschuldigung. Please forgive me." I quickly pursued the rolling potatoes and onions along the sidewalk, gathered all into my apron and returned them to the string bag she held open.

Her hands shook. Without a smile she nodded. "Danke."

I saw her glance down the street at the synagogue engulfed in flames. On her lapel, the word "Jude" printed on a bright yellow star flashed in the light. Suddenly, she spat toward the fire. I stared at her, as she turned and walked away.

With relief I realized that none of the brownshirt devils were chasing me. Maybe they are people, I decided, since they didn't have horns or long tails.

I had learned all about good and evil in the daily lesson from our Lutheran teacher, tall skinny Miss Duboirs.

"Each devil is evil," she told our third grade class, "and his looks can be deceiving. Sometimes you can't even see him. That's when he whispers temptations in your ear." Her index finger pointed upward. "Always listen to your angel."

I stopped at the next cross street and looked to the left for oncoming bicycles. Oh no! Here they were again! Yelling and screaming, young men dressed in brown uniforms were throwing bread and rolls into the narrow street from the Konditorei, the coffee shop on the corner. A cheesecake splashed against the wall on the opposite side of the street. I saw the filling, all white against the red brick, and I wanted to scrape some with my fingers. Gleefully, the brownshirts trampled cakes and pastries. Why didn't they eat the goodies? Or give them to someone?

How often had I pressed my nose against the now-shattered display window, yearning for the cakes covered with fluffy frosting and almonds, wanting to taste just a little piece of that Torte Mamma could never afford. Now they lay splattered on the sidewalk between liverwurst and pieces of broken glass. Wasted.

More men appeared down the street—some wearing swastika arm bands, all shouting, tossing meat and sausages out of the delicatessen shop. A salami rolled in front of my feet. I stared at it, longed to pick it up.

One of them grabbed my arm. "Don't touch it. It's kosher!"

I thought I better get home fast. Leaving the men's demoniacal laughter behind, I fled from the squandered food, the senseless violence.

A few blocks away a voice yelled, "Extra! Extra! Saboteurs! Read all about the latest roundup." Although the man at the newsstand shouted at passersby, not many bought. Instead, people watched a paperhanger paste a red poster with black print over the existing ads on a Litfassaeule, a ten-foot high advertisement column.

Should I read the news or continue home? Last time I was late, Mamma scolded.

The man with the newspapers repeated his shouts.

What are saboteurs?

Curiosity won. I stopped to read the banner headlines: "Enemies of the State arrested and transported to the KZ, the Konzentrationslager, in Matthausen." Then, in smaller letters: "Concentration camp takes prisoners charged with treason against the Nationalsozialisten, the National Socialists." In small type were listed hundreds of names, alphabetically, with age and address—and affiliation. Communists, Socialists, Doctors of Theology and Philosophy, artists, homosexuals, priests, pastors, Jews.

Puzzled, I stood reading as others approached, until men and women surrounded the column, the ones in back stretching to read over the shoulders of those in front. The silence was eerie. Some shook their heads; others shuffled away with heads bowed; a few put balled hands in coat and pants pockets and moved on with somber faces. A sad-looking man gently pulled me aside. "Hurry home, little girl," he admonished. "This is no place for you."

Obediently, I walked fast to the next big street, a block from home. Stiftstrasse, street of seminaries.

The tall, stout traffic cop in the white uniform strode toward me from his post in the middle of the bustling intersection. I could always count on him to guide me across the busy street. In the morning, on my two-kilometer trek to school, there were rushing trucks and cars, bicycles, a few motorcycles, and pedestrians hurrying in all directions. In the afternoon it was less congested. Now the street was almost empty.

"Anneliese, you're late," the policeman said. "Been daydreaming again— gazing at the store windows, have you?"

I looked into his friendly face, saw his warm smile. "Not today," I said. "I've been running from demons. They're roaming all over the streets, beating people, smashing cakes, and…" I glanced down the street lined with shops, "…on the Borneplatz, there is a gigantic fire burning—like hell."

He frowned. "I heard."

My hand firmly in his, I felt safe.

He stepped off the curb, raised his white-gloved hand against the traffic, and blew a whistle.

The part I liked best was the shrill sound that made the cars and bicycles stop. I skipped beside him, trying to keep up with his long strides of authority. How shiny his boots were! He was my king and I was a princess. He didn't ride a horse, and his sword was but a big stick—but it didn't matter. He had a whistle!

Midway across the street he stopped. I knew the ritual. Don't move until he tells you to. Palm out, he brought the oncoming traffic to a halt. "Go straight home, angel," he urged. "And say hello to your Mamma." He waited for me to reach the sidewalk.

He must like my Mamma, I thought as I hurried along. Some days I would stand and watch him direct traffic on that square box in the intersection. One arm up, turn one quarter to the right, blow the whistle, spread both arms to stop traffic. But today, I didn't even stop at Kaufhaus Schneider, the big corner department store right across from Woolworth. Instead, I turned the corner of Stiftstrasse.

It was deserted. Usually, small groups of boys between fourteen and sixteen loitered in the street, trying to block my way, making scary noises. Once, when out of fear I hurried across the street, a delivery truck almost ran over me. I'll never forget the squealing brakes, my scraped knees seeping blood, and the driver shouting angrily from his cab.

Mamma called the boys hoodlums. She said they belonged to street gangs fighting each other for power. Today, I wondered where all the bad boys had gone.

"Anneliese!" It was the shopkeeper from the smoke shop calling. "Here is another empty cigar box for your Mamma and Pappa."

My heart still beating wildly in my chest, I stopped beside him. "Thank you, Herr Schultze." I curtsied.

"It's nearly four o'clock. Where have you been, child?"

"Don't you know about the big fire and the broken glass and bad people?" I looked down the street toward the butcher and bakery shops." I saw them stomping on sausages and cakes. They were laughing. I shuddered. "Oh, it was scary!"

Herr Schultze scratched his head. "Sounds like hell has descended upon us," he said slowly, letting out a long sigh. "Run along now. Your Mamma will be worried about you."

Clutching the box, I ran past the flower shop and the grocer to Little

Eschenheimer Strasse, the street where I lived. A long, narrow, and crooked street it was, lined on each side with about fifty old row houses. Most were five stories tall, with attics and cellars, the first floors occupied mostly by shops or taverns.

Number 14 was my house, the seventh on the right, with entrance doors big enough to accommodate a delivery truck.

I turned the corner—and froze in terror.

Is there a fight?

No. It's the hoodlums! Most of the older boys were dressed in civilian clothes, not uniforms. Only two wore the brown shirts of the storm troopers. Immediately, I recognized the gang members I most feared. Milling in front of my house, they held the long iron pole Herr Goldschmidt used to close the shutters of his leather goods store. A small crowd had gathered.

Pushing through them to the entrance, I looked for my nine-year old friend David. Two years my senior, he was like a big brother and always waited for me. His parents owned the store, and on Friday, when Mamma washed the floors of the shop, Frau Goldschmidt furnished cookies and milk. Then David would get the box of multi-colored leather buttons from the shop and we'd sit on the doorstep to play. We pretended the buttons were people, with names and faces. The biggest was the Pappa, the prettiest the Mamma, and the ugliest the boys in the street who threw stones and yelled, "Juden Junge, Jew Boy," after David and his older brother.

Someone shouted, "Watch out!" The crowd moved back from the large store window.

Crash! Sheets of glass shattered on the ground as a long, heavy pole hit the pane.

I shivered in horror and watched a brownshirt jump through the opening. Standing on the big work table, he shouted hatefully, "Down with the Jews!"

No one clapped, no one cheered, there wasn't even a jeer. But neither did anyone try to stop them.

Gripped by fear, I cried, "Mamma! Mamma, where are you?"

"She's inside, little one, by the stairway," whispered Frau Mueller, our third floor neighbor.

Pushing through the crowd, I reached the building entrance. The two front doors hung wide open. People from neighboring houses milled about or sat on the staircase.

I recognized a loud voice. "You hoodlums!" Mamma could not hear well in one ear, but always made sure she was heard by others. Hands on hips, one-

13

hundred-and-fifty pounds, she yelled. "Punks and thugs, that's what you are. Tagdiebe. Pigs!" She spat on the floor.

"Keep quiet, Johanna," said a tiny, frightened neighbor.

Inside the leather shop, the agitators pulled down the work bench with a long hook, scattering tools and supplies across the shop.

Mamma turned her back to the store and faced the onlookers. "I worked all afternoon washing those floors and windows. Who is going to clean up this mess?" She thumbed her chest. Her four-foot, ten-inch frame seemed to grow. "I'm the cleaning woman around here."

"Mamma." I wriggled through the crowd into her arms. Safe at last.

"You're late, Mausi." Mamma's voice softened. "Where have you been?" As always, she straightened the big bow in my hair.

From the store came muffled cries and shouts. "Get on your knees, Jew, and pick up every needle and thread, every scrap of leather, all those buttons. Schnell! Hurry up!"

Peeking from behind Mamma's apron, I tried to get a glimpse inside. What I saw was Herr and Frau Goldschmidt crawling on the floor gathering tools and buttons. Then I spotted David's jacket on the coat rack, the yellow star clearly visible. The first day David wore it, I'd asked him, "Why can't I wear a pretty star like this?"

"Because you're not a Jew," he said.

"What's a Jew?"

David hung his head. "My mother says they're not Christians."

I remembered that during religion period my class was divided into Catholics and Protestants. "Why can't I have a star that says Protestant?"

"The word doesn't fit the space," David explained. He was so smart, I thought in admiration.

Where was David? My eyes searched inside the store. There! Crouching behind some boxes. "David!" I called as Mamma's hand muffled my scream.

Too late. The brownshirt standing at the side door had followed my eyes. "What have we here?" he said, dragging the nine-year-old boy kicking and screaming from his hiding place.

"Leave him be, you bully!" Mamma's loud voice raged as she shook a fist at him. "He's only a child."

Furious, the uniformed youth booted David across the store, grabbed the iron rod and slowly, but deliberately, stepped in Mamma's direction.

Trembling, Mamma pushed me toward the open corridor leading to the back of the house. "Quick, to the backyard. Hurry!"

I hesitated.

"Go!" hissed Mamma and watched me retreat. Then she turned and braved the approaching youth, with the rod lifted above his head. "I know your mother," she lied. "You should be ashamed!"

He threw the rod before her feet, clicked his heels, raised his right arm, and shouted, "Heil Hitler!"

Lugging a box, Frau Goldschmidt emerged from the store.

The brownshirt spun around and demanded. "Halt, Jew! What's in the box?"

"Junk for the trash cans in back." Head downcast, she shuffled past the workshops of the broom maker and carpenter. "Anneliese," she called in a whisper.

With my face tear-streaked, I appeared from behind the receptacles. Shocked by the horror, the violence, and the humiliation heaped on this good woman, I felt small and frightened.

Frau Goldschmidt beckoned me to come close. Her hands shook as she hurriedly stuffed my apron pockets with leather buttons.

She still likes me! I trembled. Clutching the empty cigar box, I opened my mouth to thank her, but she silenced me with a finger across her lips. To my astonishment, she filled the box to the brim with more beautiful buttons.

Why is she giving them away, I wondered? She'd always told David and me how expensive they were.

"It's my gift to you." Frau Goldschmidt's voice was barely audible. She pointed to the fire escape in back of the flat were I lived with Mamma, Pappa, and my younger brother. "Hide them," she whispered, gently patting my cheek as she'd done so often in the past.

"Danke schoen," I said, my eyes filling with tears of shame and gratitude. For a brief moment, I felt a sense of normalcy return and clutched the buttons with pride to my chest. They're my badges, I thought, she gave them to me because I'm special to her.

The woman, whose face had turned ashen, whose mouth had sagged in the last twenty minutes, wiped away a tear and emptied trash into the junk bin.

Weeping, I closed the box lid and scampered up the steep fire escape to hide my treasures. "David…" The word was a whimper.

What were those shouts and screams? Was that my friend crying?

Hearing squealing car brakes, I quickly descended the flight of metal stairs, ran around the corner, and arrived at the entrance of the leather shop in time to see two brownshirts jump from a truck and storm inside the store.

"Move back!" The crowd, fearful but curious, pressed against the wall lined with mailboxes. A man shouted at the cowering Goldschmidts. "Raus! Get out! Schnell !"

In disbelief, I watched as David passed by, eyes downcast, not saying a word.

Gasping for breath, I reached out, tried to scream, "David!" But Mamma's hand clamped over my mouth and the name remained locked in my throat. All I could do was sob as I watched the young hoodlums shove my friends, David, his brother, his Mamma and Pappa, one by one, into the canvas-covered truck.

"When will they come back?" I asked between sobs.

Mamma shook her head and mumbled. "Something senseless is happening. Something insane."

"God have mercy on their souls," said a neighbor, making the sign of the cross.

With grim expressions, the crowd slowly dispersed. Mamma took another look at the looted store, the gaping window, the toppled showcases. A coat rack stood naked in the corner. "My best customer," she sighed. "Gone. Kidnapped."

I picked up a swastika pin that had fallen on a piece of cloth with a yellow star.

Taking the crooked cross out of my hand, Mamma threw it against a wall and shook her fist to heaven. "The devil shall have these pigs!"

She took my hand and together we slowly ascended the worn wooden stairs that led from the side of the shop. As she unlocked the door of our second story flat, Mamma mumbled, "Some day they all burn in hell."

"Please God—" I prayed in bed that night "—please protect David and his family." Against my cheek I pressed a soft leather button that was as black as David's curly hair.

I closed my eyes, waiting for night to pull a blanket of peaceful slumber over me. But instead, a nightmare of fire, smoke, and destruction sabotaged my sleep. I had seen and heard my parents argue and fight violently at my home, but this was worse. The world wasn't safe anymore.

Blinking, I saw a light shining through the open door connecting our living and sleeping rooms.

"We must burn the books our friends gave us," I heard Pappa say. "Especially the ones by Jewish authors."

"We have so many," said Mamma. "The carbon may clog the chimney."

"We'll burn a few at a time," Pappa decided. "We must do it soon. But we have to be careful. The city is crawling with informers."

Burn books? I slipped out of bed, crawled under it to retrieve my Grimm's Fairy Tales, and hid the story under my mattress. Nobody was going to burn my favorite book!

CHAPTER TWO—Aryans—Winter 1938

"It must be the coldest day yet this December." Mamma's friend, Paula Kinkel, shivered as she layered pieces of kindling in our kitchen stove to start a fire. "Wonder what's keeping Johanna?" She rubbed her hands over the top of the stove, lifted one of the lids to add more wood, then turned to warm her back. "Your Mamma must be doing some extra cleaning at the Himmelmanns. She'll be tired."

At the wooden table in the corner of the long, narrow kitchen, I did my homework. Beside me, a window overlooked the shops as well as family flats to the right and left. On warm summer days, when the windows were wide open, we could hear mothers admonishing children or arguing with neighbors, but not tonight.

Warming my hands under my armpits, I stopped practicing penmanship. "Mamma had a conference with my teacher," I told Paula. "Miss Thyssen was busy all day talking to parents outside the classroom—something about the questionnaires we returned on Aryans and Jews. So I had to stand in front of the class and assist the teacher by telling stories."

Paula stood by the chipped enamel sink near the window scrubbing potatoes under running water. "Which one of Grimm's fairy tales did you tell?"

"All that I could remember from my book. Some I told twice. At the end of the day I made up my own."

After Paula carried the full pot to the stove and added coal to the burning wood, she sat next to me at the table. "Tell me one of your stories," she coaxed, putting an arm around me.

I blushed. Must I? "It's just make-believe about a little girl. She has long blond braids and blue eyes." That's how I want to look—my very own secret.

Adjusting the big white bow clipped to the top of my short hair, Paula's blue eyes showed kindness and acceptance. "I like brown hair. And I love little girls with dark brown eyes." She kissed me on the cheek. "Brown reminds me of chocolate."

I shook my head. "It's ugly. The man in the uniform said true Germans are blond and blue-eyed."

"Bah! What does he know about true Germans?" She rubbed my hands until they were warm enough to continue with homework.

Doing word drills, I recalled how Mamma and Paula disagreed over the questionnaires I had brought home from school two days ago. They asked for names of mother, father, brother, sister, birthplace, and birthday. Three generations of relatives. Each question ended with: Aryan. YES. NO.

Even the grownups had wondered what an Aryan was. All were puzzled.

"It's a Jew," Paula guessed.

"No," Mamma argued. "Jews are Jews. Aryans must be Christians."

"Nonsense." My stepfather, Albert, squinted with steel gray eyes from behind frameless spectacles and brushed a strand of hair from his high forehead. "I heard them talking at the factory," he said with authority, waving the stump of his right forearm. "Aryans are the blond, blue-eyed, super race of the new regime. Hah!"

"Well that leaves us out," Mamma said. We all had inherited her father's dark brown eyes.

Paula fetched the dictionary. "Aryan. Noun. A member of the Caucasian race," she read.

"What's Caucasian?" Again they looked at each other, puzzled.

"That settles it." Mamma circled 'NO' for Aryan. "If I don't know what it is, I say no. Better safe than sorry."

Now, hearing familiar footsteps coming up the stairs, I hurried to the door, and turning the large key that protruded from the keyhole, unlocked it. Mamma and Walter stood shivering in the cold.

"It's nice and warm in here," said my six-year-old brother as he removed his mittens and woolen stocking cap. A shock of blond curls frames his face, and eyes as brown as mine begged for attention. He was tiny and frail for his age. Mamma told people his growth had been slow because he was born prematurely.

Tonight, Mamma seemed more tired than usual. She took off her coat and hung it on one of the hooks next to the door, tossed some forms on the table, and sat down heavily. "More papers to fill out. This time from the Government child care center. They want to know everything about Walter's father." Elbows on the table, she buried her face into cupped hands and began to weep. "It's been one hell of a day," she cried, pulling a handkerchief from her pocket to blow her nose.

19

Paula lifted the lid off the boiling potatoes to allow the steam to escape and stop the rattling. "What happened?"

"I lost another cleaning job." Mamma's voice sounded dull. Sniffling, she pressed out the words. "The Himmelmanns' are gone. Left overnight. Disappeared into thin air." She walked to the stove to warm her hands. "Some say they fled to another country. Probably America. Damn!" She blew on the hand she'd burned from getting too close to the pot. "Now I have only one customer left. First, the Goldschmidts downstairs were forced to leave to hell-knows-where, then old Silberstein hanged himself while the brownshirts were kicking down his door, and now the Himmelmanns have left. Abgehauen!" Her voice, usually loud and excited, was low and lifeless.

Paula set the table, rattling tin plates that didn't match. "Put your homework away, Schatz," she told me. I liked it when she called me "precious."

"And don't dilly-dally," added Mamma.

She's in a bad mood, I decided, quickly putting away my book.

Mamma set what was left of a jar of jam on the table. "Where are the men?"

"Probably having one beer too many," sighed Paula, draining water from the potatoes into the small kitchen sink.

As always, Walter wiggled back and forth in his chair, kicking against the wooden legs, dropping his fork on the floor.

"Why can't you sit still, wiggleworm?" Mother was truly irritated now. She scraped the last margarine out of the butter dish.

Paula started peeling the hot potatoes. "What happened at the teacher's conference?"

Mamma gave me a funny look. "Why don't you take your brother to the toilet?" she said.

"I don't have to go," protested Walter. One community toilet on each floor was shared by three families of the four-story tenement house.

"Go anyhow!" commanded Mamma, pointing to the door.

Reluctantly, but obediently, I took my brother to the unheated toilet at the top of the stairs. It was cold. While he peed, I put my ear to the kitchen door entrance and listened to what Mamma was saying that I wasn't supposed to hear.

"They are trying to take away my Anneliese." A tin plate clanged to the floor.

I tried peeking through the large keyhole to better understand.

"Who is doing that?" Paula's voice was laced with fear.

"The Government." Mamma grabbed the potato peels and threw them in the trash pail. "I went to see the principal at Anneliese's school."

"And?"

Mamma began to sob. "He called Anneliese a bad name. And he made me out to be a tramp, insinuating I sleep with the husbands of my employers."

What are they talking about? I wondered.

"That Schweinehund!" Paula's voice seethed with indignation.

Mamma's voice shook with rage. "That's too good a word for him. He's a Waschlappen. A wash rag. A wimp!" She searched for a more descriptive word. A Schlappschwanz! That's what he is. A limp tail!" She filled the kettle with water and slammed it onto the hot stove.

Walter called for me to lift him up so he could pull the toilet chain. Cold and hungry, we returned to the kitchen.

Paula put jam and potatoes on our plates.

"Hurry up and finish your meal," urged Mamma. "I have things to discuss with Paula."

We did as told, gobbling down our food, hardly tasting it.

Trying not to make noise, I stacked the plates in the wash bowl under the sink and even offered to do the dishes.

"Where do they want to take her?" I heard Paula whisper while she wiped the table.

"I'll tell you later." Mamma wrapped an old towel around a heated brick to warm Walter's bed.

Usually, I was allowed to stay up a little longer than my brother, but tonight we both had to go to bed early. Together we recited an evening prayer that I had learned in school. "Dear God. Bless me so that I may join you in heaven some day. Amen." As usual, the door was left open a gap, allowing not only heat and light to filter inside, but also muffled conversation.

"They want to put her in a school for gifted children, called Adolf Hitler Schule. But first I must prove that her no-good father is not Jewish." Mamma's cry was somewhere between a sob and a wail. "Anneliese's birth certificate says 'FATHER UNKNOWN.'"

"You must go and see her real father," urged Paula.

"No!"

"For the sake of Anneliese's life, you must plead with him to admit his fatherhood. Beg him on your knees!"

After some silence, Mamma stammered, "No, I—I—did that eight years ago when I learned I was pregnant. He wouldn't listen. I took him to court, presented my case. The judge appeared to be deaf. I prayed to God. He didn't hear me."

I sat up to better understand. I seemed to have two fathers—a Pappa and a no-good father.

Walter interrupted my thoughts with a whisper. "What are they talking about?"

"Something about my no-good father," I whispered back. What were they talking about? I wondered. It must have to do with that questionnaire I brought from school.

Miss Thyssen, the teacher, had been upset. Very upset. I heard her lament to the principal that the parents don't know the difference between Aryan and Jew.

He questioned all students about what church they attended.

"None," I answered.

He turned to my teacher. "What's her grade average?"

"She's a straight "A" student."

"Do you like studying the Bible?" The principal stepped closer to my desk.

I nodded with enthusiasm. "I love the stories in the Old Testament."

His bushy eyebrows furrowed as he looked at the questionnaire. "Why is your last name different from that of your mother and brother?"

"I don't know." Somehow, I had never realized I had another last name.

Miss Thyssen whispered something to the principal and handed me a note to give to Mamma.

From the kitchen, I heard Paula's voice again. "You must get Anneliese's father to admit his parentage, Johanna. Tell him to shove his money. But convince him the life of his daughter is in his hands. It's her only chance."

"I hate him! He's no good." Mamma's voice quivered. "She may be illegitimate—" her voice grew louder "—but Anneliese is no bastard." She screamed, "Her no-good father's the bastard!"

Paula agreed. "But if the fanatics pin the fatherhood on a Jew, Anneliese's fate is sealed. And you'll be another name in the column of undesirables for the good of the State. Another number. The two of you will join little David and his mother—wherever they may be."

My ears perked up at the mention of David. Goodness, I'd forgotten to pray for him.

Louder than ever, Mamma's voice carried to the bedroom. "They wanted me to become a member of their party. I am not joining anybody or anything. That's what I told that Scheisskerl, that shithead in uniform at the principal's office." Mamma paused for a moment, then continued dramatically. "You'll get my daughter over my dead body," I told him, "and I'll make sure to take her with me."

Where is she taking me after she's dead? Who is my no-good father? I felt confused. As I scooted down into my bed, I thought I heard Mamma say, "I'll see her no-good father tomorrow."

A week later, I had a State-appointed guardian. Mamma noted that the much-despised man's rosorial features, from beady eyes to receding chin, were aptly suggestive of his character—a rat. At random intervals, he checked my progress and behavior in school and followed up with visits at home. Neighbors were queried. I learned that Pappa was my stepfather.

Mamma began to receive aid for children from the State, but she was not happy. "Snoopers and informers, that's what they are," she fumed. "Now they are going to tell me how to run my life. Always remember, Anneliese," she lectured, "nothing in life is free. There's a price attached to everything."

I was so intent on watching Mamma mixing batter to make Christmas cookies that I paid little attention to her life philosophy. She kneaded and pounded the dough until it was the right consistency, and I got to help. Using the rolling pin was hard work, but cutting out the shapes was fun. Stars and half moons filled the empty spaces between Santas on the cookie sheet. Walter helped decorate with sprinkles of red and green sugar.

We gave the figures names of boys and girls we knew, like David, and my best friend Hannelore. And there was a Mamma and a Pappa—even a no-good father. But I didn't tell Mamma about that. Once in a while a cookie crumbled after it was baked—a good excuse to eat it. My no-good father cookie lost his legs. So I threw it in the trash. Fathers are supposed to be perfect, I thought.

Oh, how I loved Christmas time! In school, we were encouraged to practice old Germanic rituals, but at home it started on the eve of the first Sunday in December with me lighting a candle to hail the advent of Jesus Christ. The fresh smelling evergreen branches of the wreath were bound by a red satin ribbon and decorated with small pine cones and silver bells.

Soft shadows danced on the wall as the light flickered to our songs, bringing to life the peaceful promise of "Holy Night." When the dripping wax started making little red spots on the table cloth, Mamma told Walter to blow out the candle.

St. Nicholaus, the Santa Claus, came on the sixth of December to collect our wishing list. With anticipation we'd wait for him to come stomping up the stairs.

"Who's knocking on the door?" Mamma always acted surprised. "Oh, it's Knecht Ruprecht, the Christ Child's helper."

On his back, he carried a heavy sack filled with goodies. The story goes that he'd put you in his big bag and carry you away if you'd misbehaved during the year.

"Have you been obedient to your parents and teachers?" His deep voice scared me, but his knowledge put me in awe. He seemed to know everything: fibbing, breaking things, Walter's bed-wetting, good report cards. He even admonished Mamma to smoke less and swatted her with a switch. His eyes, curiously enough, sparkled much like those of Paula.

There seemed to be angels everywhere to oversee the Christmas preparations. "We must help them make toys," was Mamma's excuse for sending us to bed early.

Paula and her husband, Heinrich, would visit nightly after supper, when we were in bed. Soon, the rasping sound of a small coping saw made it difficult to listen to what was said in the living room. It reminded me of the cabinet shop downstairs. The smell of glue and wood shavings sometimes penetrated to the bedroom.

While I listened to what was said, Walter peeked around the door gap. "They're cutting up cigar boxes," he reported, shivering in the dark. "Looks like Mamma just finished a tiny chair."

"Quiet in there!" Pappa's voice commanded.

Quickly, Walter hopped into my bed to get warm faster and soon fell asleep.

I continued to listen.

"Did you see the newest name on the 'Enemy of the State' list? It's Pastor Martin Niemoeller. He's working with the underground," he said in a low voice. Pappa had a way of being well informed.

I didn't always comprehend what he meant, but I tried to understand. Some things were so confusing. According to what we learned in school, Jews were bad, and enemies were people who didn't agree with our Fuehrer.

"Niemoeller is the most outspoken critic of Hitler's anti-Jewish policy," said Mamma. "Other Protestant theologians have joined him."

Must be something about religion, I thought. But how do they work under the ground? Was there a tunnel somewhere? I crouched close to the door gap.

Heini—short for Heinrich—got up to check the fire in the potbelly stove. "The coal is red hot," he said. "Time to tear up and toss a few more of the condemned books in the fire."

Condemned. Where had I heard that word before?

"Better burn a few pages at a time," cautioned Paula. "We don't want to clog the chimney with carbon."

Why are they burning the same books Pappa had been reading only a few weeks ago? Grownups sometimes don't make sense! Shaking my head, I checked for my book under the mattress, found it was still there, then scooted into my brother's bed.

A week later, Mamma took Walter and me to a Christmas party given by the State for disadvantaged children. Mamma insisted we wear our best outfits—something not patched.

We were greeted by a smiling, uniformed lady. Handing us a plate filled with hazelnuts, gingerbread, and an orange, she pointed to the table laden with toys. "You may each choose one thing from all those lovely gifts."

Spotting a thick volume of fairy tales by Hans Christian Anderson, I ignored the dolls and teddy bears and instead turned the well worn pages of the book. Looking at the beautiful pictures and ornate script, I asked timidly, "May I have this book?"

"She loves to read," said Mamma.

The lady put a little doll in my arms. "Wouldn't you rather pretend you're a mother rocking her baby?"

I hung my head in disappointment. She'd told me to pick anything. Now she was trying to decide for me. I felt like a dummy as I picked up the doll that had fallen to the floor. Apologizing, I handed it back to her. "Can I have the book instead?"

Looking from the doll to the book, she shrugged. "You may have it," she said curtly.

Mamma sighed. "God knows we have enough books. Might as well get another one."

Paula's words echoed in my mind. "Better burn a few pages at a time…"

Quickly, I grabbed the book and looked up at Mamma. "You won't burn it, will you?"

Frozen silence filled the room.

Mamma frowned. I knew that whatever I'd said should never have been uttered.

The uniformed lady frowned also. "Who would burn books?"

Mamma tugged at my hand—a signal to keep quiet. "I told her she reads so much, her eyes may some day set the pages on fire."

Sometimes Mamma says the most peculiar things, I thought, as I followed her and Walter to the exit. Mamma turned and smiled at the lady. "Thank you. And Merry Christmas! Froehliche Weihnachten!"

It was the day after Christmas when it happened.

I was standing by my doll house, complete with furniture, thinking about the tiny lamps that would light up if hooked to a small battery. Pappa knelt on the floor with his back against the bookcase, helping Walter wind up his train set, and Mamma was taking a nap in the adjacent family bedroom.

Heavy footsteps up the stairs. Pounding on the door.

Had Saint Nicholaus returned?

Bang! The kitchen door crashed open. Two men dressed in civilian clothes flashed their badges. GESTAPO! GEheime STAatsPOlizei. Secret Police.

Pappa jumped up, while Walter and I froze with fear. The runaway engine banged against the foot of the table.

At first the men didn't say anything. From the kitchen, they rushed to the table in the middle of the living room. One kicked aside a chair, the other flung open the door to the bedroom, its handle hitting my hand that was wrapped around the dollhouse wall.

Suppressing the pain, I stood petrified.

From the other room, I heard Mamma let out a blood-curdling scream. "Albert!" She yelled for Pappa. "Help! Thieves! Thugs!"

Pappa stepped toward the bedroom, shouting but one word. "GESTAPO."

The rotund man with the flabby face and frog eyes pushed Pappa to the floor. He stomped behind the taller accomplice and followed him into the other room. "Halt' s Maul," his raspy voice croaked. "Shut up!"

What is he doing to make Mamma cry out? Nursing my sore knuckles, I peered around the open door into the bedroom. Where is she?

Next to the dresser that contained linens, I saw her standing in her stocking feet, trying to cover her slip-clad body with a rumpled housedress. While her fingers fumbled with the front buttons, her dark eyes darted between the two men—who pulled out dresser drawers, dumping their contents on the floor. Her mouth opened and shut without a sound. Her always ruddy complexion had turned white.

My lips began to quiver. I wanted to cry. Swallowing hard, I blinked away the tears. Anneliese is too big to cry.

When Mamma spotted me, she rushed to where I stood and protectively pressed my face to her body.

Then came a crash and a clap. We both jumped and stared in disbelief as the overturned wardrobe spilled winter coats, scarves, and woolen caps over Walter's bed.

Will they make us leave the house the way David's family left the store? The memory prompted me to cling even closer to Mamma. In horror I watched as the men tossed things about, looked under beds, lifted mattresses. Under mine they found my book.

"Fairy tales," said the tall, skinny one.

I started to shiver. Even my teeth began to clatter.

Holding my book, he strode toward me. "Anneliese."

How did he know my name?

"Anneliese," he repeated, "why do you hide your books?"

Afraid I'd get yelled at later, I didn't want my parents to hear my answer. In a voice barely audible, I answered, "Sometimes I read in bed."

"In the dark?" His voice was soft, yet mocking.

"I have a flashlight." I lowered my eyes as tears welled up. Now Mamma and Pappa were going to spank me.

"Speak up!" Pulling me away from Mamma, he grabbed my shoulder and shook me hard. "Who is burning books in this house?"

From his corner of the room, Pappa yelled, "Stop it!"

Mamma struggled to free her arms, pinned back by the other Gestapo man. "Leave my daughter alone!"

Walter started to whimper.

I looked in his direction. He crouched on the floor, holding onto one of Pappa's legs that straddled in front of the always locked bookcase.

"Aufmachen! Open it!" demanded the man who still held me.

Pappa couldn't find the key, so the pudgy one with the frog eyes and drooping jowls smashed the glass. Buried under files and magazines he found two books: a much-thumbed dictionary and a little used medical book.

"No Bible?" His mocking question was directed at Mamma.

"I live by The Ten Commandments. That's good enough for me," she said.

Walking to the Christmas tree, he asked cynically, "You do believe in Christ, don't you?"

"We celebrate His birthday." Her voice quavered. "I believe in The New Testament."

He flung my books at the tree, causing it to fall. "What did you do with the ones in that bookcase?" His face turned crimson as he looked at Pappa. "You burned them, didn't you?"

"Check the potbelly stove in the living room," called the man in the kitchen where pots and pans clanked to the floor. We could hear him shovel through the coal bin, turning the waste receptacle upside down, sifting through ashes under the kitchen stove. "Nothing," he said, as he walked into the living room.

"Same here. Nothing." The tall one brushed the ashes off his trousers, then walked over to where I stood. "Nice doll house," he said, peering into the different rooms. He picked up a piece of furniture, threw it back, looked at another, lifted the tiny coverlet from the little bed. It was a red, square piece of cloth covered with lace, no larger than a handkerchief. Flipping it back and forth, he examined it carefully.

"Communists!" he snarled, looking at Mamma. "You thought you could fool us by removing the hammer and sickle embroidery. The outline of the pin marks are clearly visible."

Mamma was holding onto a chair. "I found it in the trash can."

"You're lying." He strode towards her. "We know that your ex-husband is a Communist. Where is he?"

Mamma's face turned ashen. She glanced at Walter. I divorced Fritz Hoehn right after my son was born."

"Tell us, where can we find that pig of a Communist?"

"I don't know."

They took Mamma away.

I started to scream, but Pappa clamped his hand over my mouth. "Schweinehunde!" he said through clenched teeth and kicked the damaged kitchen door that wouldn't shut.

Terrified, I wanted to run after Mamma but couldn't move. As the sound of her footsteps faded away, I wondered, what will happen to my Mamma? What will these bad men do to her? They didn't look like the gang of hoodlums I'd seen earlier—hoodlums wearing swastika bands, smashing windows and hurling wares—but they acted the same. I turned and looked at the toppled tree, the looted doll house, the smashed engine. Horror crept over me. Stifling a sob, I wiped away an angry tear. Slowly, I followed Walter into the living room to gather the tracks to his train.

He pulled my sleeve. "Don't worry," he whispered. "They won't find him."

"Who are you talking about?"

Walter placed a forefinger across his lips. "Last week, while I was playing marbles in the downstairs entrance hall, a man stopped me and said he was my real Pappa."

I recalled the papers to obtain a certificate of Aryan ancestry. Mamma and Walter's last name was the same. "His name was Hoehn?"

"Yes," Walter nodded. "He gave me a hug and handed me a Groschen."

"A whole dime?"

"When Mamma saw him from upstairs, she screamed at him. Real bad words!"

I gasped.

"She told him he'd better hide or she'd tell what he did and they'd lock him up."

Pappa entered from the kitchen and asked us to help him upright the overturned wardrobe. "Let's clean up this mess," he said in a voice void of emotion. Had he overheard our whispers?

Without a word, each masking our fears with work, we put things in order until darkness slowed our efforts. Too tired to eat, we nonetheless nibbled on Christmas cookies we found in a tin that had tumbled on the floor.

"Go to bed," said Pappa.

I recited the shortest prayer I knew. "Dear God. Make me pure so that I may enter Thy Kingdom. Amen. Und bitte, Lord Jesus," I pleaded, "don't let them hurt my Mamma."

In the morning, I woke to the aroma of malt coffee that wafted through the room. Was that the sound of dishes clattering? Could it be? Barefooted, I hurried through the cold living room, flung open the kitchen door—and stopped. That stooped woman with the pinched face, swollen eyes, and disheveled hair...Was she my Mamma?

Without a word, she bent and drew me to her bosom, patting my hair, stroking my face, her mouth forming words that remained locked behind quivering lips.

She refused to talk. We never learned what had happened.

"I saw Fritz Hoehn's name on the latest list of politically undesirables," Pappa mentioned one evening. "He'll end up in the concentration camp, the KZ in Matthausen..."

Mamma remained silent.

CHAPTER THREE—The Assault—January 1939

Flags, flags, flags. Everywhere. Each red and white, each with a black swastika in the middle. They waved from poles at schools, decorated post offices, police stations, and every government building. They hung from windows of homes, apartments, even tenement houses, and were displayed in stores next to life-sized pictures of Adolf Hitler, the Fuehrer, our leader. It was January 30, 1939, the sixth anniversary of Hitler and his party coming to power.

Walter and I counted flags as we walked past the fifty houses to the end of our street. He held up a finger after I reached one hundred. Then two, then three. We stopped counting. Some flags were small and limp, like the one outside the pub across our street; others looked proud and prominent. The window of the beauty shop was covered completely by a banner.

Inside, Mamma said, was not so patriotic. The air buzzed with the latest satire of the Third Reich. "Did you hear the one about Josef Goebbels, our Minister of Propaganda? His wife's blood line is a quarter Jewish, but they made her an honorary Aryan." Sitting under their hair dryers, they'd snicker behind cupped hands.

When we met Pappa at the streetcar stop near the newspaper office building, Walter said, "I wish we had a window out front so we could show a flag." Our stepfather was working the day shift and always bought an evening paper that smelled as though it had just rolled off an inky printing press.

"Even if we could afford a flag, we wouldn't display one," said Pappa, folding the General Anzeiger expertly with his only hand.

I could read the headlines. "It says there's going to be a big parade tonight. Can we go?" I pleaded. "Bitte?"

"It will be dark and too cold."

"Our teacher told us to be sure to see it," I insisted. "It's a class assignment."

Pappa gave the front page a quick glance. "We'll see." He slipped the folded paper under his disfigured forearm. "We were planning to play cards tonight with Paula and Heini."

Perhaps they'd persuade our parents to go, I hoped.

When we arrived home, I mentioned it to Mamma. She stopped stirring the stew and glared at me. "Parades," she fumed. "More propaganda. I've been hearing Hitler's voice all day long. Loudspeakers on every street corner barking out his speech. The sound of his voice makes me gag."

"Me, too," agreed Pappa. "My fellow workers are laughing at his Austrian accent."

Heini, who'd been quiet all through supper, said mockingly, "Remember, Austria is part of Germany now."

"As far as I'm concerned, Hitler's a foreigner." Mamma had the last word this time. But after much begging from Walter and me, she eventually relented and allowed us to go to the corner in front of Woolworth's to hear the tramp of marching boots.

Bundled in scarves and mittens, we watched column after column of uniformed young men, sixteen abreast, goose-step down Main Street toward the Opernplatz, the Opera Plaza. They carried tall torches, flames shooting above their heads, giving the cold night an eerie glow.

My chest swelled with pride as I stood on the pavement and watched the young men and women march to the beat of drums. Will I be one of them some day? I quickly put the thought aside. I could never march for hours in such tight formation. But I would be proud to carry a banner, or better yet, hold one of those flaming torches.

Not everyone had similar feelings. Most older folks standing behind me emanated an icy blast. "Youth in uniforms, indeed!" Their voices laced with indignation, they grumbled, "Hitler's little puppets."

Others murmured in admiration as they watched stern-faced soldiers under steel-grey tortoise helmets stare ahead while marching. "What discipline!" Lines were straight, and black polished boots kicked in step to somber pounds of drums. "Welche Macht!" The columns of young men seemed never ending. "Such power!"

"This spectacle is truly a sight to see." In mixed disbelief and awe, Paula shook her head.

"So is the carnival parade just before Lent," said Mamma. "At least the

31

clowns and costumes give you a laugh, and the bands make you want to dance. This—what is this but boots? A thousand polished boots."

"I like pretty girls sitting on top of decorated floats," snickered Heini. He elbowed Pappa and winked, then pointed to an approaching tank flanked by artillery cannons. "Here come the instruments of the new regime."

"Halt's Maul!" The shout to shut up came from a stout man holding between his fingers a fat cigar. "I'm proud of what I see!" He flipped the accumulated ashes, took several short puffs, and blew a cloud of smoke into the frosty air. "This is the future of our fatherland!"

"Beware of overbearing pride!" The shaking voice from the man standing near to Pappa sounded old and raspy. Watery blue eyes were enlarged by thick lenses inside wire spectacles. A raggedy coat too large for his decrepit body hung loose from stooped shoulders. Like a prophet, he lifted his steel-tipped cane in the direction of another tank rolling by. "Less than twenty-five years ago," he said, "I saw the result of these weapons scattered across the battlefields of France and Russia. Hands and heads blown off. Legs mangled."

Lowering his gnarled hand, he coughed and spit out a wad of green mucous before continuing his gestured lament. "War. The carnage of civilization."

I didn't know what those big words meant, but from the library, I'd obtained books on Germany's war history. Most battles were not won by the Germans, I learned. Before Christ, the Romans conquered most of German territory. There were the Crusades between Catholics and Protestants; Napoleon pushing across Germany into Russia; and the longest war, during which the Swedes overran Germany from the North, lasted thirty years.

The old-timer slowly shuffled away. He's just an old man, I thought. What does he know?

For another hour, we stared at the pompous procession. Mesmerized by the crashing tread of feet, flickering light from torches, and the rousing display of flags, I wanted to stay longer. But Mamma said she had seen enough.

I obeyed—as always. But the songs—with melodies at once aggressive and sentimental—stayed with me throughout the night, reappearing in my dreams.

Next day, we all had colds. When sneezing didn't stop and coughing got worse, Mamma took us to the doctor. Our General Practitioner used to be Dr. Gruenbaum, but because he was a Jew, not allowed to practice anymore. Our new physician was Dr. Luise Klein. Contrary to the meaning of her last name—Little—she was tall and slender, with not only a soft voice, but a pretty face and friendly smile. I liked her immediately and decided then and there to become a physician.

The waiting room was crowded. To pass time, I looked at pictures on the wall, studied a black-framed doctor's degree, and memorized a verse in a simple mounting next to the reception desk. It said:

A doctor has three faces:

When giving advice to the ill, he looks angelic;

When healing the sick, his image is that of a God;

But once he asks for his reward,

His face changes to that of the devil.

Regardless, I wanted to be a family practitioner like Dr. Klein. She was my idol—though her prescription to get rid of the flue tasted awful. Drinking bitter camomile tea, and covered with two layers of feather coverlets, we literally sweated out our cold. I felt at times as though I would suffocate, but I was too weak to even whimper.

I couldn't go to school until I had completely recovered. That made me sad. I loved to read poetry as much as history, enjoyed memorizing multiplication tables, and even liked German grammar. But most of all, I missed carrying Miss Thyssen's briefcase on my way home. I longed to chatter with my best friend, Hannelore.

The public school I attended was near the Jewish ghetto, a two kilometer walk. It was the only place that accepted students younger than the minimum age. To Mamma's delight, the classes were fewer than twenty-five, but best of all, girls and boys were segregated—not like the school in our district that was not only overcrowded, but had students of mixed gender.

"I don't approve of this modern train of thought," I'd hear Mamma say. "Boys and girls in the same classroom, indeed! "Nix!" She shook her head emphatically. "Besides, I don't want Anneliese to associate with the dirty riffraff of our neighborhood. Bad enough we have to live here."

Mamma prided herself that she cooked and cleaned and sewed for her family. Hot oatmeal every morning. Mondays with milk and sugar, Tuesdays without milk, and no sugar the remainder of the week. "My children will never look ragged and dirty like those thirteen on the upper floor," she'd tell Paula. "Three families, all on welfare, most don't know who their fathers are!" Inevitably, she'd add, "One of these days I'll get a good job and move out of this rat hole. Einestages!."

"And one of these days, "I said looking up from a book I was reading, "I'll be a physician, Mamma, just like Dr. Klein." I was determined. "We'll move by the park to one of those nice houses with big front windows."

Mamma smiled ruefully. "Get the doctor idea out of your head, dear. We're not people of the upper class—we're plain working folks with little money. She looked into the small mirror above the sink and twisted her hair into a tight knot. "Perhaps you can become a hair dresser, or work as an apprentice in a butcher shop."

I grimaced. "What kind of people are we?"

"A foolish question, Anneliese." Mamma became defensive. "I work hard. I don't want you to have to scrub floors for other people. There are better ways to make a living." She picked up a loaf of bread and started to slice it. "What about a job in a butcher shop or a bakery? You know how to weigh goods and make change."

Discouraged, I promised to think about it. Kneading dough and shaping it into bread and rolls could be fun, I reasoned. And to sell delicious-smelling baked goods must be a delight—though it would mean getting up before dawn.

Slicing sausage and placing hunks of meat on a scale, on the other hand, sounded awful. Besides, I didn't like that old woman who sometimes helped behind the counter. Her hands were covered with brown blotches and looked all wrinkled when she weighed and wrapped goods. And it was always cold in that butcher shop.

What about becoming a beautician? I always got Walter's part straight when I combed his hair. But I had trouble with mine. It was short and wavy, and that big white bow of synthetic satin always slipped. How I wished to have braids! All the other girls wore them. Except Hannelore. Her hair was curly without ever using rollers. No, I decided, fixing hair is not for me. I'd rather bury my nose in books.

Pappa encouraged me to study. He not only monitored my homework, but had me read aloud to him daily.

I preferred reading to myself, but feared his mean temper. It flared up quicker than Mamma's—and often without warning.

When angry, Mamma screamed and yelled. Once, during a disagreement with Pappa, she flung a kettle with boiling water across the kitchen floor. Another time, several dinner plates slipped out of my hand while lifting them from a high shelf. Incensed, Mamma smashed the last one over my head. For awhile, my scalp sprouted a bump the size of a goose egg.

Pappa rarely raised his voice, but his words could be menacing—similar to a snake attacking its prey. Sometimes, he used his powerful hand to vent his anger. Like a hammer, his fist pounded blow after blow on Walter's head because he couldn't memorize time tables.

One evening before supper, Pappa took the medical book from the locked bookcase and showed it to me. "If you want to be a doctor," he explained, "you must learn about the body. You may not be able to read all the words yet…" he casually flipped the pages…"but you can study the pictures."

The drawings were graphic, the medical language difficult to pronounce. At first, it seemed like fun to learn something new.

He seemed eager to help with the correct pronunciation and interpretation. "You're so smart, Anneliese," he said. "You read so well." He pointed to his crotch, and coached,"Geschlechtsteil. Say it again. Sex organ."

I began to feel uncomfortable and tried to turn the page.

"Not so fast," he said, pointing to the drawing of human anatomy. "Touch your neck, your chest, your buttocks." He scooted his chair closer to mine and unbuttoned his shirt. "Touch my abdomen."

Soon, the reading sessions turned into a game of not only repeating words and identifying body parts, but also of showing and touching. The more he delighted in the game, the more I began to hate it. Fidgeting in my seat, I stumbled over the word vagina.

"Concentrate!" It was a command. "A doctor must be disciplined. Don't look up. Don't move. Just keep on reading." Slowly, he walked around my chair, then stopped, facing me. Jutting out the stump of his left arm, he hissed. "Caress it." His face contorted. He groaned. "Rub it again," he demanded. "It feels so good."

Just looking at that stump gave me the creeps. I felt shame, but dutifully, I rubbed the ugly scar some more.

Mamma called from the kitchen to stop doing homework and come for supper.

Cooked cabbage. I could tell by the awful smell—but was glad to obey!

At the table, I poked around my food. "I'm not very hungry."

"Eat anyhow." Mamma heaped more vegetables on my plate. "You're so skinny, people will think I don't feed you."

"Mamma, I'm full," I protested meekly, stuffing my mouth with more of the bad-tasting stuff.

A spoon dropped to the floor as Walter wriggled in his chair.

"I'll teach you two to sit still." Pappa seemed greatly agitated. He fetched four blocks of wood and jammed them under our arms.

Walter's head began to wobble. My lips quivered with fear.

"We'll take care of that," said Pappa and placed a book on each of our heads. "Don't move," he threatened. "If either one of you drops an item, I'll knock your head off."

His eyes looked wild. Did he mean it?

Her head low, Mamma sat in silence. Was she as afraid as we were?

Staring at each other, beads of perspiration covering our foreheads, Walter and I sat motionless for what seemed hours. Fighting back tears, I glanced at Mamma. Why doesn't she shorten our sentence? She could at least yell at him, I thought.

When Pappa left the kitchen, Mamma removed the books that were still balanced on top of our heads, and allowed the objects clamped under our armpits to drop. "That's enough discipline," she said and locked the books in the cabinet.

Glad to be able to move my head and arms again, I wanted to hug her—but she was busy clearing the table and filling the dishpan with hot water from the kettle.

"Please take care of the dishes while I clean the bakery across the street." Placing her apron on the hook next to the towels, her voice sank to a whisper. "Don't make any noise. Pappa is taking a nap in the bedroom." She closed the door softly.

I stood on the stool to better reach the sink and carefully put the first dish in the tray to dry. It was Mamma's favorite—a gift from one of her former customers.

Pretending the dish towel was a flag, Walter bounced around the kitchen and started to sing the new national anthem about raising the flags up high, marching and uniting against Communism and reactionaries. He could be such a clown!

"Shhhh. You'll wake Pappa."

As I tried to grab the towel, the stool wobbled and I lost my balance. The plate slid to the floor and broke in two.

"Kaputt," was all I could say. "Broke." I froze with fear. Did the crash wake Pappa?

"Mamma is going to scream her head off," Walter whispered. "For sure, she's going to spank us."

I don't know which I feared more—her loud voice or the spanking. With trembling hands, I picked up the pieces. Glue, I remembered. I had seen Mamma combine flour and water to create a mixture that repaired stoneware.

I made the paste. First it was too thin and wouldn't stick. I added flour. Now, it was too thick and dried immediately. In despair, I started to cry softly. "I'm afraid."

"Not me," said my little brother. "The spankings don't hurt any more."

"What's going on in here?" Pappa's threatening figure appeared in the doorway.

Everything happened so fast. I tried to hide the broken plate behind my back. Walter jumped in front of me. "I did it," he said.

Pappa's fist came crashing down on little Walter's face. Again and again and again.

I screamed. "Stop it. Please—stop."

His open hand flew out and hit me so hard I flew across the room. Crashing against the wardrobe in the living room, I crumpled to the floor. If Walter cried, I didn't hear him. My ears felt plugged. I raised my head to see my brother. I couldn't. The room began spinning as I staggered to rise. Vomit gagged my throat. Blood trickled from my nose.

"Look over here, Anneliese." Pappa's ominous shadow towered over the formless heap that was my brother, ready to strike again.

"No," I pleaded, dropping my head. "Don't hit him any more. Please. I'll do anything you want me to. Anything."

"What did you say?" He now stood next to me. "Anything?"

My head throbbed. Did I hear a sob from the bundle on the floor that was my brother?

"Look up," Pappa snarled, unfastening his suspenders.

I recalled the whip with the five straps the woman upstairs used on her children. He is going to beat me to death. I shuddered, waiting for the first blow.

It didn't come. Instead he commanded, "Look at my hand!"

Although afraid, I raised my head to look. His long fingers opened the top button of his fly.

Before I could figure out what was going to happen next, the front door opened and I heard Mamma shout. "Grosser Gott! Great God! What has happened here?"

"How can anyone sleep in this flat with all that racket?" Pappa kicked the broken plate across the floor.

Crawling on the linoleum, I collected the shattered pieces. It's all my fault, I thought. I'm the guilty one.

Mamma yanked a fragment from my hand and flung it across the room.

"It's just a damned dish!" Fetching a clean cloth and soaking it under the kitchen faucet, she continued to rave and scream at Pappa.

What she said, I didn't bother to understand. Cradling Walter's head in my arms, I murmured words of comfort while waiting for the tirade to subside.

When it did, Mamma knelt before Walter and put cold compresses on his bloody face. After the bleeding stopped, she tucked us each into bed.

I lay there stiff and frightened.

A moonbeam cast soft light through the window. I could see the washcloth had slipped from Walter's puffed face.

Cold eyes staring from swollen slits, he whispered through cracked lips that barely moved. "It didn't hurt a bit."

"He'll never beat you again," I promised, replacing the cold cloth. Tears of fear burned my eyes as I searched for Walter's favorite bright buttons to put in his hands. He loved the smooth texture of the leather. For me, they were happy memories of playing house with David and snacking on cookies and milk Frau Goldschmidt provided.

Trying to go to sleep, I lowered my eyelids. "God," I implored, "what must I do?" I thought of running away, but where to? Feeling the button in my hand, I remembered the bad people who had beaten and dragged David from the store. Who'd help me and my brother?

I could talk to my teacher. No. She would have to tell the authorities. They'd take me and Walter—where?

My head hurt. The pain pounded like the beating of the drums at the parade.

From the living room, I could hear Mamma and Pappa argue violently. Something—or was it someone—crashed against the wall. Would they never stop?

Why do people fight?

Life was sometimes hopeless.

CHAPTER FOUR—The Yarn—Spring 1939

"Singing in the street? My Mamma?" Could Mamma's friend be right? "What kind of song?" I dropped a few loops of the skein of yarn Paula was winding into a soft ball.

"A lullaby. You've heard her sing it many times. It goes like this." Mamma's friend patiently unraveled the tangle I'd made while she hummed the melody.

Recognizing it after the first three bars, I sang the words. "In the garden, dear Mary was weeping; in her lap, the sweet child was sleeping."

"That's it." Paula nodded. "Your Mamma used to sing that song walking up and down the streets, carrying Walter and holding you by the hand. You'd pick up the coins and paper bills people threw out their windows and put them in your Mamma's apron pocket."

"Did you help her sing?"

"Me?" When Paula laughed, her whole body shook as laughter rippled up and down her large frame. "I can't tell one note from another, much less carry a tune. But your Mamma! She has a big, powerful voice. A beautiful voice." Paula shifted her fingers on the ball of yarn and leaned closer. "That was at the end of 1932. Times were bad and there was fighting in the streets between the Communists and National Socialists. Die verdammten Schweinehunde won in the end. Damned Nazi pigs."

Paula was so agitated, she discovered she had wound the yarn too tight. Redoing it, she mumbled, "And how awful was the inflation. German marks lost their value by the hour. And printing presses all over the country kept printing more, so that each mark was worth less. The numbers on the bills increased by the thousands, but a handful wouldn't buy a bottle of milk."

"What did Pappa do?"

Paula ignored the question. "Schatz," she said, "Concentrate on the skein around your arms or the yarn will get tangled up again."

"What about Pappa?" I insisted. "Where was he?"

"There was no Pappa then, Anneliese." Paula took a deep breath. "It's hard to explain—and more difficult for you to understand. You see, your real Pappa is the one your Mamma refers to as 'no-good father.' Right after you were born, she married Walter's Pappa. I don't know exactly what happened, but your Mamma divorced him."

"Was he mean to her?"

"Probably." Paula leaned back in the chair and dropped her arms to her side. "You can relax for a while." She looked into space for a moment. "Your Mamma is a brave and proud woman. She survives by her own set of rules. No politics, no religion, no free handouts. Ja, ja, she is too good." Paula nodded as she again speedily rolled the yarn over her fingers while I moved my arms back and forth, right and left, in rhythmic motion.

"She has good looks and a big heart, but no luck when it comes to men. You ask me, she treats them too well. Ja, ja." She looked at me. "Are you getting tired, Schatz?"

I shook my head, wanting to hear more about how it used to be. "Did you dance while Mamma sang?"

Paula chuckled and looked at her ankles. "These fat feet don't dance. Never did. No. Your Mamma did the dancing. When she got tired of singing, she took you and your brother to the playground to build castles in the sandbox. I just sat on the bench outside the park and waited for one of my men friends to come around."

Her voice hardly a whisper, Paula's eyes clouded. She didn't notice the yarn was looping round her fingers instead of the ball. "It paid the rent for my little room under the attic." She smiled at my questioning eyes. "Your Mamma lived in the room next to mine. That's how the two of us became friends. We helped each other—even shared the sink and toilet in the hallway. You remember visiting my place right under the attic, ja?"

I did remember climbing the five flights of stairs to the two rooms apart from each other. The bedroom was unheated, but the main room had a couch, table and chairs, and a pot-bellied stove. On the way to the attic, Paula would stop between floors to catch her breath, while Heini raced ahead to light the fire in the potbelly stove.

In the evening, I loved sitting by the window under the slanted ceiling, looking at the twinkling lights and rooftops below. The stars seemed close enough to touch and the moon was so near—I could almost see the face of a man. The pressed-glass kerosene lamp bloomed like a sunflower on the kitchen table, while we ate beef stew. After dinner, I watched Heini wash the lamp chimney, until it gleamed, and trim the wick. Then Paula would spread a deck of cards in a special way over the table to read Mamma's fortune.

Untangling a knot in the yarn, Paula continued. "I met my Heini on that bench by the park," she said, letting her hands become idle again. "His heavenly blue eyes looked so innocent in that young face, and when I touched his upper arms, I could feel the muscles through his threadbare shirt. Ach, it was love at first sight. Ja, ja.

"He said he had no money to spend. But I told him, 'You need no money, Liebchen,' and invited him to my room." She smiled dreamily. "We were married within a month and I've never looked at another man since."

I remembered seeing all the newlyweds on Saturday morning pull up in front of the photographer's near the flower shop. "Did you wear a long white dress and a billowing veil and ride in a silver coach pulled by white horses?"

"No, precious. We had barely enough money to go to the Buergermeister's office and pay the fee for the license." She caressed my cheek. "Happiness is not measured by how much money one has."

"But what did you wear?"

Paula shrugged. "I owned only the dress I was wearing." Her face broke into a mischievous smile. "I washed and ironed it the day before my wedding."

"When I grow up," I said, "I want to get married in a long white gown, and ride in a horse-drawn carriage, and have my picture taken at a studio."

Paula didn't hear my prattling. "I almost called off the wedding."

"You did?"

"Heini showed up at my door wearing a uniform. Jawohl! He dared to cross my threshold wearing scheiss-braun pants and a matching shitty-brown shirt, shiny black boots, and a black leather strap across his chest. And on both his armband and that ridiculous pill-box hat, a swastika."

Her fingers were shaking as much as her voice. "Raus!" I told him. "I'm not going to marry any dammed Fascist. I fought against them in the streets and protested in demonstrations, proudly waving the red hammer and sickle of the working man."

Pulling on the yarn hard, she broke the thread. "But my Heini had reasons. He tried to explain that he had to join the movement to get a chance at a bricklayer's job. 'I'll do anything so you don't have to make money sitting on that bench,'" he said.

Paula shook her head. "Nix, "I told him. "Better sell your body than prostitute your soul." Straightening, she breathed hard. "Take off that damn uniform," I said, "or I'll kick you down the stairs."

Never had I seen Paula in such a state. "Did you throw him out?"

"I didn't have to." A smile crept over her face. "He changed his clothes."

Playfully, she tossed the finished ball of yarn to me. "That's enough for today," she said, patting her hair. "Wonder what's keeping your Mamma? I must get home to cook for my Heini."

"What a day!" Carrying her old string bag, stretched to capacity, Mamma came in and pushed the door shut with her behind. "Schlepp, schlepp, schlepp. My arms are about to fall off." She dropped her burden on the table. "My lady paid me in sheets today, Nice sheets. Towels, too. Thick ones." She spread them out and sat down. "I told Frau Lilienbusch that sheets aren't going to pay the rent. I needed money. After all, her husband is a banker! She told me, no more. The Reich took over the bank or some such thing. The end of her lament was that they have no money. All her other domestics left long ago. All but me."

Mamma rummaged in her purse to fetch a handkerchief. "I hate to leave her. She needs me. Especially on Saturdays. You know how they are during Sabbath. Can't even turn on the light switch." Mamma shook her head, mumbling, "Funny ways they have, those Jews."

"She gave you a bonus at Christmas," Paula said.

"Ja. She's always treated me good." Mamma sneezed.

"Gesundheit," nodded Paula.

Sneezing after a statement always proved it true, I remembered.

"But you need money today. How will you pay the rent? The Hausmeister will be here soon."

Mamma ignored her. "Oh, the mail. I forgot to unlock the box."

"I'll get it." I fetched the key and ran downstairs. There was a light blue envelope, our address written in beautiful script and the postage cancellation clearly read, Heilbronn.

"Where's Heilbronn?" I asked, handing the letter to Mamma.

Mamma's face lit up as she grabbed the letter. "It's either from your grandparents or from one of my four sisters," she exclaimed, opening the envelope with a jagged fingernail. "It's from Lina, my favorite!" she burst out. "She's coming to visit us this summer." Out came the handkerchief. "Why am I crying? I'm so happy."

She gave me a big hug. "Lina is your godmother," she explained. "You'll like her."

My family is growing, I thought. Besides a no-good father, I have a fairy godmother!

Mamma walked around the flat looking here and there. "Ach Du Lieber!" she fretted. "Goodness, this place is a mess. The walls need a whitewash. That good-for-nothing landlord promised two months ago he'd send the painters to do it. And the windows look bare. I must cover them with curtains. And I need linens—" She looked at the sheets and towels on the table. "Frau Lilienbusch! I'll clean her house from top to bottom! Since she has no money, she can pay me with household things. I don't want her Rosenthal. Her everyday dishes are plenty beautiful. She may even give me that nice tablecloth I ironed today. It has a little hole, but I can patch it."

"Remember, Johanna, you need money for the rent first," said Paula, motioning toward the door. "What will you do?"

"The landlord," I gasped. "He's here." Even I recognized his voice as he argued loudly with the tenant next to us.

"That fatso wants all my money," Mamma grumbled, letting him knock twice before opening the door.

He entered slowly, the thick gold chain of his pocket watch drooping across his huge belly. "You keep the place nice," he said, giving the flat a sweeping glance.

"It's a pigsty," retorted Mamma, standing in the middle of the room with her hands on her hips. "You promised to whitewash two months ago."

"You're stalling," thundered the landlord. "The rent is due today."

"The paint was due last month," Mamma shot back.

A heated argument followed, rising in crescendo to shouts of rage.

"Put the money on the table."

"Fix up the flat!"

"I'll evict you!"

"Who'd rent this rat-hole?"

"The money!"

Mumbling something about his taking food out of her children's mouth, Mamma slammed part of the rent on the table.

The landlord grabbed the money quickly and muttered, "Unglaublich!" before leaving. Unbelievable!

"Vollidiot," she sneered after he'd left.

Two days later, a crew of painters appeared. Soon, walls gleamed white, windows sparkled under lace curtains—compliments of Frau Lilienbusch— and floors were polished with wax Mamma had bought in installments from a door-to-door salesperson. Every week the man softly knocked on our door, offered soaps and brushes, and waited patiently for his weekly payment.

Each time, Mamma would rave with great theatrics. "Do I look like I'm made of money?" Or more dramatically, "Didn't I just pay you my last Groschen, my last dime, yesterday?" Or with finality, "Kein Geld—no money."

"Ach, give the poor Jew his Pfennigs," said Paula, digging into her purse for some coins. "He earned them."

Before spring, Mamma lost her last cleaning job. Fear of the "nightly knock" must have scared the Lilienbusch family away. The flat was still furnished when Mamma arrived to clean. But the people were gone.

Mamma took a feather duster and walked from room to room. What about that small table lamp in the parlor? I've always admired its ornate porcelain base and fringed shade. It was promised to her in exchange for work. And she did spend money for streetcar fare. Mamma turned on the bulb. It's beautiful, she thought. Before she could change her mind, she quickly pulled the plug and wrapped the lamp in a sheet. Cradling it in her arms like a baby, she carried it home. It will always remind me of Frau Lilienbusch, she thought.

Meanwhile, the Office of Race Investigation had received enough proof to decide I was Aryan—whatever that meant. Mamma got a job at the main Post Office, located immediately behind the street on which we lived. They were training her to be a letter carrier, a Brieftraegerin—one of the first women ever. Proudly, Mamma slung the huge mail bag over her shoulder— and even got used to wearing a uniform with slacks instead of a skirt. But she would not don the hat with its swastika pin. "It gives me a headache," she told her supervisor.

Young men, who had been mail carriers, exchanged their blue postal uniforms for grey ones—the Wehrmacht, the German Army, the new military force.

It was spring, 1939.

CHAPTER FIVE Lina—Summer—1939

When I first met my Aunt Lina, I stared with wonder—she was so beautiful. Her large brown eyes, accentuated by extra long lashes and artful pencil-thin eyebrows, were the most striking part of her face. Chestnut black hair was carefully coiffured in an upsweep that ended in soft curls on top. I remember Mamma telling me Lina's nickname was "Schwarze" because she had the darkest hair and eyes of the five sisters.

Lina's mouth was as expressive as her eyes. The lower lip looked smaller and fuller than the heart-shaped upper one. And when she smiled, pearly white teeth complemented a soft rosy complexion.

"This must be little Anneliese, my godchild," said Lina, bending down and taking my hand into hers. "I've always wanted a little girl just like you." The gesture and words evidenced warmth and sincerity. Her eyes revealed her love.

My heart swelled with pride and joy. I felt special, and pretty, and good all over. She wants a girl just like me! "Guten Tag," I said, wishing her a good day. Her hand felt firm, but gentle.

Lowering herself to a sitting position, she put an arm around me. "Where I come from, in Heilbronn, the daily greeting is 'Gruess Gott.' It's God's blessing." Her voice was soft and sultry. Nice. But I had to listen carefully to what she said. She talked funny.

I soon learned that it was her Swabian accent that made her sound different. "le" was added to most nouns, making a child, or Kind, a Kindle— which is a small child. Soon Mamma began to talk funny as well, mixing the Frankfurt, or Hessian, dialect with that of her native Swabian.

Lina was about the same height as Mamma, but slimmer. She had the figure of a model. The beautifully tailored dress she wore made her not only look taller, but elevated her appearance from mundane to regal. I continued to stare at her as she walked through the rooms, admiring Mamma's curtains and tablecloth, filling in the near empty wardrobe with her dresses. "You have a nice place, Johanna," she assured Mamma.

Lina's husband, Bert, agreed. Admiring my dollhouse and Walter's grocery shelves, he stepped behind the counter of the make-believe store and addressed me. "What will it be today, Gnaediges Fraulein?" he mocked. "Would the young lass like some flour or sugar? Perhaps a loaf of white bread for your company, and real butter instead of margarine?"

I didn't know which I liked most. The game of shopping or his undivided attention to Walter and me.

"All those tiny shelves and small drawers took a lot of skill and patience to make," Uncle Bert commented to Mamma. "Who gave you the idea?"

"Albert drew up the plans. He treats Walter as though he was his own son and thought the boy would enjoy playing shopping with Anneliese."

Uncle tussled my brother's curly hair. "You're a fine lad." He winked. "Thanks for letting me play with your store."

Rearranging some flowers in a glass vase, Mamma beamed and then served Kaffee und Kuchen in Frau Lilienbusch's everyday China—Mamma's pride and joy. The cake, of course, had been made from scratch the day before—with me stirring the batter about twenty of the required hundred times. It was my job to carefully grease each ridge of the cast iron Bundt pan before Mamma filled it with batter and carried the pan to the baker's oven across the street. The best part was when Walter and I were allowed to lick the inside of the bowl.

After everyone had a second helping of coffee and cake, Lina's husband, Bert, and Pappa decided to take a walk through the neighborhood to check out the various Wirtschaften, or pubs, for a Schnapps or two. Walter trotted along for a lemonade, while I preferred to stay with Mamma and Lina.

I was fascinated by their conversation.

"Tell me about our sisters—Else and Erika, first," pleaded Mamma, grinding beans for another pot of coffee, not the synthetic Ersatz we usually had. "Did Else finish her apprenticeship as a seamstress?"

"Ja, natuerlich. Of course. You know our Else. She always was obedient, the most chaste and sweetest, the one never getting into mischief."

"I remember," sighed Mamma. "Our mother thought she had the goodness of a saint."

Lina broke into a deep laugh as she rummaged through her purse for some photos. "She's the only one of the five of us who could wear a white dress on her wedding day—you know what I mean." Lina produced a picture. "She sews all my dresses. I just show her the latest style in a fashion magazine and she copies it—sometimes even improves on it."

The kettle whistling on the stove interrupted. "I always wanted to be a tailor, instead of going to school to learn alterations," said Mamma as she poured boiling water over the coffee in the filter. "But mother wouldn't let me."

Somehow, I knew how Mamma felt. When I wanted to be a physician, like Dr. Klein, I was told by the receptionist to settle for nurse. However, I knew better than to interrupt. Little children were to be seen, not heard.

Pretending to read, I retreated to a spot not too far from the table—where I could learn much from listening to Lina's answers to Mamma's numerous questions.

"Is Else happy? Why yes. She has a caring husband and Ursule—not Ursula—is adorable. Blond curly hair and eyes as blue as the heavens. How old is he? About two?"

And so it went, as the two sisters caught up on family facts and gossip. "Erika?" Yes, she's still the favorite, the baby—and spoiled. The youngest always is. She's living at home with mother and father. Is she married? No. But she has a little boy—I think he's three. His name? Roland. Blue eyes and blond hair. His Oma and Opa idolize him."

I have grandparents, I thought. Wunderbar. I almost clapped together my hands in joy, I was so excited. My girlfriend, Hannelore, has grandparents. She always tells me how wonderful they are. I wonder what Opa and Oma look like? Probably old, and stooped, false teeth, grey hair. So far I counted three aunts: Lina, Else, and Erika, and two cousins: Ursula and Roland. Mamma poured another cup of coffee. I'm glad their thirst helped me to know more about my ever-growing family.

Adding cream and sugar to the brown brew, Mamma slurped with delight. Lina sipped daintily. "You haven't asked about Hedwig."

"Is she still bossy?"

Lina shrugged. "Yes. And as serious as always. Takes on her responsibility of being the oldest."

Suddenly, Mamma started to cry. "You know what they say: All good things come in three's—the fourth is hexed. I am the fourth born. I don't think any of my sisters care about me—except you. The others picked on me, got me in trouble with Mutter." Mamma cut herself another piece of cake. "Even mother called me Dicke, or 'Fatso.'"

"Johanna," said Lina, "we all had nicknames. As a child, you were overweight. Always eating. Perpetually getting in trouble."

Mamma put the untouched slice of cake on her plate. Both seemed oblivious of me. "Do you know how I felt having to do all the cleaning and scrubbing while you all went to your jobs, or school, or apprenticeships? Like Cinderella, that's how I felt. Only there was no fairy godmother."

Lina tried to wedge in a word, but Mamma's lungs had recharged with oxygen. "It was 'Johanna do this,' and 'Fatso do that.' Wash the windows, darn the socks, fetch potatoes from the cellar. I was treated like a scullery maid."

"You're exaggerating," interjected Lina. "You lay around reading romance novels all day while we were out working." She thumped her chest. "Remember, we handed our weekly wage envelopes to Vater. Father would dole out a little pocket money—if we were lucky." She picked up the coffee pot and poured until coffee spilled over the edge of her cup.

"You all ganged up on me the night we had that big fight." Mamma pointed into the air with the cake knife. "And Hedwig told me to get out."

"That's untrue, Johanna. You left of your own accord. You ran away." Lina's soft voice became firm. "I remember so well that last argument. Granted, we probably picked on you more than we should have. Sometimes treated you badly. But you stormed out of the house and slammed the door behind you—like you'd done so many times before."

I couldn't believe my ears. Mamma running away? Mamma, who always faced problems head-on. Turning her back in defeat?

Pushing her cup to the middle of the table, Mamma spit out the words. "Jawohl! Yes, I left like so many times before. But this time I didn't come back." Her body straightened in defiance.

Lina's cup rattled as she set it on the saucer. "You scared the wits out of us. We waited and waited for a word, a letter, anything. We felt responsible. Everyone worried what had happened to you. Usually you came back after a day or two. But this time you simply disappeared. Vanished into thin air."

A soft sob escaped before Mamma was able to wipe the tears off her face with the back of her hand. "I made it to the big city. Frankfurt. Got jobs cleaning houses during the day. Thank God for rich Jews. One of them found me work waiting on tables in his Gasthaus." She raised her head with pride. "Always good tips."

After some silence, sad again, she said with a glance at me, "That's when I met her no-good father."

The room was so quiet, time seemed to stand still.

"Have you heard from him?"

Feeling Mamma's eyes on me, I turned a page and lowered my face closer to my book, but extended the invisible antennae of my ears so I didn't miss a thing.

"I had to contact him." Mamma whispered. "Had to get an Ahnenpass for Anneliese. You know, that certificate of Aryan ancestry. Ach nein? Oh yes! GESTAPO? Oh no? Ach ja! They put me through hell." Mamma's knuckles rapped the table. "Someday her no-good father will pay for that."

Lina put her hand over Mamma's clenched fingers. "Why didn't you ask for help? There are places for that. Salvation Army. Churches. Government Welfare."

"Welfare? Me? Take a handout? Never! Churches? My motto is, God helps those who help themselves. Salvation Army? I'd never spend a night there. They did find me a place in the hospital in Limburg. I worked till the day I went into labor with Anneliese." A smile of pride crept over Mamma's face. "She weighed over five kilo. I nursed her and someone else's baby besides. Earned enough money to make it back to Frankfurt." Mamma nodded. "Anneliese was a healthy baby—not like her brother. Walter was weak and sickly from the day he was born. I should never have married that Fritz Hoehn. I just wanted a father for my daughter. Instead, I ended up with a crook—a Communist to boot—as well as another child."

Lina stroked Mamma's arm. "They say you should not suffer through the past. Wear it like a loose garment instead, so you can take it off and let it drop. Forgive."

Mamma was unrelenting. Arms folded under her enormous bosom, she muttered, "I curse the day I laid eyes on Fritz, that Schweinehund." After a long sigh and a couple of "Ach ja's," she picked up where she left off. "Let's get back to Hedwig, our oldest sister. How many children has she by now?"

"Three. Heinz, Sonja and Ellen. The girls range in age the same as Anneliese and Walter."

Three more cousins, I counted.

"Heinz is bright," continued Lina. "Learns fast. He spends most of the time with our mother and father. They adore him, and treat him more like a son, than a grandchild."

"Whatever happened to Franz? Is he still in Russia?

"Last I heard, our brother is on his way back to Germany," said Lina. "With a wife and child."

They chattered on.

"Ach nein! Oh ja! Musja is the wife's name. Russian? Ja! It means Maria in German. She has a daughter Tamara. Ach was! You don't say! Another

Russian? Ach Du Lieber! Why is Franz coming back to Germany?
More relatives for me. I almost dropped my book. How exciting!

It was a busy week with everyone buzzing about making plans where to go and what to see. One day we took the streetcar to visit the Palmengarten, a botanical garden near the House of Rothschild, on the west end of Frankfurt. Later in the week, at the Zoo, Uncle Bert lifted Walter high enough to place peanuts in an elephant's trunk. He encouraged us to growl at the lions and make faces at the monkeys. He told us that we talked funny, adding a diminutive 'che' to nouns, instead of 'le'—which was much easier to pronounce. But we did communicate. He bought us an ice cream cone every time the man pushed by with his cart. "What flavor this time?" he asked. "Vanilla or chocolate?" Cocking his head, he closed his eyes while we decided. But the results were the same. "One of each," he'd tell the vendor, and as far as we were concerned, Uncle Bert was a big spender. With a smile on his face and twinkle in his eyes, he always carried change in his pocket.

Aunt Lina also loved spending. She would shop for hours. Especially for hats—outrageous hats. The bigger, the better. I watched her try on one after another. Some were adorned with fashionable feathers, while others were glamorized with veils, lending a mysterious look. Eventually, she chose a creation having flowers and a veil. Mamma almost fainted when she saw the price tag.

Uncle Bert didn't. "You look gorgeous," he told Lina. "Like a film diva. You can wear it whenever and wherever you want. But don't expect me to walk next to you when you have that monstrosity on."

I thought he was kidding, but he wasn't. Sunday afternoon, when the sun was shining out of a cloudless sky, we went for a walk along the river Main that runs through Frankfurt. It was customary to promenade and show off one's latest finery. Walking with the dignity of a queen, Lina received much attention wearing the latest style dress from Paris, high heels, gloves—and chapeau. Some people turned and looked while others simply stopped and stared. Bert watched the spectacle from a few paces behind.

"I'll fix him," said Lina. Smiling graciously, her head held high, she informed the gawkers, "The short fat one walking behind me...that's my husband. Ja, ja."

"Ach du liebe Zeit," sputtered Mamma, shaking her head. She stopped and sat on a bench facing the river. "Goodness gracious!"

Lina joined her. "Ach, my bunions hurt."

Mamma looked at Lina's high heels. "I'd go barefoot before I'd wear that kind of shoe."

"Good idea," said Lina, nonchalantly taking them off. Dangling shoes from one hand, purse from the other, she continued walking down the promenade, telling eyebrow-raising passersby, "My feet hurt," leaving them clucking and strutting in the other direction.

Sitting on a bench, I started to take off my shoes, but one look at Mamma's stern face made me change my mind.

At home, I marvelled at everything Lina did, said—and sometimes sang. Like when she wanted to go to the opera and Bert didn't. "Why don't you like the Nibelungen Ring?" she sang in a clear soprano voice, dramatically repeating, "Why not?"

In his best baritone, Bert bellowed back, "Because Die Walkuere gives me a headache."

"How come?"

"Because!"

"Why not?"

"Because!"

"Please try!"

"Not me!" To emphasize his point, Bert took the lids of two pots and clanked them together. That did it.

Lina asked Mamma, as well as Paula, to accompany her to the opera.

And how I loved Lina's daily ritual of applying makeup! My eyes were glued to her every move. I watched her cleanse and dab, smooth and rouge, powder and paint from bottles and boxes containing magic potions that transformed her face into a picture of beauty.

"Always go easy on the mascara," she'd advise, brushing layer over layer on long lashes.

Mamma stood watching from the kitchen. "You're putting crazy ideas into Anneliese's head."

"Every morning before we go to school, Mamma puts gobs of Nivea cream all over our face," I told my aunt.

Pappa entered the room. "You know what the new regime says about women painting their faces…they belong in a French brothel! German women are to look natural." It was hard to tell whether he was joking or being serious.

Lina refused to be intimidated. "Some German women, with their blond braids and pale cheeks, could benefit from a little rouge." She carefully outlined her lips with a painted stick. "French women know how to enhance what nature provided.

Mamma scorned. "Our Fuehrer would like to turn all blue-eyed blondes into breeding machines. The rule is, marry a cold blonde, keep her pregnant. But have a hot brunette for a mistress!"

"Our Fuehrer has a screw loose," retorted Lina.

After the women left for the opera, Heini got a mug of draft beer from the Bierstube across the street, Bert bought Coca Cola for Walter and me, and we all ate some open-faced sandwiches spread with liver sausage or Limburger cheese.

As always, they talked politics. Austria joining the German Reich. After all, they spoke German and it was Hitler's country of birth. Germany moving into Boehmen and Maehren to rescue Bohemians and Moravians of German ancestry from being tortured. Dr. Goebbel's strident voice of the propaganda machine screeching out abuse by Czechs and Poles.

Heini lit another cigarette. "When will Hitler's appetite stop gobbling up countries?"

Pappa played the host and poured beer. "I predict we'll have another world war." Bubbly foam rose to the rim of his glass and spilled over. "We just added a third shift at the ball bearing plant."

"Partial mobilization is in full swing," sighed Bert. "I'll be one of the first ones drafted because of my medical training.

"I won't be far behind," nodded Heini. "My age group is next in line. It will break Paula's heart."

"And I'll keep cleaning lavatories at the factory," said Pappa, finishing his beer. "Prost!"

All they ever talk about is Hitler and war, I thought.

CHAPTER SIX—War—September 1939

Screeching, the war began coming to us in pieces. When the air raid siren howled, I saw it as a roller coaster rising, rising, rising, terrifying in its upward climb until it reached some kind of peak and fell again, plummeting and dropping as horribly as it rose. The sound went through my clothes and raised goosebumps on my skin. None of us could escape it. It filled our ears, drove routine thoughts from our heads. While the siren blared, there was nothing else to think about.

I remembered watching sirens being installed on top of school buildings. Schools, it seemed, were strategically important. Mamma told of search lights on the edges of the city. And Pappa had seen anti-aircraft cannons set up near the factory. They called them FLAK for Flug-Abwehr-Kanone.

All the families living in our building assembled in the large entry hall of the apartment house. The cranky, older couple from our floor sat on the bottom step complaining about the noisy children. Herr Schmidt's wife and daughter ignored all and prayed the rosary. Frau Rech, with four toddlers clinging to her apron, whacked Willie on his behind for misbehaving. And Frau Wessely's brood of five—or was it six—were, as always, running all over the place.

Over and over the sirens wailed their litany of woe. As yet, the sirens were but a test—the war was real. It was September 1, 1939, the day the German armies rushed across the Polish border to "liberate the world."

I was scared—so scared I almost wet my pants. And I didn't know what I was afraid of. Covering my ears to shut out the painful wail, I started to sob. Hansi took one look at me and let out a howl. The other children joined in. Mothers screamed. Men yelled. Why is everybody upset?

A rude voice commanded, "Ruhe!" Everyone quieted down. Even the siren ceased.

"He must be our new air raid warden," said a neighbor.

Mamma raised a hand to shield her mouth and whispered to the person next to her, "Informer is a better word." She turned to me, shaking her finger. "I never want to see you cry again, Anneliese. You're the oldest. You need to set an example for the little ones!"

Nodding, I wiped away tears with the back of my hand and promised. The younger ones have to be protected, I thought. I must be brave just like Mamma.

The droning voice of the warden continued. "In the event of an air raid—" he glanced at the cellar door, then the little ones"—women and children go first."

"There's no light down there," objected one of the mothers.

It was true. I couldn't remember the reason for being punished—only the darkness. Locked in that damp, musty-smelling cellar, I had felt the terror.

"There are mice in that hole," someone shouted from the back.

"I've seen a rat," added another.

"Ruhe!" The warden's face turned red as he took a deep breath and blew a shrill whistle. Pulling a sheet from his briefcase, he posted instructions on the wall, next to the house rules that told us what we must do before, during, and after an air attack. "Number one," he said, "I'll set traps for vermin. Number two: Everyone must have a flashlight. Number three: Each family must give up two meters of their assigned basement storage space and provide chairs." He stopped to scratch his behind. Sheets of paper scattered to his feet. As he squatted to retrieve them, a loud Furz broke the silence. Ignoring the involuntary chuckles and snickers, he continued in a blustery voice. "The landlord shall supply one bunk bed, but it's only for the old or sick."

Showing the speaker no courtesy, Mamma commented loud enough for the others to hear, "Hermann Goehring, our great Air Defense Minister, told us in his last speech that his name will be 'Meyer,' if a single enemy aircraft penetrates Berlin's air defense."

"Ja, ja," they all cackled, each adding a bit of sarcasm of his own.

"Goehring, the fat one, with all the medals."

"Hermann promised us a net of protection."

"We'll call him by the common name of 'Meyer' from now on. Or Schmidt. Hah, hah. Verstehst?"

Even the cranky neighbor nodded and grinned.

Mamma said, "He and his endless speeches! Screeching day and night from loudspeakers on every street corner."

"Quiet!" Oblivious of his shoes getting splashed, the warden hit a shovel alternately against buckets filled with water and sand. "Number four." His voice lowered an octave. "The occupants of each floor must make sure these buckets are filled at all times." He pointed to the house order posted next to the mailboxes. "Add this responsibility to your weekly schedule of cleaning the stairway and hallway toilet. Number five: Blackouts. All windows must be covered with black shades that will allow no light to pass through. All street lights will be turned off." He itched his nose, then droned on. "But don't worry, police patrols will be enlarged.

"Number six: Emergency tunnels will be dug in cellars from one house to another to provide escape routes."

Why would we be trapped in the cellar? The mere thought of that possibility paralyzed me with fear. It confirmed, however, what I'd overheard Mamma and Pappa discuss not long ago. Bombings!

A high-pitched, but monotonous siren signaled the "All Clear." Not a loud lamentation—just a somber sound, like that of a tired teakettle. Mothers herded their children around them and clambered up the stairs, ignoring the warden's clicking heels, stiff arm salute, and "Heil Hitler."

"Good evening!" Herr Muller secured his bicycle to a rack before picking up his son, Hansi. He kissed his wife Helene, patting her bulging belly. "They're putting me on night shift with overtime," he said as the family climbed the stairs ahead of us. "We'll earn extra food ration stamps!"

Holding her huge stomach, Helene stopped to rest for a moment at our floor before attempting the second flight. "One more month," she sighed.

Mamma embraced her. "Knock on the pipes when your time comes. I can help."

Inside our flat, Mamma studied the new ration cards. Overnight, it seemed everybody had one. Adults, youth, children, toddlers, infants—all were categorized. Expectant or nursing mothers and heavy equipment workers received more, the elderly and retired, less. Adolescents received the most.

"Miss Thyssen explained all about calories in school," I said. "In four years I'll be old enough to get the highest quota."

"Heaven forbid the war lasts that long," said Mamma scrutinizing the cards. They came in a kaleidoscope of colors and sizes with detachable coupons. Brown for bread, white for eggs, yellow for butter or margarine.

Staring into space, Mamma said quietly, "The Nazis have been planning this for a long time. Ja, ja," she sighed. "I was only two years old when my father was called to fight the last war."

She's talking about my grandfather, I thought. "Did Opa earn medals?" In school we'd learned about heroes.

"No. He was captured by the Russians and sent to work on a farm. I didn't see him again until I was eight—same age as you are now."

Mamma placed the ration cards in a drawer next to where she saved the monthly rent, and a down payment on a sewing machine.

In her new job as a postal worker, she now had a steady weekly income and despite the heavy mailbag slung from her shoulder, she walked tall and proud in the carrier's uniform.

Pappa, like Herr Muller, worked longer hours at the Kupferwerke, a ball-bearing

manufacturing plant outside Frankfurt. Having more money, my parents purchased furniture from the second-hand shop.

The open shelves in the kitchen were replaced by a china cabinet with windows and curtains. A moving van delivered a complete bedroom set: glass-topped nightstands, a dresser with attached mirror, and a three-door wardrobe. Though our home was not a palace, we didn't feel like paupers anymore. In fact, Mamma now considered herself rich in the poor neighborhood.

Mamma still knitted and sewed for her old customers in the evening and on weekends. Her fingers were never idle. But a new form of entertainment, called radio, made the work easier. The Sunday afternoon two-hour Wunschkonzert, a concert by request, was all of our favorite. Greetings from families were transmitted to their men far away on the war fronts, and songs wished for by the soldiers broadcasted.

The new media also provided the listener with news about the war. Joseph Goebbels made sure everyone had a government-controlled Volkshoehrer. We were encouraged not to call it a radio—a foreign word. The one-station apparatus appeared in living rooms at the same time autos began disappearing from the streets and the Autobahn. "A temporary loan to the army," explained Dr. Goebbels. "The little propaganda minister with the big mouth," Pappa called him behind closed doors. Listening to foreign broadcasts over a short wave wireless, however, was strictly forbidden. STRENG VERBOTEN!

Walter and I were not allowed to turn the knobs of the radio. "How do you think the people talking and singing get in there?" he asked me one night. I knew what he was thinking. When Walter was curious, he started to take stuff apart. Numerous times he had been in trouble for disassembling things that were hard to put back together.

"I don't know," I answered, wondering myself how a whole orchestra could fit inside that little box. Then I remembered the book I had recently read about the Lilliputians. "They are smaller than a little finger," I told him. We peeked through the penny-sized holes of the board that covered the back of the radio. "They're hiding behind and inside all those tubes. When the knob is turned on, they become invisible," I whispered, half-believing it myself.

Blitz! Lightning! The war slashed through Poland. Drums of war rolled, mercilessly tearing families apart.

It was my duty to read the daily war bulletin in school. While I read, Hannelore, my best friend, added or advanced small Swastika flags.

Within one week, Poland, at the east border, was covered. The advancement of the flags moved slower as the season grew shorter. In April 1940, the German war machine invaded Denmark and Norway. Victoriously, the little flags quickly covered those countries to the north.

"It's the Huns fighting in good German style," hailed the teacher. "We must give our lives to our Fatherland and Fuehrer! As in the Niebelungen saga, we must suppress any fear of death with pride, honor, and fatalism."

Except for the weekly air raid siren tests, the war was exciting. People discussed and argued each offensive as if it were a Sunday soccer match—and our team was winning. And it all happened far away, in other countries; we felt quite safe.

In school, we started the day with a prayer, and ended with another—asking a blessing for our brave soldiers fighting far away to protect our country. Then we always prayed for the Fuehrer.

Second period started with a Heil Hitler. Like little puppets, we popped up, right arm extended, and sang the German national anthem, "Deutschland, Deutschland, ueber Alles," followed by the new National Socialist song—something about raising the flags, tightening the ranks, and marching to the pace of the storm troopers. The song ended with a reminder of those killed by the Red Front Reactionaries. I didn't mind singing, but keeping my arm extended all the while we sang was torture.

"Jesus," Mr. Schneider, the second period teacher, said softly with a hint of reverence. He was short, thin, almost bald, with blue, penetrating eyes, behind thick glasses. Despite suspenders, his pants hung baggy and his shirt always looked rumpled. He once taught history, starting with the Germanic tribes long before the time of Christ. But Dr. Goebbels, who was also in charge of education, had decided that history now had to start with the present time, namely the National Socialist dictatorship.

"Jesus," Herr Schneider repeated slowly.

I wondered if he was going to teach Catechism.

"You learned about Jesus," he said a little louder. "The son of God." He pointed upward. "Do you know who killed Him?" His penetrating eyes were as sharp as his voice. He paused, stalked to the chalkboard and quickly drew the Star of David. "The Jews killed him."

The next day, he changed his tune. "Jesus was but a Jew," he sneered. "He's not worthy to be worshipped."

Something isn't making sense, I thought. The messages contradicted each other. But one thing I understood. Everyone should hate Jews. All of them.

Why? I recalled reading about a Jewish butcher, named Harman, who chased little children with an axe. After he caught them, he chopped their bodies into small pieces to make sausage. "I read it in this paper they handed out at the streetcar stop," I told Mamma.

She took one look at the title of the weekly and stuffed Der Stuermer in the cold stove, mumbling something about anti-Semitic nonsense. The Stormer prints but scandals," said Mamma, "intended to agitate people with lies and cartoons of bad taste. Don't read that trash!"

I promised, but nonetheless, I felt scared. I remembered once taking a shortcut to school through a narrow, dark street flanked by tall buildings. Its dull windows looked as foreboding as did the gaunt people with long straggly beards. Dressed in black robes that blazed a yellow star, and heads covered with small caps, they hurried past without a smile. Could one of them be a butcher? Never will I take this sinister-looking route again, I swore.

Herr Schneider still droned about our great Fuehrer, the wonderful gifts to his countrymen and party members—the Volksgennossen and Parteigenossen. The new tract houses that gave the unemployed work and shelter.

I knew of this, too. I'd heard Mamma tell how my grandfather toiled long hours to complete hundreds of duplex homes outside Heilbronn. The mortgage payments were affordable, enabling my grandparents to own a home.

A Volkshoehrer and Volkswagen meant a radio and car for all the folks. Autobahn highways crisscrossed Germany.

"A proud army, navy, and air force are protecting our fatherland from its unfriendly and pushy neighbors," said Herr Schneider.

He lectured on Hitler Youth, the proud future of the German Reich, and distributed notices when and where to report for the next meeting.

Hitler Jugend.

Now it was compulsory to be a member. Without membership, higher education was denied. I was glad when he dismissed the class. "Heil Hitler." Arm up. Click. March out.

Since there was no history class scheduled, Miss Thyssen, our home room teacher, suggested we go to the library and read books about the past. "Study the old kings and kaisers: Barbarossa, Charlemagne, Frederic the Great. Go back to the Germanic tribes as far as you can," she encouraged us. "I'll be available to answer questions."

I told Mamma what Mr. Schneider had said about Jesus and the Jews. Also that Miss Thyssen had suggested getting books about history at the library.

Mamma took a moment to think while stirring the stew. "I don't like that Herr Schneider." She slammed the lid on the pot. "The library charges a fee to check out books. You'll have to wait until I get paid at the end of the month."

Paula, who was visiting as usual, pulled out her coin purse and handed me a fifty-Pfennig piece. "That should be enough to get a membership card and one book. Better start with ancient history. As far back as the Iron Age."

I looked at the alarm clock ticking on the kitchen table—the only time piece in the house. "If I hurry, I can be back before the air raid siren gets tested again."

Mamma gave an approving nod. Covering her ears, she said, "I hate that sound."

Helping me with my coat, Paula mumbled. "With all the protection Reichsmarshall Goehring brags about, I wonder why these tests are necessary.

CHAPTER SEVEN—Victory—Spring 1940

It snowed. Not the delicate frozen flakes that covered the countryside like a white blanket, and that could be molded into snowballs and snowmen; not the cold fluff that delights children. What filled the air that warm spring night in May 1940 was a blizzard of white leaflets. To the staccato bursts of anti-aircraft guns, millions floated downward through the beams of searchlights, performing a lazy ballet as they silently landed on Frankfurt.

When the sirens sounded the ALL CLEAR, Pappa tramped in, catching us coming up from the cellar. "I had to wade ankle deep through that paper slush," he said, as he distributed a fistful into eagerly outstretched hands.

Outside, loudspeakers blared from cars and street corners: "Gathering and reading of flyleaves is strictly prohibited. Streng verboten! Offenders will be arrested and punished."

The leaflets disappeared into pockets quicker than they had appeared on the streets. Tempted by curiosity, I hid one inside my light overcoat and went upstairs to undress and return to bed. By the light of my flashlight, I read the forbidden:

GERMANS. FOR NINETY-TWO DAYS YOU HAVE RAINED BOMBS ON ENGLAND. NOW IT IS OUR TURN. SIGNED AIR MARSHALL A. T. HARRIS, BRITISH.

I was stunned. What does it mean, I wondered rereading the message.

For weeks everyone had been trilling and shouting the catchy lyrics to a peppy tune, but lately it had begun to sound like a hymn of hate.

"Do you hear the motors sing?

Attack the enemy!

Do you feel your eardrums ring?

Attack the enemy!

Bombing, bombing, bombing old Eng-l-land."

Still shaking from earsplitting explosions of anti-aircraft fire, I scooted under the featherbed. I had to escape the anxiety-ridden voices of neighbors in our living room and the constant blare of loudspeakers. Finally, I slept.

At dawn, Walter woke me. "Let's hunt for shrapnel," he urged, and pulled the pillow from under my head.

"It's too early," I protested.

Walter rattled the cigar box that contained our souvenir collection. "I checked outside," he said. "Hundreds of kids are prowling the neighborhood."

I dressed hurriedly, not bothering to wash my face or comb my hair. Rushing outside, I saw children of the Hitler Youth Brigade—not looking for FLAK splinters, but picking the city clean of every printed leaflet.

On May 16, Holland capitulated. The next night, the British launched their first air raid over Frankurt.

Lately, we hadn't bothered going to the cellar every time the sirens wailed.

"What city is getting bombed this time?" Mamma would wonder aloud, and tell us to go back to sleep.

But Walter and I crept through the dark to the bedroom window, lifted the blackout curtain, and watched the searchlights crisscross the sky, ready to zoom in on their targets. Suddenly, the sky was filled with the droning of airplane engines. "They must be British bombers." Walter stood on a chair to see better.

A flash, a crash, a pounding roar. Was it a bomb? Or a plane that exploded? A Junker or Spitfire? We had learned in school that the English fighter plane could out-maneuver our Messerschmitt 109 and a Focke-Wolffe 190. But not to worry—the German planes were faster. I didn't take time to figure out which was which. At the first sound of gunfire, I took Walter's hand and fled downstairs into the cellar.

The air battle raged. "They got another one," boasted Walter, a mixture of fear and excitement in his voice.

"Hope it wasn't one of ours!" Mamma's whole body trembled as another explosion shook the air.

Huddled in our deep cellar, I quivered with fear. Screaming children and mothers competed with the explosions above. You can't show fear or cry in front of the younger ones, Mamma had told me months ago. Instinctively, I put my palms over my ears to muffle the human cries and the inhuman explosions.

Wide-eyed, Hansi copied me.

I crouched next to tiny Lieselotte, who held her breath in terror. "Cover your ears," I advised, guiding small hands. Screams waned to faint sobs. Mothers rocked the wee ones in their arms. I walked from child to child and folded their little hands. "Dear God," I prayed with them, "please protect us." Silently I said, "God, please make it stop."

For a few seconds it was quiet above, except for the humming of aircraft. I watched the flickering light from the dripping candlestick. Shadows quivered on the wall. Then anti-aircraft cannons opened fire. Pappa could tell the difference between explosions. "Our fighters must have run out of ammunition," said the warden, edging closer to the emergency exit that led to the adjacent cellar. He was ready to squeeze his fat body through the narrow opening.

What if he gets stuck in the hole? The thought made me shudder.

The air battle lasted twenty minutes, but seemed like hours. Later we learned only three bombs were dropped that night, but many planes were shot down, doing more damage to homes than did the bombs. According to news reports, British bomber and fighter casualties far outnumbered German.

"Good!" cheered the populace. Few questioned the numbers.

Two weeks later, shortly after midnight, we had another bomb attack—a major one. Machine gun fire from fast-moving fighters mingled with the droning engines of bombers.

A few seconds of silence. Anti-aircraft cannons bellowed. "The reception committee," said Mamma, putting protective arms around Walter and me. Hell came crashing to earth. Explosion after explosion shook the air. I was convinced it meant the end of the world—and dared not to breath.

"Bombs!" chocked the warden.

Drowning out the sound of FLAK, they mercilessly pounded the earth, a heavy downpour laced with deadly explosives.

Two hours after the attack began, we stumbled up the cold cellar steps.

The warden yelled. "Hurry! Come outside!"

Walter and I squeezed through the crowd of grownups to catch a glimpse of the awesome sight. At the far end of our narrow street a fierce blaze spewed huge flames. Tongues that licked and hissed like a fire dragon. Smoke billowed, stinging nostrils and scratching throats. "How soon will it be up here?" Walter coughed, rubbing his eyes.

"I don't know." I grabbed his hand like a security blanket. Would the fire burn out like it did at the synagogue? Terror gripped my mind at the memory. Or would it spread to neighboring buildings?

Fire engines blared their familiar warning. "Da-dee, da-dee, da-dee, da-dee." Hoses were connected to hydrants and soon water gushed, torpedoing the flames with a vengeance.

Helmeted men shouted commands.

The wind howled, driving the fire column closer.

I clutched at Mamma's apron in fear.

Holding me close, she shouted, "I need a cigarette. Someone please give me a smoke." The warden handed her his cigar—and she puffed.

"A bomb hit the newspaper building, the General Anzeiger," yelled a boy across the street.

"Bravo! Those Tommys just wiped out one of Dr. Goebbel's propaganda machines," snickered an old man.

Mamma poked him with an elbow. "Careful!" she whispered. "The walls have ears!"

Flames leapt skyward, devouring bales of paper. Roaring winds increased their ravenous appetite as the fire spread to adjacent buildings—crackling, licking, exploding, moaning like the lowest notes of a gigantic pipe organ.

The increasing smoke brought more tears to my eyes. I reached for Mamma's hand. "Will the fire eat our house, too?"

"Not tonight," Mamma's voice quavered.

From then on, I added a prayer before going to sleep. "Please, God, don't let a bomb fall on our house."

The next morning at school, our religion teacher taught us to listen carefully and consistently for the angels God sends. "Everyone has a guardian angel," Miss Duboir assured us, "especially the little children." She copied the psalms on the blackboard.

He shall cover you with His feathers.

And under His wings you shall take refuge.

His truth shall be your shield and buckler

You shall not be afraid of the terror by night.

Nor of the arrow that flies by day.

"How big is a guardian angel?" I asked. I had always pictured angels to be small, pudgy cherubs with little wings.

"They come in different sizes, with more than one set of wings of various spans, and their hair matches the color of those powerful wings," Miss Duboir explained.

I imagined my own angel to be big and strong, dressed in a gold gown, with wavy blond hair flowing above vibrating feathers. Each time I pictured this angel, it was guiding me gently to safety.

The raids on Frankfurt continued. Six more in June. The propaganda news kept daily records. When British planes approached, screaming sirens pierced nerves rubbed raw from lack of sleep. At times, we spent most of the night in the cellar.

Scrambling out of bed, we dressed quickly or just grabbed our clothes and ran. To get to the shelter, we had to cross a short span of open space. That meant dodging the falling shrapnel spread by FLAK bellowing fiercely at targets on the dark horizon. Sometimes the planes unloaded their explosives over Frankfurt; other times they passed high enough to be silent and bring terror to another city farther south.

When the armada returned after dropping its deadly cargo, the FLAK again tried to shoot down as many planes as possible. Still taking cover in the cellar, we knew when anti-aircraft cannons hit their target. A long whining sound was followed by a crash.

"Kaputt!" The block warden glowed and yelled. "Got one!"

Mamma didn't cheer. "A mother will cry for her son," she said softly. "A child may have lost a father."

For the first time, I realized that our enemies were humans, too, that they fought for their country, and suffered over missing loved ones.

Eventually, Walter and I didn't bother undressing at night. Instead we took off our shoes and slipped under the bed covers, hoping to sleep. Others, like the old couple next door, spent all their nights in the cellar.

After repeated raids, school sessions were re-arranged to start an hour later, so that children could catch up on lost sleep. The first period of instruction was cancelled

"Who needs religion?" Mr. Schneider sneered. "Who was Jesus Christ anyhow?" he screeched. "A Jew! A rotten, stinking Jew!"

I began to wonder. I was certain I hadn't misunderstood him when he'd denounced the Jews for killing Christ. Something was wrong.

CHAPTER EIGHT—Hannelore—May—1940

"Will the war be over soon?" I looked at Mamma, sitting near the radio, knitting needles clicking furiously in her hands.

She fumbled with the yarn. "I hope so!" she muttered as she retrieved the dropped stitch.

This was such an exciting time, I thought. In school, each day started with the Wehrmachtsbericht, the news bulletin from the front.

Victory!

German forces liberated Belgium and The Netherlands.

Victory!

The mighty army out-flanked the Maginot Line and entered France.

Victory!

A large British cruiser sunk by a small German U-Boat.

Heil Hitler!

My friend, Hannelore, got to move the little Swastika flags west across France, and added another where British warships had crossed. Although we didn't learn much history, we became experts about current events—and geography. For homework we drew detailed maps of the countries surrounding Germany and memorized names of cities, rivers, forests and lakes.

When Pappa turned on the radio, thoughts about school were broken by hysterical trumpet fanfares—that's what Mamma called them. Ta, tara ta, tara ta, tara ta, tara taaaa!

"Achtung! Achtung!" the news announcer shouted. "Attention! We interrupt this program with a special announcement from the war front! Victory! Paris surrenders without resistance. France has capitulated."

I accepted the news matter of factly. Germany always wins, I thought. Our army was invincible.

Pappa studied the calendar on the wall while the radio blared, "Six weeks of fighting. That's all it took to bring the French to their knees!"

Turning down the volume, Pappa said, "It was on my birthday, the twelfth of May, when our armies swarmed across the Western borders. I remember it well!"

I looked at today's date. June 18, 1940.

"I hope this is the end of the war," said Mamma. "I'm getting tired of the British bombing the hell out of us."

The radio credited the quick defeat of the French to the Luftwaffe. 'STUKAs, or Sturzkaempfer, are the heroes of the day," the announcer shouted. "When on the prowl, they create havoc wherever they strike."

One afternoon I saw a full-length movie glorifying our dive bombers, featuring the good-looking movie idol, Karl Raddatz, as the star pilot. All the kids thought it was an exciting movie, full of heroic deeds, with the good guys being the Germans and the bad guys everyone else.

Miss Thyssen, our home teacher, said she didn't have time to see movies, but steadfastly continued to teach Poetry and Music. I began to study scenes from Goethe's "Faust," and learned singing Lieder by Franz Schubert that revealed the composer's profound union with nature and its beauties.

Drills in Math were administered by an older teacher, Herr Becker, who was grumpy most of the time. Someone said he had suffered shell-shock during the First World War.

Geo-politics, primarily of National Socialism, was taught by Herr Schneider, an honorary party member. His beady blue eyes cast a hypnotic spell over us. One minute soft-spoken, the next instant shouting words with machine gun rapidity. "Rassenschande! Racial Shame! Hate! Brutality! Terror! Today Germany, tomorrow, the world. Heil Hitler!"

The lesson always started with questions about our Fuehrer—and he liked calling on me. "Eisenkramer!"

I stood. "Jawohl!"

"Birthdate of our Fuehrer?"

"Twentieth April, 1889."

"Birthplace?"

"Braunau am Inn."

"Book he wrote?"

"Mein Kampf. Written while in prison." I knew what would be the next question and could've recited the answers in my sleep.

Satisfied, Herr Schneider, told me to sit down.

Hannelore was called on next. Usually, she had the assignment of reading the war report from the newspaper. "The latest advances and victories of the German army…"

My eyes followed Mr. Schneider's pointer on the wall map of Europe. It moved north across Denmark to England while Hannelore read on. "British bombers continue their scattershot bombing patterns on German cities. In retaliation, English industrial areas were attacked last night by the Luftwaffe."

The civilians seemed to be taking more of a beating than the soldiers at the front, I thought.

When we did have a night without an alarm, Miss Duboir resumed religious studies during first period. It was the only time the class was co-ed. Boys sat to the left, girls to the right. I always felt shy around my classmates, especially the boys, and moved as far away from them as I could.

I watched with envy as the boys in class bragged about making the loudest screech by wetting a finger and rubbing it across the laminated desk. The girls just giggled and made their own little screeches. Could I get their attention by making a squeak?

A devil sat on my left shoulder and whispered in my ear. "Do it," he urged.

"Don't! It's rude," warned the angel on the right.

Too late. The devil won. He forced my wet middle finger across the desk. "Screeeeeeeeeeech!" It was the longest, loudest, most beautiful squeak ever made.

My heart pounded. I looked up. Had I really done that?

"Who is responsible for that?" Miss Duboir's high-pitched voice silenced the students' cheers.

All eyes blamed me. "Eisenkraemer did it," they shouted, pointing.

On no, not me, I thought, slumping down in a heap of guilt, staring at my finger and the desk. How could I have done such a dreadful deed?

Miss Duboir glanced at me. "Eisenkraemer would never do such a thing," she said scornfully. Turning to the blackboard, she made the white chalk screech across the slate as she wrote the lesson for the day.

Silently, I debated. Should I stand up and admit that I was the one who produced that wonderful terrible sound? She would be disappointed. I was one of the others now, not so perfect anymore. Shoulders still hunched, I glanced around wondering. Would they accept me? The need for acceptance won. I kept silent. In my heart, however, I made a promise to be good and never, never make another screech.

I liked the tall, Protestant teacher with the French-sounding name. She had a kind face, although she rarely smiled. "God loves all people—even the poor and ugly," she began, "regardless of belief or origin."

Her lesson always gave me comfort and hope. Sometimes I felt so small and helpless in this world, so filled with terror that I could hardly breathe—afraid of bombs bursting over our house, fearful of fire burning me alive. And always scared of Pappa.

We prayed before the bell announced the end of the period. "God protect us from the perils of war," the teacher added quietly. "Provide safety for our soldiers, and guide ourFuehrer to lead us to peace. Amen."

On my way out, Miss Duboir stopped me. "Anneliese," she said, extending a damp sponge, "please help me clean the blackboard."

She watched and waited while I scrubbed until the slate gleamed like ebony. Ask her for forgiveness, pleaded a voice inside. Finally I turned to her. Eyes cast down, I looked at my shoes, and in a voice barely audible choked, "I'm sorry."

"God bless you, Anneliese." She lifted my chin and softly stroked my hair, her dark eyes glowing.

The stone that weighed my heart with guilt rolled away like magic.

On the playground, Hannelore jumped rope.

"Acht-und-achtzig, neun-und-achtzig,neunzig,'" she counted before she missed.

"You're going to be ninety years old, wow!" We all laughed at the time-word ritual.

Hannelore was good in sports. She jumped the highest, ran the fastest, and everyone wanted her on their handball team. She would shinny up a pole in the gymnasium with speed and ease, then slide down even more quickly—black,

shoulder-length hair encircling her head like a halo. "I learned to climb from my brothers," she'd laugh.

Uhlandschule, our school named after the poet Ludwig Uhland, was in a neighborhood of merchants. These families earned more money than those in the working class neighborhood where I lived. I was almost ten and beginning to realize that I was not dressed as nicely as my classmates. We couldn't afford store-bought clothes, so Mamma sewed my entire wardrobe by altering hand-me-downs. The only things purchased were underwear and shoes.

I was never invited to my fellow students' beautiful homes, except when I helped with their homework. Conversely, I was not allowed to bring anyone to our modest flat, not even Hannelore.

"We may be the rich people of this neighborhood," Mamma would tell me, "but we're poor in comparison to the feine Leut', the people of status in the suburbs."

Hannelore and I loved learning. She excelled in math, but I was best in spelling. When we were not helping slower students with their homework after school, we'd walk together to her house. Hannelore's large family lived on the top floor and had a beautiful roof garden with a view over the city. One could see the cathedral on one side and the burnt out synagogue on the other. I tried to see the street where I lived, but the distance was too great.

We collected pictures of movie stars. Black and white photos the size of postcards. "I'll trade you Marika Roeck, the Hungarian dancer, and Zarah Leander, the Swedish singer, for Karl Raddatz," Hannelore bargained.

"No." I pressed the blond movie idol to my heart. "He's mine for ever and ever. I'll never part with him."

"Where did you get him?" Hannelore spread her collection across the floor. Hers was much larger than mine. But I had the favorite!

"The man in the tobacco shop saved him for me." I sorted my few cards in order of best looking, with Karl Raddatz on top. "He cost my whole week's allowance. Ten Pfennig."

Berthold, one of Hannelore's eight brothers, arrived with his collection of miniature war weapons: artillery, tanks and anti-aircraft; STUKA's and fighter planes; ships of all sizes—big destroyers and small submarines.

My brother, Walter, and I had a cigar box full of these same models. Like Hannelore's brothers, we begged them from people who had bought one, two, three, or more during the monthly money drive for the "good cause." Hitler Youth, boys and girls as young as ten, would walk the streets offering an assortment of trinkets: flowers, birds, animals, weapons, for a Groschen—ten pennies. The trinkets wobbled on a string fastened to coat or sweater buttons, signifying the stamp of approval for the war effort. No one would dare be without one, lest they be considered disloyal to Fuehrer und Vaterland.

"Let's have a sea, land, and air battle," said Berthold, lining up his fleet of ships, columns of tanks, and squadrons of war planes. "I'm going to be a fighter pilot in a Messerschmitt 109."

"Our Mutti doesn't want us to play war," cautioned Hannelore.

"My Mamma threw our collection in the trash after Walter and I had a fist fight," I said. "He drew most of the planes and wiped out my army. I told Walter that since I was Germany, I had to win—but he didn't let me." I rolled up my sleeves. "See, he scratched me after I hit him back."

Berthold's brother Willie joined him in the war game. "When I am old enough, I want to be a gunner in a Messerschmitt dive bomber," he said, maneuvering one of the STUKAs over the battlefield. "Rat-tat-tat-tat-tat. Volltreffer!"

"Direct hit!" Berthold feigned dying and took one of his tanks out of the battle formation.

"Ewald received his draft notice today," Willie said to his brother. "I wonder if he'll be in the infantry, like Egon, or the cavalry, like Alex?"

"Mutti cries a lot lately." Hannelore sighed. "'They're stealing my boys for Kanonenfutter,' she says."

"What's cannon fodder?"

"I don't know."

Hannelore rummaged in a box. "I found it," she exclaimed, holding up a slim book. On its cover was a picture of a beautiful woman in the arms of a handsome man.

With our backs to the boys, we read the title. "Die grosse Liebe." A Berlin movie studio was making a film named after this book. "The Great Love."

"How did you get it?"

"My sister left it on her nightstand. Mutti gets a new romance novel every week and she and Sofie read them all the time."

"Mamma reads them, too. She even turns the pages while knitting stockings." I whispered so the boys wouldn't hear me. "Sometimes the man and woman kiss."

"Really?" Hannelore broke into giggles. "Once I saw Sofie smooch with her boyfriend on the couch in the living room."

"Did they have their arms around each other, like in the books?"

"How did you know?" Hannelore gasped.

"It's in the stories. I've been reading them when Mamma and Pappa are gone." I looked into Hannelore's eyes, blue as forget-me-nots. "Promise not to tell."

"I swear." She crossed her heart.

"I have another secret."

Hannelore moved closer.

I hesitated. How can I tell my best friend Pappa fondles me while Mamma is at work. How can I tell her about the things he coaxes me to do to him. No. She won't believe it. I shuddered with shame and told her a good secret. "I'm writing a story myself. Eight pages are done, but I don't have any more paper to write on."

Hannelore jumped up. "I have some in my book bag." Handing me a few sheets, she asked, "Is it a love story?"

I nodded. "It's called "Angels Unawares." I'm hiding it under the mattress with some of the books."

"What if your Mutti finds it?"

"Since Mamma broke her leg on the ice carrying mail, she works long hours during the night-shift sorting letters, and sleeps during the day. She never makes beds any more. I have to help her with the housework."

"You do? I never have to help Mutti. She and my big sister do everything. But I do get to cut out cookies for my brothers in the military and knead dough on the weekends when Mutti makes Apfelkuchen. Apple cake is Vati's favorite."

"Mine, too."

Slowly, I gathered my things to leave. "Does your Pappa ever beat you?"

"Never!" Hannelore looked shocked. "Sometimes he gets after the older boys. But my Vati would never lay a hand on me. Never!" She grabbed my arm. "Does yours?"

Slinging the book bag over my shoulders, I nodded with downcast eyes. Inside, just a little bit more of me died.

CHAPTER NINE—Surprise Assault 1940

"Aha!" exclaimed Pappa reading the newspaper. "The British are concentrating on the Northwest: Essen, Duesseldorf, Wuppertal. That's where the steel mills churn out weapons." No wonder Frankfurt is only averaging two raids per month.

Pappa continued to read. "It says here forty-seven bomb-proof bunkers will be built in Frankfurt through the winter of 1940-41!" His fist pounded the dining room table. "Only last week we were promised the war would be over before the end of the year." He slammed down the evening paper. "It doesn't make sense."

"Empty words," grumbled Mamma. "I don't trust those grubby little climbers in Berlin. All I hear are hymns of hate."

I recalled how our teacher, Herr Meister, with eyes ablaze, parroted Herman Goehring. "We'll fight until the last British bomber crashes!"

Bunkers? Bombs? Battles? I didn't like the sound of it—too scary. Better not think about it. Besides, two afternoons a week I was busy attending Hitler Youth meetings where I learned of the good things our leaders did. We sang hiking and marching songs, and sometimes practiced parading.

Singing was fun. I always enjoyed songs that praised the nature and its elements: tall trees swaying their majestic crowns in the wind, birds praising the morning dew, and fields spreading green, yellow, and brown patchwork quilts across the countryside. The poetic lyrics of the sun bathing hills and dells with life inspired me to walk briskly, even bounce a little, inhaling the panorama with wonder and joy.

The new patriotic tunes, however, with words of loyalty to our leaders and pride in our country forced me to march in tight formation, body straight and rigid. "Left! Left! Turn!" shouted the youthful leader in uniform, her braided blond hair securely pinned to the top of her head. A shrill whistle commanded the beat to endless verses, dampening the feeling of glory in our Fatherland with boredom and sweat.

Weary, but determined, I marched and sang, sang and marched, like a true German trooper following its master's orders.

"Ja, ja," cackled old women leaning out of windows and doors as they watched us parade through the narrow streets. Tongue in cheek, they chanted, "This is Adolf's proud new youth? The future of Germany?"

Before winter, we'd go on field trips, collecting medicinal herbs in the woods. Camomile plants were easy to spot because of their mustard-yellow blossoms, and the fresh fragrance of mint lead us to clusters of green foliage. "Watch the nettles," cautioned Hannelore. "Their leaves resemble those of Mint and create large welts on skin when touched."

Too late. Scratching my arms and hands furiously, I twisted a dance of agony to the sting of burning nettles. "I want to go home," I whined.

Spring tiptoed into the city and countryside, spreading new hope that peace was just around the corner.

Hannelore and I lingered longer than usual on the roof garden, enjoying the warm sunshine. She told me about her sister's wedding, and the man Sofia married. It all sounded exciting.

"What did she wear?" I asked.

Hannelore showed me a photograph. Sofia wore a short, light street dress and the groom wore a small spray of Maybells in the buttonhole of his military jacket. "He's training to be a pilot." Proudly she showed me more pictures.

"He looks handsome in his Luftwaffe uniform!" I exclaimed. "Are they going on a honeymoon?"

"There was no time. He had only a three-day leave, so they didn't even have a party. They'll have a big wedding with presents and dancing after the war is over." She started to giggle. "The City of Frankfurt gave them a wedding present—a copy of Hitler's Mein Kampf. Vati uses it as a doorstop in his workshop."

Hannelore strode dramatically across the floor. "When I get married, I'm going to have a big church wedding with bells ringing, a long dress, and flower girls—and everything."

"I'll never get married."

"Why not?"

"Because I'm going to be a teacher like Miss Thyssen. And teachers don't get married." Besides I don't want to have to sleep with a creep like Pappa.

"I thought you were going to be a scientist, like Madam Curie, or a medical doctor," teased Hannelore.

"Mamma won't let me go to a high school, much less a university. She says we can't afford it." What's the use of getting good grades?

Hannelore interrupted. "But you received a scholarship—just like me. Why can't you go?"

"Because my family is not a party member—just like yours."

She looked disappointed. "That means we can't attend the Frankfurt Academic Gymnasium for girls."

I nodded. "I heard Mamma tell Paula she won't ever join the Nazi party. It's like selling your soul to the devil." I shrugged in defeat. "And without membership, there's no chance of getting a higher education. Besides, Mamma doesn't trust the State schools. Says they'll turn me into a little Hitler puppet and that I wouldn't feel comfortable with those fancy people of high breeding." I folded my arms in defiance. "She just doesn't understand me."

"My parents aren't thrilled about my going to that school either," said Hannelore. "We're not rich—even though Vati owns his tailor shop." She signed. "I rarely see him anymore. Day and night he sits bent over the sewing machine making uniforms for officers."

Although we were alone on the roof top, Hannelore lowered her voice. "Vati hates the Hitler Youth. He won't have anything to do with the Nazis. Didn't want Mutti to accept the special commendation for having ten children."

I started whispering, too. "Mamma didn't even let me wear a uniform to the meetings. You know what she did?"

"What?"

"She went to the group leader and put on a show. 'I'm just a poor working woman and don't have the money to buy a uniform,' she lamented. I was so embarrassed!"

"Where'd you get the one you wore last week?"

"They gave me a second-hand one. But as soon as Mamma learned that I was recommended for leadership, she shrunk it! Can you imagine? How humiliating! Sometimes, I just don't understand her."

The big cast iron bells in the cathedral nearby announced five o'clock Vespers.

"Gott im Himmel!" I grabbed my book bag and skipped down the five flights of winding stairs. Am I going to be in trouble? I ran all the way home.

My brother sat on the steps outside our flat. "Dicke Luft," he said, not smiling. "They've been arguing."

I sat down next to him and asked, "What about this time?"

74

"You." Walter hesitated. "They found the love stories under your mattress."

Fear paralyzed my speech. How could I forget the monthly laundry day routine? Mamma stripping the beds, Pappa helping turn the mattress. I could see her fury when she discovered the books.

My heart began to pound faster. Never mind the books. What about my manuscript? Thirty hand-written pages or more.

The door crashed open. "Where have you been?" Mamma's voice was loud and accusing as she pulled me inside. She held three thin weekly issues of romance novels in her hand.

But where was my manuscript?

"Is this what you're looking for?" Pappa tapped the rolled up pages on the stump of his arm. He didn't look angry, like Mamma. He didn't even raise his voice. Except for that sardonic grin on his face, he almost seemed benevolent. "It's quite good."

"It's trash," said Mamma. "I want you to burn it."

I gasped. "But it's just like fairy tales, with dukes, and counts, and barons." I wanted to protest more, but the words remained locked in my mouth. Never talk back to your parents, I remembered—especially when Mamma appeared exasperated.

"Perhaps she wants to be a writer," mocked Pappa, filling a bucket with water from the sink faucet.

Mamma arranged the white soiled sheets and clothing in the oval wash tub on the floor, all the while fussing and fuming. "Anneliese, what is to become of you? Your head is always in the clouds." She emptied the pail in the tub, then sprinkled soaking powder all over the wash. Pappa drew more water.

Looking down at my feet, I stood there feeling small and useless, glancing at Mamma, waiting for my punishment.

Finally she straightened with a groan. "Ach—mein Ruecken, wie weh—my back aches. She untied her apron and hung it on the rack attached to the back of the door. "I forbid you to read any more of those trashy love stories," she said in a stern voice. "You're not old enough—you understand?"

I nodded. I was getting off easy—no spanking. Mamma must be tired.

She looked at Pappa getting ready to leave for his job. "Will you have to work overtime again?"

"Most likely." He put a Blutwurst sandwich and my manuscript in his lunch bucket. "Don't expect me before sunrise."

While Mamma heated leftover soup on her new gas stove, I set the table.

As always, we ate without conversation. Then Mamma broke the silence. "First time my mother caught me reading a romance novel I got a hard spanking." Rubbing her eyes, looking tired, she nodded in my direction. "It hurt," she said.

"I'll do the dishes quietly so you can take a nap before going to work, Mamma."

"Good. I need the sleep." She wound the alarm clock and set it for ten. "It will be a long night." She sighed. "Hope we won't have an alert so we can work through the shift. Tomorrow is laundry day."

Walter and I went to bed at nine as usual, making sure we could find our clothes and shoes in the dark—in case the sirens wailed. Since we shared the large bedroom with Pappa and Mamma, we had to be very quiet so that she could sleep.

"We forgot to pray last night," Walter reminded me.

"Better say our prayers three times. We might forget again," I said.

The room was dark and quiet.

"Wake up, Anneliese, wake up!" In the dark I recognized Pappa's voice. Like a robot, I reached for my clothes. Why didn't I hear an alarm?

"Walter…" I called.

Pappa's hand clamped tightly over my mouth. "Shshsh! Come with me," he whispered, pushing me toward his bed.

Not again, I thought, tripping over my shoes. Panic gripped my heart.

He turned on the bedside light. "Take off your night shirt," he urged. "We'll play a new game."

A deep chill, cold as a ghost's breath, struck me as he approached, and I clasped my arms to silence a shiver. Eyes closed, I shook my head and said, "I'm cold."

"Look at me!" He breathed heavily, his glassy-looking eyes gleaming.

Shaking with fear, I glanced at his naked body.

"Touch it!"

I'd never seen his penis erect. Something awful was going to happen, I thought, and backed away.

With his one hand, he grabbed my gown and pulled me close. "I won't hurt you," he said.

Whenever grownups say that, it always hurts. I started to whimper. "Guardian Angel," I prayed silently, "Where are you?"

"We'll play a game called doggie," he said, trying to pull up my nightgown. "Remember the two dogs humping in the street?" His eyes were blocks of ice hazed with molden lava. They narrowed into slits as he stroked his monstrous-looking organ with the stump of his arm. A groan escaped his throat.

Satan. He's turned into Satan! I must run away.

"Kneel!" His commanding voice was raspy, his breath short. Steel fingers dug into the flesh of my buttocks as he tried to straddle me.

"CRASH!" The whole house shook and the light went dead.

Pappa jumped up and yelled. "The fucking bastards forgot the siren."

Windows shattered. Jagged slivers ripped through blackout paper. Explosions flashed through the darkness. Hell came loose again.

Bang! Anti-aircraft cannons boomed.

Walter screamed.

I grabbed his hand and we ran.

In the dark hallway, howling children crawled to the steps, pushed and pulled past fearful mothers carrying babies. Everyone ran, stumbled, fled, cried, and screamed. Crash! In bare feet, I hurried over broken glass.

"Hansi!" Cowering in a corner, he sat sobbing hysterically. I let go of Walter's hand, picked up the little bundle of Angst, and stumbled down the stairs.

"Mamma!"

Unafraid, she had run home from the post office across the street.

"Run, Anneliese, run," she screamed, helping to lift someone who had fallen. "We're being hit! I saw the target flares light up like Christmas trees."

Fearfully, I stopped at the open air space between the hallway and cellar door. Rat-tat-tat-tat. Were those our Messerschmitts joining the bombing barrage?

Angel, where are you?

My protector was invisible, but I felt the wings hovering over my head, firmly prodding me to the door, down the steep stone steps into the cave of safety to escape the hell that rained from heaven.

Suddenly, my angel was gone.

The explosions were muffled now. On the cellar floor we waited for the next wave of bombers to strike. In anticipation of block busters slicing the air, I covered my ears to stop the penetrating whine.

Rocking back and forth with fear, Hansi sat on one side of me, while Walter clutched at my legs. Silently, I prayed. "Please God, don't let a bomb fall on our house." From the corner of my eye, I saw Pappa standing close to the escape hole with a blanket wrapped around him. It was then I realized that the surprise bomb attack had saved me from his assault. Thank you, angel.

After the ALL CLEAR sounded, Walter and I ran upstairs to dress and join the crowds in the street. We wanted to help, too, filling buckets with water, clearing rubble, or retrieve someone's belongings.

The night sky glowed red. Boiling air spewed from hot flames as tongues of fire tore through rows of houses with hurricane speed. Columns crashed. Windows shattered. Children whined while mothers wailed. From beneath burning debris, animals whimpered. Everyone ran to escape the nightmare, gathering what belongings they could carry.

"Tara—tara-tara-tara," blared the fire engines in the distance as they raced to attack the menacing flames. All was chaos.

"Form a bucket brigade," someone shouted. The pails raced through a chain of hands—clanging, banging, splashing waves of water on the howling fire storm. But it was never enough.

"Achtung! Here comes the Fuehrer!" The shout came from the window of a burning house.

Momentarily, everyone froze at attention—then roared with laughter as the framed picture of Hitler came crashing into the street.

Galgenhumor, they call it—gallows humor.

The next morning, Pappa was gone. And so was the rent money.

"He's on another of his drinking binges," cried Mamma, her voice shaking. "This is it!" she thundered. "Schweinehund! I won't take him back."

"That's what you said last time," Paula reminded her.

"This time I mean it," Mamma bellowed, slamming her fist on the desk. "No matter how much he begs and pleads—even down on his knees. It's over. Fertig!" She breathed heavily. "You know the saying: The crock draws water from the well until it breaks. Kaputt!"

Three days later Mamma entered our flat, her face ashen. Salty rivulets streaked her hollow cheeks. "Pappa—they found him in the woods," she told Paula. "He took poison!"

Paula gasped. "No! Where did he get it?"

"He emptied the medicine cabinet."

My heart soared. Never again will he wake me in the dark of night. Never again will I have to fondle him. Never again will I feel shame. I wanted to scream. Hallelujah! He's dead. I'm free.

"The doctors said he'll live," said Mamma, her voice dull and lifeless.

No! The word pounded my head like a hammer. I almost threw up. For the blink of an eye, I'd glimpsed freedom. His death lifted the giant prison gate. Then reality slammed it shut again—locking me in my private pit of hell. The devil had won again!

Defeated, and filled with guilt for having wanted him dead, I sobbed uncontrollably.

"Why are you crying, Anneliese?" Mamma wiped my tear-streaked face with the corner of a rumpled cotton handkerchief. "I didn't think you loved him."

I covered my face with both hands. Oh Mamma, I thought, turning back to her. I hate him—I hate him! Don't you know? My head throbbing with pain, I ran to my bed. I felt so alone.

CHAPTER TEN—Summer 1940

Bombarded with war news, we kept track of our armies occupying France to the west, Holland, Belgium, Denmark, and Norway to the north, Poland and the Balkan states to the east.

Dr. Goebbel's propaganda machine constantly buoyed our spirits with hopes that peace was just beyond the next victory. After each radio address by the Fuehrer, new strength streamed into us.

In school, Miss Thyssen talked about people of the past: German thinkers and poets who searched the truth, composers who painted pictures of strife and tranquility with musical notes; inventors who put the word God into print; and scientists who developed X-rays for the betterment of mankind.

When I grow up I want to be like one of them, I thought, feeling proud of my German heritage, and trusting our leaders to bestow honor to our country.

Life in my own home went on differently—and not nearly so well. My terror was the threat of Pappa.

He'd been gone since Mamma threw him out two weeks ago. Then one night, while Mamma was at work, he reappeared at the bedroom window after he climbed up the fire escape and crept along the metal platform. Tapping on the panes, he begged to be let in.

At first I thought it was the wind and rain that drummed against the glass. But then I saw the shadow and recognized his voice. "Go away!" I yelled, my heart pounding.

"He's cold," Walter pleaded.

"Let him freeze."

"He says he's hungry."

"Let him starve!" I screamed.

The tapping stopped. I didn't move—barely breathed. All was quiet.

Closing my eyes, I tried to return to sleep, but the fear of Pappa trying to molest me again kept me awake. Should I tell Mamma what happened? Tossing and turning, I wrestled with the question.

I'll tell her tomorrow after I get back from school, I decided, while she's in the kitchen doing the laundry. Sometimes, while I help her scrub, rinse, and wring the small items, Mamma tells me stories about her childhood, about how she got into all kinds of mischief when she was little.

Outside I heard a scraping sound, sat up, held my breath and listened. Could Pappa still be on the ledge? Would Mamma take him back? The thought put me in a state of panic. Terrified, I buried myself in the bed covers.

I'd run away. I'd go some place far, where he couldn't find me.

But where? To Aunt Lina in Heilbronn? I didn't have her address. And how would I get there without money?

I'd kill myself—jump out the window.

I remember our teacher, Mr. Schneider, telling us to report our parents if they did mean things to us—or talked bad about our Fuehrer. But I don't trust that Mr. Schneider. Besides, Mamma said she wouldn't take Pappa back. The thought lulled me to sleep.

When the alarm clock rang at seven, I got up and pulled the cover off Walter—it was the only way to wake him—and splashed my face with cold water from the kitchen tap. "Get ready for school," I urged Walter, who was now up but tried to slip back into bed.

"Where's Mamma?" He sleepily rubbed his eyes.

"She must have worked all night," I said, slicing two pieces of bread for breakfast, and four for lunch.

With a match Walter lit the gas burner to heat the ersatz coffee, while I spread the bread with home-made marmalade and wrapped sandwiches.

Rushing down the stairs, I met Mamma and stopped. "Pappa was outside by the back windows last night," I told her. "I was scared."

Walter threw me an angry look. "Anneliese wouldn't let him in," he said.

"Verdammt!" I rarely heard Mamma swear. Now she looked angry enough to hit someone. "Don't worry," she added, adjusting the bow in my hair and smoothing back Walter's curls with spittle. "I'll be home tonight." With a quick kiss on the lips and the words, "Be good!" she sent us off to school. "Come right home, Anneliese," she called after me. "I need your help with the laundry."

When I returned from school that afternoon, Mamma was bent over the oval tub that sat on two sturdy kitchen chairs, scrubbing clothes. Pulling a pair of Walter's trousers over the foot-wide wooden washboard, she looked up and smiled. "I'm so glad you did as I asked." Groaning, she arched her back briefly, wrung out the pants, and tossed them into the sink.

81

I hung up my book bag, changed clothes, and carried the footstool to the tub. "I'll do the socks," I offered.

With the edge of her apron, Mamma wiped away sweat from her brow. "I need a rest," she sighed, checking the fire under the wash kettle.

I knew the ritual. Before nightfall, Mamma would have the white wash hung on the clothesline outside the kitchen window. Screech, squeak—the rope moved over the roller. I handed the clothespins to her, while she reached to put the sheets on the outer line so they'd hide the underwear from the eyes of the neighbors. "You never show them to anybody," she lectured.

Watching me toil away, she sat down a moment, all the while rubbing and stretching her lower back. "Want me to finish?"

"No." I fished for another sock. It was one of Pappa's. "Is he coming back?" I asked, making swift downward strokes with the scrub brush. The long stocking seemed so dirty.

"You worry too much, Mausi." Mamma stoked the fire. "He was a big help on laundry day, your Pappa. His one arm had the strength of two when he helped lift the heavy kettle from the stove."

"What if he comes back tonight while you're working?"

Mamma lifted the lid from the tall, squatty laundry pot, and added rinsing powder to the water. "It'll make the sheets lily-white," she said with satisfaction.

"I'm afraid of him," I said.

Not responding, Mamma stacked some dishes on the sideboard.

Didn't she hear me? A little louder, I added, "I hate it when he wakes me and…"

Taking the brush out of my hand, she changed the subject. "What did you learn in school today?"

I liked talking about school. "We're studying poetry."

"Oh? Which poem?"

"Goethe's "Gefunden," We had to act out the story in class. I was assigned to play the part of the young man finding the flower in the forest. He wanted to break it off, but the blossom asked not to be wasted. So he dug it up with all its roots and planted it near his home where it could grow and multiply." I sighed. "I really wanted to be the beautiful blossom whose eyes shine as bright as stars, not the man wandering around in the woods."

My teacher, Miss Thyssen, must not think me pretty enough for the flower, I thought. Sadness clouded my vision. She chose Trudi, the tall blond girl with the big smile and the fancy clothes, while I silently pouted, feeling pangs of jealousy.

Mamma laughed. "You be the flower, and I'll play the philosopher's part."

"You know the poem!" I was astounded.

"I know them all," said Mamma, "Goethe, Schiller, Heine, Uhland, Rilke—I liked Goethe's Erlkoenig best."

"You never told me." I knew Mamma remembered all the verses to many folk songs, and would even harmonize while I sang. But poetry! I was impressed.

She not only recited, but put melody to all the lines of the poem. My part was but one question. "Shall I be picked too soon—to wield?"

I remembered Miss Thyssen explaining that the flower symbolizes a young maiden, and secretly I swore to never let a boy steal my heart.

Mamma started emptying the washtub with a bucket. "Wonder what's keeping your brother?" She sighed. "Probably loitering in the park again. That boy is nothing but trouble."

As if on cue, Walter crashed through the front door and said, "I'm hungry. I lost my lunch."

That's what he said yesterday, I thought—and jumped when I heard the familiar knock on the door. Could it be Pappa?

Wiping her wet hands with her apron, Mamma opened it.

"Sorry I'm so late," said Paula and put down a package of meat and sausage. "The queue for horsemeat is getting longer every week."

"How long did you have to wait this time?" Mamma poured equal parts of vinegar and water into a large bowl until the marinade covered the meat, and added sliced onions, bay leaves, cloves, salt and pepper.

"Four hours!" Paula slumped on a wooden kitchen chair.

I dropped to my knees and massaged her tired, swollen feet, especially the toes, the way she rubbed mine many times when they were cold.

"I guess word got around that horsemeat makes good sauerbraten," said Mamma. "Besides getting double value for ration coupons." She stood and carried the bowl to the bedroom where it would cool. "It'll be perfect for Sunday dinner."

While I set the table, Paula sliced the bread and cut chunks off the horsemeat sausage.

"It tastes good," said Walter, attacking his food.

"Yes," agreed Paula. "Much like salami."

After supper, Paula and Mamma siphoned the dirty tub water into the sink and emptied the kettle back into the tub. I watched them work together, wringing out more sheets and pillow cases by twisting the heavy material as tightly as they could. Soon, I'd be able to help, I thought.

Before they finished, Mamma told Paula she better leave early. "The Tommies in all likelihood will send their bombers again. They seem to prefer the warm summer nights."

Why can't Paula spend the night here, I thought? While Mamma is at work, I could tell her about my fears and shame. My heart beating fast, I waited for an opportunity to interrupt their conversation.

Rummaging in her purse, Paula produced a letter. "I almost forgot to tell you," she exclaimed. "I received a note from my husband today." Recovering her glasses, she reread the letter. "Heini expects to return on a one-week leave by the end of this month," she said, bubbling with excitement.

"That's but a couple of days from today," said Mamma.

"I know! Not much time left." She brushed through her straight hair. "On my way home, I must make an appointment at the beauty shop." Her face lit up as she continued reading silently. "He seems to think the war will be over soon and we'll be together again." Paula looked at Mamma and added in a more subdued voice, "He sends greetings to you and Albert."

I decided this was not a good time to ask Paula to stay and tell her of Pappa's abuses. Some other time.

When I came home from school the next day, Paula was there and Mamma was in a bad mood. I could tell by the way she pushed and pulled the hot iron across the bed sheets. "Truant," she snapped. "How could he skip school? Three days! Wait 'til he gets home. I'll beat his brains out."

Paula tried to calm her. It wasn't easy. "Don't you understand? The boy misses his Pappa. He feels sorry for him."

"How do you know?" Mamma put down the iron with a thump.

"He told me."

"What else did he tell you?"

"He gives his lunch to Pappa."

"What! Why didn't you tell me sooner?"

Anger blocked my hearing. Pappa—that monster! Picking on my little brother. Taking his lunch. I never came so close to telling Mamma what a beast he really was. Why is Walter protecting Pappa? Why am I? I stomped into the family bedroom and looked at my brother's unmade bed. He had wet it again. I hate them both, I thought—Walter for skipping school, Pappa for talking him into it and taking Walter's lunch. How could Walter feel sorry for him? Then another thought crossed my mind. What if Mamma takes pity on Pappa and decides Walter needs a father after all? Before returning to the living room, I closed my eyes tightly and clenched my fists to block out the unthinkable.

"Thief," Mamma screamed at Walter, hitting his hands with a big wooden cooking spoon. "You lied to me." Her rage escalated while she smacked him repeatedly across his mouth with the back of her hand.

Blood seeped from his swollen lips as Walter pleaded. "No, please, no. I won't do it again."

Paula wedged her plump frame between Mamma and Walter. "Stop it, Johanna. This is why I didn't tell you." She put a protective hand over Walter's head. "He's but a boy trying to be loyal to both of you."

"You keep out of this," Mamma threatened, waving the long-handled spoon in Paula's direction.

I couldn't believe what I saw. I had seem Mamma lose her temper before, had heard her yelling and screaming, but this time she seemed uncontrollable. Though I feared for my brother and Paula, I remained motionless. Silent. Just wanting the anger to go away. What could I do?

In a flash I remembered how, when I started to cry because Walter got a severe spanking, she grabbed me, pulled me over her knee, and pelted blows on my behind until the wooden spoon broke. "Now you have reason to cry," she'd screamed.

The memory filled my eyes with tears. Will she beat me again?

Frantically, I looked for an escape, ran to the open window and climbed out onto the ledge.

"Have you gone mad, too?" Mamma got hold of my apron strings and pulled me back. "Kinder," her voice quavered. "Sometimes I feel like running away myself and never come back." She looked defeated as she sat by the table, laid her head on folded arms, and cried.

Bewildered, I sat on the floor and stared, watching Paula put compresses on Walter's swollen face. He didn't flinch.

In June, we received an invitation from my grandparents to visit them during summer vacation. Grandpa's handwriting was in the ornate script, the type I had mastered in first grade. Later, the school system changed to Latin—a more uniform system used worldwide with rounded letters easier to form than the pointed m's, n's, and i's of the Arabic.

"We have chickens and rabbits, even a pig," Grandpa wrote in his letter. "And the garden is brimming with fruit and vegetables."

I hoped there weren't too many of the latter—I hated to eat anything green.

The sheet of paper dropped from Mamma's shaking hands. Did I see tears in her eyes? Trumpeting into a large handkerchief, she sniffled, "It's been more than ten years since I left my parents."

"Why did you leave?"

"It's a long story." She blew her nose again. "I feel like the lost sheep returning home." With a long sigh she looked into the small mirror above the kitchen sink. "My hair looks a mess. Lina told me I should get a permanent."

Now I remembered! Long ago, Mamma got into an argument with her sisters and ran away from home. I wondered what my grandparents looked like, but Mamma didn't have any pictures. Will they like me? Will I like them?

Mamma, Walter, and I, took the streetcar to the station. We were dressed in our Sunday clothes, Walter had a haircut, and I a new bow in my hair. Together we had the responsibility of carrying the bag with sandwiches and apples Mamma packed for lunch. "I saw Mamma put in a bar of chocolate for a treat." I whispered into Walter's ear.

At the crowded station, she checked large time tables to find the platform for the train to Heilbronn.

I watched with fascination as people bustled in and out of the station, some carrying small packages, others lugging large suitcases, all in a hurry. A soldier lost his cap while kissing his sweetheart goodbye, and a grey-haired gentleman took off his horn-rimmed glasses before wiping his eyes; then, swinging his grey felt hat, shouted farewell to his sailor son. Next to the stairs, an older woman received her grandchild with outstretched arms.

A square-faced clock hung suspended from the multi-colored glass cupola covering the station. Slowly, its second hand moved from point to point. It won't be long now, I thought, waiting for the big hand move to the next numeral.

Walter couldn't stand still. Jumping up and down, he asked the same questions over and over. "When will the train come? How long is the ride? Can we eat right away?"

"It's a three-hour ride to Heilbronn," Mamma replied patiently. "Then, we'll have to take a streetcar that connects to a bus that takes us to Boeckingen, the outskirts of the city. It's another half hour walk to their home. Now! I will not answer you another time."

She always meant what she said and Walter knew better than to test her. Silently, we watched her rummage in her purse until she found the letter. She pulled out a picture of her parents' house. "It looks so pretty," she said. "All white stucco, with forest green shutters. I can hardly wait to see it."

With the conductor's help, Walter and I got window seats, Mamma sat next to me. When the train's whistle blew, the station master held up a large sign and called, "Alles einsteigen! All aboard!" Slowly, we started to move.

Sitting across from each other on polished benches of light wood, Walter started fidgeting with the front of his pants. "Is there a toilet in the train?" he asked meekly.

As I watched Mamma take him down the long corridor, I said a little prayer that he wouldn't wet the bed at our grandparents' house. He went to a sanatorium to cure his

bed-wetting, but he still had occasional accidents.

Inhaling a whiff of 4711 Koelnish Wasser, I knew Aunt Lina couldn't be far. It was her favorite cologne.

She greeted us all with a hug and kiss, then stepped next to a man not much taller than herself.

At first Mamma and her father just stood and stared at each other. Neither spoke for a long time. Finally, Mamma blinked. Sniffing, she extended her hand. "I came back."

He clasped her hand into his and said in a voice that slightly quivered, "Herzlich willkommen, daughter."

Seeing him was love at first sight. He shook Walter's hand and patted me gently on the head. "Gruess Gott, Kinder," he said. Because he was short in stature, I didn't have to look up to him. A large handle-bar mustache dominated his small face, and dark brown eyes winked a friendly welcome.

My heart pounded as I took his outstretched hand. Not letting go of it, I walked proudly alongside. I might not have a Pappa anymore, but I had an Opa—who looked truly "grand."

The grownups talked incessantly. After what seemed like hours of walking and lugging the suitcase, we reached a double-tracked railroad crossing. Behind it, rows and rows of white two-story houses stretched up the hill like steepled boxes covered with powdered sugar. "Ours is the sixth one from the bottom," said Grandpa. He pointed to the one with green shutters. "I picked one on the bottom row so your Oma wouldn't have to climb the steep streets.

Multi-colored dahlias and tree roses bloomed beside the long walk leading to the back entrance and flower beds screened a large vegetable garden. Grandma, wearing a dark Sunday dress that fit loosely to hide her ample frame, waited under the arbor covered by a lilac bush that stretched over the squatty gate.

She greeted us with outstretched arms, and when she smiled, her toothless grin was the shape of a quarter moon; but her face shone with love as she pulled each one of us to her soft bosom.

Mutterle!" is all Mamma said, as she hugged her mother and burst into tears.

Why is everyone crying? I wondered, watching the grownups pull out handkerchiefs to wipe away tears and blow noses.

In late fall, I met another member of the family. Mamma's only brother, Franz, with his wife and child came to visit us in Frankfurt. He had just returned from Russia where he worked as an engineer for several years and married a Moscow woman with a child. More relatives!

I don't know which was more eventful: the short visit to my grandparents' house, or the arrival of my Uncle Franz with wife and daughter.

One day, Mamma packed a picnic for all of us. Then we took the streetcar to the forest that surrounded the city. The tall trees were shedding their lovely coat of yellow, red, and brown, the fallen leaves rustling and crunching under our feet.

I was in awe of my Uncle Franz. How handsome he was! His bushy black brows matched the color of his eyes and his hair was as dark as Aunt Lina's. With white teeth sparkling when he smiled and talked, he reminded me of a movie star. He and Mamma talked non-stop.

We had bologna sandwiches and hard-boiled eggs at a small Gasthaus near one of the walking paths. Uncle Franz bought Coca Cola for us children—a first-time treat—while the grownups enjoyed beer from cool steins, its white foam slowly spilling over the rim.

"How old are you, Tamara?" I asked, trying to make conversation with my cousin, but she couldn't understand me, since she didn't speak any German. Uncle had to translate.

"Tell me about Russia," said Mamma. "What made you come back?"

"The Bolsheviks," said Franz. "But I really don't want to talk about it." Ruffling his hair with long fingers, he added, "Sometimes I think I jumped out of the rain into the gutter."

"Our father will be glad you no longer believe in Communism." When she lowered her voice, I always pricked up my ears. "Vater is still a staunch Social Democrat. Has nothing but disdain for National Socialists. Doesn't trust our Fuehrer."

Uncle nodded. "Neither do I." He paused and looked around before continuing. "Hitler's hordes are looking east for more land."

Mamma shook her head. "When will this war end? Hitler's going mad. Power hungry!"

CHAPTER ELEVEN—The Axis Cracks—1941

"Unbelievable!" "Something horrendous is happening." People whispered the news in lowered voices: in the grocery store, at the hairdresser, outside the flower shop.

In May, radio Berlin had trumpeted to the world: "Premier Molotove has been replaced by Josef Stalin." Newspapers showed the new leader and Hitler shaking hands on a non-aggression pact. But now, one month later, Hitler ordered German tanks to attack Russia. One June 22nd, the assault was followed by a declaration of war.

The German people shivered with fear. "The evil tentacles of war are reaching even further," some mumbled.

While newspapers extoled news about German battalions mobilizing from the Arctic to the Black Sea against the Russian barbarians, Mamma worked hard to create a sense of normalcy at home. She took pains making Sundays special, this one in particular. It was Paula's birthday.

A small bouquet of carnations decorated the table covered with white linen. Cups and saucers replaced the daily mugs, and today the aroma of real coffee wafted in the air. Feeling fresh and pretty in my clean underwear and Sunday dress, I patiently waited for Kaffeekuchen to be cut. Did I smell hot chocolate? What a treat!

From the cathedral downtown I heard the powerful bells toll for high mass, followed by the call for Lutheran services from nearby Peter and Katarina churches. "Ding-dong, ding-dong," we counted the time of day and forgot all about armies waging a war in Russia, submarines sinking ships, and airplanes dropping bombs. Our small world seemed at peace.

Mamma worried about summer vacation. The standard six weeks were cut to four to make up lessons lost during periods of air alarms. "The raids are expected to increase during warmer weather," she said to Paula. "I'm concerned about the children being by themselves, especially during the night. The Post Office established a summer camp for the children of its employees. It's up north, near the Baltic Sea."

My heart pounded. Is she sending us away? "I'll wake Walter the moment the siren sounds," I said.

Mamma put her arm around me. "Every time the alarm goes off while I'm at work at night, I'm concerned about you making it to the cellar in time."

"At least when Albert lived here, he would watch over them," sighed Paula.

"At the sound of Pappa's name, Walter started whining. "I wish our Pappa would come back."

The thought of him returning made me cringe. Better be in camp than here, I decided quickly. "Will we go by train again?" I remembered what fun it was to look out the window when riding to our grandparents in Heilbronn. "You'll be taking the night express to Berlin," said Mama, "have breakfast at the Post Office, then board another train in the direction of Stralsund by the Baltic Sea." She pinched our pale cheeks. "The ocean breezes will make your skin rosy again…"

On the day of departure, Mamma snapped shut the lids of the two suitcases, made sure Walter's fly was buttoned, and once more fanned the bow in my hair. "You'll probably be in separate buildings and won't see much of each other." Mamma looked straight at me as she talked. "But promise to keep an eye on your brother whenever you can…"

Nodding, I dutifully took Walter's hand.

Paula handed the two of us a small paper bag before helping Mamma with the luggage. "A little surprise in case you get hungry," she winked.

"You're spoiling them again," said Mamma.

As we approached the station by streetcar, a new banner stretched across the entire frontage of the building. RAEDER SOLLEN ROLLEN FUER DEN SIEG! Walter and I chanted the words. 'WHEELS MUST ROLL FOR VICTORY!"

Inside, Mamma spotted a group of children and adults near the designated meeting place. Our baggage was collected and tagged; a third hug and kiss from Mamma and Paula, some tears, a promise to be good from us. Then the conductor shouted, the train whistled, the wheels turned. "Write as soon as you can," I heard Mamma call before she faded out of sight.

I looked at the other girls assigned to my compartment. Was I dressed as nice as they? My worries dispelled quickly when our chaperone complimented each one of us on our outfits. We learned each others names, took turns at the window seat until dark, sang several slumber songs, and finally bedded down on the polished, but hard seats. "Clickety-clack, clickety-clack," sounded the wheels as they rumbled across the rails.

The next morning, we had breakfast at the post office cafeteria in Berlin. Women in postal uniforms talked in an accent loud and boisterous, much different from ours. My dress rumpled, rubbing eyes still filled with sleep, I felt too timid to open my mouth and answer all their questions—much less eat. But when baskets of fresh-baked crusty rolls lined the table, I developed a hearty appetite.

Heaping blueberry jam on buttered bread, I proudly talked about Frankfurt, my city, and that we lived right behind the post office where Mamma worked every night, sorting mail.

"Iss und trink, Kind," urged one of the women as she refilled my cup with milk. "Eat and drink. It will be several hours until you reach your destination."

On the train, we had sandwiches, hard-boiled eggs, and an apple. "Where's my brother?" I hadn't seen him at breakfast.

"The boys are in the next carriage," I was told. "Don't worry."

The camp had several small buildings and I wondered how I'd find my way around. But our group leader put us at ease. "Just stay close to me," she said, leading us to the community dining room that had large windows.

We slept in long, narrow, dormitories—ten beds on each side, with a large circular washbasin and lockers in the adjacent room. "Before going to sleep," explained the nice lady, "You hang your coat on the hook with your name above it and place day clothing on the chair next to your bed."

"Which way to the cellar in case of a bomb attack?" I didn't want to get lost in the dark.

"You're safe here," said our leader. "War planes never come this way…"

Rules in the camp were enforced without harsh words. I liked and trusted our camp counselors who neither wore uniforms, nor made us march through the nearby village.

At breakfast time, we each had to swallow a spoonful of cod liver oil that tasted awful. The food smelled different than Mamma's cooking, but was good and plentiful. Except for that white flat fish on Fridays, called flounder. "It's a delicacy," the cook assured us. But we hated to look at its sad eyes that reminded me of the wise flounder who granted all wishes of the greedy fisherman's wife—until she demanded to be God himself.

My brother sat with the boys. Sometimes we had a few minutes to talk, but mostly we just waved to each other across the dining room.

Then a new person appeared at camp—the first I'd seen there in uniform. The stocky man snapped his heels together and, thrusting his arm out to salute, said, "Heil Hitler!" Facing the assembly in the dining hall, he paced the floor. "Today," thundered the officer, his eyes moving from face to face, "One of your comrades insisted that Germany will lose the war."

"...Germany will lose the war." Where had I heard those words? Through the wide open windows, I watched ominous clouds gather, turning the sky from deepest blue to sultry grey. Pearls of perspiration crept down my forehead.

Outside, the black clouds became thicker. The room grew dark.

"We are here because of the generosity of our victorious leader, Adolf Hitler," bellowed the officer.

The first lightning streaked across the sky.

"Sieg Heil!" As if on command, we parroted the grownup's words.

Another Blitz bolted outside, followed by a distant rumbling. Was it thunder or bombing? A stern look from the supervisor halted our feet from shuffling and our hands from twitching.

Strutting up and down the room in his knee-high boots, the uniformed man stopped in front of the boys' section and shouted, "Germany is not only going to win this war—our Fuehrer is going to conquer the world!"

The thunder of colliding clouds outside drowned out the victory hails of Sieg Heil.

Now I remembered. We were having a small get-together for Mamma's birthday. Even Pappa visited.

"Herr Hitler is making a big mistake fighting a war on two fronts," argued Paula's husband, Heini, home on a three-day leave. "I don't care how many tanks he's built, it's infantry—" he pointed to himself "—it's the little guy that gets stuck doing the fighting after the big boys run out of gas. Just like Kaiser Wilhelm, Bonaparte, and the other warlords."

"Heini's right," someone interjected. "Our armies are spread much too thin. Russia is a huge country, too big to conquer. Napoleon tried it. Sure, he beat Germany, overran it, but his soldiers froze in Russia, and the horses mired in the mud of the spring thaw."

Someone else at the party interrupted. "Relax. Let's have another beer. It's going to be all over before the winter sets in. Tanks move faster than horses."

I was listening hard, trying to decide who was right.

"Our Fuehrer's a genius!" The blond woman seemed a little tipsy. "Look how fast we broke through the Maginot line in France. And we have those good-looking allies in Italy."

His face red, Heini pounded the table with a fist. "Hitler's a demon! An egomaniac wearing a red cape and tights! He's underestimating the Russians and overestimating the Italians."

"For goodness sake, stop talking politics and war." Paula had to shout to be heard. "This is Johanna's birthday. Let's celebrate!"

Everyone agreed. Beer glasses clinked and cheers of Prost! resounded. "To a long life! To shorter queues! An end to bombing! To victory!"

Pappa stood up. Glancing around the table, he lifted his mug and said quietly, "I predict Germany will lose the war."

No one moved or spoke. It was as if he doomed us all.

My thoughts returned to the dining room. "What is your name?" I heard the officer shout.

The voice answering was all too familiar. "Ich heisse Walter Hoehn," said my brother, looking terribly frail as he stood in front of the man.

Feeling my heart thump louder than the rain pounding on the windows, I thought, he's in real trouble.

The man towered above Walter. "Who told you we're going to lose the war?"

"Nobody."

Were those tears rolling down Walter's cheeks?

"Stand up straight and tell the assembly who is going to win the war."

"We are going to win the war."

"Who?"

"Adolf Hitler is going to win the war." His lip trembled.

"Louder!"

What was that dark spot on the front of Walter's short trousers? I looked again and saw a small puddle at his feet.

Walter shrieked, "Germany is going to win the war!"

"Heil Hitler!" Up flew the arm; click went the heels. The officer turned, stalked to a table across the room, and talked to Herr Schmidt, the head of the camp, a stooped man with perpetually baggy pants, whose grey hair always looked uncombed.

"Heil Hitler!" echoed the children and their leaders.

While the storm outside continued to rage, the two men at the head table conferred, sometimes looking at Walter, who was still in the middle of the room, other times glancing in my direction. Will he make us leave? I trembled with fear. The swastika on the officer's sleeve reminded me of the Gestapo who once interrogated Mamma.

In the distance, the sound of squealing brakes brought back the terror of another event. He'll shove Walter and me in a van the way they did David and his family. Terrified, I wanted to hide under the table or run away—but I stood perfectly still, as though my feet were glued to the floor and tried to will the man in uniform away.

Suddenly, he left. Without looking back, he strode through the room, with Herr Schmidt shuffling close behind him. Opening the door for the person of authority I saw the older man return the Hitler salute, and they patiently waited for the car to speed away.

"Sit down, children," said Herr Schmidt, as he walked past the tables to the middle of the room. "You, too, Walter." He ruffled my brother's blond locks and continued to the kitchen. "Start serving—the children are hungry."

Relieved, we banged spoons against dinner bowls and started a chant we'd learned. "We are hungry—we want to eat."

Outside, the sun pushed through the clouds, its rays dancing.

Before we ate, I asked permission to take Walter to the boy's dormitory so he could change.

"You're such a showoff," I scolded, still worried about what might happen to us. "You'll get our whole family in trouble. What will Mamma say when she hears about this?"

Stubbornly, Walter stomped alongside me. "She agreed with Pappa. We'll lose the war!"

"Halt's Maul." Putting my hand over his mouth, I stopped and hushed him. "Shut up!" Good thing Mamma couldn't hear me use this language, I thought.

He sat down on the graveled walk and started to sob. "You don't love me. Nobody loves me. I make everything come out wrong."

Tear welled up in my eyes—but I didn't allow them to spill. Being the big sister meant I had to be strong. Instead, I sat next to my little brother and wrapped my arms around him, rocking slowly back and forth. He wasn't the only one in need of love. "I'll never leave you," I promised.

Soon he stopped crying. Together, we smoothed a few stray pebbles in the path. "We should get back," I said.

He dragged to his feet.

"Let's race to the dorm," I tried to cheer him. "Bet I can beat you."
We ran on the damp packed gravel. I let him win.

So did Mamma. In a conciliatory mood, she took the train to the camp and met with Herr Schmidt. Miraculously, she cleared up the misunderstanding. Like Walter, Mamma's tongue often got her in trouble, but she had a way of talking herself out of it.

"I'm glad you're in a safe place," Mamma told us before she returned to Frankfurt. "We had three air attacks the first week you were gone."

Every day after the noon meal came nap time. Stretched out on one of the lounges set up on the veranda, I'd watch the clouds above and imagine I saw the face of God. With His long white beard, billowing hair, and loving features, He seemed kind and gentle, giving me comfort. He watches during the day, I reasoned, and rests at night. Testing, I'd close my eyes—then look at the clouds again. They'd shift a little, but I could still make out His image. If only He'd stop the bombing! Quietly, I prayed for Mamma and Paula's safety.

Twice a week, we climbed the sandy dunes, weaved through grasses taller than us ten-year olds, and tumbled down the other side onto a gigantic sandbox—the beach.

In awe I stood on my spindly legs, feeling the sea breeze tug at my hair, watching white seagulls dive into the sea. What fun I had digging my toes into the fine sand, making footprints where sprays of water had wetted the surface, and jump with joyful shrieks into the surf. Soft swooshing sounds followed.

The war was tucked somewhere in the recesses of my memory. Forgotten were the howling sirens, the booming anti-aircraft guns, exploding bombs, and sleepless nights.

Dream-like days of peace flew by. I felt safe.

"Over here, little seagulls," called our instructor. That was the name of our team, the second youngest at the camp.

Sand caked to our wet feet, we gathered in a circle around her. "Next week," she announced, "we'll have a contest between boy and girl groups to see who can build the biggest, most beautiful sand castle."

That sounded exciting, but when we sized up the older teams, especially the boys, we became discouraged. "The other kids are so much taller," Ilse whined. "We'll never win."

"Let's gather seashells today," suggested Fraulein Schultheiss. We need them to decorate our castle."

Eyes glued to the sand, I spotted a small pebble that glittered in the sun. "It looks like gold," I exclaimed, showing my find to the others.

"It's a little piece of amber the sea washed ashore," explained the Fraulein. "You'll find many more after the tide rolls out."

The next day, we started early to dig and shape, added water to the pile and patted it into a mold, and finally decorated the creation with our treasures from the day before.

Except in pictures of my book of fairly tales, I'd never seen a castle, but I thought ours to be the most grandiose in the world. It glittered with pieces of amber, shells of various sizes, and boasted a crown of white seagull feathers. We received an award for the most beautiful.

The first prize went to the Wild Ducks, a girls' team whose castle had turrets and deep moats flanked by tall watch towers. Their king carried a scepter and the queen's brown sea weed hair cascaded across her shoulders. Knights in armor stood guard.

Suddenly, balls of wet sand pelted our creation. Pretending they were shooting cannons, the boys played war.

Angrily, we counter-attacked by dousing their fortifications with pails of water, and soon all the sand castles were destroyed.

I crawled up the dunes and took one last look at the battlefield, strewn with corpses, the castles in ruins. War brings nothing but destruction, I thought. Head hung low, I marched back past the pine woods where we had picked plump blueberries the day before. I licked my lips—and tasted bitter salt.

After we returned to Frankfurt at the end of August, two more night bombings occurred before school started, two more in September, and one in late October.

When Pearl Harbor was attacked by the Japanese in December, many wondered if the Americans would join the British and begin bombing. Most people thought not. America is too far away.

CHAPTER TWELVE—Winter 1941

Winter came early in 1941. Subzero temperatures turned dripping snow from roofs into icicles in minutes and the blustery wind swept through every nook and corner of the house. It was cold, bitter cold. Especially in Russia, where snowdrifts and ice slowed the advance of German infantry, tanks, and machinery on their fast track to Moscow and Stalingrad.

On the home front, behind frost-painted windows, mothers, wives, and sweethearts knitted sweaters, vests, stockings, and pulse warmers for sons, husbands, and friends.

I wanted to help, too. But the harder I tried to master knitting, the more stitches dropped off the needle—much to the chagrin of Mamma, who could read weekly romance novels while making socks.

"What's to become of you, Anneliese?" she'd sigh, checking tension and counting stitches. While her ball of yarn disappeared under flying fingers and clicking needles, the stocking magically took shape. When it came to knitting or sewing, Mamma considered me a disgrace to the family.

I redeemed myself, however, when the task became beating the batter for cakes we baked in loaf pans and mailed to our growing family of soldiers—whenever we saved enough from our ration cards. The list of relatives and friends grew longer as the war dragged on.

Lina's husband, Bert, still served as a medic on the Russian front. Uncle Franz, Mamma's only brother, was ordered to serve as an interpreter for Russian soldiers—who surrendered by the thousands.

His wife, Musja, pleaded with him. "We left Russia to escape the Communists. Their armies are infiltrated with partisans."

"I'll be considered a traitor to my Fatherland," he explained. "I volunteered to join Rommel's Corps in Africa—where I'm told it's hotter than hell—but the request was denied."

When he was served his draft notice, it broke my Aunt Musja's heart. "I love my Franz," Musja sobbed. "But me born and raised in Russia. I teach in Moskau." Her limited German and heavy accent made her speech difficult to understand, but her tone of voice was clear. "Me German citizen…" She thumped her chest. "…but inside here, it still beats Russian."

With tears streaming down her lined face, she strummed her guitar and sang folk songs in her native language. "Ej, uchnem, ej, uchnem," her beautiful voice called, echoing the chant of weary boatsmen pulling their loads down the Volga.

"When will I see my Franz again?" Musja wailed

How romantic. How sad, I thought. The love for my uncle is stronger than her homesickness.

Paula spent a lot of time with us that winter—partly to conserve coal, but also to escape loneliness. "I'm getting too old to climb up and down five flights of stairs and then run several blocks to the shelter," she complained. "I wish we had a cellar with an arched ceiling and thick walls like this old building. At least it's safe from fire and collapse."

One evening, Paula brought home a kitten she had found in the rubble of a burnt-out building. The little grey and black-striped creature was scrawny and scared, and when I picked it up, tried to scratch. We fed it milk with my doll's baby bottle. Once it got used to the rubber nipple, it drank two bottles and soon curled in my lap looking like a ball of Mamma's yarn. Only this one purred.

"Ach Du lieber!" moaned Mamma when she first saw the mewing little bundle. "One more mouth to feed."

I called my kitten Muschi after a female cat in a nursery rhyme—though it turned out to be a male, much to Mamma's relief.

"Kittens become cats," Mamma fussed, but put an old towel in a carton for its bed and placed it next to a litter box filled with sand. "If he smells up the house, he goes."

"I'll change the litter," I promised. And I did. Sometimes I'd get sawdust from the carpenter shop downstairs, and other times I'd use cold ashes from the kitchen stove.

I pretended to be Muschi's Mamma, making Walter the good Pappa. We'd bathe him in the all-purpose sink, but Muschi didn't like the water. When we tried putting clothes on the wiggly bundle, Muschi let us know he preferred his own fur coat. Against Mamma's orders, he snuggled with us under the plump, feather-filled bed covers. But no matter how much we begged and pleaded, Mamma always checked and Muschi was picked up by the scruff of the neck and banished to the kitchen.

99

"Raus!" Mamma would yell. "Out!"

Her voice was stern, but not like when she kicked out Pappa a few months ago after another of his drinking binges. "Get out and stay out!" Mamma had shouted when he picked up his clothes. In spite of my fear of his violent assaults, I sometimes wondered where he was.

"Have you seen him?" I once asked my brother.

Walter nodded. "Mamma invited Pappa for Christmas dinner."

No! My heart sank. Why did she throw him out and then invite him for dinner? He'll be back to stay. I tried not to think about that possibility all day long and prayed Mamma would change her mind. Later, nightmares tormented my sleep. Why do I have a bad Pappa and a no-good father? Mamma never called Walter's father no-good. On second thought, she never says anything about him.

Often, I wondered about my no-good father. What did he look like? Was he tall or short? Good-looking? Probably not. Since he was no-good, he must be ugly. Why did Mamma hate him so?

Then, as if someone heard me, one morning I heard Mamma say to Paula, "Guess who's a lieutenant in a tank division?"

"My Heini's not in that class, that's for sure."

"Her no-good father!"

"No!"

"Jawohl! I saw him this morning in the post office."

"How does he look?"

"Handsome, as always," Mamma sighed. "Didn't think his long legs would ever fit into the small space in a tank."

He must be tall, I thought. And handsome. Did I resemble him? Why didn't Mamma invite him for Christmas?

CHAPTER THIRTEEN—Day Attack 1942

On April 20, 1942, the Fuehrer's birthday, a new law dictated that all boys and girls aged ten automatically joined the Deutsche Jungvolk (German young people) and Deutsche Jungmaedel (German young girls), and swear allegiance to Hitler. The ceremony took place at the Huthpark—a large meadow on the edge of the city, surrounded by sturdy Chestnut and wispy Linden trees.

It had been a place for Sunday picnics, a place where men kicked soccer balls across the grass while women sat around and chatted until the last crumb of Wurst und Brot was picked off by a fat sparrow. Now it had become a place for mass youth rallies, with the accompanying pomp of flags and sound of drums.

When asking for some change to go to the youth meeting, Mamma frowned. "I have no money for streetcar fare." With a thump she replaced the iron on its cradle and wiped her brow.

I knew she didn't want me to attend. I had learned long ago that her porte-monnaie, as she called it, snapped shut fast when the word Hitler Youth was mentioned. And she continued to refer to her coin purse in French, never calling it Geldbeutel, the proper German word. Neither would she use Gehsteig for sidewalk. "Trottoir is easier to say," she'd insist. I decided it was her way of defying the authorities.

"I'm amazed that you care to be present at all," she fumed. "Don't you have homework to finish?"

I didn't answer, because she knew my assignment was complete.

"Don't expect me to buy you a uniform," she added. "I've seen those Hitler youth march in three ranks along the Kaiserstrasse, stamping as loudly as possible when passing the houses of the rich Jews. I don't want my daughter to be part of these harassments."

"In school we were told that, besides the meetings and field exercises, we'd have hikes and weekend outings with campfires—even youth hostelling." To me it sounded like fun, but Mamma wasn't convinced.

"The State is exercising too much control over my children," she insisted.

I jogged all the way to the park, only to be late for the oath—but in time for a fanfare of trumpets, and the rolling beat of drums. Hypnotized, I watched the spectacle.

Then it happened. Thousands of leaflets descended from the sky. If a plane had dropped them, I didn't see or hear it. Grabbing one of the sheets in mid-air, I started reading.

"Terror! It is Hitler's weapon over London and Birmingham.

Now comes Churchill's answer: Bombs. Bigger Bombs. What you experienced last night were but the first drop of the storm to come. The drops are still small. But they'll get more powerful, more devastating until you're on your knees. Watch out!

Signed, Sir Arthur Harris."

Quickly, I crumbled the paper into a wad and tucked it inside my blouse. I knew it was forbidden to read—much less keep—any written materials dropped from British planes. STRENG VERBOTEN! The warnings were posted on every street corner. But few people took heed.

I must show this to Mamma, I thought, disobeying the commands of the loudspeakers. "Turn over all leaflets to your leader immediately!"

Would the prophesy of the propaganda leaflets come true? I trembled as I picked up another stray piece. Until now, the air raids concentrated on military targets. But rumor persisted that the British Air Minister had threatened to focus night time saturation bombing on residential areas to break civilian morale.

Sirens wailed what had been predicted. But the new and more ravaging bombs—incendiaries and blockbusters, did not so much breed fear and a desire to bow before the storm, but rather a certain fatalistic cussedness and a dogged determination to survive.

Mamma sat at her Pfaff sewing machine, racing the needle across the material as though her life depended on it.

"Bombing homes and civilians," she mumbled. "Cowards!"

I sat next to her, making cross stitches on a table cloth stretched over an embroidery hoop. The radio droned a commentary on the latest battles—as colored by the German News Bureau. They blared of Japanese victories on land and in the air. Surabaya bombed, Singapore taken, Sumatra oil centers captured.

Where are those places? I wondered.

The commentator began chiding the citizens. "Germans! Stop

complaining! Even in wartime, we have a standard of living superior to any other country of Europe. The home folks have thus far felt the war very little. Shed no tears if heavier sacrifices are now asked of us."

The sewing machine stopped its tack-tack-tack. "That sounds like something straight out of Goebbel's loud mouth," Mamma said.

"My feet are freezing." Walter rubbed his toes.

While she searched for extra sweaters and socks to keep us warm, the newscaster continued to ramble. "In the cities, the coal situation is critical. The schools may be forced to close. Production may stop in some of our munitions factories."

Moving closer to the dying embers in the stove, I wondered if the news was a foreshadowing of worse things to come. I must be brave, I thought— like a good German girl!

Then, without a knock, Pappa entered, carrying a burlap bag full of black coal. Though he was living with us again, he spent most of his time at the factory. "I snitched the few pieces that spilled near the coal bin," he said as he kindled the fire in our little potbelly stove.

Pretending not to hear him, I didn't return his greeting, but buried my nose in my book.

Mamma didn't let me get away with the pretense. "Say, 'Guten Abend,' to your Pappa," she admonished.

"Good evening," I mumbled, glancing in the direction of Pappa.

Greeting him with a kiss and embrace, Mamma said, "You haven't been home for three days."

He massaged the stump of his forearm. "They're offering premiums of cigarettes and schnapps as incentives to work double shifts."

From the radio came more: "Dr. Goebbels is appealing for national discipline and reminds every citizen of his duty to increase production," the newscaster rambled on.

"I hear the same crap at the post office during the night shift," said Mamma. Scheisse! It stinks!"

War had now become a way of life for all of us. Over the winter, the bombing had eased, but food and fuel shortages eroded our morale. Ration coupons were reduced and queues grew longer. We wearied of the so-called glories of war.

Paula came in, and without uttering a word of greeting, headed straight for the warm stove. "I waited five hours to buy one kilo of meat. It may be the last for awhile," she said, taking off her heavy, woolen mittens Mamma had knitted for her.

Walter helped remove the shoes from her frozen feet and I poured hot ersatz coffee, so she could wrap her icy fingers around the steaming mug.

"Sometimes I miss the aroma of real coffee beans," she said, "but this brew hits the spot." With pleasure, she slurped the hot drink until the cup was empty. Looking at the meat in the paper wrap, she sighed. "I hear due to lack of fodder, they're butchering a lot of cattle."

One of Mamma's customers arrived. I shut the door quickly while Frau Schaub removed her coat and draped the fur over a chair. "A present from my husband," she said. "He sent it from France."

Probably because he couldn't hear over the chatter, Pappa turned up the volume on the radio. "German submarines shelled vital oil installations at Aruba in the Caribbean, and sank seven Allied tankers in the Atlantic."

We all cheered. "Hurrah for the U-boats!"

"The U.S. East Coast is a shooting gallery." From the bravado in the announcer's voice, he, too, seemed glad to deliver good news. "Ships sail at night with lights on. Lighthouses operate as normal. Radio messages are sent without codes. There are few U.S. warships on patrol."

Standing on a footstool to have the hem of her skirt adjusted, Frau Schaub almost lost her balance with laughter. "Americans are so stupid," she roared. "Playboys! Weaklings! We don't need to fear them. Besides, have you heard? The Japanese are beating the breath out of them."

"Roosevelt has plenty of money to build planes and tanks," Paula insisted. "Remember, America is a big country, with lots of people!"

I recalled the brief lesson in demographics our teacher put on the board: Major cities: "New York, Los Angeles, Chicago. Population: Gangsters and Jews."

"They're a mongrel race." Frau Schaub's blue eyes blazed as she adjusted hairpins in her blonde chigon.

Mamma re-measured the length of the garment and said, "Please stand still or the hem will be crooked."

Frau Schaub bent down to Paula. "I hear their skin is all shades. British masters mixed with their black slaves." She whispered the last word. "Mulattoes."

"What colors?" I asked.

"Rassenschande ! A shame to their race—that's what Americans are." Frau Schaub's features turned red in disgust.

"Quiet!" Pappa pointed to the radio.

"The two German battle cruisers, Scharnhorst and Gneisenau, and the heavy cruiser, Prinz Eugen, successfully escaped from the French port of Brest. They eluded the British fleet in the English Channel." The announcer paused a second. "Both battle cruisers received slight damage from mines before returning to port."

"Slight probably means heavy," Paula said. "Just like 'slim' retreat in Russia means great losses."

Pappa shook his finger at her. "You're becoming more cynical all the time."

Pins held between pinched lips, Mamma marked the skirt hem at the back. Darting warning looks at Paula and Pappa, she pointed to Frau Schaub.

I sensed that something was said that shouldn't have been and tried to change the subject. "In school, we talked about Field Marshall Rommel," I said. "He's the hero of the Africa Corps."

Pappa turned down the radio. "Erwin Rommel—now there's a good commander!"

Wanting to share what I'd learned in school, I said, "Herr Schneider showed on the blackboard how the Axis forces launched an offensive in Lybia, catching the British by surprise."

Frau Schaub said proudly, "My son was awarded the Iron Cross, First Class, for his precision target bombing on Malta. He flew many extra missions."

"First Class! Donnerwetter!" With that compliment, Mamma ushered her customer into the bedroom to change.

Pappa turned up the radio volume again.

"We turn now to our Eastern front—Russia." There was a slight pause before the newscaster continued. "The German offensive against Moscow has been halted as temperatures plunged to 30 below zero, freezing tank engines and the guns of three Panzer groups and three infantry armies."

"Poor Heini," Paula moaned as she collapsed into a chair. "I haven't heard from him for weeks." She started to cry.

Mamma pulled out a handkerchief. "The mail isn't coming through from the east. We haven't had a letter from Franz or any of my brothers-in-law in a long time."

"From besieged Leningrad," the broadcast continued, "the Soviets began mass evacuations, trucking refugees over frozen Lake Ladoga."

"I've listened enough to this nonsense. Turn off that Quatsch." The word "nonsense" was one of Mamma's favorite words when the talk centered around war news.

"Listen to this," said Pappa. "On the eastern front, German divisions have established a dug-in defensive position. The propaganda machine issues an order." He read aloud from the newspaper. "We must only refer to our soldiers in Russia as brave soldiers. It is forbidden to pity them.

"More German and Italian warplanes were sent to Malta," he continued to read. "Rommel's Afrika Korps wiped out a British Brigade in combat in Lybia. Those are the 'victorious soldiers.'"

Looking over his shoulder, Paula read aloud. "At home, food and coal rations will be cut again."

Now I picked up my ears. Will that mean less bread for school sandwiches? Less meat, like slices of ring bologna in potato soup?

Pappa turned the page. "British bombers have begun a new style of air raid," he read, "using incendiary bombs to light the way for night time attacks on the Krupp armament works in Essen. Yet a raid of more then a thousand bombers caused little damage to that industrial city and nearby targets."

"Will we be next?" I asked, though I didn't even want to think about it.

"It's just a matter of time." Mamma nodded, pulling another sock out of the darning basket.

I thought about what she had said and changed my nightly prayer. "I don't want my neighbors to be hurt," I prayed. "And since some night a bomb will fall on us, please make it quick, God. Send the biggest bomb you have so I'll be blown to nothing in an instant."

The bombs did become larger. Four-thousand-pounders were dropped on Essen in late April, reducing the few remaining buildings to rubble. Cologne and Hamburg were assaulted in May by up to a thousand bombers a night, leaving the cities in ashes.

"When is it our turn?" I didn't have to wait long.

On May 5th, Frankfurt was hit.

It has started, I thought, and waited for doomsday's total destruction. The distant rumbling of high-flying aircraft turned into a thundering roar, interrupted by shattering belchs of huge antiaircraft guns.

How many planes were up there? Where were our Messerschmitts?

Hannelore's brother, Egon, a gunner, told us he volunteers for extra missions all the time. "We have but few squadrons left to protect civilians. Most fighters have been dispatched to the Eastern front. The Americans are building those bombers faster than we can shoot them down."

"How big are their planes?"

He thought for a moment. "Picture them flying in tight formation. A thousand planes is about twenty-five kilometers long and ten kilometers in breadth. It would take an escort fighter thirty minutes to pass the armada from beginning to end."

Those numbers were too big to comprehend. I didn't even try.

But when the bombing over Frankfurt didn't continue, I reasoned that it must've been just a scare.

After the attack on the old port of Luebeck in Northern Germany where many ancient buildings and monuments once stood, the people demanded revenge.

The Luftwaffe got even. German planes battered the Allies' historic cities like York and Bath which, according to rumor, were selected from the Baedeker tourist guide.

"An eye for an eye," said some.

Mamma said, "Madness!"

In late July, just before school vacation started, our class studied poetry.

"I recommend you read Schiller's poem, The Song of the Bell, thoroughly, but we won't memorize those fourteen pages," said Miss Thyssen. "Like the motto in Longfellow's The Building of the Ship, the work calls to the living and bemoans the dead." She looked at me. "Anneliese, by tomorrow, I want you to recite the four pages that deal with the element of fire."

That's a big assignment, I thought. But I loved the challenge.

"Schiller finished the poem in 1799. The fear of fire felt by people then is the same as today. Too often," Miss Thyssen lectured, "we despair over lost worldly possessions instead of rejoicing in the living."

Mamma needed me to help with chores but took time to listen to me practice my lines.

"I marked the places in the book," I said, following her into the kitchen.

"I don't need to read it—it's all stored up here." Tapping her forehead, she started to recite from the beginning. Festgemauert in der Erde, steht die Form aus Lehm gebrannt..."

The printed words matched her memory. "Mired to the earth, stands the mold cast from clay..." Her love and knowledge of poetry continued to astound me.

In class the following day, before I could open my mouth to recite the poem, sirens wailed. I froze, unable to think or move. Feet shuffled around me and Miss Thyssen shouted orders. "Go to the shelter next to the school!"

We'd had many fire drills, but this was the real thing. Walking down the stairs, I remembered the threats on the leaflets: a thousand planes, bigger bombs. I thought of my family. Where is Mamma at this time of day? Probably sleeping—she stills works the night shift. Paula may be trapped in a food queue. And Walter? Is he as scared as I?

As we'd practiced, two hundred girls from grades one through eight walked down the stairs in orderly fashion, and crossed the asphalt-covered school yard, heading for the shelter. The younger ones were at the front of the line.

Suddenly, the air was filled with a sound like a million bumblebees. The sky darkened.

"Airplanes," yelled Herr Schorndorfer, the Math teacher, a veteran of the First World War. His white hair flapping in the air, he bolted to the shelter, shouting, "They're not British. I can tell by the sound of the engines."

Frightened, the little ones stampeded after him. Crying and shoving, everyone ran for safety. I didn't dare raise my eyes to the sky. Don't be afraid, I told myself over and over, increasing my stride.

"Where is the FLAK?" someone shouted. "They must be taking a nap or playing a game of cards."

Just as the first-graders descended the cellar steps, I watched in horror as some of the older girls pushed past them, knocking the smaller ones down.

"Langsam!" Miss Braun, the physical education teacher shouted and started helping the scared children to their feet.

Some cried for their Mamma. Others crouched in corners, screaming. Above the chaos and confusion, teachers tried to restore order.

I stood near Miss Thyssen. She blew her whistle. "Start reciting, Anneliese," she said in a voice that was steady and firm.

The children quieted down.

Shaking from head to toe, I rose. I had to do it. Outside, muffled explosions continued. Bombs? Flak? In panic, I looked at my teacher. I couldn't remember the words.

She seemed to read my mind. "I'll help if you get stuck." Her smile was reassuring as her hands gestured to hush the frenzy in a far corner.

"Wohltaetig ist des Feuers Nacht…" Timidly, words spilled out of my mouth describing, the might and benefit of fire as long as it was harnessed and contained by man.

As the explosions multiplied, I grew unsteady. The earth shook and rumbled under my feet.

"Go on," said Miss Thyssen, reaching for my hand.

I drew strength from her.

In a voice stronger than the outside thundering, I continued with the story.

"What happens when fire roams free? The elements hate to be tamed by man," the story unfolds. "Without resistance, the fire spreads."

How well we knew! How often had we heard the growing crackle, seen the raging inferno, smelled the acrid smoke. Eyes smarted, nostrils stung. Everywhere moaned the sights and sounds of hell.

Yet, spellbound, everyone listened to the story the poet had created.

I continued. "Clouds give sunshine and rain—both a blessing. But, without warning, lightning may strike."

More explosions outside. An aircraft crash? Was it the enemy or one of ours?

Miss Thyssen squeezed my hand till it hurt. "Keep going," she whispered.

The story continued with the fire storm, the bucket brigade, and the fright and flight of people—and the flames growing to giants.

What was happening upstairs? The children grew restless. So did I—but I had to stay calm and be an example to the younger ones. I couldn't show fear.

"Helpless and without hope," I recited, "man retreats from the strength of the Gods and idly watches his works drown in flames."

Suddenly, all was quiet. Even my voice stopped shaking.

"Burnt out is the place that's been the bed of wild storms. While the clouds watch from high above, the new resident of the ruin is called horror." A tear choked the last word.

"Once more man looks back at the grave of his belongings. Joyfully, he reaches for his hiking staff. No matter what fire's wrath has robbed him of— one sweet consolation remains. He counts the heads of his beloved—and see, not one is missing."

After I finished, Miss Thyssen stood up. "On your way home today, think of what Schiller said in that last stanza about the element of fire. There is hope!" Eyes moist, she looked around the room and added, "God bless you all—and thank you, Anneliese."

When the ALL CLEAR sounded, we moved reluctantly upstairs to the nearest exit. The little ones still seemed anxious, the older girls climbed out slowly.

I waited until the crowd had thinned.

"You have the farthest to go, Anneliese," said Miss Thyssen. "Do you want to wait with me at school? Perhaps your Mamma will come for you."

Seeing the fire and smoke ahead of me, I shook my head. Trembling, I said, "I need to count heads, too."

I started to run home, my feet flying faster than the day of Crystal Night. Taking a shortcut through the park, I passed the Holy Ghost hospital on the left and raced down the broad Zeil boulevard to the corner of our narrow Strasse. Near the post office stood Mamma, peering anxiously up the street. Walter stood at her side, I ran even faster until I was safe in her arms. Bursting into tears I said, "I didn't cry in front of the little ones, Mamma, I was brave."

CHAPTER FOURTEEN—Russia—Winter 1942

While delivering mail. Mamma had slipped on ice and broke her leg—a good reason for Pappa to move back.

"He promised not to drink any more," Mamma assured us.

I wanted to protest. It won't work. You have taken him back so many times. But she looked so pitiful lying on the makeshift bed in the living room with her leg propped on pillows, I swallowed my words and tears.

Death to the German invaders! Pappa heard the message from the Soviet Union on a wireless at a friend's home.

"Time is Russia's strongest weapon," said Pappa. He lifted Mamma a few centimeters so I could spread a clean sheet over the sofa.

"How?" I asked, as I tucked and pulled on the white cotton to remove the wrinkles. War news seemed as important as the weather report—and as unpredictable.

"As knee-deep snow covers the land, winter becomes their ally," explained Pappa. "History has shown that armies can't combat winter in that vast country." He fluffed Mamma's pillow. "Russia has only dirt roads. After the frost thaws, the ground turns to quagmire. Tanks, artillery, all motorized equipment will be swallowed in the morass."

"Surely, the war will be over before spring," said Mamma.

That's what everyone said last year, I thought.

In school every day, we followed the German blitz as troops methodically dug deeper into Russian territory.

Herr Schneider, our teacher of current affairs, pointed to Leningrad, Kiev, Stalingrad, and Moscow. "Our brave soldiers have been fighting on a front two thousand miles long—they're now standing in the shadow of the Kremlin." His finger moved across the Ukraine to Crimea on the south. "My son manned one of the 1300 cannons that shelled Sevastopol. The battle lasted 28 days. He wrote this port is decisive for the success of the Russian campaign."

No doubt Herr Schneider was proud to be a member of the Nazi party. Flipping the map to Africa, his voice shook. "Tobruk. That's where my other son gave his life for our Fatherland." He wiped his brow despite the cold temperature. "With 200 tanks of the British to our 100, our victorious soldiers continue to battle the British forces in the North. But as soon as Fieldmarshall Rommel gets more tanks, he'll push them back." He struck the map so hard with his pointing stick, several of our flags fell to the ground. Striding up and down the room, he started reciting the latest battle hymn:

"We'll continue to march on,

Until all is shattered and gone,

Today we belong to Germany,

Tomorrow the world belongs to us!"

But the words were hollow now, I knew the tide in Africa had turned. I'd overheard people whisper behind cupped hands, "For the first time we're losing."

Sirens interrupted our lesson. Round-the-clock air raids were a way of life. Ports like Hamburg and Bremen, as well as industrial centers were systematically demolished. Duesseldorf had been targeted fifty times. Miraculously, Frankfurt suffered few direct attacks.

Would we be next?

Sitting in the air raid shelters, I worried about our home. It would be just a matter of time, I reasoned, till we were hit.

In the privacy of the kitchen, we aired anxieties over loved ones in Stalingrad. Twenty-two Axis divisions began a siege of that city in late August. It was now close to Christmas.

"I don't think we're being told the truth," Paula said. Her face red with agitation, she waddled to the stove to add a briquet. "Our poor men are starving inside the pincers the Soviets laid." Closing the lid on the coal bin with a bang, she sat next to the fire and cupped her flushed face in her hands. "I'm worried about Heini."

Mamma tried to calm her. "According to his military mail code, he's not in Stalingrad." She picked up the last letter from Uncle Bert. "But I'm not so sure about Lina's husband. He wrote this three months ago." A tear trickled down her cheek as she reread the lines. "I'm glad he received the small mouth organ I sent him last summer."

It was now Paula's turn to comfort Mamma. "Bert is a medic. They won't harm him."

"I hope not."

"Have you heard from your brother?" Paula asked.

"No, not a word." The tears turned into a flood. "We don't know where Franz is. His mailing address has a secret code."

Coughing and sneezing, Pappa entered the kitchen, a newspaper clamped under his arm. Verfluchte Kaelte!" He handed the paper to Paula and blew his nose. "Cursed cold!"

Mamma ladled hot pea soup into a dinner bowl and sat next to him. "What's the latest rumor at the factory?"

Before he could answer, Paula jumped up from her seat. "Did you read this?" Her voice was shaking.

Pappa grabbed the paper from her and adjusted his glasses. Looking over his shoulder, I read the headline. "The ring must be broken."

In a voice barely audible, Mamma said, "Our men are encircled outside Stalingrad. Completely cut off. Trapped!"

Pappa read aloud. "Field Marshall Paulus, head of the 6th Army, swears his men will fight to the bitter end. If anyone surrenders, his family will be killed." Under his breath, Pappa muttered, "Schweinehund!"

I wanted to cry, but couldn't. I thought of prayer. No, I had stopped praying a long time ago. At eleven, I felt old and reasoned that God was busy listening to people like the British, the Russians, and Americans. The way I saw it, the whole world was against the Germans.

How big was Germany compared to other countries? The Soviet Union alone could put Germany in her hip pocket. We had no map of America, but clearly, they were making airplanes faster than we could shoot them down. Surely their people were praying "Death to the enemy!" as hard—and to the same God.

Our soldiers were outnumbered. By now, twenty-eight nations had declared war on Germany. Some were countries, like Mexico, I'd never heard of. Where in the world was that?

On February 2, 1943, after 153 days of fighting, Paulus' army capitulated. They had been surrounded for 93 days. Twenty-four German generals were captured by the Russians. Of the 280,000 German soldiers trapped, 150,000 died, 40,000 were wounded, and 90,000 surrendered.

"Nobody got away," said Pappa. "The prisoners will not survive the forced labor camps in Siberia." He took off his fogged eye glasses and began to furiously wipe them.

We rushed outside to talk with others. People collapsed in the streets, crying openly. Everyone knew someone in the Sixth Army.

Mamma, her face covered with tears, trembled with pain. A woman standing next to her fainted; others shrieked. Some just sobbed quietly.

Throughout the city, wailing filled the air. Not sirens, but women weeping for their men. The sound penetrated to the darkest rooms—from the smallest attic to the deepest cellar.

Three hundred and thirty thousand perished in Stalingrad.

"Cry, children, cry," said Mamma and put her arms around us. Rocking back and forth, she whispered, "The dead deserve our tears."

For many weeks, page after page of the newspaper's obituary section listed those considered dead. Little black crosses followed the names. One of them read: Albert Duerr, Medic, Private First Class. Uncle Bert. I wanted to cry out his name. Sob. Whimper. But not a tear squeezed out. All I felt was pain, a crushing ache inside of me.

Escorted by P-38 and P-47 fighters, American B-17's continued strategic daylight bombing over German cities. After an alert, we often gathered at the parking place behind the post office. The boys knew all about how ME109 Messerschmitts swarmed after the enormous planes.

"Those big bombers are vulnerable to head-on attacks because of their size and weight," said one of the older boys, showing off. "Flying Fortresses, the Americans call them. Their fighters are faster in the chase, but ours have better maneuverability."

"Jawohl!" A red-headed kid bragged from behind. "Our black crows can't be beat!"

"What's a black crow?" Walter asked.

"It's what the British call our Luftwaffe."

"Why?" Walter persisted.

"'Cause they fly low when attacking," explained the boy with the red hair.

"How do you know all that?"

"Because my father is an officer in the Luftwaffe. He flies fighter planes and volunteers for extra missions all the time." He pulled a crumpled picture of a Junker fighter from his pocket. The other boys crowded around him.

"Maybe he shot down one of theirs this morning!" exclaimed a little kid missing his front teeth.

"No," said the older one. "He's fighting in Africa."

It must be nice to be proud of your father, I thought. I wish I could brag about mine.

Using their hands as bombers and fighters, the boys started their favorite game of air attack.

114

"EEEH-OOOH-EEEH-OOOH,' warned the sirens. "BRRMMM-BRRMMM

sounded the heavy engines of the B-17's. Then the sound of Messerschmitt machine guns. "Rat-tat-tat-tat." Crash!

While the children played war across the street, the grownups talked reality in the kitchen. "The RAF discontinued their thousand-bomber-raids," said Pappa. "I've heard they've run out of trained pilots. It takes more than a gunner and a bombardier to complete a flight crew."

"Perhaps they're out of petrol," Paula conjectured.

"No." Pappa shook his head. "They have to train new pilots, gunners, and navigators to man their planes. Some recruits come all the way from Australia."

"Don't forget the bombardiers," Mamma chimed in as she pulled the black-out drapes over plexi-glass window panes.

Whole squadrons were wiped out, we were told. But the Americans kept coming. The rumbling of B17's became a thunderous prelude to shattering roars of huge antiaircraft guns. Casualties on both sides were always heavy. Loaded with tons of explosives, the planes shot down by the FLAK and German fighters did as much damage to homes as did the bombs.

Power outages after air battles were common and wax candles became scarce. When the water lines broke, we carried buckets from the nearest working fire hydrant over three-hundred meters away. The heavily loaded wire handles cut into our hands and water slopped onto our shoes.

"We must boil the water before drinking it," cautioned Mamma.

"Why?" I asked.

"Typhus. It's a killer."

As the city deteriorated, mobile field kitchens appeared. They were designed to feed those without shelter, but Walter and I always managed to get some bread and soup. We survived.

CHAPTER FIFTEEN—Evacuation—Early Spring 1943

In big, bold letters, Miss Thyssen wrote the word on the blackboard.
E V A K U A T I O N.

"It's a new word for most of us," she said.

Why was her round, kind face frowning?

"It means departure, leaving, parting, exodus, flight." She seemed to choke on the words. "Our Fuehrer wants you children to be safe." She spoke slowly, pausing between each phrase. "The Reich is providing camps in the country for you, far from bombs and destruction. The schools in Frankfurt will close completely." Unable to meet our shocked eyes, she shuffled a stack of paper around on her desk.

Some girls cried out in delight.

I was too stunned to react. No learning? How awful. Reading poetry, writing compositions, or using math to count calories to me was more fun than dusting or doing dishes. True, sometimes it was an escape from the miserable world around me. I would rather become absorbed in a book than to deal with the realities of fetching and boiling water.

"Some of you will be living with relatives in rural areas," Miss Thyssen continued. "Others will be evacuated to permanent camps, such as the one located in the Alps, near Salzburg." She showed us the area on the map and then passed out notification slips to take home.

Mamma was furious. She screamed and slammed the paper on the table. "Now Adolf wants our children." I knew Mamma was upset by the way she called Hitler by his first name—an act of disrespect to grownups unless given special permission.

Paula read the note. "It says the children will be supervised, get nourishing food, and will continue their education."

"Adolf is stealing my children," Mamma screamed again.

"Lower your voice," said Paula. "Informers are lurking in every corner."

"Kanonenfutter! That's what the young boys will turn into."

I pictured Walter being stuffed into a large barrel as food for a cannon.

Mamma looked at Paula. "I've heard some rumors about the goings-on in those camps."

They glanced at me.

"She's too young to breed babies for Adolf's armies. Besides, she's too skinny," said Paula.

What are they talking about? Were they going to feed me until I got fat? I thought of Frau Wessely upstairs. She had a big stomach again. Perhaps my teacher could shed light on some of my questions—except, lately, she was so busy making evacuation arrangements.

After a conference with Miss Thyssen, Mamma pooled the clothing allotments to buy material and started making new clothes for me. She cut out patterns, measured and pinned, basted and sewed, until the cloth turned into lovely dresses, blouses, and jackets. Sometimes she rubbed her tired eyes—often the sleepiness turned into tears.

I had mixed feelings about leaving home. I would miss my teacher, I thought. Miss Thyssen was my role model, often more important than Mamma. School without her was unthinkable.

I wouldn't miss doing the housework every day. Certainly, it would be nice not to be frightened out of sleep by the howl of sirens.

What made me feel especially good was that Hannelore was also going. We swore loyalty to each other a long time ago, even devising a secret language. We'd sign the alphabet with our hands to talk to each other. Hannelore and I had great fun doing this in front of our classmates, friends, and even her brothers.

Walter had to stay home because of his renewed bed-wetting and poor health. What would he do without me? Who would make breakfast for him? Pack his lunch for school? Help him with homework? Dry the sheets he wet during the night? I worried about him a lot.

I'd also miss Paula. Trying to express my love for her, I embroidered her a tablecloth with flowers and hearts.

My stepfather? I pondered how to hide my joy. I will have to pretend being sad, I thought. I don't want to hurt Mamma's and Walter's feelings. They care about him. In reality, I wouldn't miss being slapped by his powerful hand, making him supper in the middle of the night, or darting from his advances. All I wanted was to get as far away as possible. How I hated him!

Mamma lamented my leaving. "When will I see my little girl again?" she'd sighed.

Reversing roles, I put my arms around her. "As soon as the war is over," I said, patting her back.

She reviewed the list of items to pack one more time. "Writing paper," she read. "Promise to send a letter every day."

The week before it was time to leave, she cooked all my favorite dishes: Lentil soup with small dumplings. Mushrooms. Vanilla pudding. No sauerkraut—her favorite dish.

We were not told which camp we were assigned to until a few days before the schools closed. Handing me a slip of paper, Miss Thyssen beamed. "My best friend will teach at the place where you're going. I told her about you and Hannelore. Her name is Timpelmann. I wrote it down, and also my address so you can write to me. Tell me how you like her."

"Where are we going?" I wanted to know

"To Kaprun-am-See, a little village in the Alps, named because it's near a lake."

Hannelore squeezed my hand until it hurt. "It sounds so exciting," she whispered. "Yet I'm scared. I've never left my family."

"No matter what, we'll stick together," I whispered back.

At the train station, we waited at the appointed place. I observed the gaping roof that once had been panes of all colors; read the Nazi slogan banners screaming from walls WHEELS MUST ROLL FOR VICTORY, and looked at tired faces of people crowding the platforms. A female Hitler youth leader in uniform met us.

"Just a snot-nosed kid," Mamma said. "I don't like her."

After roll call, the luggage was tagged and put in the rack above our wooden bench seats in the train compartment.

"It's going to be a long ride," said Paula, patting my cheek.

As I hugged Walter, he started crying. "Wish I could go with you," he sniffled, as the train hissed steam.

Hannelore's small and frail mother leaned on Mamma. "I've said good-bye to most of my boys because of the war. Never did I imagine I'd see my youngest leave—my daughter at that."

The whistle blew. "Alles einsteigen!" The conductor stepped aboard and shut the door.

Inside, we crowded around the open window. Some girls giggled; others sobbed. I pulled out my handkerchief, waved, managed a brave smile.

The wheels began to turn, grinding and screeching against the iron tracks, moving at a snail's pace at first. Hobbling alongside the train, Mamma forced a smile, but then her smile slipped and her face crumpled. The tears she had been holding back trickled down her cheeks.

When the speed picked up and the train moved away, she stopped and waved, "Auf Wiedersehn!"

CHAPTER SIXTEEN—Austria—Spring 1943

Shouts and girls' chatter woke me. "Look at the snow-covered mountains! It's like in Heidi! Look down there! A brook!"

I rubbed my eyes and sat up. Where was I? I felt the train's rhythmic rumble that had lulled me to sleep the night before, and quickly scrambled atop of the wooden bench, my bed for the last ten hours.

I held onto the net of the luggage carrier above and stretched across the heads of my companions to look outside. "How beautiful!" Never had I seen such a sight, never had I felt so much wonder.

Completing a curve, the train jerked and began to slow down. I was struggling to regain my balance—when I felt a firm hand steady my back. Turning, I looked through my tangle of brown hair into soft amber eyes exuding friendliness. I'm going to like my new teacher, I thought. "Oh— thanks," I said and returned to the panorama unfolding outside.

Miss Timpelmann nodded. "I promised you the Alps would be magnificent, especially in the morning sun."

The others in the compartment bombarded her with questions. "When are we going to be there? How much longer? When is breakfast?

Everyone wanted to know the same thing.

"Let's sit down," Miss Timpelmann suggested, helping me off the bench. We're getting close to Salzburg where we'll have something to eat at the station. Afterwards, we change to a slower train that'll take us to our final destination."

"Where's Salzburg?" a girl with thick, blond braids wanted to know.

The teacher pulled a map out of her briefcase, "It's near Vienna," she pointed, then proceeded to tell us about the rich salt mines in the region.

"Is that why it's called Salzkammergut?" Hannelore obviously had studied her geography.

Miss Timpelmann looked pleased. "Yes, and the city is also named after the castle sitting high on the side of the mountain. Folklore tells us in medieval times its occupants were under siege from a neighboring lord. He was trying to starve them into surrender. 'Women can leave the castle without being harmed,' the warlord promised, 'but they may take only what they can carry on their backs.'"

The train whistle interrupted the story.

"Another tunnel!" Little-girl shrieks filled the compartment as the train entered the darkness.

"It's like a blackout," I whispered, scooting close to Hannelore.

Once the train was out of the tunnel, Miss Timpelmann peered into our questioning faces. "What do you think the women carried on their backs?"

"Jewelry," said the girl with the fashionable Mozart-style braid.

"Potatoes," ventured Hannelore.

"Salt?" I felt foolish after saying it.

"Good guesses," she nodded and smiled. "On their backs, they carried what they most loved—their husbands!"

As we laughed at the story, the train grunted to slower speed and finally stopped. One of the young uniformed leaders opened the compartment doors and yelled, "Alles aussteigen!" Time to get off.

We scrambled for jackets and coats.

"Better put them on," advised our teacher, "March can be very cold up here."

She was right. The air was brisk, and the wind biting—not at all warm and pregnant with Spring, like the breezes in Frankfurt the day we left.

At the station we received a crisp roll, and hot malt coffee, generously laced with milk and sugar. For the time being, our appetites were satisfied. We were all anxious to get to Kaprun.

"Let's follow our teacher," I urged Hannelore, who had begun to draw a hopscotch grid on the platform with a piece of charcoal. Despite being a couple of months older than I—almost twelve—she usually followed my lead. I guessed it was because she had all those older brothers and a big sister to tell her what to do.

As we boarded the train, so small it looked like a toy, we watched the engine driver feed wood into its boiler. Slowly, the locomotive chugged its way across the mountain, huffing and puffing before the town disappeared behind as we rounded the bend. We doubted the engine's power to make the next rising turn, and when Miss Timpelmann remarked with a sober face we might have to push the train, we all began to giggle.

Someone started singing the first bars of a song. Another remembered the lyrics, which told of a young lad who climbed the steep mountain cliffs to fetch an Edelweiss for his sweetheart living in a storybook village below. Even the train seemed to hum along, ending with a melodic whistle as it crept to a halt at a tiny station platform, barely big enough to hold a dozen people.

A small sign spelled the name of the place—Kaprun am See. Not far away we could see a cluster of three buildings with steep roofs and farther back, a few farm houses were nested between straggly evergreen pines. As we piled out of the train, a female shouted, "Uhlandschule!"

I poked Hannelore in the ribs. "That's the name of our school."

The woman in charge was about seventeen, and wearing a Hitler Youth uniform. Two rows of blond braids were pinned tightly to the top of her head. "Heil Hitler! My name is Inge," she announced. "From now on, I'm your leader. We occupy the second floor of that three-story building. Some rooms have two bunk beds, others three, and the largest has four. Each has a sink with running cold water. Heil Hitler!" She gulped a breath. "Follow me!" she shouted and marched off.

When we arrived at our assigned building, she led the way upstairs. "Pick your bed and locker and then assemble in the dining room by noon. I'll blow my whistle at twelve."

We soon learned to live by that sound. The shrill tone woke us at six each morning. Changing quickly from nightgowns into training suits, we ran downstairs and lined up outside.

The whistle started and ended our fifteen-minute jog over mountain trails. Sometimes we did calisthenics instead. Afterwards, we had half an hour to sponge-bathe with cold tap water, get dressed, make our beds, and clean up our area. It didn't leave a lot of time to talk.

A quarter of an hour before our seven o'clock breakfast, the whistle blew again, followed by a voice as shrill as her mouth instrument. "Room inspection!"

One more time, Hannelore pounded the straw-filled mattress and pillow sacks to smooth out the hills and dells that regularly appeared after you slept on them. Even spreading the grey army wool blanket across the bedding straw didn't smooth the lumps and bumps.

Whistle in hand, Edeltraut, the inspector, entered. Her thick glasses extended her eyes like light bulbs as she checked the sink for scum, the table for dust. Stopping short in front of my friend's bunk, her eyes narrowed to a slit. "You call this a properly made bed?" In one sweep, she jerked blanket, pillow, and straw mattress on the floor. "Do it over so it resembles the shape of a giant-size cigar box," she ordered, and strode to the four lockers that looked like single-door wardrobes without locks.

Will mine pass inspection? I knew the underwear had shifted a little when I lifted out a pair of panties.

It did not. Without a word, the inspector overturned the closet that contained my belongings. "That will teach you to stack your things in proper order!" snarled Edeltraut.

Every passing second, I began to dislike that name more, wanted to snap back or yank the piece of yarn that tied back her red frizzy hair parted in the middle; but without blinking an eye, I stood straight and said, "Jawohl, Fraeulein Edeltraut!" Hourly indoctrination during the first day had imprinted the message—insubordination of one member will lead to harsh discipline of the team.

A good example was mealtime. We were to remain silent while in the dining room, but when a girl at our table whispered something after the whistle blew, all eight of us were punished.

"Table Six," shouted the group leader, "you will not receive mail for the next five days."

Letters from home was an event we looked forward to every day after supper. It was the only link to the outside world since we had no access to newspapers or radio. Even the daily lesson plan did not allow for discussion of the war front.

School started promptly at eight and lasted until dinner at noon. "What's our assignment for homework?" I asked Miss Timpelmann.

"No study time has been allotted." Our teacher let out an audible sigh and shrugged, "There's no library, no books, no periodical. I don't even have teaching materials."

Hannelore pointed to the schedule on the wall. The afternoons were filled with drills, Nazi doctrine, more physical workouts, or sometimes long hikes—fair weather permitting.

It was our turn to moan and grumble. "I want some free time to do nothing," said Hannelore.

"Me, too," I said. "But most, I miss reading books."

Once a week, we had two hours of unstructured time which we used to write letters to our families.

"Dear Mamma," I wrote. "We live in a place that once was a fancy mountain resort. It's supposed to be next to a lake, but I haven't seen it yet. The hotels have been converted into a youth camp. I share a room on the second floor with three other girls."

What would Mamma like to know? I didn't want to tell her about the humiliating inspection event. Knowing Mamma, I knew she'd take the next train and give that girl a piece of her mind. Like the time she stormed into a Hitler Youth gathering in Frankfurt and loudly complained about the nonsense being taught in these meetings.

Chewing on the tip of my pencil, I remembered her disdain as she'd glared at the girl in uniform who couldn't have been a year over sixteen.

"You're not old enough to be dry behind the ears," Mamma taunted.

I will never forget the silence that filled the room like a ghostly presence. Bulging eyes widened behind the glint of spectacles. "Youth must be led by youth," retorted the pudgy troop leader. Her voice turned icy. "It's the National Socialist principle. Sieg Heil!"

Drawing little swastika crosses around the border of the letter, I recalled Mamma's dark eyes flashing with anger. "Pin your principles on your own hat," she retorted. Over the protest of the leader, Mamma yanked me from my seat and, not letting go of my hand, stomped out. "Rotznase," she hissed. "Snotnose!"

What embarrassment! All I wanted was to be like all the others.

No, it wouldn't do to get Mamma upset. The cuckoo clock on the wall of the assembly room announced the hour. Not much time left to write. Food! I thought. That's an important issue with Mamma. "We line up one table at a time, to get our portions," I continued writing. "Often, we have little dumplings made of flour instead of potatoes. Sometimes they make stew. It's good, but I like yours better. They put in too much cabbage and too many carrots. We do get a second helping when there is enough."

Mamma knew I hated vegetables. What else? "The weather is still cold, but we warm up in the morning by doing a lot of running and jumping."

She was aware that I don't like exercising either.

"Do you have many air raids? We had a thunderstorm the other day that sounded as bad as the bombing because it echoed in the mountains. I was scared."

I had to start a second page.

"All of our leaders are young, except our teacher, Miss Timpelmann. She's the only older person in this camp. She says our generation was fatally lacking in contacts with mature people."

Then I remembered my brother.

"How are you, Walter? I hope fine. What do you do all day with the schools closed? Are you taking good care of Muschi? I miss stroking her soft fur and hearing her purr."

What else?

"I don't know anything more to say. Please send me a book, Mamma. And write more often. You, too, Walter. I promise not to look at the spelling mistakes. Love, Anneliese. P.S. We get mail every other day—except when we make too much noise in the dining room. Then the mail is withheld from everyone for punishment."

Miss Timpelmann approached the table where Hannelore and I were sitting. "Would you girls like to add a few lines to a letter I wrote to Miss Thyssen?"

"You first," said Hannelore, looking at me. "I want to write a letter to my brother, Berthold. He's only fourteen and received a notice to do his one-year labor duty. Vati is trying to fight it."

The whistle blew. "You have ten minutes to finish your correspondence. Make sure you address the envelopes properly—but don't seal them."

"Why not?" I turned to my teacher with the question.

"Censorship. All outgoing letters are read before they leave," she answered.

I immediately scratched out the part about punishment in the P.S.

Sometimes I longed for privacy—time to think, watch clouds drift to nowhere on the horizon, listen to the birds and wonder what they were saying to each other, talk to God.

Once in a while, before going to sleep, I felt homesick. Some girls missed their families and cried. For me this place was a solution—to be away from Pappa.

There were many things to feel good about, like my friendship with Hannelore. At night, she delighted in telling stories about ghosts prowling in dark corners of the deathly quiet room, their low moans beckoning, "The erlking wants you."

While fearful squeals emanated from Liesel and Erna in the upper bunks, goose bumps raised the skin on my arms. Quickly, I pulled the blanket over my head, pressed my face into the straw pillow—and sneezed.

"Gesundheit!" Hannelore's laughter broke the spell.

"We want to hear another one," Erna called.

"Let Anneliese recite the Erlkoenig," said Hannelore. "It's so scary!"

"And sad," added Liesel.

We had studied Goethe's poem about the enticing king that day in Miss Timpelmann's class. The erlking made promises. The feverish child believed. And the father raced on his horse against the ruthless tyrant—but lost. On arrival, the child lay dead in his arms.

"Better wait until tomorrow night," I whispered. I hear Edeltraut, the night watchman.

Every night 'til dawn, we sleep peacefully. No more sirens, no antiaircraft, no bombings. No Pappa. A time of healing and sanity—I felt safe.

One morning, Hannelore didn't want to get up. "I feel dizzy," she said.

I coaxed her to at least make roll call. "You know how upset the exercise leader gets when someone reports sick," I said. "Remember yesterday? How Gerda screamed about the ill being lazy! She made us all do ten extra pushups."

Listlessly, Hannelore dressed while I helped her fluff, shake, and smooth the straw mattress.

Outside, we shivered in the morning mist that shrouded mountains and meadows with hues of silver and gray, dripping from trees in tingling droplets.

Two girls didn't appear for lineup before exercises. When their names were called, Inge yelled, "Sick!"

Gerda, the training leader, scowled. "There seems to be an epidemic of laziness. We'll have to do something about that!"

Small raindrops started falling. She looked at the sky. "A little rain won't hurt anyone. We're going to jog despite it. Let's go!"

I stayed close to Hannelore. Her fair complexion looked ghostly this morning. Twice, I helped her up when she slipped. "You can do it," I encouraged.

With her blue eyes shaded a dull grey, she managed a small smile and nodded.

The jog did bring color to her cheeks. By the time we entered the dining room, her face was flushed. She hardly touched her breakfast—only sipping a little warm milk.

Sitting next to her in class, I noticed beads of sweat covering her face; she shivered. Carefully, I draped my sweater over her shoulder.

Miss Timpelmann walked to Hannelore's desk and felt her forehead. "You have a fever," she said, looking worried.

"I'll take her to the nurse," I offered.

The sickroom had six beds, all occupied with feverish-looking girls. "It must be influenza," sighed the helper, an older woman from the village. She read the thermometer, shook it, and put it back under Hannelore's armpit.

This time the robust-looking camp nurse looked at the silver streak.

"Maybe the mercury is stuck," she mumbled, shaking it again. "We better take your temperature rectally. It's more accurate."

I watched her carefully cover the thermometer with Vaseline and insert it. Mamma always took our temperature that way. Peering inside the gloomy room with all the beds, I observed a woman apply cold compresses to the foreheads of her patients.

"We need to call a doctor," said the assistant as she helped Hannelore to her feet. The nurse agreed. "Please stay with the children until I return." Turning to me, she asked, "Can you take Hannelore to her room?" She raised her hands in exasperation. "We've no more accommodations in the sick room. And Hannelore must go straight to bed."

Holding back tears, I nodded. "Lean on me," I said. She was so weak. Slowly we walked to our building, up the stairs, and down the hall to our room. I helped her undress and put on her nightgown.

"I'm thirsty," she said, so I filled the communal tin cup at the sink with water. She drank it, asking for more.

The whistle blew. Even though I knew I'd miss dinner, I stayed.

Bringing a bowl of porridge to our room, the nurse said, "The doctor will be here soon." She wiped Hannelore's face with a cold cloth and said in a soft voice, "I must look after the other patients, little one." She turned to leave. "Try to finish the food."

Hannelore refused to even taste it. Propping her up with another pillow, I held the spoon to her lips. She turned her head to the wall.

What was the game Mamma played feeding little Hansi? Remembering, I felt a rush of homesickness as I put a spoonful of the mush in my mouth and swallowed. "One for me," I said.

Hannelore stared at me with glassy eyes. Again, I filled the spoon. "And one for you." This time she opened her mouth.

"One for me and one for you." We played the game a little while longer until she started to cry.

"You don't have to eat any more," I said, wiping her mouth with my handkerchief. "I'll finish it."

Outside the door I heard voices. "They're dropping like flies," Miss Timpelmann said.

"The ambulance will take them, two at a time, to the nearest hospital," said an unknown female voice.

It must be the doctor, I thought. Quickly, I brushed Hannelore's dark, curly hair away from her face with my hands. It was matted and sticky with sweat. I wanted my friend to look pretty.

"This is Dr. Schimmel," said Miss Timpelmann. "She'll take care of Hannelore."

She didn't look like a doctor at all, I decided. Dr. Klein in Frankfurt was tall, thin, and smiled. Dr. Schimmel was short, fat, wore horn-rimmed glasses, and frowned. Besides, she looked old and wrinkled. Why did we have such a prune for a doctor?

I didn't even like the name Schimmel. It reminded me of that white and grey mold that grows on cheese in humid weather. Even her hair was the color of mildew.

The empty porridge bowl with the spoon inside was sitting on the bed. "She ate all of it," I lied.

Miss Timpelmann took my hand and gently suggested I go to the dining room before the food was all gone. "They have Knoedel and fruit compote," she said. "Dumplings are your favorite."

Watching Dr. Schimmel pull a stethoscope out of her black bag and place the ends into her ears, I slowly backed out of the room. Before closing the door, I got a glimpse of the doctor bending over the bed. Guess she's a proper doctor, after all.

When I returned, Hannelore was gone.

I tried to see her at the sick station, but wasn't allowed. The aides were busy wheeling someone into an ambulance, while another girl, too weak to walk, and delirious, was lifted inside. Helplessly, I watched—and waited.

That night, I crawled into her bed, pulled the covers over my head and cried until the straw reeked like rotten hay. No one told me not to.

The next morning, they came to gather Hannelore's blanket, lumpy mattress and pillow. A day later, her belongings were gone.

Staring at the vacant bed and empty locker, I was worried. Why was my best friend gone? Where did they take her? What was wrong? Was she dead?

My roommates whispered and wondered. "Who'll be missing next from roll call?"

"Nothing to worry about." Inge gave one of her spunky speeches. "You are the future generation. Our Fuehrer will take care of you. Heil Hitler!" After the fifteen-minute jog, she announced that in the afternoon we'd go on a long hike.

The weather was beautiful when we started, not a cloud in the sky. In spite of worry, we were in good spirits.

Miss Timpelmann decided not to join us. "I have to prepare lessons for tomorrow's class," she said, looking tired and drawn.

No wonder, I thought. She's helping at the sick station every minute she can spare.

We sang and hiked—sometimes on a path so narrow, we had to go single file. Shouting into nowhere, we enticed the echo. "Hannelore," I called.

"Lore, Lore, Lore," the mountains answered.

Then it was still. Only the wind could be heard, as it whistled through the canyon. Below, cows grazed in a pasture.

The day grew dark. Black clouds gathered on the horizon. Thunder bounced off mountainsides, multiplying the crashes. One more lightning bolt, then rain poured out of clouds in buckets.

There was no shelter. The troop trudged back with just our light jackets as cover. We arrived at the camp soaking wet—and cold.

With a stack of towels, Miss Timpelmann waited at the bottom of the stairs. She even managed a small smile, but appeared exhausted. "After you've changed your clothes," she said in a voice that sounded as tired as she looked, "come to the dining hall. Our cook has hot chocolate waiting for you."

Holding the hand rail, I climbed the stairs slowly. My legs felt leaden. Inside my room, I removed my wet clothes and put on a warm dress and sweater. My head ached. I wanted to sleep. But the shrill sound of the whistle wouldn't let me.

Slowly, my legs moved my body through the door.

"Mach' schnell," urged my two roommates. "Or the cocoa will be cold."

From my room, I made it to the top of the stairway. Then everything around me started to spin. My knees buckled and I collapsed.

CHAPTER SEVENTEEN—The Erlkoenig— Late Spring 1943

Gently sleeping, I rocked from side to side until something bumpy jolted me out of my slumber. What was that hum I heard? It purrs softly—now louder. Could it be the engine of an airplane?

I tried to see something in the inky blackness. Licking my hot, dry lips, I blinked. Were those stars framed by a window? No. They were eyes; evil eyes; coming closer. Frantically, I tried to sit up—but couldn't. Sweat covered my body. The world spun around me. I screamed. "Go away!"

"Be calm—it's only the light of heaven."

"Miss Timpelmann?" I turned my head and saw the outline of someone sit beside me.

"Yes, Anneliese." She stroked my hand.

Her voice faded away, but her warm touch gave me comfort. "I'm glad you're here," I said.

The rhythmic rocking lulled me back to sleep—until something lurched and jolted. Grasping my teacher's hand tighter, I cried out, "Are we on a horse?"

"We're in an ambulance." The voice sounded far away, but her face was close, and the cloak and crown where white.

Cold sweat covering my face, I cried out, "Ein Geist ! A ghost is coming after me."

"No, dear child, it's a nurse," said Miss Timpelmann. "She's taking your pulse."

The round face of the moon grinned at me through a small window of the vehicle.

More ghosts! "Go faster," I begged. "The Erlking's trying to touch me."

"It's the fever," said the nurse.

"How much longer?" asked Miss Timpelmann.

"We should be there soon."

"We've arrived," boomed a male voice from somewhere.

Miss Timpelmann squeezed my hand. "We're at the hospital."

The rocking ceased. The humming stopped. Peace came in an envelope of darkness.

Where am I? Turning my head toward the light, I saw a wall of windows. How long had I been there? Hours? Days? Weeks? I was in a room full of beds.

A voice interrupted my attempt to count them. "Anneliese. Can you hear me?" A figure in a floor-length black gown, face boxed in a white-winged hood, stared down at me.

Staring at the apparition, I thought I must be in heaven.

"You're in the Salzburg Hospital. I'm Sister Josephine. We're taking care of you."

A vision in white joined the angel in black. "You're getting better." She smiled. "Let's check your temperature." Pulling down the cover, she turned me on my side, and inserted the thermometer. Carefully, with fingertips pressing, she said, "Let's see what your pulse is."

Someone in a white frock with stethoscope around her neck appeared. By now, I knew these were not angels.

Cool hands gently touched my face and pulled down the skin under my eyes. "I'm Dr. Huebner."

"I'm checking the pupils of your eyes," she said, as in answer to my thoughts. Winking, Dr. Huebner added, "You have pretty eyes."

Nobody had ever complimented my eyes, I thought. But my grin disappeared as I felt a sharp jab in my hip.

"There," said Sister Josephine, lightly patting me. "That didn't hurt."

Dr. Huebner looked at a chart. "Temperature still decreasing?" she asked.

"It's down to forty-one Celsius," said the nurse.

On my back again, I pulled the cover up to my chin and looked from one to the other. I listened to what the doctor told the nun and nurse, all the while wondering what I was doing there.

Finally, I asked the question aloud.

"She can talk!" exclaimed the nurse, scribbling on the chart.

The Sister made the sign of the cross. "G'lobt sei Jesus Christus," she whispered. "Praise be to Jesus Christ." She kissed a shiny crucifix extending from a string of black beads that looked like a necklace.

As Dr. Huebner sat on the edge of my bed, she thumped my chest and listened to my heart; but when she finished, she said something to the nurse about congested lungs.

Turning back to me, she said, "Your fever is called typhus. That's why we have to give you shots every four hours. We're also treating you for pneumonia and asthma."

I looked at the bed next to me, where the nurse had wheeled her little cart with instruments. "Is Hannelore here?" I asked the doctor.

"Is she your friend?"

I nodded. "She got sick before I did. I helped feed her."

Dr. Huebner was standing now. "I'll have someone check on Hannelore." She paused, skimming the chart. "I ordered some rice and applesauce for you. It's good!"

I liked applesauce. Mamma made it often from overripe apples that dropped off heavy branches. But I had never heard of rice before.

She winked again and smiled, then turned toward the person in the bed next to mine.

After what seemed like a long time, another nurse with a large tray entered the room. She cranked up my bed to elevate my upper body. "Now you can look at your roommates."

I counted five occupied beds, all in reclined position, and stared at faces as white as the pillows their heads rested on. Where was Hannelore? "Why are they all sleeping?" I asked the nurse.

"They need lots of rest—like you." She rolled a cart close to my bed. "Here is your dinner—let's try it."

I had my first rice and it did taste delicious. The woman fed me from two bowls, alternating between the white fluff and applesauce, and every time I swallowed another spoonful, she praised me by saying, "Good girl."

"Do you know someone named Hannelore?" I asked.

"What does she look like?"

"She's pretty." I took another swallow. "Curly black hair and blue eyes."

"No," the nurse answered. "There are so many of you. Every room on this floor is filled with ill girls from your camp. All have typhus."

"How many?"

"Too many to count." She sighed, placing another portion of rice in my mouth. "More than seventy."

"Seventy! Do you have to feed all of them?"

"Not anymore," she said. "Most can feed themselves now."

"Can I try?"

"Sure." She placed the spoon in my hand. I tried to grasp it, but it fell to the bed covers. "You're still too weak." She wiped my mouth with a cool washcloth and fluffed the pillow.

Discouraged, I turned my head to the wall.

She cranked down the bed till I was horizontal. "Soon you'll be big and strong again," she whispered.

Every day I quizzed whomever came into the room about Hannelore: the nurses and nuns, the doctor, the person who fed me, made my bed, and came running with the bedpan—which was often. Every time I had a bowel movement, someone took a sample and put it in a little bottle.

I even asked Frau Mueller, the woman who came to mop the floors. She reminded me of Mamma, always asking questions.

"Tell me about the street you live on in Frankfurt," she'd prompt. Or, "What subject do you like best in school?"

I didn't want to talk about things. My home and family seemed so far away, so unreachable. I remembered my teacher in the ambulance. She, too, had a fever. "Where is Miss Timpelmann?" I asked.

"Miss Timpelmann?" Frau Mueller bent down to reach the farthest corner under the bed. Straightening, she said, "I heard there was an instructor admitted. She must be on another floor."

"She's here? Please, will you find out her room number for me?"

"I'll check with Mother Superior," promised my friend. "She's in charge here." Quietly, she closed the window shutters. "Go to sleep now. You need lots of rest."

Slowly, I settled into the hospital routine of around-the-clock serum injections, blood tests, stool samples, sponge bath, and examinations. Between long periods of sleep, I wondered about time and calendar days. "How long have I been here?" I asked the person bringing the meals.

"Several weeks."

How long is that? How much longer until I go home?

Dr. Huebner calmed my anxieties. "First, your temperature must return to normal; next, you will slowly regain your strength once your system tolerates solid food. It will take many more weeks to fully recover."

Determined to speed the process, I learned to feed myself—a painfully slow experience.

When caraway was added to the rice, I picked the little seeds out of the porridge one by one and threw them under my bed. "Mamma hates those, too," I explained.

Frau Mueller didn't mind the mess. "Tell me about your mother."

"I want to know about Hannelore and Miss Timpelmann. Did you find them?"

"The sister is still checking." She put down her broom and rearranged my pillows. "Soon, you'll be strong enough to transfer to a larger ward." Her face broke into a wide smile. "Lots of nice girls there—and no more caraway seeds in the rice."

"Will you take a note to my friend and teacher?" I could hold a pencil and write now.

Nodding, she folded the sheet of paper and put it into her apron pocket. "I'll give it to Dr. Huebner," she said.

The day came when I was to transfer out of the critical room. "Please, Dr. Huebner," I pleaded, "put me with Hannelore."

Grave-faced, she gently placed her hands around mine and said slowly, "Hannelore's no longer with us."

"You mean she went home?" I didn't understand. Would not allow the possibility of...

The doctor shook her head and looked into my heart. "Her new home is in Heaven."

At first I felt numb, then anger flooded my mind, until my whole body trembled with rage. Recalling the poem about the father riding with his feverish child from The Erlkoenig, I said through clenched teeth, "The Erlking grabbed her. She's dead!"

"She's an angel."

I snatched my hands away screaming. "God stole her! I hate Him! I hate God! I hate Him!" My voice turned into a screech. "God—I hate you!" Unshed tears burned my eyes and clogged my throat. No more skipping rope, no more shared confidences. What would I do without my best friend? How much more would God take before He was satisfied?

Sister Josephine entered the room. Making the sign of the cross, she knelt and picked up a bead of her Rosenkranz. "Would you like to say the rosary with me?"

Ignoring her invitation, I asked, "Did God take Miss Timpelmann, too?"

She didn't look at me, but nodded and started the litany. "Heilige Maria Gottes..."

"God—I hate you."

"Hail Mary, full of grace..."

The nurse appeared, holding the familiar syringe.

Automatically, I turned to my side and raised my gown.

"This will calm you down," she said, rubbing the puncture with cotton soaked in alcohol.

The drug worked for a while. When I opened my eyes, Frau Mueller sat next to me, wiping my brow.

"Please stay with me." My voice sounded hoarse, my head hurt. I wanted my Mamma.

She squeezed my hand. "I'll sit with you all night, if you want."

Glancing toward the window, I viewed an outside gloom which matched the sadness I felt. Raindrops were the tears I couldn't shed.

"I got a letter from my son, today," said Frau Mueller. The wrinkles on her face momentarily smoothed at the mention of him. "He's somewhere in Russia." She dug the letter out of her purse and reread it. "Near the Volga River."

Frau Mueller started humming a haunting melody. Homesickness overcame me. It was a song Mamma used to sing about a soldier standing patrol at the banks of that river—protecting his Fatherland. I remembered the words.

"The night was dark, and he was alone—

So far away from home.

Neither moon nor stars lit the sky,

He whispered 'Why?'

Silent remained the barren land,

And he wiped away a tear with his hand…"

My eyes grew moist while I watched heavy rain fall on the open veranda. A voice inside my head admonished, German girls don't cry! It was too late— the emotional impact of the soldier's song hit me, and I started to sniffle. The song went on….

"You must have forgotten all about me—way above,

My crying heart, it yearns for love."

I remembered Uncle Bert…Hannelore; Hansi and family who perished in the bombs…Hannelore; Miss Timpelmann…Hannelore. And David. Hannelore.

I pleaded silently with the soldier's song.

"You have so many angels in heaven with Thee—

Please send Hannelore back to me."

Tears tumbled down my cheeks, first making soft ripples, then flooding, mingling with Frau Mueller's, whose face was pressed to mine. We clung together sobbing.

Outside, the rain poured down.

"Heaven is weeping, too," said Frau Mueller, turning my soaked pillow.

"The moon is hiding behind the clouds," I said.

She kissed my cheek softly. "So are the angels," said Frau Mueller. "They're polishing the star lanterns until the storm disappears. God will show the way."

CHAPTER EIGHTEEN—Recovery— Summer 1943

"Important visitors will be arriving soon," said Frau Mueller as she cleaned the double windows of our hospital room that led to the outside corridor.

"Who?" The six of us asked in unison. We longed to see someone other than doctors, nurses and hospital staff whom we saw daily.

"Don't tell that I told you." The twinkle in Frau Mueller's eyes matched the sparkle of the glass panes she polished. "Your families are coming."

We shouted, clapped, and cheered. "How soon?"

Frau Mueller wiped one more spot, then turned and whispered, "In three days. That's why I'm making these windows so clean."

Thinking about our mammas and pappas, and brothers and sisters, the six of us in the recovery ward filled the air with questions.

"Can't Mutti come inside?" The girl next to the window asked. She was the most homesick and always called her motherMutti, like the children from upper-class families. Working-class people preferred the more common "mamma."

"You're still under quarantine. Typhus is very contagious," explained Frau Mueller. "Even the letters you write must be disinfected before they're mailed. But you will see your mammas through these shiny panes."

My bed, the third from the window, was against a solid wall. I visualized the distance and wondered if I could see Mamma from that far away. Would she recognize me? My arms and legs were thin as spindles though I always finished my bowl of soup and rice porridge. I longed to look in a mirror to study my face and check how much of my hair had grown back. Once thick and healthy, it now felt thin and greasy. Will I ever be well enough to have it shampooed?

According to the chart on the wall, I had been in the hospital two months. By now I was able to eat by myself, wash my face, and even comb what hair I had, but getting out of bed was still not allowed.

In anticipation, I counted the days. I also began to worry. What if Mamma has to work? Sorting all those letters at the post office was important. Maybe she can't come.

"Don't worry," whispered Frau Mueller. "She'll come. Her boss will give her time off."

"What about money?"

"The Fatherland will take care of everything," she assured me. "Close your eyes and think of beautiful things so that you're well rested when your Mamma comes."

While taking a long nap two days later, I dreamed of skipping across a meadow in the Alps with Mamma trying to keep up with me. In the distance, cows grazed, the big bells around their necks clanging as though they, too, were playing a game of tag. "You're good as new again," said Mamma, stopping to catch her breath. Her healing hands, rough from hard work, brushed across my brow.

When I opened my eyes, Frau Mueller stood by my bed with a fresh hospital gown. "Wake up, little one. We must get ready for our company."

Hair brushed and tied back with a blue ribbon, I sat in my bed with pillows propped up, waiting. One mother after another arrived, smiling and waving to my roommates, while I stared at the glass wall and swallowed to prevent the tears spilling from my eyes. Where was my Mamma?

"She'll be here, soon," said the nurse who walked back and forth between window and beds to relay messages. "She must wait her turn."

I saw my brother first. He leaped up and down like a jumping jack, making funny faces that caused everyone to laugh, including me. Then I saw Mamma. She seemed shorter than I remembered her, and much slimmer. As she blew kisses, she blinked back the tears. Her lips formed the words, "I love you."

"Come home!" shouted Walter, and pressed his nose against the glass, marring its clear sparkling surface—but somehow he seemed closer.

If only I could leave my bed and walk to the window, I thought. Instead, I nodded and asked, "How's Muschi?"

Mamma didn't understand, but Walter mimicked, "Meow," walking like a cat with its back arched.

He held up an envelope without stamps. "It's from your teacher," he said, pointing to Miss Thyssen's name.

The nurse promised to deliver the letter to me as soon as it went through the sterilization process. "We don't want any new germs," she said.

I communicated to the nurse to please ask Mamma how bad the bombings were in Frankfurt.

Mamma frowned so much, her eyes turned into little slits. "Schlimm!" She brushed away the word with her hand. "Terrible!"

Running up and down the corridor, Walter demonstrated by extending his arms like wings. I watched him purse his lips many times to make the sound effects of engines. He then crouched on the floor and covered his ears.

"Salzburg hasn't had any bomb attacks," the nurse told Mamma. "Not even an alarm."

"Das ist gut," said Mamma.

Waving and blowing more kisses through the window, Walter and Mamma left, but promised to come back the next day.

Only a week later, I woke to the howl of sirens. Air raid!

A nurse rushed into my room and helped me out of bed. Holding onto the rail, I tried to walk—but couldn't.

"You can make it," she said, walking off to push a stretcher down the long corridor toward the elevator.

People shuffled and hobbled to the lift, but when I tried to take a step, my legs buckled. Gathering all the strength I could, I rose to my knees and crawled.

What did it matter that my buttocks were exposed when I bunched my gown around my waist to prevent it getting tangled under my knees? The goal was to get to the staircase, to safety.

Pearls of perspiration dripped from my forehead as I inched along the wall past the doctors and nurses helping older and disabled patients to safety in the cellars.

An aide stopped and in one motion lifted and carried me to the elevator. Outside, FLAK bellowed.

In the darkest corner of the cellar I sat shivering, my hands clasped over my knees, head down to my lap, waiting for the inevitable explosions of bombs and the thunk of airplanes crashing.

They never came.

After what seemed like hours, strong arms raised me to my feet. "The alarm is over," said the nurse, and helped me up the stairs to my bed.

Back in my room, I wrapped the sheet and blanket around me to get warm. I want to get out of here. Soon. Tomorrow.

139

A month later, I was one of the sixty-three girls who had survived the epidemic. We were transferred from Salzburg to a small town called Unterach-am-Attersee.

Our new home, a two-story guesthouse converted to a convalescent hospital for children, was surrounded by tall trees. From my upstairs bedroom window, I spotted a pond, and behind it clear blue water sparkled from a lake. Soon after, the sun dropped behind the distant fir trees and the moon cast a soft glow across the landscape.

At first, the fearful croaking of frogs robbed me of sleep. I thought of Mamma, Pappa, and Walter sitting in a moldy-smelling bomb shelter in Frankfurt, while here my room was filled with the fresh scent of pine. Outside, I heard the soft breeze murmur the sighing of tall firs. Gradually, they lulled me to sleep with their secret whispers.

I woke to the sound of birds twittering. They must be having a conversation over breakfast, I thought, quickly getting dressed so I wouldn't miss mine in the dining room. Before leaving, I read the posted schedule. Morning: looking for polliwogs, it said.

What a big word. Are they plants or animals? Hearing someone explain that they were baby frogs, I decided to stay away from them. Suppose one jumped on me?

Later, wading at the edge of the pond, I shaded my eyes from the climbing sun and watched the ducks glide across, trailing a miniature wake, to the other side of the pond. The drake led the way, then the duck and her babies. A whole family, sure of themselves and their place in the world. Where was mine?

For an entire month, we took daily strolls through the woods, gathered pine cones, and frolicked in the fresh water of the lake when it was warm enough. Once, we even hiked to the village. I felt safe again.

We didn't march to the orders of Hitler Youth leaders, nor sing patriotic songs of conquering the world. Instead, we strolled past shops displaying souvenirs of the rare Edelweiss and unique wood carvings by the local mountain folks.

The day Mamma came to take me back to Frankfurt, all we girls in the temporary home put on a show for the families. I had watched the tap dancers practice for hours, always hoping they'd teach me, too. Instead, our thespian leader selected me to take the part of the witch in the fairy tale, Hansel and Gretel. I practiced until I knew my lines, but didn't like being pushed inside the oven by Gretel.

"You did a fine job with your part," one of the special guests, a man in uniform said.

"Especially the mean voice of the old hag," his woman friend chuckled. Compared to the young, bossy Hitler Youth of the camp in Kaprun, these people were kind and generous.

Mamma bragged that my performance was outstanding.

Still, I didn't like being a witch.

Leaving my friends and the comfortable house in the woods made me sad, but I was anxious to get back to the city to be with my family again. Surely, the war will be over soon, I thought, and the bombing will stop. What about Pappa? He was never mentioned during Mamma and Walter's visit. Perhaps he no longer lives at home.

Home again! That's all I could think about.

Mamma helped me pack my few belongings. We walked to the station and boarded the slow mountain train to Salzburg, a faster one to Munich, then transferred to an express to our final destination.

She put an arm around my shoulder to protect me from the shoving crowd. The compartment was crammed with women returning from the country to buy fresh vegetables, or to visit their children. An infant wailed in its mother's arms until comforted by nursing. We could hear the sound of suckling. A young soldier leaning against the door fumbled in his rucksack and brought out a mouth organ. He banged it on his knee, pursed his lips, and began to play the most haunting of all soldier's songs. 'In the homeland, in the homeland, there we shall meet again.'

I remembered Mamma sending Uncle Bert that same small instrument for Christmas last year and wondered if it was buried with him. Wiping a stray tear, I gently hummed along, with Mamma naturally slipping into alto harmony. 'In der Heimat, in der Heimat, da gibt's ein Wiedersehn.'

All night I tried to sleep, but every time I dozed off, a sharp blow from the elbow or foot of the boy crouching next to me jolted me awake. The baby started crying again. Grunts and sporadic snores, followed by long melodious whistles emanated from the floor where soldiers on furlough slept. The air smelled like an open sewer. As the train rumbled into the Frankfurt railway station, I anxiously peered out the window, looking for Walter and Paula.

Climbing over people sitting in the aisles, Mamma pushed her way to the platform.

"Woman, wait your turn," the conductor snapped.

"My child just recovered from typhus," Mamma said with importance as she elbowed her way out, dragging our suitcases down the steep steps.

At the station, I noticed the beautiful glass dome of many colors that covered the station was no more. Instead of sparkling prisms illuminating the interior, the wind whistled though the glassless, twisted steel grid.

"Anneliese!" The familiar voices rang out over train whistles and loudspeaker announcements.

Dodging through the crowd, I spotted Walter. Not far behind was Pappa, and far down, at the exit, Paula waved an oversized handkerchief.

A combination of love and fear surged through me. I wanted to run away from Pappa and into Paula's arms. How much loyalty is expected of me? Clinging to Mamma, I for a moment longed for the safety of the house in the mountains by the lake.

When Walter reached me, we joined hands and danced around the station platform, ignoring the angry shouts of people we bumped into. From his pocket, Walter produced a large splinter of antiaircraft shrapnel. "For our collection," he said, proudly handing me the piece of jagged metal.

I pretended surprise, for I had forgotten how important that hobby once was to both of us.

Pappa walked toward us to fetch the suitcase. Before lifting it, he extended his hand. "Good day," he said, and grasped for mine. His calluses pressed hard against my soft palm.

Avoiding his eyes, I timidly returned the greeting. "Guten Tag."

The first night at home, I crouched in the cellar listening to the staccato sounds of FLAK. This time the bombs rained down. Explosion after explosion ripped the air. I couldn't believe some children and grownups slept through the whole attack. I was terrified.

Walter wasn't. "Always remember," he lectured me, "as long as you can hear the crashing of bombs, it means they're falling in another part of town." He could hardly wait to get upstairs and survey the damage done to the city. "Let's go," he called, pulling me along. "Look across the river. A good place to hunt for more treasure." Anxiously, he shook the cigar box that contained the metal splinter collection.

Mamma objected. "Anneliese needs to rest. We have a doctor appointment tomorrow. Besides, she's not used to the flames and smoke. It's bad for her lungs."

"We just want to look for more shrapnel," Walter pleaded.

"It's too dangerous," said Pappa, his voice stern and commanding. Turning to me, he locked his right arm around my waist and looked into my eyes. His voice turned sweet as honey. "Anneliese needs to go to bed."

As his face came closer, I heard the blare of a fire engine drown Mamma's shrill screams scolding Walter. Smoke exhaled from Pappa's cigarette burned my nostrils and throat. His breath and grip felt like a dragon choking me. I screamed and screamed and screamed. "Let me go! Let me go!"

"She's hysterical," said Mamma, trying to comfort me.

"Don't touch me," I sobbed, shrinking away from her, too. Choking, I fought for air, longing for my hospital bed.

Paula approached and took my hands. "It's been too much for her," she said to Mamma. "The long trip. The bombing. The fire. She needs to be away from here. Let me help you, Anneliese," she coaxed and took my arm.

Exhausted, void of will, empty of tears, I nodded and walked up the stairs with Paula.

"I'm waiting for word from her grandparents in Heilbronn," said Mamma. "She will be safer there.

Oh, please, Oma, I thought. Write soon.

CHAPTER NINETEEN—Heilbronn—Late Summer 1943

"Kika-ri-kee." Is that a rooster crowing? There it was again!

Pushing back the feather ticking cover, I leaped out of bed, rushed to the window, and unhitched the wooden shutters. Slowly, I pushed each panel open from the inside, letting sunlight flood into the room. Now I remembered. I was at my grandparents' house in Heilbronn.

In the garden beyond the yard, a rooster strutted among a dozen hens in an area fenced off by chicken wire. Chasing a hen, he crowed once more while showing off his beautiful tail and flip-flopping the bright red coxcomb atop his head.

I watched with wonder as a familiar woman entered the yard and threw handfuls of grain to the chickens, causing them to cluck, push, pick, and run after the feed. The woman shook what was left from her apron, wiped her brow, and turned toward the house.

It was grandmother! I recognized her by the braided bun at the nape of her neck. "Oma," I called from my upstairs window. It was easier to pronounce than Grossmamma and sounded friendlier.

Grandma waved and called, "Gute Morge!" in her Swabian dialect. Her round face breaking into a toothless smile, she added, "Come down."

My heart pounded as I approached the narrow staircase leading to the kitchen. Had I overslept?

She waited below with outstretched arms. "Langsam," she cautioned, "The steps are waxed and very slippery."

Clutching onto the handrail, I wanted to climb down as fast as I could, but by the second step I knew I had to take one step at a time, until my feet landed on the last one. "Guten Morgen," I said in my best school-German. Grandma had trouble the night before understanding my Frankfurt dialect.

Hugging my face to her large, soft bosom and squeezing me gently, she patted my head. "I'll make breakfast," she said. "Warm milk, and bread with butter and home-made jam." She pointed to the door across from the bottom of the staircase. "But first you should use the toilet."

Dutifully, I climbed the two steps leading to the small place, lifted the detached round lid and peeked inside. Not nice. I crinkled my nose, but placed the wooden top on the polished bench next to the hole and scooted up on the seat. There was paper, but no chain to flush—it was nothing more than a fancy outhouse placed inside.

"Don't forget the cover," called Grandma. "We don't want to stink up the house."

Hopping down the steps and into the kitchen, I was greeted by my four-year old cousin, Roland, a strikingly handsome boy with a shock of flaxen hair and eyes bluer than heaven on a cloudless day. "I like your cat," he said. "May I pet him?"

"Sure," I said. "He likes it."

We found Muschi under Grandma's flower stand by the kitchen window, where the potted geraniums showed off their bright red blossoms. As we approached, the cat rose, arched his back, stretched, and walked between my legs, purring and meowing as he brushed against me.

"Grandma won't let him come inside," said Roland, squatting next to me.

"I know. Oma wrote me." Stroking Muschi, I remembered the letter. "You can bring your pet," she'd written, "under one condition. He must stay outside." Nonetheless, I was grateful to have him with me.

I looked at Muschi rubbing against my cousin. Such a good cat—just like he'd been on the train. During the three-hour ride from Frankfurt, Walter and I took turns holding him in a cloth bag Mamma had sewn. Against her orders, we gave him some of the sandwiches she packed for us—and prayed that he wouldn't mess. He must have sensed our stress because he didn't.

Grandma brought out a few table scraps in an old dish which was for the Katz,' as she called him. "He must learn to catch mice," she said. "We have lots of them running around."

The thought made me shudder, but after a few days, Muschi did hunt for his own food. I'd watch him crouch down, stalk, wait, then streak across the yard after his prey.

Caught, the trapped rodent would try to get away, but Muschi played with it relentlessly until finally the mouse lay motionless. I couldn't watch after that.

How cruel, I thought, and walked away from the scene. The hunt was fascinating, the cat and mouse game was not. I didn't want to stay for the meal.

My older cousin, Heinz, however, could hardly wait to tell me all the details about the feast. Baring his teeth, he'd say, "Muschi carried the mouse in his jaw—and then crunched its bones. Lick, lick, went his tongue."

"Oma, please, make him stop," I cried.

But she wouldn't take sides. Heinz, fourteen, was her oldest grandson—and the apple of her eye. He was huskily built, with eyes matching his brown hair—and curls and lashes that were the envy of most girls. I loved to hear him play the accordion, but held my ears when he practiced the trumpet in the house.

"Go outside," I told him.

"He'll scare the chickens," said Grandma. "They'll stop laying."

Heinz returned the instrument to its case. "I'm going to be a jazz player some day," he said with determination.

"Jazz?" I asked. "What's that?" It sounded foreign and a little crazy.

"It's what they play in America." Lifting two wooden spoons that rested next to pots on the stove, he started drumming on the lids.

"Stop that infernal noise this instant," said Grandma retrieving her cooking utensils. "Get Uncle Bert's accordion and play a nice Kaiser march like from the good old days."

Heinz liked to tease, but complied with Grandma's wish. While he played, Grandma sang the old songs—some cheerful, some sad, but all with a distinct marching beat.

A violin under his arm, Heinz's best friend, Dieter, entered the kitchen. He gave me a wide smile before asking my cousin to join him with his squeeze box to do some practicing on the strip of grass across the unpaved road in front of the house.

That night, before going to bed I tiptoed into my grandparent's bedroom and peeked through the slanted shutters that covered the open window. I shivered a little in my long cotton nightgown—though the evening was warm and balmy. Dieter was even more handsome than Heinz, I thought, opening the slats a little wider to see him better. He never teased me like my cousin did.

Watching and listening intently, I didn't notice my grandparents had entered the room. Startled to hear the clearing of a throat, I turned from the window and felt the color creeping into my cheeks.

"Did you notice, Luise," Grandpa said, "ever since we've had a young girl in the house, the boys are hanging around every night playing serenades."

His deep chuckle quickly eased my embarrassment. But when Grandma added, "That's because she's such a pretty girl," I couldn't stop the blush from returning to my face.

Life at my grandparent's house on the outskirts of Heilbronn seemed so peaceful in comparison with the pressures I'd experienced at the flat in the big city. No one ever criticized or yelled at me. No matter what I said or did in the Haeusle—that's what everyone called the compact, two-story duplex—it was received with praise. I felt worthy.

In Frankfurt, I never could do enough to please Mamma. Although she was proud of me, I was always too slow, too shy, a dreamer building castles in the sky.

But here in this small community, when we walked to the corner dairy, Grandma loved showing me off to the neighbors. "Gruess Gott, Frau Lapple! This is my granddaughter from Frankfurt," she told the woman who lived in the house on the other side of the tall beanstalks.

"Gruess Gott, Frau Eisenkramer! You mean that little one is Johanna's daughter?" Playfully, she pinched my cheeks. "We need to fatten you up a bit, don't we? And put color in your face. Ja, ja!"

Then they'd talk about how good the cabbage crop promised to be or what a nice head of cauliflower grandpa had picked that morning. And as always the conversation turned to those away in the war. "Have you had any news from your Franz?" Frau Krueger's voice was filled with concern.

It had been weeks since Grandma received a letter from her only son. A shadow crept over her face. "My Franzle must be busy interpreting and translating on the Eastern front."

"If you can believe the war news," said Frau Lapple, "the Russians are surrendering by the thousands."

Grandma carefully looked around before she spoke. "My husband learned Russian while working on a farm in the Ukraine during the last war." She glanced over her shoulder before continuing. "He hears horror stories from the Russian workers he's training and supervising in the factory. When will it end?"

"Schlimm, schlimm," whispered Frau Krueger. "It's getting worse. Who'd have thought the Nazis would turn into such Schweinehunde!"

Nodding, they parted with the daily greeting to God, "Gruess Gott!"

Close to Grandma, I skipped past the black-shingled, look-alike duplex homes that were built up a slope in rows of twenty. All looked alike, except for landscaping and exterior color. Ours was green with a lilac bush trellised over the small entrance gate.

As expected, I removed my sandals outside, placed them on the shoe rack inside the back entrance, and hung up my coat.

To the left of the vestibule was a large laundry and utility room with a real bathtub. Grandma was the proud owner of a magic apparatus that squeezed the water out of the clothes so that she didn't have to wring them with her arthritic hands. "It was a Christmas present from the whole family," she told me. I wanted to help her crank the handle, but she wouldn't let me touch the wringer for fear I'd get my fingers between the rollers. "You can help me hang the sheets on the line outside," she said.

I was glad for the opportunity to be useful. Usually, Grandma would tell me, "You must take it easy because your heart is still weak. You aren't well yet."

Not used to being treated like an invalid, I protested. "I can peel potatoes, do dishes, wash floors, make beds, lots of things."

"You mean your mother made you do all that at your tender age? The dragon!" She gave me a tight hug. "You need to be spoiled a little."

One by one, however, I collected little chores, like sweeping. I could always count on Grandpa's comment as he pushed his bicycle down the long walk beside the house to park it in the shed.

"Since Anneliese lives here, we have the cleanest yard in the neighborhood," he'd tell Grandma after he kissed her lips. I wondered if his long mustache tickled her face.

Before supper, I'd follow him into the garden to watch how he used a hoe to loosen the ground around the flower beds, then fill a large galvanized can and attach a spray to its spout to water the vegetables.

"I want to help," I said, proudly picking up the spoils of the earth. But when I pulled out a young white radish instead of a weed, he sent me to the kitchen.

"Grandmother needs help chasing flies while she's making jam," he suggested.

My favorite place remained the kitchen. It was roomier than the one we had in our flat in Frankfurt. The Terrazzo-stone sink was large, with an extension to drain dishes or prepare food. Besides the table and chairs, there was a cupboard and a radio sat on a small cabinet. Occasionally, Grandma took a nap on the couch behind the table.

After supper, Grandpa read the paper and later listened to the news. He didn't say much during the broadcast, but often shook his head, twisted his handle bar mustache, and gave a little grunt. I soon learned it was his way of disagreeing with what he heard. When the announcer named the cities that were bombed during the last twenty-four hours, I anxiously listened, hoping Frankfurt was not one of them.

My grandfather became my idol. I rarely heard him raise his voice, much less strike anyone. "Donnerwetter!" He sometimes thundered at Heinz. "You forgot to feed the rabbits again."

Grandpa was proud of his rabbits. Especially the big white one, called Max. He'd won a prize at the garden show and had a certificate to prove it. The rabbit wouldn't bite, he assured me. So I petted Max often.

Opa knew I was afraid of the animals in the barnyard and preferred watching rather than feeding them. Especially that cocky rooster. He not only chased the chickens, but often jumped on them, causing them to cackle and flutter their wings as they ran all over the yard.

"He's not hurting them," Grandma assured me as she gathered eggs. "We need that ornery cock to have baby chicks in the Spring."

One morning I tried to prevent the rooster from chasing a hen. "Get away from her," I yelled, trying to separate the two with a stick. He turned on me with vengeance and I ran screaming from the coop, leaving the small gate open. Most of the chickens and the rooster escaped from the pen into the garden, pecking on carrot sprouts and lettuce leaves. Shouting and waving, Roland and Grandma ran after them, even Frau Lapple, the neighbor, helped with the pursuit, and for a while we didn't know who was chasing whom.

Humiliated, I sat on the front steps when I heard grandpa say, "That old rooster is getting too mean. I've been wanting to replace him with a younger one."

"You're right. It's time that old cock hit the pot," agreed Grandma, and the following weekend we had chicken soup for dinner.

I ate nothing but the noodles.

Sundays were special. Whenever possible, the whole clan came to visit from different directions. It was the only time I'd see my brother, since Walter had gone to stay with Aunt Hedwig on the other side of Heilbronn.

I envied my cousins, Sonja and Ellen's beautiful blond, thick braids. My hair was still short and straight, parted on the side and pulled back by a clasp. But at least I didn't have to wear that big bow anymore.

"I wish I had hair like you," I told Sonja as we strolled across the fields gathering blue corn flowers, yellow buttercups, and red poppies for grandma's dinner table.

Sonja didn't respond. She flung back her waist-long braids and picked a few stems of oats to add to the bouquet. While I didn't know one grain from the other, she even knew the difference between wheat and rye. I was impressed.

In the distance, Walter called. "Wait for me."

But Sonja continued walking. "I don't like your brother," she said.

I was alarmed. "Why not?" Did he fight with our cousins the way he used to fight me? I recalled the two of us getting into some bad squabbles, the times he kicked my shins, his fingernails digging into the flesh of my arms until blood trickled from the long scratches.

"Every night he wets the bed," said Sonja.

I was mortified. "My Mamma always put a rubber sheet over the mattress."

"The sofa in the living room is beginning to stink from the piss," she snapped, tossing back a braid that had slipped forward. "In school and in the neighborhood, he tells false stories about our family."

Embarrassed, I stopped and waited for my brother, while she stomped ahead without me. Walter waved and shouted as he ran toward me. How small and frail he was in comparison to other eleven-year olds, I thought.

"I wish I could stay with you," he said. There was a sadness in his smile I hadn't seen before. "Or go back to Frankfurt."

Playing the role of big sister, I tried to console him. "Frankfurt isn't safe for kids because of the bombing. Besides, all the schools are closed."

"I hate school! The kids tease me about the way I talk. I hate them, too. And I hate Sonja and Ellen, and…"

"Stop it! Why can't you adjust to your new surroundings, like me? What's so difficult about cooperating? We ought to be grateful we can live with relatives and be away from the bombs," I reminded him. "Don't cause trouble—and don't wet the sofa."

Walter hung his head. "I can't help it." He looked dejected, but his words were laced with sorrow and anger. "I want to go home to Mamma and Pappa," he insisted.

"Have you written to Mamma?"

Breaking the small limb of a branch in two, Walter shook his head. "No. She doesn't ever write to me. Remember, you always were her favorite, the shining star with the superior report card, outstanding even in deportment, the model child." He kicked a clump of earth and crushed the remaining dirt lumps under his sole. "I'm the rebel, the troublemaker who takes things apart, the idiot who can't spell or remember timetables."

Now I really felt guilty. In a letter to Grandma, Mamma had addressed me. "Be a good girl," she wrote. "Clean your plate—even the leftovers. And help your grandmother." She finished the note with, "I miss you very much."

Sonja approached, showing off her beautiful bouquet of field flowers. "We better return to the house," she said. "Dinner will be waiting."

Silently, we walked back.

Overhearing a conversation between Grandma and Hedwig, I realized that my brother was creating a lot of problems at home and in school.

"He's rebellious, like his mother," said my youngest aunt.

Grandma agreed. "Johanna was a difficult child." She sighed. "Why can't Walter be obedient and adapt like his sister?"

Protectively, I took his hand. What was to become of him?

CHAPTER TWENTY—School—Fall 1943

Summer was over and the first day of school finally arrived. I so looked forward to meeting my new teacher and classmates. As I hurried into the room I saw written on the chalkboard: Herr Hoffer, Seventh Grade.

A short man, slight build, with little hair, Herr Hoffer's eyes glinted like forged steel. No welcome smile softened his face as he raised his left arm and shouted the official greeting, "Heil Hitler!"

"Heil Hitler!" We answered in unison and sat. I liked Fraulein Thyssen's Guten Tag much more—but this was not the Uhlandschule in Frankfurt.

From my seat in the back of an all-girl class of twenty-three students, I watched him pace the length of wooden desk rows. His rigidity scared me a little, not knowing what to expect.

Suddenly, Herr Hoffer stopped in front of me, his small stature growing to a straddling giant. Squinting over narrow spectacles that had slipped to the tip of his nose, he said, "So you're the new addition to our class of seventh graders." He pulled the lobe of his ear. "What's your name?"

I rose. "Anneliese." My eyes fixed on the right sleeve of his jacket. It hung limp against his side.

"Anneliese what?"

"Eisenkraemer. Anneliese Eisenkraemer."

With his left hand, he tucked the empty sleeve into the coat pocket. "Relationship to Franz Eisenkraemer?"

"I'm his granddaughter—from Frankfurt." Nervously, I brushed a wisp of hair from my forehead.

"Aha. You're from the big city. That must be the reason for the short hair and fancy dress. We're simple people here in Heilbronn-Boeckingen."

I knew I shouldn't have worn my Sunday best, but I had wanted to look nice, especially for the first day. I bowed.

He stalked back to his desk. "Come here, city girl. Tell us about Frankfurt."

Slowly I walked to the front of the class, turned, and looked at the sea of round and oval faces framed by long braids in shades of blond and brown. I'd been worried about hostility from the girls, and experienced relief when I was acknowledged with smiles.

To make sure I was being understood, I talked in my best high German taught in all schools and spoken by newscasters. "Frankfurt was once a big beautiful city on a river called Main. Our dialect is not Swabian, but Hessian."

Encouraged by attentive faces, I continued. "Because of the constant bomb attacks, my school building was destroyed and the children were evacuated."

Herr Hoffer's face reddened. "That's enough. Go to your seat." Emphasizing every word with his left arm, he bellowed, "Germany has been in a state of total war since May of this year and we will spur on any flagging spirits to fight to the bitter end." He pulled the empty sleeve out of his coat pocket. Shaking it at us, he screamed, "We'll not quit or surrender like we did in World War I. Never!" His face beet-red now, he looked at me with disdain. "You remember that, Eisenkraemer. We all must sacrifice."

His glance reminded me of searchlights, sweeping the Frankfurt sky for a target. "Bombs!" his voice exploded. "Air raids!" He looked to me. "What has your family ever done for the Fatherland?" Standing erect, with head held high, he pointed to the
gold-rimmed swastika on his coat lapel. "I'm an honorary member of the party. I believe in our Fuehrer and support our national socialistic system." He shook the empty sleeve. "I have sacrificed for my Vaterland."

Pausing for a moment, he pinched the bridge of his nose, then continued in a voice shaking with emotion. "And I've given my two sons, my only children, to the Third Reich. Both were brilliant university students before joining the Luftwaffe. Both earned the Iron Cross First Class for bravery in air battles. They downed hundreds of British and American planes." His bottom lip quivered as did his voice. "Helmuth was an officer, a fighter pilot, like his older brother. His plane was hit over Stuttgart a week ago. And here we are safe because of such brave young men." The teacher's fist crashed on his desk.

I jumped.

"There is no greater glory than death on the battlefield." Each word was accentuated by his knuckles pounding on hard wood.

I sat motionless. Bewildered. Scared.

153

What was this tirade all about? I wondered. This was school, not war. And why was he so angry if he was so proud?

Suddenly, Herr Hoffer stopped. He picked up the chalk and began writing problems on the blackboard. "Let's have a math test."

That evening, when I told Grandma about my teacher, she said, "Herr Hoffer's been an instructor at that school for a long time. He was Else's teacher for two years."

"I had him in eighth grade," said Erika. "He was tough and assigned a lot of homework."

"Else did some sewing for his wife," Grandma added. "They live in a nice villa near the school. While Else took Mrs. Hoffer's measurements for a dress, the boys used to practice the piano. Now they're dead. What a waste!" Grandma looked at the picture of her own son, Franz. "I feel for their mother."

Erika poured hot water over soap in the dishpan. "I didn't like him. He always talks about the party and the superiority of the Germans."

I helped clear the kitchen table to do my homework, a composition about courage, while Grandpa talked about his job.

"They've brought in another load of forced laborers from Russia," I heard him tell Grandma. "I'll have to put in extra hours to train them on the machines. The production quota is high and the foreman is on my back all the time."

"Are the laborers skilled?" Grandma sounded concerned.

"No," answered Grandpa. "But most cooperate with me. Especially when I tell them I learned Russian while in captivity working on a farm in Ukrania."

"When were you a soldier?" I asked.

"In the Austrian infantry in 1914, during World War I, Maedele. Our platoon was surprised by a Russian commando and I was captured."

"You were a prisoner-of-war?"

Nodding, he continued. "I was just like these Russian laborers. I think that's why they give me no trouble."

Images flashed through my mind as I tried to form the scene of Grandpa as a prisoner with his hands locked behind his head. I waited for him to pack his pipe with tobacco.

"Were you behind barbed wire?" I asked timidly.

"No," he said. "But I worked hard for a Russian family plowing their fields, bringing in their harvest, and maintaining their equipment. The owner of the land was a prisoner-of-war in Germany, and when he returned in 1918, he said he had been well treated by the Germans. He gave me clothing and papers and helped me escape. It wasn't easy. There was a revolution going on in Russia and no one knew whom to trust. But lucky for me, I'd learned enough Russian to make the long trek back to Heilbronn."

Grandma poured hot herb tea into mugs and said, "I will never forget the day I opened the door and saw your Grandpa standing there." She set down the teapot and laughed. "Because of his bushy beard and long hair, at first I didn't recognize him—then my heart exploded with joy."

"How old was my Mamma?"

"Johanna was six and she didn't recognize her father either. She screamed and kicked when he tried to hug her. Lina was eight, Franz ten, and Hedwig twelve.

Four-year-old Else had never seen her Pappa."

Lighting his pipe, Grandpa puffed smoke rings. "Yes. I'll always be grateful to that farmer. Now it is for me to do the same." He drew on his pipe again and exhaled. "The workers call me Pappa in Russian. They're easier to deal with than most of my German superiors."

"Promise to be careful," said Grandma, busily darning socks. "Frau Schroeder told me her husband has a list of undesirable Germans to be eliminated as soon as the war is over."

Grandpa twirled the ends of his mustache. "I don't trust old Schroeder. He's some big shot in the Nazi party—like Anneliese's teacher."

"Schroeder is a Drecksau," mumbled Erika. "A dirty pig."

Picking up his pipe again, Grandpa said, "Most likely, I'm on that list because of my former affiliation with the Social Democrats." Jaw jutted forward and rapping his knuckles on the table with every word, he said, "but they won't get rid of me." He took a quick puff from his pipe. "Not yet," he said between clenched teeth. "They need me too much."

Herr Schroeder was one of grandpa's neighbors. The mention of his name brought to mind the time I'd seem him passing on his bicycle while I walked to school with my new friend, Gertrude. "Gruess Gott, Herr Schroeder," I said, proud to remember the common greeting in this part of Germany.

Without a return greeting, he braked his bike abruptly and started lecturing me. "It's 'Heil Hitler!" he shouted, raising his right arm to shoulder height.

Suppressing giggles, we both mimicked, "Heil Hitler!" and continued to walk. Gertrude was a year younger than I, and had no parents.

"Why are you an orphan?" I asked her.

Looking at the ground, Gertrude took slower, but longer strides. "My mother deserted me and my older sister."

I stopped walking and tugged on her coat. "You mean she just left you with your grandparents? Where's your sister?"

"She's with my other grandmother in a small village near Hamburg. I haven't seen either of them since my mother left."

I was shocked. How could a mother leave her child? "Why didn't she come back for you?"

"The way I understand it, my parents emigrated to America where they met and married. When my Hamburg grandfather died in 1939, my mother took us girls and returned to Germany to help with the farm. Dad stayed in Chicago to sell the house and furniture.

"And when the war broke out, my father thought it safer for our family to go back to America. He never did like Hitler and his regime.

"But mother could only get tickets for herself and my baby sister. A Norwegian freighter gave them passage." Gertrude shrugged in resignation. "I was visiting with my Schroeder grandparents here in Heilbronn, while my older sister was staying at the other grandparents on the farm up North."

Gertrude kicked a stone across the road. "They're people of prominence, and own a lot of land. They don't like Grandpa Schroeder because he's a party member." She picked up a pebble and threw it at the railroad track that ran parallel to the street.

I didn't ask any more questions.

The scent of freshly brewed peppermint tea and cups rattling on saucers returned my thoughts to the kitchen. My teeth clamped on the top of my pencil, I stared at the blank sheet in front of me.

"Anneliese," said Erika, "What are you daydreaming about? You haven't written a word."

"It's time for bed," said Grandma, searching for another hole in the sock that needed darning.

Hearing the mantle clock in the living room chime nine times, I put away my books, brushed my teeth, said good night, and was about to go upstairs when the air raid siren began howling. Before the second wail even began, I bolted for the basement.

Grandpa stopped me. "Where are you going?"

Shaking all over, I covered my ears to drown out the wail and cried, "Quick, quick, Opa, we must go to the cellar."

"No need," said Grandpa, leading me to the long sofa that sat behind the kitchen table. "The planes are just passing over."

"It's the Tommies on their way to Munich," added Erika. "The Americans have been pounding Strassburg all day."

Not hearing any explosions, not even a single shot from FLAK, I calmed down and rested on the sofa until the sound of the "All Clear" wailed an hour later.

The next day we had a practice alert at school. Since it was considered safer for students to scatter in different homes than in the one cellar at the school, we went in small groups to the neighboring houses. Thereafter, we spent much of our school time sitting on doorsteps of our assigned shelters counting squadrons of planes flying south. We'd wonder what the target was—Stuttgart again? Of course, Herr Hoffer encouraged us to study while waiting. But we found other things more interesting to read than textbooks. Heidi, one of my class mates, brought fifty-page romance novels. Her mother subscribed to a series called "Every Week A New Romance." We took turns reading out loud.

I held the paperback and began to read. "Sieglinde's eyes filled with tears when Count von Winkelstein told her it was time for him to lead his men in the cavalry to victory. How handsome he looked in his uniform decorated with tassels and shiny medals."

Heidi sighed, "Oh, I can see him ride on his white stallion…"

"The Count wiped away a tear from Sieglinde's cheek," I read with feeling, "and brushed his lips against her…"

"Turn the page," urged a chubby Lisbeth. Her already ruddy complexion had turned a crimson red.

"…forehead," I continued. "'Please wait for me, Beloved. Some day I'll return with medals of silver and gold and lay them at your feet as a sign of my love,' THE END."

"Read the line with the lips once more," swooned Lisbeth.

"I can hardly wait for next week's book," said Heidi.

"My Grandma lets me read the continuous romance in the newspaper every day," I confided.

"Really? Tell us!" Heidi broke the tension as the "All Clear" sounded and we headed back to school.

Anxious to hear the next installment about a U-Boat Captain, I skipped home. I always looked forward to the daily ritual of Grandma opening the section of the paper that carried the love story. Only after she had read and censored it, was I allowed to read.

"Oma, do you think the heroine will be true to her hero while he's away in the war?" I loved asking her questions because she always knew the answers.

"Absolutely!" said Grandma.

Watching her fold the newspaper carefully to give Grandpa the illusion that he, as the man of the house, was the first to open it, I asked, "But what about him, Oma?"

"The hero?" He's a good boy, too. After all, who's he going to meet in a submarine in the middle of the ocean?"

Cocking my head, I contemplated for a moment and giggled, "A mermaid!"

Grandma chuckled along with me, but it was a long time before my Oma laughed again.

CHAPTER TWENTY-ONE—Trains—Fall 1943

On a bright day, I'd see the steel rails gleam in the sunlight. The melodic sound of the steam engine's whistle always made me stop and wave, hoping a passenger or two would return my greeting. At night, its melancholy, retreating blasts lulled me to sleep.

Lately, the open flatbeds carrying tanks, artillery, and cannons, were a sight to see as they trundled west. The young soldiers guarding the weapons smiled and waved, while the older ones gave a short salute by lifting their crumpled caps.

"Opa, there were fifty tanks," I exclaimed excitedly.

Roland, as always, contradicted my count. "I saw sixty-five and lots of giant-sized artillery. Also some minnies."

"It's Minenwerfer," I corrected him. He thinks he knows it all.

"Everyone knows minnies are mine throwers." Roland had to have the last word.

Looking up from his newspaper, Grandpa interrupted the argument. "Which direction were they heading?"

"West."

Grandpa frowned. "A year ago, when they moved east, to Russia, the number was ten times greater." Pulling the ends of his long mustache, he added, "They're getting ready for something on the Western Front."

"Our leaders have gone mad," said Aunt Lina, "not me." Her draft notice had come soon after she'd become a war widow. Now a nervous breakdown had brought her home on a medical leave from the Luftwaffe.

For many months she had been holed up in a bunker on the North coast of The Netherlands, tracking the flight path of attacking aircraft and searching for German fighters lost in the air battle.

Now, while she stared into space, her fingers tapped dots and dashes of the Morse code on the kitchen table. "They won't make it," she mumbled. S.O.S.

"The Luftwaffe is kaputt." S.O.S. "Goehring is a pompous ass!" S.O.S., S.O.S.

Seeking to distract her, Grandma said, "I wonder what's keeping Erika?" She added another briquet to the pot belly stove in the parlor.

"Probably stopped to look in on Franz's wife," said Grandpa. "Musja hasn't had any news from her husband. She's half out of her mind with worry that, as an interpreter, he'll be a prized captive for the Russian underground."

The fire had died down again by the time Erika entered the room. Eyes clouded, hands shaking, she picked up her brother's picture from the mantle and draped it with a black scarf.

Lina turned off the light and tapped. "Dot-dot-dot, dash-dash-dash, dot-dot-dot."

"God save Franz's soul," Erika whimpered, groping in the dark for a candle.

I found a box of matches and with a shaking hand, lit the wick, then wiped away a tear.

Grandma sat motionless, eyes dull, face hard.

"When?" Grandpa looked so small standing behind her chair, his shoulders hunched, his back stooped.

"They don't know." Erika's voice was barely audible. "His patrol never made it back."

"Partisans," said Grandpa. The whisper of the word hung in the air like a dangling shadow cut up by a giant henchman.

S.O.S., S.O.S. Lina tapped.

It was late September, 1943. After living with my grandparents for several months now, I had learned much of the local dialect. In school, I worked at being accepted by my teacher and classmates, and at home, I tried to make myself useful.

Some chores were hard, but fun—like beating rugs. Once a week, the small carpet pieces that felt so soft when I jumped out of bed on them, hung over the clothes line and everyone took a turn pounding the dust out of them.

"I pretend the rug is the Russian who killed my Bert," said Lina. With both hands wrapped around the handle, she pelted until she had to stop to catch her breath.

Roland attached different boys' names to his quick swats. "That's for Willie, and that one for Fritz, and one more for Horst, the meanest kid on the block." He seemed to have fun.

I held the rug beater overhead and swung at the mat so hard, it flipped and dropped to the ground. "I hope it hurts, Pappa," I said between clenched teeth.

Erika took her turn next. She must be mad at her boss again, I thought, watching her swing the tightly woven beater against the rug until no more dust scattered.

Grandma didn't want to participate. She stayed in the kitchen—her domain—preparing preserves. In Frankfurt, I'd helped Mamma with the canning during the summer, but to see things grow and ripen in my grandparent's garden was a new learning experience.

Grandpa let me help pick red currants from the bushes sprawling near the apple and pear trees. Removing the small bunches from the waist-high bushes was tedious work, and every time I crushed one of the tiny berries, my fingers became sticky with red juice. But I felt useful and didn't complain. I was hoping he'd harvest the peas and beans as soon as they were fully grown. Working with Grandpa was fun.

I did learn to pick peas—but not at home. A note from school informed parents and guardians that more farm hands were needed in the fields. For two weeks we were trucked early each morning to farms covered with green bushes as far as the eye could see.

"Here come the pea pickers," said the overseer, a burly man dragging a wooden leg. "You'll get paid ten Pfennig per bucket," he told us the first day.

The calculation was easy. I'd have to fill ten buckets to get one Reichsmark, which was the right amount for two cheap seats at the movies. It was an incentive to work fast. So was the contest to win a bonus for the highest number of bushels picked. Yet no matter how hard I worked, I couldn't keep up with my classmates. Soon, sweat dripped from my forehead, dust entered dry nostrils, and dirt caked around my cracked lips.

I had helped Grandma shell peas—it was fun breaking the plump green shells at the seam and remove the kernels with my thumb nail, but when it came to finding the pea pods on a vine, I had a difficult time crouching and creeping between the bushes. The peas were camouflaged by large leaves, and I missed many.

"You must lift the branches by their vines," said Lisbeth, picking a handful from a spot where I saw only one.

By evening, every muscle in my body ached, and the yield of peas was so low. I was so frustrated, I felt like crying.

I had left the house at daybreak and returned just before sundown, and now I was too exhausted to have supper. "I just want to wash up and go to bed," I said meekly.

Grandma put a steaming bowl of potato soup in front of me—one of my favorites. "First you eat," she coaxed. "It'll make you feel better." She filled the large kettle with water and lit the gas burner. "Later you can take a warm sponge bath."

Turning to Grandpa, she said, "I want you to go to the authorities tomorrow and file a request for exemption from farm labor. Anneliese is but a child, barely twelve years old. She hasn't fully recovered from the ravages of typhus."

"Oma," I said between blowing on a spoonful of soup to cool it, "please let me go back tomorrow. We were told by Herr Hoffer no excuses will be accepted." Besides, I thought, I want to win the contest.

"Nix," said Grandpa. "Nothing doing. We'll go to the Labor Office first thing in the morning."

Fortified with medical records from the Salzburg hospital, Grandpa stood in front of the stern-looking official. "The work is too hard and the hours too long," he pleaded. "Look at how frail she is."

"Working prepares our youth for tougher times to come," retorted the woman with starched stiffness, an allegiance to duty written all over her frowning face. After studying the documents with raised eyebrows and giving me a few quick glances, she handed the papers back to Grandpa. "Request denied," she said curtly. "Heil Hitler!"

Meekly, Grandpa returned the official greeting, took my hand and left the office without the slightest protest.

I was surprised my Opa didn't at least raise one objection—inside his home he had acted furious. I pictured Mamma shouting with indignation at the government official. Is Grandpa afraid of them?

Silently we walked to the streetcar stop. "No sense arguing with those people," Grandpa grumbled, and after a few grunts and mutters, added words only angry grownups are allowed to say.

Without telling anybody, I felt glad I could return to pea-picking as part of a team to do my duty for the Vaterland. I wanted to be like my peers: strong, healthy, and productive.

The next day we picked until noon. Bucket after bucket emptied into a bin by a big fellow named Jupp. Hopefully, we compared scores. Mine was so low, I felt humiliated and hung my head in shame.

"I'll put some of my peas into your bucket this afternoon," said Mariele, the girl sitting next to me during lunch time.

I remembered helping her with fractions after class. She was a slow learner, but tried hard. "Thanks," I said. "I wish I could pick as fast as you." Swallowing one's pride is a painful process, I thought, and quietly wondered if that was why Grandpa had remained silent.

Mariele took another bite out of her liverwurst sandwich. "It's easy," she said, munching her lunch. "Don't bother to count, just look and pull on the vines with both hands."

We were dangling our feet inside an angle-shaped trench, built to provide cover from American fighter bombers. JABOs, the news media referred to them, short for Jaeger-Bombers. The people in Heilbronn called them Bomber-Karle. These small bomber-Charlies were quick and had developed the fine art of hunting whatever moved on the ground. A whining dive, a burst of fire…. Their specialty was trains.

"It's a cat and mouse game," said the big Jupp. When one of the JABOs approached, he'd yell, "Run. Schnell! Faster. Or Karle-cat will catch you."

Too scared to cry, we would grab a handful of branches to cover our heads, scurry like mice to the nearest ditch, and jump in. Sometimes the JABO's didn't dive at all; other days were filled with strafings.

Inside the narrow trenches it was hot and stuffy and during a rain shower, the branches covering the openings slipped inside, draping our heads and arms with greens reeking with rot. The stench coated everything: hair, eyes, teeth—gagging us and bringing tears. I tried to get some fresh air, but a strong hand pushed against my shoulder. "Stay down!" Above, the planes whined down to another and yet another attack. Then the quiet—except for choking sobs from little girls.

When the boss shouted, "Alles raus! The sky is clear," I scrambled out of the trench as fast as I could, looking like a pig that wallowed too long in the mud. Running across the field, I lost one of my sandals in the wet soil. But I didn't care. The earth smelled sweet, crows circled and cawed above, and I was alive.

At the end of two weeks, I had filled more than a hundred buckets—enough to earn over ten Reichsmark. I felt rich!

"You can keep it all," said Grandpa. "You earned it."

Aunt Erika suggested I open a savings account in my name.

"Spend it," said Grandpa. "Go into Heilbronn with Gertrude and see a funny matinee."

I liked going into town as much as seeing a picture show. The film was Japanese, with German subtitles.

"What was it about?" Erika asked.

"War," I answered. "These small Japanese soldiers first kissed the earth, then climbed into a plane, zeroed onto the target, and dived. They were proud and brave. But I felt sad."

"Propaganda trash," grumbled Grandfather as he turned up the radio to hear the news. It was October 4, 1943.

"Yesterday, Anglo-American terror bombers hit Frankfurt three times—morning, afternoon and night."

I stiffened.

"Between 400 and 500 planes attacked the city, raining down phosphor and fire bombs for two solid hours. A sea of flames sucked up the oxygen from the east end of the city. People, trapped in their cellars with no chance of escape, suffocated."

My body started shaking. Fire death, destruction. Fear! For a moment, I relived it all. I felt Grandma put her arms around me. Clinging to her large apron, I felt comforted and protected—but what about Mamma and Walter? Because he couldn't get along with my aunt, he'd returned to Frankfurt during summer break and stayed in the city.

We waited anxiously for news. Would a letter ever come?

Finally, I read Mamma's writing. "I thought the world was coming to an end," she wrote. "The air vibrated with the sound of airplane engines. FLAK roared with all cannons during the first attack. The house shook as if in a fever."

"A few hours later the city was doused with phosphor. The third bombing damaged the cathedral. We have no light, no power. I feel so tired and helpless. The river is still on fire."

At my school here in Boeckingen, the little Swastika flags on the world map slowly retreated from the Eastern front toward the German border. By October, all German troops had left the Caucacus. Russian troops continued to push Germans back from gained ground and Allied forces crept up to Naples on the Italian mainland.

As the Axis began to crack and crumble, people reacted with fear and anger and screamed in indignation: "The Italians are traitors!"

Strutting back and forth in the classroom, Mr Hoffer bellowed, "We must retain solidarity against the common enemy on land, on sea, and in the air! We shall never give up!" He raised his good arm shoulder high. "Sieg Heil!"

According to the news, carpet bombing of cities continued. In later November, Frankfurt suffered another heavy raid. Among the hits was the famous Goethe's Haus, birthplace of our famous philosopher and poet.

"Damaging a cultural monument is sacrilege," roared Dr. Goebbels. "There's nothing one can do about it! Air raids have blunted our feelings and hang over us like fate."

Outside of Weimar in Thuringen, a magnificent old beech was felled. "Goethe often sat and contemplated under that tree during the last years of his life," said a small notice in the newspaper. "It had to die to widen a road leading to a place called Buchenwald." The once beautiful beech forest was now the site of another concentration camp.

Why do we need so many prisons? I wondered.

In the privacy of their homes, some people whispered, "We want to quit."

But from radio broadcasts, Goebbels, the Nazi mouthpiece blasted, "Germans must fight to the bitter end!"

"Trust me," cajoled Goehring, the formidable minister of air defense. "Our scientists are developing a secret weapon that will erase whole cities from the map."

Whom shall I trust? The people or our leaders?

December was cold and wet. Outside, trees bent and shuddered before a howling wind.

Inside, I hovered close to Grandma. She made little conversation and neither laughed nor cried. Whenever she looked at the picture on the mantle, pain clouded her face. I could almost hear her silent thought. Who would be next?

I didn't want to think about it.

Anxiously, I waited for the mailman to bring a letter from one of Grandma's sons-in-law.

"Keine Post heute," called the letter carrier, trotting on to the next address.

Watching him hand a letter with a black border to the neighbor, I thought, getting no mail is better than getting a death notice.

In the evening, while Erika brewed the nightly herb tea, and Grandma darned and redarned, turned and patched, we sat in the kitchen anxiously listening to the radio. No longer did we sing folk songs in harmony, not even the beautiful and haunting "Lili Marlene."

Why is everyone so serious, I thought. Surely the war will be over soon—and we'll win. After all, our teacher tells us so every day.

On our way home from school, Gertrude and I talked about our families. "There are no more fun times," I said, "like when Grandma allows us to rest elbows on the table and slurp the soup at lunch. Or when she pretends she doesn't see us dip a wet finger into the bowl filled with sugar."

"They're all worried about the war," sighed Gertrude.

We stopped in front of our house—the sixth from the railroad crossing, where Grandma and Aunt Lina were waiting by the white picket fence.

"Gruess Gott, Oma," I said.

She tightened the woolen scarf around her chin. "Greet God, Maedele," she answered. In mellow moods, Grandma called me little girl.

"You two must be half frozen." Gradually, Aunt Lina had stopped tapping the Morse code and talked more and more like the rest of us.

From the west, we heard the familiar sound of an approaching train, but no friendly whistle announced it's arrival. Shivering in the wind, we waited as it noisily rambled over the frosted steel rails.

"It's just one of those slow-moving cattle trains," said Gertrude.

"I see no animals," I remarked. "Just people." I could make out sad eyes in gaunt faces, with heads wobbling like scarecrows over bodies clad in what looked to me like striped pajamas.

"Good God!" Aunt Lina clasped a hand over her mouth. "Grosser Gott!"

"If they are people, why aren't they smiling?" Gertrude pulled out a crumpled handkerchief. "Let's wave to them."

"Halt!" We recognized Herr Schroeder's voice immediately. His face distorted with hate, he grabbed the kerchief out of his granddaughter's hand. "They're Jews." He got off his bicycle and picked up a handful of pebbles. "Probably on their way to Buchenwald," he sneered, pelting the train.

"Stop it!" Grandma's voice was sharp and clear. She snatched off the scarf from her head with such a jerk that hairpins pulled down her bun. Hair blowing in the wind, she fluttered the woolen cloth wildly. As tears streamed in rivulets down her face, Grandma cried, "Wave, children, wave!"

I waved. Gertrude waved. Lina waved.

Some waved back. I paused and squinted. Who was that little sad boy with dark curly hair? Could it be? Dear God, was it?

Wheels squealing, the train jerked on.

Running along the hedge, I called, "David, David," until the icy wind cut off my breath.

CHAPTER TWENTY-TWO—Trapped—Spring 1944

It was Easter 1944. The air was unusually mild for late March. Sun and shadow flooded the roads and the sky sparkled as clear as if the angels washed it that morning. Even the sparrows twittered.

In the makeshift Lutheran church that once housed a printing press, Pastor Burkhardt opened an old, leather-bound songbook as her eyes swept over the small congregation. "Let's stand, please," she said, "and sing the verses from 'A Mighty Fortress is Our God.'"

She appeared frail and pallid in her black, shapeless wool dress that she'd bought two months ago—right after receiving notice that her husband, also a Protestant chaplain, had been killed on the Russian front.

I looked over at her three-month-old son who lay sleeping in his carriage next to the lectern. Singing with joy and faith our hymn abruptly ended as the air raid siren howled.

Hastily, Pastor Burkhardt said, "Please join me in a prayer. "Jesus Christus, please protect our homes from the perils of war and watch over our children." Her voice trailed off. "Dear God, keep the enemy from our borders, and guide our leaders, especially our Fuehrer, in right decisions."

How I longed to sing more songs, but our pastor urged everyone to hurry home, and since Gertrude and I lived in the same direction as Frau Burkhardt, we three walked together. We girls took turns pushing the baby buggy.

"I love babies," I said, peeking inside the covered carriage. "My Tante Else just had another little girl. I visit my aunt every weekend and help her take care of my little cousins." Playing mother gave me the sense of being needed.

Gertrude lingered by the baker's house admiring the first blooming daffodils and crocuses.

"We best keep going," cautioned Frau Burkhardt. "The alert has not been called off." Listening, she turned and raised her head, her beautiful chestnut hair shaded with veins of gold glistened in the sun. "Look!" She pointed to the tight formation of airplanes high above. Glittering in the sunlight, something silver fell from one of them. First we thought they were bundles of propaganda fliers. Tumbling and turning, they seemed to take forever to reach the ground.

Then there was a bang and a crash, followed by a thunderous explosion that shook the ground. Smoke billowed to the sky.

"Our church!" In disbelief, we all looked down the road, horrified.

This is God's house, I thought. Where had I heard those words before? Smoke billowed. A lone fire engine whined in the distance.

I began to tremble. Five minutes sooner, and we all would've been wiped out. Had the guardian angels whispered in Pastor Burkhardt's ear to dismiss us early?

"Thank you, God, for Your guidance," our pastor said, her voice sounding raspy as she grabbed up the baby and clasped it tightly to her breast.

Gertrude, not used to bombing, sobbed uncontrollably. "Our beautiful church. Where will we study our Catechism?"

"I'll make room in my home," said Frau Burkhardt. Turning her back to the fire, she laid the baby carefully in its carriage. "We'll start meeting after school next week." Her shaking voice belied her outward calm and confident composure.

Gertrude and I could hardly wait to tell our families about the bombing and how we were saved and ran home as fast as our legs let us.

Excitedly, I opened the door—but then I stopped, frozen in my tracks. Who was this, sitting on a chair in the middle of the kitchen? No, I thought. It couldn't be! Ends ragged and singed, her dark hair was matted and covered with black soot, and a tattered coat covered with dirt and grime reeked of ashes gone stale in the stove.

"Mamma!"

Slowly, she turned her soot-covered face toward me. Tired eyes peered from behind swollen lids, and blisters on cracked lips seeped blood. "We lost everything." The dull voice carried a ring of defeat. "Alles kaputt," she repeated over and over. "Everything's gone!"

"Mamma!" I cried.

Ever since the daily war news reported Frankfurt had three major air attacks in the past five days, I had been waiting for word from her.

Tears flooded Mamma's face as I cradled her head in my arms and cried with her. "You're safe! You're safe! I'm so glad you're safe." My eyes searched the large kitchen for my brother. "Where's Walter?"

"Taking a bath in the laundry room," Grandma said, putting a bit of honey in the camomile tea. "Here, drink," she told Mamma, "it's guaranteed to soothe the nerves."

Grandpa rose from his chair. "I better look after the boy. I'll check the fire under the kettle so Johanna has hot water."

Drinking tea and smoking another cigarette, Mamma nervously wiped her swollen eyes. "We've been in and out of trains so many times, hiding in ditches from the dive bombers, every bone in my body feels bruised. Twice, the engine was hit and we had to stand around and wait until it was repaired. It'll feel good to soak in the tub and shampoo my hair."

"It'll take more than one shampoo to get rid of that smut," said Lina. "You reek of smoke."

"So does my coat." Reluctantly, Mamma stood to remove it.

Erika helped, pulling at the sleeves until the garment dropped on the floor. Something fell out of a pocket and clanked to the terrazzo.

"My house keys!" Mamma quickly retrieved them. "I thought they got lost," she cried.

For a moment, no one spoke. Everyone stared at Mamma, pathetically holding onto the bundle of keys as though they were made of precious metal.

Slowly, Grandpa approached her. Patting her shoulder, he put an arm around her and gently took the key ring from her hands. "You won't need these any more, Johanna," he said in a voice filled with compassion. "You lost your home—not your keys."

With a wail that flailed my heart like a whip, Mamma slumped to her knees. Rocking back and forth, face lifted to the ceiling, fingers clawing her scalp, she sobbed uncontrollably. "We're homeless! Obdachlos! Without a roof!"

During all the commotion, I hadn't seen Walter enter the kitchen. He stood in the doorway, holding a wet towel and wearing a shirt and a pair of Heinz's pants that were much too big. Shyly, he greeted me in his Frankfurt dialect. "Guten Tag."

I ruffled his wet hair and pressed his head against my shoulder. "You haven't grown much," I teased him. "You'll have to grow a lot more to fit into those clothes."

He grinned. "I shampooed my hair three times before the soap made bubbles. Then, looking at the table, his face broke into a wide smile. "I smell food. What's for dinner?"

169

"Spaetzle and pot roast—and lots of gravy." Whispering, so Mamma couldn't hear me, I added, "Without lumps."

Sunday dinner was usually in the early afternoon, but because of all the excitement, it was almost two o'clock before we sat down to eat. Everyone was ravenous.

Afterward, Mamma and Walter were so exhausted that their afternoon nap extended through the night.

Next day, the three of us shopped in Heilbronn with the emergency coupons all homeless citizens receive. Mamma bought each of us the two sets of clothing allowed. Then we went to visit Aunt Hedwig, Mamma's oldest sister.

"I have to get back to work in Frankfurt as soon as possible," Mamma told her. "But I cannot take Walter with me. Children are no longer allowed in the city shelters."

I remembered Mamma's sudden decision last Christmas to take Walter back with her after she and Hedwig had a disagreement about his behavior.

Mamma looked up from the kitchen chair. "You and Walter go to the playground across the street."

We left without shutting the door completely and sat on the stairs outside the apartment.

"I don't want to stay here," Walter said.

Inside, the discussion continued. "He's changed," said Mamma. "The child's been through hell."

"I feel for the boy," said Hedwig. "But he simply cannot get along with my girls."

"Please. Give it another chance," urged Mamma.

"It won't work, Johanna. He's too defiant, too difficult. Besides, he spreads lies about us mistreating him. The neighbors told me."

"He promises to obey. And he must get back to school."

"That's the biggest problem. He continually skips his lessons and doesn't do any of his homework," insisted Hedwig.

As the volume of voices inside increased, Walter covered his ears. "I want to go back to Frankfurt," he cried.

A draft slammed the door shut. "Let's go outside," I said. Taking Walter's hand, I pulled him after me down the stairs.

The playground was crowded because of Easter vacation, but we found a vacant swing. Slowly, gliding back and forth, Walter started to sing. The song was a melancholy one—about a sailor longing for his homeland. Softly he sang the words.

In the land of Hessia,
By the river of the Main
Lies a pile of rubble called
Frankfurt.
Covered with ruins
and burnt-down houses—
lies my home called
Frankfurt.
The swing soared higher as his voice became stronger.
Tears running down my cheeks, I hummed along.
Where the cowardly Tommy
Kills women and children;
Where we mourn
So many casualties;
Where windows are shattered;
And the power turns off—
lies my home called
Frankfurt.

Jumping off the swing, he repeated, "Frankfurt am Main—it is my home, my home, my home."

"You have no home," I reminded him. It occurred to me that even I didn't consider Frankfurt my home anymore. I had been away too long. First the camp in Kaprun-am-See, then the hospital in Salzburg. Home to me, I realized, was at my grandparents house in Boeckingen where I felt safe, protected, and loved. Obediently, I accepted the rules of the house, conformed to school standards, and tried to please. I felt happy living with the relatives—Walter did not. Unable to adjust to new surroundings, he rebelled, lied, skipped school, wet the bed.

We stood and watched the children play.

I remembered a letter from my brother. He had been evacuated with other children to a farming community outside Frankfurt.

"Whatever happened on that farm near Oberursel?" I asked him. "Why didn't you stay there?"

"It was awful," he said. "About twenty of us—some younger, some older than me—were driven in an open truck to several villages. When we arrived at one of the destinations and climbed off the truck, the farmers walked around us, peered into our faces, felt our arms and legs. 'I don't want this skinny guy,' said one old farmer. 'I want a girl,' said the wife."

I poked Walter in the ribs. "I think you are making this up!"

He shook his head. "They'd pick a few of us and the rest scrambled back into the truck and we'd drive to the next village. Same thing. 'Too big, too little, too frail, not smiling enough, too ugly.' Finally there were two of us left. Me, and a red-headed, mean-looking girl." Walter swallowed hard. "We went to the next village. That farmer got stuck with us. And we knew it."

"You did get good food, though, didn't you?"

"Plenty. But after school we had to help the farm hands with chores until late in the evening, and I didn't get along with any of them."

"Is that why you ran away?"

Walter nodded. "I also had fights with the kids in school. Those farm kids were bigger than me; I never won. I was always scared. It wasn't just the boys beating me up, I hated that long walk to school. To avoid the dive bombers, we had to go through shaded woods. That was even worse than the dark cellars in the city. Early one morning, I hid between big milk containers on a dairy truck and made it back to Frankfurt."

"What did Mamma say when she saw you?"

"Oh, she was mad and slapped me. But Paula made her stop. She always takes my side."

Spying an empty bench outside the playground, we sat down. "What did you do all day while Mamma and Pappa worked?"

Walter thought a moment. "Aunt Paula was on a cleanup commando. I went with her and helped clear rubble off the streetcar tracks and sidewalks."

How awful, I thought, picturing the strenuous, dirty work in the bombed out city. He's so small and Paula has trouble breathing. How peaceful it was here in comparison. Pangs of guilt pierced my conscience.

I put my arms around his bony shoulders. "Where will you live in Frankfurt? In the cellar?"

"I dunno. It's flooded now," he said. "But I suppose Pappa will fix it!"

"Pappa?" The memory of my stepfather filled me with rage. "Pappa!" I choked out the words through my suddenly dry throat.

"We'll use buckets and pails, how else?" Walter became very animated. "Pappa explained it to me. He'll clear the rubble until he finds the entrance to the stairs…"

I interrupted. "You like Pappa, don't you?"

"I love him!"

"But—he used to beat you! Bash your head against the wardrobe until you threw up! He kicked you…. "

Shouting, Walter jumped up. "He saved my life!" A sob escaped his throat. "Yes, he saved my life. And Mamma's. And Paula's. And everyone else in that cellar." He sat back down. "Didn't you hear Mamma talk about it in Oma's kitchen?"

"No." My whole body trembled with shame. "That must've been before I returned from church." I was silent for a moment. "How did Pappa save your lives?"

Walter squirmed and fidgeted. He never could sit still. "It happened during the second attack. The bombs howled and whistled; then there was a pounding. A crash. Everything rattled and shook like a thousand hungry lions crunching bones.

"I was scared. The lights went out." Walter shuddered, remembering. "You know how I hate the dark. People from the cellar next door climbed over the short ledge of the crawl space. Their basement began flooding from a broken pipe."

"It was pitch black and the bombs kept coming. I could hear water running over the ledge. It spread around my feet. Slowly it filled the cellar floor, slushed around my ankles. I held onto Mamma's hand—she was scared, too. 'Don't talk,' she said. 'We must conserve oxygen.'

"When the bombing stopped, we were trapped. Upstairs, I heard a noise— like scraping and scraping. We lit a candle and waited."

Walter moved closer to me on the bench. "I was so scared. The water kept coming higher and higher, and the light of the candle grew smaller."

I knew what that meant. Without oxygen, the flame would go out—and the people would fall asleep and never wake up again. "How long were you down there?"

He shrugged. "I don't know. It felt like forever."

"How'd you get out?"

He grew excited. "You remember the coal chute?"

I nodded. "The one you sometimes peed in."

"That's the one! Well, Pappa was outside and had already started clearing the rubble. He shouted down the chute. We yelled back and before we knew it, eins, zwei, drei—maybe it took an hour, or only minutes. But when he and some others widened the opening, Pappa pulled me out first!"

Pappa, I thought. Pappa. There was goodness in him. I should love him. But I do despise him!

I remembered Pastor Burkhardt's words at one of our lessons. "Within every dragon," she lectured, "there is a princess; and within every inferno there is a paradise—if we know what to look for and if we have the eyes and the heart to see."

CHAPTER TWENTY-THREE—Invasion 1944

Huddling on the doorstep of our grandparents' house, my cousin Sonja and I flipped another page of the book that our neighbor, nurse Bauer, insisted we read. "You're coming of age," she told us—whatever that meant. "Start with the first two chapters and be sure to look at the pictures."

"The beginning pages are all about bees buzzing from blossom to blossom," I told Sonja, "It's called pollination."

"What's that?"

"It makes a tree bear fruit." I pointed to the drawing of a pear tree.

"I thought bees make honey."

"Me, too." I turned the page to the next chapter.

"It's about birds," said Sonja.

"And nesting," I added.

"I saw a swallow's nest under the eve of the storage shed. Let's find out if the eggs have hatched."

Carefully we climbed up the ladder and stretched our necks to spot any life in the nest. There, in the center, a swallow twittered persistently as another one flew around, shrieking.

Sonja and I decided to return to our book, doubting we had much to learn from the birds and bees.

"Let's skip to the third chapter," I suggested.

Pointing to a picture, my cousin exclaimed, "Look. It's about a baby growing inside the body of a woman." Sonja combed one of her two long braids that had come undone.

"Your hair must be below your hips," I said, looking enviously at her long blond tresses.

"I can sit on it," she said. "But it's a bother to brush and braid every morning. Mother says I can get my hair cut for confirmation next year, right after eighth grade graduation." Sonja was a year older than I, almost fourteen. We went to different schools, but because I started at a younger age, we attended the same grade.

Her disposition was sometimes solemn—even moody. I liked the serene beauty of her face. The boys liked her—especially lanky Wally who had a cute smile, bright blue eyes that always teased, and a voice that often burst into song. Whenever Sonja visited, he'd walk back and forth in front of our house, singing up a storm about Sunny Sonja.

She was taller than I, and already breasts pushed at her thin sweater.

"Are you wearing a brasserie yet?" I asked enviously.

Her eyes riveted to the book, she folded her arms over her chest and nodded. "Yes, but it's a nuisance."

"I can wait," I said. Looking over her shoulder, I read the word menstruation. "I started that," I said.

"Your period?" Sonja stopped reading. "Tell me all about it! Does it hurt? I hear it's messy!"

"It's a big inconvenience. And bloody. You have to wear a big band-aid, called a sanitary napkin. Aunt Erika and Lina complain that it's nearly impossible to buy them at the drug store anymore."

"Sounds awful," said Sonja. "I can wait."

Turning another page of the chapter on childbirth, I started to giggle. "You think this book wants us to be mothers?"

Catechism lessons at Pastor Burkhardt's were more than a study of the New Testament. We'd sit in a circle and discuss our experiences, our aspirations, and ourselves. We hoped and prayed—not for victory, but for peace.

I shared with the others the horror of bomb attacks in Frankfurt, and the tragic typhus epidemic at the evacuation camp that turned Hannelore and my teacher into angels. For a brief moment, I thought of talking about David—I often wondered where he and his family were—but decided against it. Long ago I had learned that certain subjects were not discussed. One of them was Jews.

When Pastor Burkhardt asked about our goals in life, I expressed disappointment that I was offered a scholarship to a high school by the State, but Mamma wouldn't let me go. "All she had to do was join the Nazi party—but she was stubborn and wouldn't. Why?"

"Sometimes," said Pastor Burkhardt, "we don't understand our parent's wisdom while we're young. Then we must trust in God."

175

I couldn't comprehend the meaning of the words, but her gentle voice spread a cloak of comfort and hope around me. I put my grudges aside and listened to what others had to say.

Some girls wanted a typist position, others opted for work in the local shoe factory because it paid more money. Neither appealed to me. I saw myself doomed for the assembly line, working next to Aunt Erika and Aunt Hedwig.

Pastor Burkhardt suggested an apprenticeship at a doctor's office as a receptionist. "For three years, you'll get on-the-job training while enrolling at a trade school for eight hours a week. You'll even get some pocket money every month, which will be raised as you progress toward completion of the program."

"Mamma won't sign such a contract," I pouted. "She said I must contribute to the family income."

"I'll talk to your grandfather," said Pastor Burkhardt. "But first you must finish elementary school. Your teacher, Herr Hoffer, is a fine teacher—despite his eccentricities."

As if in contemplation, Herr Hoffer slowly strode back and forth in the classroom—his right sleeve dangling from the shoulder, his left arm bent behind his back. The expression on his face was somber and his eyes, usually sharp and piercing, today they were dull and sad. Even the Heil Hitler lacked its usual vigor.

I had begun to like this teacher; he was less intimidating and appreciated a student who wanted to learn—and I absorbed knowledge like a sponge. He rewarded me with good grades, that earned me a lot of praise from the family.

Herr Hoffer stopped pacing. "I've been a teacher most of my life," he said, his voice without luster. Shaking the empty sleeve of his coat, he continued. "I served my Fatherland during the First World War."

Because of his words and gestures, I knew he was upset.

He walked to the European map on the wall. For the last few months, the little swastika flags had retreated close to the German border on the Eastern front. The Soviet Union was covered with empty pinholes where once German armies had advanced. From Italy, the Allies pushed North toward Germany's Southern border. But France, to the west, was still under German occupation. It was May, 1944.

Herr Hoffer pointed to Hitler's picture on the wall. "And I've sacrificed my sons for our Fuehrer." His once proud and arrogant voice was now harsh and cynical.

The class sat silent, waiting for a tirade of words.

Instead, he pulled from his pocket a glass case and removed a pair of small round rimless spectacles. He cleaned the lenses, holding them this way and that, and, meeting his approval, he carefully set them on his desk, took off his black-rimmed ones and replaced them with the other pair.

We all waited patiently, fearing to make a sound.

For a long time, he quietly stared at us. Directly, through the glasses, he gazed at each one of us. One by one. Row by row.

"As a teacher—" his voice was but a whisper "—this is the saddest day of my life."

I had to strain to hear.

He turned away, blew his nose, and wiped his eyes. Picking up a crumpled sheet of paper from his desk, he smoothed it, and started reading. "You are herewith advised that your eighth grade class has been selected for special employment for the general war effort of the German Reich." Still staring at the students, he started pacing again.

In surprise, we looked at each other. "Special employment? General war effort?" Questions flew across the room and hung suspended in the air.

What does it mean? No more school? I shuddered in the silence.

"What does it mean?" His brow compressed, his expression somber, he stopped in front of my desk.

He must've read my mind, I thought.

"It means that your formal schooling is over. Schluss! Finished! Kaputt ! Each one of you will replace the person serving her compulsory work year on a farm or in a household. It's a chain reaction. The replacement will relieve the person working on war efforts in the factory, and that person will be trained to defend our Fatherland." Mr. Hoffer walked to the map of Europe on the wall. "Our Fuehrer promises a secret weapon." He rapped his knuckles against the wall. "Even during war there must be hope."

A murmur rippled from student to student. "Work? When? Where? How?"

Worried, my spirits sank. How could I satisfy my ravenous appetite for knowledge? I had missed so much formal schooling already. Since third grade, class hours were shortened in Frankfurt whenever there was an air alert. In the evacuation camp, we received two hours of formal teaching. Later, hospitalization and recovery from typhus had taken three months out of my school year.

Mr. Hoffer picked up a piece of chalk. "We have until noon before official dismissal. Let's see how much of the ten months of teaching I can cram into two hours."

Library. He wrote the word on the blackboard. "You can read," he said. "Goethe, Schiller, Nietzsche—study the Classics. Even The Grimm Brothers' fairy stories have a tale to tell."

He held up the chalk. "Write! Poetry, songs, letters. Keep a diary."

Numbers. "You can add, subtract, multiply, and divide. Last year we learned fractions. You know enough to count, weigh, and measure. This year we were to tackle geometry." He drew a circle, a square, and a triangle.

I had never seen him so intense, so caring.

"Participate in the arts; listen to a symphony—Brahms, Beethoven, Mozart; see an opera—LaBoheme, Fidelio, Goetterdaemmerung ; and visit museums.

My mind wandered to the arts center in Heilbronn where Aunt Lina had taken me to the opera Aida not so long ago. She had season tickets and grandma didn't feel well enough to attend. I was allowed to wear my Sunday dress on a weekday.

"Don't even try to understand the sung words," advised Tante. "Just listen to the musical theme."

I never saw the end of Aida. Warning sirens prompted us to take refuge in a public shelter until the danger passed.

Herr Hoffer's rambling voice caught my attention again. He was giving examples of etiquette and manners, and why your hand must be cold before you can slip it into a kid glove.

Finally, he gave each one of us some practical advice to make the road of life easier.

"Anneliese," he said, holding onto my hand. "You won't have a problem making a living. But you must learn to like doing without those things that are not within your reach."

It took a long time before I understood what he meant, and, at times, I still fret when a star is too far away to be touched.

When Grandma grasped that I must work in someone else's household instead of going to school, she said, "Nix!"

For the first time, I experienced Grandma's furor.

"They call themselves leaders," she fumed, slamming the lid on a pot of boiling potatoes. "Give the Hitler people a try, they said in 1933. Why not? Things can hardly get worse."

To my horror, she even kicked the cat when Muschi tried sneaking inside the house. "Stealing the childhood of its youth to serve their inflated egos.

Groessenwahnsinn!" Power madness! Criminals. That's what they are, I swear."

I received a temporary permit to help my Aunt Else with her two children. The younger one, Ingrid, had contracted polio and required much care.

Meanwhile, Grandpa wrote a letter to the authorities and asked for an exemption because my heart was still too weak to do heavy housework.

I received a notice from the Public Health Office to be examined. My heart proved to have a healthy beat and the request was denied.

Grandpa lay low, hoping to stall long enough until all available positions were filled.

Eventually, they were. In and around Heilbronn, there wasn't a single vacancy. But fifteen kilometers away, in a small village, there was a dire need for a domestic.

"Report immediately to the home of Rolf Becker, Vice President of Bleyle GmbH, Brackenheim," read the orders. "Four children. Two elderly females, one elderly male."

"Isn't Bleyle the famous manufacturer of fine knitwear?" Grandma asked.

"The finest," Aunt Erika answered. "And indestructible."

"Fashionable," Aunt Lina added. "And expensive."

I received the letter on June 6, 1944, the day Allied troops invaded Normandy.

"Invasion!" It was no surprise. We sat glued to the radio—clinging to each word, sure our brave and courageous soldiers would push the invaders back into the English channel.

"The Allies are suffering heavy casualties," the newscaster blasted.

"Probably true," said Grandpa. "But they seem to have an unlimited supply of men and weapons."

The headline in the paper screamed, "Our wonder weapon will destroy them!"

"Hurry up!" Some whispered with fear; others prayed in silence.

CHAPTER TWENTY-FOUR
—Brackenheim—Summer 1944

The lilacs lightened their deep purples into the color of their name, shedding a tiny rain of blossoms. They were past their prime.

Grandma stood under the arbor of the drooping bush, head bent in quiet thoughts. Everything worth saying had been said. Salty rivulets streaked her flushed cheeks.

I hugged her one more time before picking up my small suitcase. "I'll be back for Christmas," I called and hurried to catch up with Aunt Lina. When reaching the railroad crossing, I turned once more and saw her remove her head scarf and wave. I'll miss her more than anyone else.

Walking the two kilometers to the station, I thought of the carefree days at the little house, the bread and warm milk prepared by Grandma every morning, her toothless smile that greeted me when I arrived from school.

At the train station, I checked the schedule, while my Aunt went to the ticket window. "One adult, round trip, and one child, one way to Brackenheim," she said.

The Bummelzug, as they call the slow train that meanders past small villages, consisted of a locomotive, a tender, and three small passenger cars. We boarded the middle car, third class.

Most of the passengers were farm women with weather-worn faces. Attired in long skirts, hand-knit sweaters, and scarves tied under their chins, they carried their wares in tightly-woven baskets: a fat hen, fresh eggs, salad greens, flowers. "Gruess Gott!" The woman with the chicken slid across the wooden bench to make room for us to sit.

"Gruess Gott!" Thanking her, my Aunt added a "Danke schoen," to the warm greeting. She held my hand and patted it gently as though I was a child in need of comfort.

Outside, the station master blew his whistle and signaled the engineer that it was safe for the train to move.

There was no talk in the compartment—except for an occasional sigh by Aunt Lina, followed by a nod of the head and the words, "Ja, ja —that's the way it is."

From my window, I watched the peaceful landscape of small farms, vineyards, and pear tree orchards pass. Clickety-clack, clickety-clack went the wheels as they tootled across the rails, around the bend, and over a hill. Will I be able to master the task that looms ahead?

The train slowed in a huff and a puff when we came to the first stop.

"Neckarsulm," called the man outside with the sign.

Two young children—she, wearing a dirndl dress with apron; he, short Bavarian leather pants with a blue shirt, skipped and hopped around the platform, arguing whose wooded sandals made the most noise.

"That reminds me of my childhood," said Aunt Lina. The smile made her look prettier than did the sighs.

"Did you wear wooden shoes?" I asked. Here comes a story, I thought.

She nodded. "During the First World War…" She stopped for a moment to think of the year. "In 1917, leather became scarce. My grandfather—that's your

great-grandfather—was a shoemaker. So he hammered all week in his workshop and made shoes for the five of us."

I interrupted. "I thought you were six."

"Erika wasn't born yet. Anyhow, we kids loved the noise the shoes made.

Klipp-klapp, klipp-klapp, all over the sidewalk we hopped, skipped, jumped and leaped, each trying to outdo the other as to whose shoes clapped the loudest. Klipp-klapp,

klipp-klapp, up and down the wooden stairs we ran, until my mother—your

Oma—covered her ears and went to her father.

'I'm going out of my mind hearing this klipp-klapp of ten little feet running up and down the stairs,' she cried. 'You must do something!'"

The woman with the basket of flowers leaned forward and asked, "What did he do? I also have five pair of feet clogging through my home all day."

"Grandfather, the little shoemaker, scrounged in each corner of his workshop and gathered every scrap of shoe leather he could find. All night, he matched and patched the pieces on the soles of our shoes, and by morning, they sat in order of size in front of our door.

"Our mother's face was etched from ear to ear with a smile of gratitude as she listened to the soft muffle of shoes descending the stairs.

181

"But we children were mad! No more klipp-klapp. No more noise. No more competition. We walked to school with heads hung in shame. After all, everybody else wore shoes that made that wonderful klipp-klapp noise. And when we returned home, we didn't speak to our grandfather—even though he told us something about elves doing the mischief during the night!"

Before I could react to the story, the train chugged to a halt. "Brackenheim!" Our trip had taken less than an hour.

Stepping onto the tiny platform, we asked the conductor for the house of Rolf Hofmann.

"Hofmann?" He scratched his head.

The woman with the egg basket called from the compartment window. "Straight through the village, around the fountain and past the dairy, then up the hill."

The house appeared formidable from the road. Like a small castle, it watched over the plots of farms below. Wide, stony steps led to the top. I counted forty-eight.

"Wonder who shovels the snow in the winter?" Aunt Lina, though slim and trim, stopped to catch her breath.

I set down the suitcase and looked up at the three-story house that now looked like a stately mansion with a double-door entrance and poplar trees taller than the building. Bay windows glistened and gleamed in the late morning sun. Was that a child peeking through the lace curtains?

The front door opened. A stout, but stately woman, wearing a crisp apron that covered the front of her patterned dress, greeted us. Extending her hand to Aunt Lina, she said, "Gruess Gott! You must be Frau Duerr." She looked at me, glanced at my Aunt, and again her eyes squinted in my direction. "The little girl with the suitcase. Who's that?"

I put down the small suitcase, stood up tall, and stepped forward. "I'm Anneliese Eisenkraemer."

"Indeed," she said, shaking my hand. "I'm Frau Hofmann's mother." Ushering us inside, she said to my Aunt, "She looks so small."

"The Eisenkraemer's come in pint sizes," joked Auntie. More serious, she sighed, "she is but a child."

A woman, tall and slim, walked briskly down the long hallway to meet us. She wore a belted housedress, but no apron.

She's at least a head taller than any of the women in my family, I thought.

Opening the door to what appeared to be a large sitting room, she invited us in. "Take a seat," she said. "I'm Frau Hofmann." She shook hands and looked at me the same way her mother had at the front door.

I was beginning to feel like a midget.

While she and Aunt Lina talked, I noticed that the furniture looked stiff and formal, but the walls were covered with beautiful paintings of landscapes that mellowed the austerity. The highly polished parquet floor was partly covered by a royal blue carpet with long fringes at each end. I was filled with awe.

"She looks so young and frail," said Frau Hofmann. "How old is Anneliese?"

"She'll be thirteen next month." My Aunt sighed once, then added with pride, "She's very good with children."

It was Frau Hofmann's turn to sigh. "Not yet thirteen!" She adjusted one of the long hairpins that held the chignon in place at the nape of her neck. "My mother-in-law takes care of the children—especially the two younger ones. The baby is six months, Rolf is three years. Six-year old Guthrun just started school, and eight-year old Anton is in third grade."

"What are Anneliese's duties?" Auntie inquired.

"The same as the older girls I had before. The last was a peasant lass who had strong legs and arms. Sofia wasn't very fastidious about housework, but she was quick!"

I straightened my slouched back, but hid my legs under the chair and my arms behind the back. I'm just the opposite, I thought. Skinny and slow.

"I do most of the cooking and shopping," continued Frau Hofmann. "Mother helps wherever she's needed."

"I'm sure, Anneliese can learn a lot from you about running a household," Aunt Lina interjected.

Frau Hofmann agreed. "Let me show you the house."

As we walked the long hallway on the ground floor, she pointed to the rooms on the right. "Mother occupies the guestroom in the front. The two older children share a room, and the baby is still with us in the master bedroom. Rolfi shares a room with Granny upstairs.

The kitchen was enormous—larger than that of my grandparents. It even had a well-stocked pantry, and was equipped with two stoves: one wood and coal burning, the other gas-powered. How much time will I spend here? I noticed the double sink, lots of cupboards, and a large wooden table and chairs by the window. Is this where I will take my meals? After all, I'm the new maid.

Adjacent to the kitchen was a large screened-in porch.

What was the noise outside? I stretched to see.

"We have chickens, ducks, and geese." Frau Hofmann's mother opened the door to the back porch. "Sofie used to feed them."

The ducks came waddling, the roosters chased the chickens, and the geese ran, their long necks extended, ahead of the feathered pack—cackling, squawking, and screaming in their individual fowl language. What a racket!

Remembering the chicken-chasing episode in Grandma's garden, I froze. Timidly, I asked, "Who takes care of them now?"

The mother seemed to sense my fear and said, "I do. My son-in-law, Mr. Hofmann, helps on weekends."

Standing by the table, Frau Hofmann said, "We don't eat in this room. Once a month, Olga, a Russian laborer from the factory, helps with waxing the floors, washing windows, and do other heavy labor. Anneliese will eat with her in the kitchen on that day. Otherwise—" she put her hand on my shoulder" —you join the family at mealtime in the dining room upstairs."

For a moment, I felt like gaining a new family, but changed my mind when Frau Hofmann continued. "We need someone to serve the dinner."

As we walked up the stairway, I glanced at my reflection in a floor-length mirror. Still too small—but I can do anything! I nodded to Aunt Lina who was right behind me and stretched with confidence.

Entering the dining room, I was struck by the silhouette of an old man sitting in an armchair by the bay window. His posture was straight, rigid— formal. The pin-striped vest over a white shirt matched his dark grey trousers. Only the camel-colored felt slippers seemed out of place. Hair like white cotton covered his head. He looked distinguished.

If he noticed us, he didn't show it. Perhaps he was hard of hearing.

Aunt Lina admired the comfortable furniture, the paneled walls, the vases and crystal bowls in the china cabinet. Several times, she glanced toward the window.

Frau Hofmann ignored the silent figure who read by the light of the early afternoon sun. Instead, she headed toward a decrepit-looking woman whose body almost disappeared inside an oversized shawl clutched around her shoulders. Her grey hair was parted in the middle and twisted tightly into a knot at the back of her head. Thin lips seemed to quiver a little, but her dark eyes sparkled with life. "B'hiet Di' Gott," she said, in a dialect foreign to me.

"God Bless You." Frau Hofmann returned the greeting. "My mother-in-law is from Bavaria." She stepped into the nursery next to the dining room where a small boy was playing with building blocks. Beyond I could see a rocking horse, fancy dolls, lead soldiers, miniature furniture, spinning tops, and a carpet crocheted from strips of old rags.

184

"This is Granny's domain." Frau Hofmann opened the door to the adjacent bedroom. "She usually stays up here with the little ones. Sometimes, she takes them for an outing in the garden."

A sharp cough from the dinning room drew our attention. Spectacles in hand, the man stood a foot from the nursery door. "I see we have company." His face beamed with unlimited goodwill.

"My uncle," said Frau Hofmann.

"Heil Hitler!" he said, with half a smile.

As if the man wasn't there, Granny turned her back. No longer old and docile, she now looked spunky and cantankerous.

"Gruess Gott!" Aunt Lina refused to give the Nazi salute of hailing Hitler.

The man's pupils constricted and he frowned as if he were not pleased.

Granny was. "B'hiet Di Gott," she said to no one in particular as we exited the room. "God protect you."

We rushed up the steep flight of stairs to the attic where Frau Hofmann opened the door to what would be my room. It contained an iron bedstead, a night stand with an alarm clock on top, a commode, a table and chair, a double-door wardrobe. My small suitcase contained only three dresses.

With relief I noticed that the bed had a real mattress—not a sack and pillow filled with straw, like the bunks at the camp. The ceiling was slanted toward the window, giving the room a cozy look.

Was that a mirror Frau Hofmann was standing in front of? When she moved away to open the window, I stared at the painting on the wall. Then I glanced at Aunt Lina. Her mouth fell open. Brown pants. Brown shirt. A swastika banded arm. Leather strap across his chest. Thick mustache. The picture was a near life-size portrait of Adolf Hitler.

"That was a wedding gift from my uncle." Frau Hofmann must have noticed us staring. "The frame is valuable," she said, leaving the room so I could unpack and spend a few minutes alone with my Auntie.

Tanta Lina broke the awkward silence. "I'll bring your new red coat next time I visit. You won't need it until winter." She picked up the alarm clock and sighed again. It was set for six o'clock.

"I don't mind getting up early," I said. It wasn't true, but I wanted to be brave.

Stepping to the window, I exclaimed about the beautiful garden below— a paradise of flowers filled with the glory of tumbling blossoms, and tall poplars shading a trail around the house that led to a white gazebo covered with climbing red roses. A free-standing, two-seat swing completed the romantic picture.

Auntie put her hands on my shoulders. "I think you'll be all right with this family. But watch that uncle. Did you see the Nazi party pin on his vest?

I nodded. "My teacher, Herr Hoffer, had one like that. It means he's an honorary member."

"He's a Seckel!" Auntie's voice was filled with scorn. "A jerk!"

I knew it was a derogatory word applied to males, but she wasn't done with uncle yet. "Viper," hissed my aunt. "I trust that old man no more than I would a rattlesnake." Pointing her right index finger at the picture of the Fuehrer, she said, "Trust my intuition, Anneliese, something tells me the walls of this house have ears. They spy and inform. Keep your mouth shut—especially around that old man."

Thank goodness, uncle didn't sleep at the house where nine other family members shared the five bedrooms. While cleaning the room uncle rented in the village, Frau Hofmann confirmed Auntie's warning. "Keep quiet around my uncle, Anneliese, and stay as far away from him as possible. Even my mother doesn't trust her own brother." She returned the broom and feather duster to the landlord and locked the door behind her.

I toiled in the Hofmann family household from seven in the morning to nine at night, seven days a week, with a three-hour break on Sunday afternoons.

Every task became a challenge—and I felt compelled to carry it out to perfection. How could I possibly disappoint my family or country? Slogans played their messages over and over in my brain. "The Eisenkraemers are a tough lot," said Grandpa; "Germans are courageous and indestructible," Mr. Hoffer, our teacher, hammered into our heads; "Don't complain," is the country's motto.

Carefully balancing dishes and food on a sturdy tray up the stairs, I talked to myself. "You must not spill a drop or anything. Look straight ahead. Don't trip on the next step. Steady your arms—they won't collapse under the load; you can do it!" Beads of perspiration covered my body as I approached the dining room entrance.

"You did it!" said Granny as she held the door open wide and followed me to the table where the family waited to be served. All except the uncle. He usually arrived from the village mid-morning with the newspaper clamped under his arm and retreated to an armchair by the bay window next to the dining room.

Sometimes I caught a glimpse of a headline that triggered anxiety in my mind. "Allied Invasion Forces Pushed Back. Heavy Losses." Where? Who?

I wanted to ask, but everyone was always busy with chores. The radio upstairs was never turned on. Perhaps it didn't work.

Mostly, I tried staying out of the uncle's way, feeling his cold blue eyes watch every move I made while dusting and sweeping. Sometimes I wondered if he was one of those spies that peered from oversized posters with the warning caption: VORSICHT! SPION!

"You missed a spot!" His reprimand startled me.

"Where?" Will he snitch to Frau Hofmann? I'd be so embarrassed!

Adjusting his screwed-in monocle with one hand, he pointed to the ledge behind the curio cabinet. Even the dark blue stone in his ring resembled that of the evil-looking man's in the picture.

CAUTION! SPY! The message played in my head.

From the nursery came the cantankerous voice of Granny. "Leave the girl alone and mind your own business." A finger, crooked from arthritis, beckoned me to come closer. "Don't pay any attention to that fat Nazi pig," she snapped. "He's as crazy as the rest of them."

I nodded and couldn't help but grin a little. She reminded me of Mamma when she made derogatory remarks about the government and its leaders. Granny's contrary words and feisty actions didn't match my image of the mother of a business executive.

From his corner I heard uncle rustle the pages of the newspaper and snap, "Communist Proletarian! They should've locked her up long ago—in a KZ!"

The ring of the last word filled me with alarm. When had I heard that word before?

"Concentration camp!…" Granny's spunky Bavarian dialect exploded explicits I'd never heard.

I gathered the soft-bristled broom and feather duster and hurriedly retreated down the stairs, almost bumping into Frau Hofmann's mother. "Granny and uncle are arguing," I said, trying to catch my breath.

"Best ignore it," was her advice. "They have opposite political beliefs and fight worse than cats and dogs. She's harmless, but watch my brother—he can be vindictive." She handed me a stiff brush and a bar of soap. "On Fridays we wash the main stairway before Anton and Guthrun come home from school. Have you done stairs before?"

I shook my head. "I've swept them at my Grandma's, but my Aunt Erika did the washing and polishing."

Frau Hofmann's mother sighed. "I miss Sofie. When she got done, the wood was as white as snow."

Sofie! All I ever hear is how fast that farm girl worked. Well—if she could do it, so can I. And better!

Carrying the bucket filled with warm water to the second floor I wondered how much more there was to cleaning this monster of a house. Water splashed over the rim on the floor. So what! I soaped, scrubbed, rinsed, and dried the first step until it gleamed spotless. "I'll show them," I grumbled and attacked the next. Never had I worked so hard, sweated so much—even picking peas must've been easier.

But I didn't complain. I was asked to do a job and I just did it. Besides, work made the day go fast with little time to miss my family. I must write and tell them all the new things I'm learning, I thought, as I dried the last of the noon meal dishes.

On Wednesday, we made sourdough bread. I began with a little leftover fermented dough from the previous week, called a starter. Adding flour and water, a little yeast, a dash of salt, I took turns with Frau Hofmann and her mother kneading loaf after loaf, punching them down—for their own good, the Hausfrau said—until the batter was of the right consistency to form four loaves. At first it was fun getting my fingers all sticky, but as the bulk grew bigger, the mass became heavier and more difficult to manipulate.

Carefully, I helped Frau Hofmann load the four round shapes onto the utility wagon. "Come with me to the village square and watch how the bread rises to meet its maker before it's baked," she said. "The community oven is not far from the village dairy."

I knew the route well. Every morning on my way to get milk, I passed a farm where two French prisoner-of-war laborers stood waiting. "Bon jour, Mademoiselle," they'd call.

"I ignore their leering eyes and crooked smiles, and look straight ahead," I told Frau Hofmann. Reminds me too much of Pappa.

"I'll have my husband report the incident to the authority in charge of forced farm labor," said Frau Hofmann after some contemplation. "Mr. Hofmann employs Russian women workers at the factory. Most are from the Ukraine and work well. Occasionally, one of them comes to help with the heavy work in the house, like cleaning windows, doing laundry, and emptying the septic tank."

I liked walking with Frau Hofmann. It was the only time we engaged in some meaningful conversation, other than about cooking and cleaning. Once a week we'd hike to the next village three kilometers away to buy groceries and fresh meat. "Your Aunt said you did well in school," she told me one day.

"What type of work do you want to get into after your year of domestic duty is over?"

What else did Tante Lina say to her? I remember her advising me to always be cheerful and do what I'm told, and perhaps Herr Hofmann could arrange an apprenticeship in the office of his factory.

I glanced at my employer. "I'd like to do research work," I said timidly.

"You want to be a lab technician?"

It sounded good, so I answered in the affirmative.

"I don't know if he has any openings," she said. "You might have to opt for a stenographer to start. He always needs help in the office."

Clerical work wasn't what I had in mind, but I felt grateful to be considered. Anything was better than working in a factory!

Upon our return to the fancy house on the hill, a letter was waiting for me. I recognized Mamma's handwriting immediately.

We dried out the cellar and now live in it, she wrote. Pappa scavenged some furniture from burned-out houses. Walter helped him install an old stove with the flue sticking out where the coal chute used to be. Paula's attic flat went up in flames when the bombs hit, so we share our lean quarters with her. You're lucky to be where you are. Work hard! Love, Mamma.

The following Sunday, during my three hours off in the afternoon, I attempted to write, but fell asleep after scribbling the first few lines. Finding a stack of books in the bottom dresser drawer, I had read for hours the night before. The stories, written for young adults, were all about cowboys and Indians. Karl May, the author, never set foot on the American continent, but his tales about natives scalping white men and cowboys attacking the savages kept me spellbound.

When I woke from my nap, I quickly finished the letter. "I'm fine and have plenty of food, but not much time to eat. Learning many new things. Miss you all. Will see you on Christmas. Please write. Love, Anneliese. P.S. How's Muschi? I miss petting her soft fluffy fur."

CHAPTER TWENTY-FIVE—Olga—Winter 1944

December 4th seemed like just another day at the house on the hill. An icy winter had settled on the landscape around the village that still lay in ebony darkness. Frost laced the window in my room, like delicate ice flowers.

Under the warm bed covers, I dressed quickly and hurried downstairs to the kitchen.

"Gruess Gott," said Frau Hofmann's mother as she filled the teakettle with cold water from the tap. She had already started a fire in the stove.

Returning the friendly greeting, I warmed my hands over the hot plate for a moment before grinding the coffee in the fancy porcelain grinder on the wall. No more pinching my thighs with the wooden box cradled between my knees.

Meanwhile, she sliced the bread; I buttered it. She brewed the coffee; I heated the milk. She stacked the tray; I carried it upstairs. We didn't talk much, but worked side by side.

"Anneliese is a hard worker and learns fast," I overheard Frau Hofmann tell her husband. My heart swelled with pride. I was eager to do a good job and earn my fifteen marks wages per month—the standing rate for domestics in training. Every month, Herr Hofmann deposited the full amount into my own savings bank, and since there were no places to spend the money, the account showed a balance of ninety mark. I felt rich!

Olga didn't think so. "Bah," she said. The large dark eyes in her round, moon-shaped

face glowed under heavy eyebrows. Mumbling in Russian, she pulled the peasant-style scarf farther down her forehead and tightened it in a double knot at the nape of her neck. "Thirty marks a month," Olga spread her ten fingers three times. "Work sixty hours a week." This time she drew the number on the table with her forefinger. "On knitting machines."

It upset me. Not that I begrudged Olga her wages, but why was she paid twice as much money for working thirty hours less than I. It's not fair! With anger I began to wonder who was the slave in our society?

Once a month, this warm and kind woman, who had been dragged from her home and family in Russia, and forced to work in the German garment factory came to help with the heavy cleaning. Zwangsarbeiter, these laborers wer called appropriately by the Nazi authorities.

"You remind me of my little sistra," Olga said. She knew few German words, but her tone of voice, expressive eyes, and gesticulating hands communicated clearly that her little sister had cried much when they were forcefully separated by the SS Storm Staff.

It was more difficult to figure out that sistra was the Russian word for Schwester, not a name. When I tried to find out what happened to the sister, Olga just shrugged and mumbled something in Russian.

Silently, we continued eating Frau Hofmann's speciality: Sauerkraut and Spaetzle. Spaetzle looked and tasted like something between a dumpling and a noodle. Baked in alternate layers with the sauerkraut in a deep dish, the casserole was covered with sauteed onions just before serving.

Olga wasn't fond of the dish and finished long before I did. Scraping what was left onto my plate, she said, "Essen, Sistra, eat!"

Quickly, I ate it all so I could help with the dishes, but she shook her head emphatically. "Olga do. Little Sistra sit."

I liked her calling me sistra —I always wanted an older sister to take some of my responsibilities off my shoulders, like taking care of a younger brother.

"Olga's one of my best workers," said Herr Hofmann. "She's not sly and rebellious like Tatiana, that Soviet witch who sabotages production quotas by tampering with machinery and weaving patterns."

Few workers were invited to do domestic work in his home. Olga was the only one to volunteer. She worked hard and was twice as fast as I—especially scrubbbing those wooden stairs that had to look schneeweiss to meet Frau Hofmann's standards of cleanliness. And who knew better than Olga how white snow looked.

Frau Hofmann liked Olga, but warned me not to become too friendly with her. "It is forbidden to engage in conversation with these forced laborers, much less to touch them. Uncle watches us closely and could make trouble for my husband and Olga."

She reminded me of the recent incident we had both witnessed on our way home from the bakery in the town square. A woman's hair was shorn in public for fraternizing too much with a farm hand of Polish nationality.

Some of the people who were there spit on the ground. "Pfui Teufel!" Who was the
bad devil?

All Frau Hofmann said was, "Schande!"

Did the 'shame' apply to the woman's deed or to those who sheared her. In any case, I thought the punishment was cruel.

Time passed quickly. Rarely did I have an opportunity to hear or read news about the war. From reading the popular Karl May stories, I knew more about what America's cowboys and Indians had done to each other a hundred years ago than what was happening after the invasion of Normandy in June.

"Don't worry," said Frau Hofmann, "our forces will push them back into the Channel." But her shaky voice belied the confidence of the words.

I heard of the attempted assassination of Hitler by Count von Stauffenberg, only because Uncle had the radio turned up high. "They should be hung alive like pigs on meat hooks," he snarled.

"The entire aristocratic family clan was arrested and shot immediately," announced the newscaster.

Heilige Maria Gottes!" The wooded rosary beads clicked in Granny's hands. "Holy Mary, Mother of God!" Was she praying for Hitler or the underground?

"They all need prayer," sighed Frau Hofmann.

At the end of August, I had glimpsed a headline that Paris had fallen to the Americans without resistance from German occupation forces. It was hard for me to believe that the enemy had come that close. Where was the wonder weapon Hitler promised us?

While German soldiers fought courageously to stem the invasion of its borders from all sides, the pace of life in the country remained virtually unchanged. Cows had to be milked, chickens fed, and crops harvested as usual by October.

Frau Hofmann, her mother, and I went to the vineyards in the hills surrounding the villages to gather vine branch trimmings. "They make good kindling for fire," said Frau Hofmann's mother. "My rheumatism tells me we'll have a long, cold winter."

I liked being outside. The fall foliage in the forests was painted in hues of yellow and green, interspersed with red and brown, creating a colorful patchwork quilt. Nature was so beautiful that I felt like singing—and did.

Soon, Frau Hofmann joined in the folksongs. Her mellow voice reminded me of Mamma, who used to sing while bending over the oval laundry tub, scrubbing and sudsing the soiled laundry. "Wherever there is song," Mamma used to say, "there's harmony. Bad people don't know how to harmonize."

We climbed up and down the hill, stooping to pick up small, dry branches and deposit them in our aprons and baskets, singing about a poor country boy who wished he had enough money to build a house for his sweetheart, Gretl, high in the mountains surrounded by flowers and meadows.

Although the ballad had a sad ending, I liked the rhyme and melody. The boy's dream to marry Gretl and have children with curly hair couldn't come true—because he had no money. Not a single girl gave him a second look. That must have hurt!

Every so often, I needed to straighten my back and stretch stiff shoulders. Shading my eyes from the afternoon sun, I looked into the still sky. "Look!" I screamed as I pointed to a couple of dark dots high above. I recalled the planes swooping down on us while we were picking peas in the fields. "Dive bombers!"

"A couple of swallows, Anneliese," said Frau Hofmann. "That's all. Hear them twitter?" I couldn't help it, but my knees shook and I felt scared for a long time.

Slowly, carrying full baskets between us, we walked down the hill. The view of broad meadows, pear orchards, an ox-drawn cart—what a delight. Bees buzzed in the last rays of sunshine. A finch chirped. I sighed and raised my eyes to heaven. It is so beautiful and peaceful here. Why can't it be like this everywhere?

Frau Hofmann put my thoughts into words. "What majesty there is in nature. What peace."

November's gray fog covered the earth as the rain fell quietly. But events outside German borders moved with frightening speed. From the west, General Eisenhower raced toward the Rhine river; General Patton pushed from the south, and on the eastern border, Russian troops thrust toward Silesia and East Prussia. A people's army, called Volkssturm, was created, drafting boys on their sixteenth birthday, and men as old as sixty, to the front—without preparation and proper arms. The bombing never stopped. The British night missions concentrated on small cities now: Aschaffenburg, Pforzheim, Bamberg. Is Heilbronn next? The mere possibility made me shudder. Trains and people, streetcars and ox-driven carts—anything that moved, became targets for American day mission bombers strafing the countryside.

December fourth. The beginning of Advent, I mused, as I climbed the stairs to my little room in the attic. Passing the dining room, I heard the clock strike nine. Feierabend, the celebration of evening; day is done.

I turned on the night stand lamp and re-read the letter from Grandma and Aunt Lina. My Aunt had written the most.

"We'll wait until you arrive before lighting the tree on Christmas Eve. The whole family will come together on Christmas Day. Aunt Hedwig with cousins Heinz, Sonja, Ellen, and your brother, Walter, from Heilbronn. Aunt Else is expecting again, but she'll try to make it from the other side of Boeckingen, with cousins Ursula and Ingrid. Aunt Musja and cousin Tamara promised to join us also. We seldom see them. Even your Mamma hopes she can spend the holiday with us. It's to be a surprise.

How exciting, I thought as I turned the page. I could see the tree decorated with silver balls and white candles in the parlor, the table set with Grandma's good dishes, smell cookies baking in the oven.

"Grandpa will have to butcher two rabbits for dinner and we'll bake lots of cookies. Love, Your family. P.S. Did you receive your red coat and other winter clothing in the parcel we posted?"

In anticipation of going home soon, I twirled around the room once, then checked the coat in the closet. Jawohl, it was there. Ruby-red and fluffy, my prized possession.

Ready to go to sleep, I removed my shoes, then took the flannel nightgown from under my pillow. Wait. Climbing on the straight-back chair, I draped my wool scarf over the picture of Herr Hitler's face. I didn't like the way he was watching me.

The room felt icy. Moving to the window I started to pull the drapes.

I stared. Froze. Trembled. Shivered. My God!

The night sky was red in the distance. Red like fire. I opened the window. Quivering and shaking, I recognized the smell. Smoke: fire and death!

Stifling a cry, I clapped my hands over my mouth. Heilbronn! No!

Once more I looked, then slammed the window shut, pulled the drapes, and turned my back. No. No. No. No. No!

In stocking-feet I raced down the stairs and almost collided with Frau Hofmann who stood at the bottom. I tried to speak. Not a word came out.

She spoke for me—confirming my worst fears. "Heilbronn is in flames." She, too, had trouble speaking, but soon regained her composure. "Let's go to the kitchen and warm some milk.

Her mother joined us and added kindling to the glowing ashes. "According to the eight o'clock broadcast on the radio, the bombardment started at ten minutes after seven and lasted twenty-five minutes." She blew into the ashes to fan the flames in the kitchen stove.

We sat and drank the heated milk, waiting for Herr Hofmann to return from the factory with more news.

I hoped for the best and prayed in silence.

Frau Hofmann met him at the door. "It couldn't be worse," I heard him say. Then their voices became muffled.

He entered the kitchen and pulled a bottle of Schnapps from the pantry's top shelf.

I waited and watched. Never had I seen Herr Hofmann take a drink.

Downing two shots quickly, he coughed and poured a third. Then he began talking. "The telephone wires are down. I told the night shift to keep trying. No one knows how extensive the damage is, except that the entire city is a sea of flames."

Numb with fear, I turned cold. My family! What happened to them? They're all dead, I thought. My family is all dead.

Like a robot, I cleared the cups from the table, while Herr Hofmann popped the cork from the Schnapps bottle and poured another drink. "Three waves," he slurred. "The next attack came in three waves. First phosphor bombs, next incendiaries—" He gulped down the fire water and smashed the glass against the stone terrazzo sink. "They finished the job with explosives and air mines."

I looked through the window pane and watched with dry eyes the thin half ring of the waning moon as it stole through the smoke—an awesome color like ashes of roses, till the fire suffused it with a burning blush.

"Stop shaking, Anneliese," said Frau Hofmann and put an arm around my shoulders. "Our home will always be your home."

My worry grew like an iceberg on my back. Somehow, I stumbled up the stairs and crawled into bed with my entire body turning into a cold mass.

Where was home? I wondered. I had a place here, but where did I belong?

The next day, Thursday, I waited for a sign of life from my family, but all forms of public communication remained silent. Uncle arrived without a newspaper, static interrupted radio transmission, and Herr Hofmann shook his head when I asked about a telephone message at the factory. "I tried all day," he said. "The lines are down, I'm told."

Doing my best not to think the worst, I kept busy to forget. As the fireball grew on the horizon, my hopes shrank.

Friday, the same. No news. What began to look like rain clouds was really black smoke. My fear mounted.

Saturday. Olga came. It was laundry day for linens.

We stood in the Hofmann's bedroom, stuffing plump featherbeds into clean covers. Glancing through the window toward the crimson sky, I pushed the buttons, one by one, through the matching holes. I missed one, and the whole row had to be redone.

Olga, stood in front of the dresser mirror, watching my fumbling efforts.

Enraged, I slammed my fist into a pillow and turned to the window. "Boom, boom." I pounded and pounded. "Boom, boom." Tears started flowing. "Boom, boom." Weeping, I walked into her arms, crying, clinging, sobbing.

Gently, strong arms pressed me to her large, soft bosom. Her body felt full and warm. Russian words caressed my ears, coarse hands felt like velvet. She didn't smell like roses, but her love seeped like perfume into my heart. "Sistra," she said, holding me tighter. "Kleine Schwester."

Suddenly, her arms stiffened.

In the mirror, I saw uncle. Don't get too close to Olga, Frau Hofmann had warned.

How long had he been watching us?

CHAPTER TWENTY-SIX—Sonja's Story—December 1944

It was Sunday, the fourth day of Advent. I always looked forward to the traditional lighting of candles atop the wreath decorated with pine cones and ribbons, while singing Christmas songs in anticipation of the holy night.

Herr Hofmann received news by word of mouth that Boeckingen, the suburb of Heilbronn, had escaped the bombing. There was some damage, but the Haselter housing development on the outskirts of the town had been spared.

I began to feel better. It meant that my grandparents, aunts, and cousin in the little house hadn't perished—or had my grandfather worked overtime and been trapped in the factory? Perhaps grandmother had gone to the theater with my aunts that evening? Their season tickets were for Wednesday. No, I told myself. Everyone is alive.

But what about my brother? He lived with my cousins and Aunt Hedwig close to downtown Heilbronn. Had my brother and relatives survived? How close had they been to the bombing? I'd overheard Herr Hofmann tell his wife that there was a shortage of track loaders to recover the dead in that area. My fears returned.

Mechanically, I performed my daily duties. Don't think, don't feel. Don't hope too much. Be prepared for the worst. Sometimes, the effort to do so made my chest feel tight, restricting my breathing. I often felt dizzy.

Carrying the tray loaded with Sunday dinner upstairs, I heard the doorbell ring. Frau Hofmann's mother would get it, I thought. She was still in the kitchen finishing the gravy. Carefully, I set the soup tureen on the table, removed the lid, and started serving.

"Anneliese! Come downstairs! You have company!"

Shaking like a leaf, I didn't move and stood as though my feet were rooted to the floor. I felt my heart pound. Don't get too excited.

"G'lobt sei Jesus Christus," said Granny. "Praised be Jesus Christ."

Frau Hofmann took the ladle out of my hand. "Go downstairs, Anneliese, go! I'll serve the soup."

"Danke," I said, gathering up a wisp of hair, tucking it back into place behind my ear—and ran.

The first figure I recognized was Aunt Lina. Dressed in black, her large brown eyes shrouded in tears, she managed a little smile. Opening her arms, she called, "Gruess Gott, Maedele!" Like Grandma, she called me little girl.

I wasn't sure whether to laugh or cry. She looked so small and frail in the dark cloth coat with the black fur trim. I recognized the hat with the veil. While in mourning for her husband and brother, she'd worn it regularly.

Rushing into her arms, I wanted to ask about the others, but, fearing the worst, all I could press out was, "You've shrunk." What a stupid thing to say, I thought, hugging her tightly.

She slipped my face between her black-gloved hands, and placed an old-fashioned Auntie kiss on my lips. "You've grown." Twirling me around, she added, "Ja, ja," and approvingly patted my behind. "You're filling out nicely."

She's stalling, I thought. What about my family?

"Why don't you hang your coat on the rack near the entrance, Frau Duerr," said Frau Hofmann's mother, "and you have some hot soup in the kitchen with Anneliese." She waved to the two silent figures standing by the door. "Come, come."

That's when I saw my cousin, Sonja, and—what was his name? He always had this cute smile and sparkling eyes.

"Remember Wally?" Sonja took off her woolen gloves and hung her coat on a hook next to Auntie's.

Smoothing my apron, I walked toward my cousin's friend and said, "Gruess Gott, Wally!"

Extending a hand, he nodded. There was a crooked little half-smile on his face—but his eyes were such a pale blue I seemed to be looking at frosted water that gave no reflection back. Moving slowly, he followed us into the kitchen.

"The noodle soup tastes good," was all he said.

"Everyone's fine," volunteered Aunt Lina.

Why the black dress?

I looked at Sonja. She was quieter than usual. Were her braids tucked under that knitted cap she was still wearing? I wondered, but didn't ask. Instead, I inquired about her family.

"They're fine."

"And my brother?"

Aunt Lina placed the spoon into her empty bowl and pushed the dish away. "Johanna took him back to the city."

"Mamma was in Heilbronn? Why didn't she visit me? How come Walter's in Frankfurt?"

"Langsam, langsam." Auntie put up a hand, trying to slow the barrage of questions. She dug around her handbag for a handkerchief. "Heilbronn is no more." She sniffled once or twice into the cotton cloth. "The little house was overcrowded when your Mamma came to check on us. She decided to take Walter back with her to live in their cellar in Frankfurt." Lina twisted the tattered hankie in her hands.

Frau Hofmann and mother entered the kitchen, carrying trays with dirty dishes and leftover food.

"Please, let me help," said Aunt Lina. "Where's an apron?"

"No. Indeed, no. You are our guests." Frau Hofmann's mother poured hot water from the kettle into the dishpan. "Anneliese," she said in her no-nonsense voice, "it's a sunny day outside. Show your cousins around the premises. Your Aunt and my daughter need to have a talk in the parlor."

Side by side, Sonja and I walked down the white-pebbled path toward the gazebo. Wally trailed behind.

"Let's go inside and sit together on the swing, the way we used to at the neighbor's garden," I suggested.

Silently, Sonja nodded and sat next to me.

As we swung back and forth, her hat slipped off.

In disbelief I looked at her ragged, uneven strands of hair—some as short as two centimeters. "What happened to your long braids?"

Sonja stopped the swinging motion with her feet. Lowering her head, she covered it with both hands. "When grandma tried to brush my hair, my braids just fell off. The fire must have singed them."

"The fire was that bad—that hot?"

"It's too horrible to describe." She closed her eyes and covered her ears with both hands. "Like a furnace. Oh, the terror! The horror!"

After handing me Sonja's hat, Wally picked up a handful of pebbles and threw them as far as he could to the other side of the rural road.

Sonja sat rigid. Carefully, I placed the cap back on her head and slid closer. "Tell me about it—please."

She shrugged. "Where shall I begin?"

"With the sirens," I said. Since the day I first heard it what seemed an eternity ago, I hated that wailing sound.

In a voice barely audible, Sonja began. "When the pre-alarm sounded at seven, we headed down the street to our friend's apartment. The building had a cellar, ours didn't. Besides, they could afford to rent a space at the bunker to spend the nights. We couldn't. So the family owning the butcher shop allowed us to use their cellar space every night. 'You'll be safe there,' said Frau Mueller."

For a moment, Sonja's voice trailed off. "We knew the planes would find us eventually."

"What do you mean?"

"The British bombers were dropping leaflets every other night over the city. 'HEILBRONN IM LOCH, WIR FINDEN DICH DOCH !'."

I repeated the threat. "'HEILBRONN, THAT HOLE IN THE DELL, WHEN WE FIND IT YOU WILL BE HELL'!" They used to drop those awful threats over Frankfurt. It's scary."

Sonja nodded. "Ten minutes after we settled down for the night in the cellar, the barrage started. Right away, we heard the explosions above us. It was deafening. I was so scared, I was afraid to breathe. When the power went out, we sat in the darkness—until mother lit a candle.

"Then we saw something oozing through the cellar door. It glowed green." Sonja drew up her knees. "Slowly, the slime slithered down the stairs. It looked like a snake dragging along its babies, spreading out in all directions. Ellen clung to Mutter and whimpered. 'It's a monster viper.'"

It must've been terrifying, I thought. I remembered ten-year old Ellen to be the fearless tomboy of the neighborhood.

"Your brother backed away. 'It's phosphor,' he screamed. 'Let's get out of here.' But the green liquid suddenly burst into flames. There was fire everywhere. The cellar filled with smoke. 'Ach du lieber Himmel,' cried mother. She grabbed a bucket and poured water on the fire. It didn't help. It spread more. We tried smothering it with blankets, but it burnt holes in the cloth. 'Don't get any of the stuff on your hands,' warned Walter. 'It'll eat your flesh.'

"We're going to be burned alive," I cried. Sonja drew both knees to her chest.

I interrupted and showed my cousin the deep scars on my ankles. "Phosphor. It happened in Frankfurt and took forever to heal," I said.

Sonja put her feet back on the ground and looked at me. "Your brother knew what to do. 'Only sand or dirt will kill that phosphorous liquid,' he warned before he ran to the crawl space and kicked down the stacked-up bricks that covered the hole. 'Fire, fire,' Walter shouted into the cellar next to us. He first helped Ellen climb across, then heaved himself over the wall to the neighboring cellar.

"'Someone find the opening to the coal chute,' Walter screamed. There was much confusion inside. People cried and yelled, shoved and cowered—but the sound of the bombardment outside sounded even worse. In our part of the cellar, the fire started licking the bunk beds. Mother yanked a sheet and blanket from one of the bunks and pushed them down in a bucket filled with water. With wet covers clinging to our bodies, coughing and choking, we crawled through the hole into the next cellar."

I felt hypnotized, yet horrified.

From the back of the swing, I heard Wally's feet crunch the pebbles. "Go on," I urged Sonja.

"The smoke started pouring through the crawl space. 'Barricade the hole,' someone yelled.

"'There's no time,' screamed a soldier home on furlong. Having found the opening to the outside, he yelled, 'Raus, raus.'

"Walter and Ellen pushed through the narrow opening first. Then the man in uniform. From the outside, he pulled until everyone squeezed through the chute. 'Run to the bunker at the Suelmer Tor,' he ordered. 'Run, run.'"

Sonja shuddered, crossed her arms and tightly clasped her shoulders to stop her trembling. Her eyes reflecting the memory glowed with fright. "I started to run, but stopped when I heard a crash behind me. Another floor of the house collapsed. There was phosphor all over the street. Fire sparks crackled in the air. Flames everywhere. I pulled the sheet tighter and ran as though the devil were chasing me."

"And all around you," I asked, "the bombs kept falling?"

"Yes, and the bunker was across the railroad tracks. Another bomb exploded. In all the chaos, I'd lost sight of mother. 'Mutter, Mutter,' I yelled.

"She heard me and cried, 'Wo sind die Kinder?'

"Before I could answer that I hadn't seen Ellen and your brother, a land mine hit near the railroad track. The force of the air pressure knocked me to the ground." Sonja covered her ears. "I felt like a dot in the heart of hell."

I knew.

Some pebbles pinged on the pavement below us. Wally, I thought.

"Did your mother find Ellen and Walter?"

Sonja shook her head. "People were sprawled on the ground all around me. The mine blast had torn off our shoes and some of our clothes. The wet sheets were gone.

"I don't know how long we were there."

"When the bombing slowed, the person next to me—I think it was an old woman—got on her knees, raised her hands to heaven and whimpered, 'Gott im Himmel, hilf uns.'

The soldier across from me leaped from the ground. 'Woman, you better pray to the devil,' he scorned. 'God has forsaken us.' Shaking his fist at the roaring planes, he swore aloud. 'I'm going back to the front,' he yelled, 'where I can fight back and kill those bastards without mercy.' Falling on his knees, he bashed his head against the ground, his fists pounding the pavement."

I put my arm around Sonja's shoulder. Huddled together, I asked, "Did you find Walter and Ellen?"

"Ja. Like lost sheep, they sat huddled in the back of the bunker.

Relieved, I gave Sonja a squeeze.

"You should have seen that bunker! It was packed. They were pushing and shoving, standing all the way up the stairway to the entrance."

"Mother decided we had better get out."

"The four of us made it to the vineyards that lead to Wattberg—you know, that old medieval lookout tower high on the hill. For awhile, we rested, watching the inferno below. Others joined us." Sonja's voice grew faint again. "As far as the eye could see, an ocean of fire—heaving, hissing, spitting sparks.

"Mother worried that dive bombers might come and hunt us. To hide, we walked farther up the hill. Crouching next to a wall at the bend of the road, we shivered and waited. Were we the only survivors?

"The next day, we didn't know what to do or where to go. Below, the river was still aflame—phosphor floated atop it. The inferno churned and roared, the church rising out of the oceans of fire.

"Finally, we decided on a route to our grandparents in Boeckingen, hoping their house had been spared."

We sat silent, trying to digest the horrible catastrophe.

I wanted to touch my cousin, at least stroke what was left of her hair, tell her how sorry I am that her belongings are gone; but she seemed strangely transformed by the story, like a statue that stands sentinel in a garden of ash.

Frau Hofmann's mother suddenly called from the porch, returning us to the present. "Time for coffee and cake."

I stood up, but Sonja leaned into the back of the seat and gave it a couple more swings.

"Where is your brother?" I asked.

"Heinz?" Sonja jumped off and looked at Wally.

He had appeared out of nowhere. "Let's go," said the fourteen-year-old. His voice sounded harsh and raspy. For a moment, Wally looked forty, bending to scoop up a handful of pebbles. His jaw set, he scattered them against a barren tree.

"We never found them," said Sonja. "He and his friend, Dieter, planned to meet after work downtown at the movie house. But they must have perished somewhere in one of the air raid shelters—I don't want to think about how."

Heinz and Dieter dead? My talented cousin who drummed to the beat of jazz, and Dieter, his best buddy, squeezing the accordion while serenading me on warm summer nights. Buried under a pile of rubble? In disbelief, my teeth began to chatter.

Her eyes staring straight ahead, Sonja continued talking in that flat tone. "The first day, my little sister came with mother and me to the burning city. Ellen started to count the corpses that lay scattered in the smoldering debris. They looked like shrunken little logs with charred, shriveled, faces. Ellen thought they were dolls. When she spotted the first headless body, she started to scream—and didn't stop.

"We took her home, then returned the next day without her."

"The bodies, battered and bruised—some brutally disfigured, were laid in rows on the boulevard, waiting to be identified. One by one, we looked into the faces of dead women and children. Except for an occasional shriek of recognition, everyone remained silent—too pained, too shocked, to cry."

Slowly, Sonja and I walked back to the house. From the barnyard, came the ubiquitous cluck of chickens, quack of ducks, and grunt of a pig. We watched as Wally fed the geese, ducks, and chickens, and the birds peck hungrily at Wally's feet.

Sonja whispered, "Poor Wally. He was drafted to dig out the bodies from the rubble. There were thousands."

My heel crunched gravel as I spun and faced Sonja. "Did I hear right? Did you say bodies? Dig for bodies? I don't believe it!"

"Ask him yourself," said Sonja.

Anneliese's cousin, Sonja, and her husband, Wally, in their home in Anaheim, California, gave details of this and the next chapter forty years later.

CHAPTER TWENTY-SEVEN—Wally's Story—December 1944

After cookies and hot tea, the three of us walked to my cold room upstairs. Sonja moved the only chair in front of Hitler's picture, while I sat wrapped in a rug, almost mesmerized by Wally's regular pacing. All through the afternoon Wally walked the room, limping a little, sometimes staring into space, other times animated, he talked and talked.

"For forty-five minutes I sat in the basement of the family home on Haselter road. The earth trembled under my feet and the house shook, like a giant with fever.

"'Oh Gott, oh my God,' I gasped, 'the end of the world has surely come.' My teeth chattered. Cold sweat soaked my pullover as I covered my ears to drown out the sounds.

"Suddenly, all was silent.

"I lowered my hands that still shook, and listened. No more explosions, no rumbles, no whistles. Nothing. I lifted my head and stared in disbelief. The walls were still standing. Even the jars on the shelves had settled to eerie quiet.

"'Upstairs!' My father's whisper had the harsh sound of a roar.

"I stole a glance at my two brothers, cowering in a corner of the basement. Kurt, the older, sat with clenched teeth, while the younger, Karlheinz, crouched with eyes wide open. No one moved—not even my mother and little sister. They're all scared to death, like me, I thought. Todesangst!

"I looked at my father, who was standing at the head of the stairway. In a high-pitched voice quivering with fear, I said, 'The ALL CLEAR hasn't sounded yet.'

"There it was! The monotone siren made the announcement. 'It's all over.'

"Everyone rushed up the stairs, the older boys taking two steps at a time.

"Running through the dark kitchen, I called, 'Where's the flashlight?'

"'Forget about light!' My father shouted.

"'Grosser Gott im Himmel!'" I stepped into the bright December night. Great God in heaven!' I gasped again. 'It's the fire of hell.'

"I stared, disbelieving, at the gigantic wall of fury that engulfed Heilbronn. For miles, wave after wave of flames leaped, twisted, ravaged and raged, until they crashed into a boiling sea of fire.

"Too scared to cry, too stunned to scream, I pulled off my sweater. The winter air had become hot and dry. Yet I shuddered. 'Zum Teufel!'

"'It's the work of Satan, all right,' yelled my father. He shook a fist at the red sky. 'It's hell here on earth!'

"Wringing her hands, my mother wailed. 'Otto and his wife are trapped in Heilbronn!'

"Frau Wolper, the neighbor, let out a scream. 'Dieter, too.' She fell to her knees and pointed to the burning city. 'My son's in there. With Eisenkraemer's Heinz. At the movie palace.'

"'My Liesele,' cried a mother. 'She lives downtown with my grandchildren. Ach Du Lieber! My Enkele.'

"'My Heinz! My Hedwig!' Frau Eisenkraemer, Anneliese's and Sonja's grandmother, collapsed next to Dieter's mother.

"Everyone ran up and down the road. They pointed, sobbed, screamed, and shouted. Some prayed, others cursed. An old lady whimpered, 'God have mercy on their souls.'

"Kurt tugged my sleeve. 'We must find Otto.'

"Not realizing the danger of our decision, we grabbed our bicycles and raced across the railroad tracks, down the long road past the Gasthaus, the baker, the butcher, the minister's home.

"We didn't talk. While courage spurred on my older brother, fear pushed me. 'I'm going to slay that fire-spewing dragon,' Kurt's burning eyes seemed to say.

"'Oh Gott, oh Gott! Mir ist Angst!' I was scared.

"Pedaling hard, we approached the burning city.

"'There's so much smoke,' I said. I slowed the wheels to a coast and wiped my tears on my shirt sleeve. 'Let's stop a minute.' I breathed hard and coughed as sizzling air ripped into my lungs.

"A fire engine tried to maneuver around some fallen debris. Against the wall of flames a mile away, it looked like an ant.

"'What's the best route to Suedstrasse?' Kurt got off his bike and helped the fire fighter clear the street.

"'Go back, boys!' yelled the captain, standing on top of the truck. 'You can't make it across the Neckar. The river has turned into a stream of burning phosphor.'

"'He's right,' I grimaced with fear. 'Let's turn back. It's too dangerous.'

"Kurt punched my shoulder. 'Let's kill that dragon,' he yelled. 'Don't be an Angsthase!'

"'I'm not a scared rabbit,' I snapped—as I soiled my pants. Pushing my bike while running past the railroad station, I screamed with my brother. 'Die, dragon, die! Die, dragon, die!'

"Sweating and coughing, we reached the river. The captain was right, the Neckar was aflame. Across it, the inferno roared and spewed like a million drunken dragons.

"Horrified, Kurt shook his head. 'Let's turn back. We can do nothing.' Searing winds whipped through our short hair. He was now afraid. For some reason, Kurt's fear showed me how important our mission truly was.

"Hiding my own alarm, I tried to shield my face from the inferno that grew more monstrous with each second. 'We must go on! Somehow! Is there another way?'

"Fire engulfed the bridges that once spanned the sixty-meter width.

"'Look' I pointed south. 'There's an opening near the ferry boat. We can swim. Hurry!'

"We dumped our bikes, ran to the spot—and jumped.

"The icy water soothed our hot skin. At first, we just splashed around, caught our breath and sized up the situation, then, with powerful strokes we swam toward the opposite shore.

"'Watch out!' shouted Kurt.

"Fighting a sudden swell of water, I glanced upstream and saw the burning mass pushing closer. Hot wind seared my face.

"'Downstream. That way!' Kurt yelled.

"I turned, dived under water, and came up beside Kurt. Silently we raced—not against each other as usual—but raced for our lives.

"Exhausted and cold, we climbed up the river bank.

"Above, a tremendous wave of heat tried to steal our breath. Devouring oxygen, the blazing mass roared down the narrow streets that formed a hellish tunnel.

"'Suedstrasse.' Kurt pointed in the other direction toward South Street.

"Turning away from the sizzling fireball, we sprinted toward the home of our oldest brother. The streets were deserted. Several houses, including the one opposite Otto's were burning. Then we spotted him atop a ladder screaming orders to a fire brigade.

"'Otto!' We cupped hands around our mouths and shouted. 'We made it!'

"'Give us a hand!' yelled Otto. 'Throw dirt on the fire.'

"'Where's a shovel?'

"'Use your hands!' Even with one arm crippled by polio, Otto worked furiously. He acquired his strength from working for Organisation Todt, the battalions that built autobahns before the war, bunkers and military fortifications later.

"For the next few hours, with Otto in command, we fought until the last flicker smothered in the dust. The two top floors of the house collapsed, but we did save the apartments on the bottom of the house.

"'Good job!' Otto smacked Kurt across the shoulder, then ruffled my hair. 'Let's go and have a beer.' Drained of energy, we trudged across the street. We didn't have to open a door or window. All of them had been blown out by the explosions of the bombs.

"Otto kicked aside the glass shards and debris, half-filled a couple of mugs for us, then finished the bottle with a long swig. 'You can bunk on the couch for the rest of the night.' He looked northward out the gaping door where he could see the inferno that had been his city. "How's everyone in Boeckingen?'

"'Mother is worried about you,' I told Otto. 'We have to get back soon and tell her you're alive.'

"'First you both need sleep,' said Otto. 'You have a lot of work ahead of you.' Scratching his head, he walked to the kitchen for another beer. 'Our Gauleiter, that big Nazi pig in charge of this area, informed me all boys between fourteen and sixteen must report at the Bauhof § early tomorrow.' Otto rubbed his lame arm. 'It's the place near the ferry.'

"'What will we have to do?' I asked.

"Through clenched teeth, Otto said, 'Find bodies and bury them.' His jaw set, he added, 'There's no one left to do it. They've drafted the sixteen-year olds for combat.'

"' The bodies?' Kurt's voice was raspy from smoke. 'You mean we must dig out the survivors.'

"Otto shook his head and looked at the fire storm that engulfed the city. 'Not a mouse will wiggle in that furnace—much less a single human being.' Beads of perspiration covered his forehead. With a rag, he blotted the sweat from his face. 'Expect the worst.'

"For three weeks, we slaved under the command of men wearing arm bands that identified them as members of the Volkssturm, a people's storm brigade for men over sixty. We received no food or water because there was none. Every hour or so, a bottle of Schnapps was passed around—not to quench our thirst, but to blur our minds. When it was too dark to work any longer, we staggered home in a drunken stupor.

"To cool the recurring fires, we shoveled dirt on the smoldering piles of rubble that sealed the doors to shelters and cellars.

"The hardest task was to find the exits. Phosphorous bombs, which burst and glowed green, had emptied themselves along walls and streets in rivers of unquenchable flame that turned the city into a giant crematorium. Carbon-monoxide seeped into cellars and quietly paralyzed and killed those who took refuge from the fire storm outside.

"Two to three meters high debris covered the residential section downtown. Kurt and I dug with shovels and bare hands. Determined, we looked for clues while digging. Where were the streets located? What were their names? House numbers? Who were those corpses—or what is left of them?

"'Thirsty, boys?' The man with the arm band passed around another bottle. This time it was wine. Without waiting for an answer, he coaxed and cajoled. "Drink up, boys! It dulls your senses!' He took himself a long swallow. 'Dig, boys, keep digging. They're roasting down below.'

"The humor of the gallows, or Galgenhumor, as the Germans called it, thrived at the rubble site.

"My shovel hit something hard. I scraped away the dirt and discovered a step, then another, and another, 'It's a staircase,' I yelled. 'It must be a cellar!'

"'We need a pick axe,' Kurt called to the old man supervising.

"Furiously, we dug and scraped until a narrow tunnel led to a cellar.

"Kurt was the first to put his head over the opening. 'Hallo! Anybody down there?'

"No answer.

"Each boy took a turn yelling into the abyss.

"No answer.

"The boss came running with a rope. 'One of you must go down there to count the bodies. Who volunteers?'

"'I'll get stuck in that hole,' said Kurt.

"'Me, too.' I squatted on the ground.

"Grabbing Fritz, the youngest and smallest of the lot, the man with the arm band tied the rope around the boy, then gave him a flashlight and another swig of wine. 'Everyone hold onto the rope,' the old man yelled. 'Kurt, go up front. You're the strongest.'

"Slowly, little Fritz descended. The rope slid through the hands of the boys above—then stopped.

"'Fritzle, what do you see?' The boss knelt next to the hole, twisting the rope around his hand.

"A muffled voice was heard, but the words were unintelligible. The rope tugged twice, the code to bring him up.

"The mouth of the hole crumbled just as Fritz climbed out. Tossing a black leather purse to the old man, he said, 'That's all I found. Lots of broken glass all over the shelves and floor. The canned fruits and vegetables must've exploded.' He sat on the ground and inspected his bloody hands.

"Pulling slivers of glass out off the boy's hand, the boss asked, 'Did you see a crawl hole, Fritzle?'

"Fritz nodded, then yelled, 'Ouch!'

"'Which side?'

"'I don't know. It was dark down there. And the stench!' He pinched his nose.

"We dug, scratched, and picked with the axe, until we uncovered another entrance.

"Again Fritz was lowered with the rope.

"Empty. Another crawl space. 'Was it to the right or left? Front or behind?'

"Every time a hole opened up, a small crowd gathered. When no bodies were found, the survivors walked away with heads hung low.

"Then, on the fourth try, Fritz had barely completed his descent, the rope tugged twice. We pulled him up.

"Gagging, he dragged himself out. Then he retched.

"The old man fetched the bottle and with Schnapps and washed away the vomit from Fritz's face. 'What's down there?'

"'Ghosts,' said Fritz. "Hundreds.'

"They enlarged the opening. 'Drink, boy,' said the man and after taking a gigantic gulp himself, handed me the bottle. 'We'll go down with you.'

"'Gott im Himmel!' I said. Covering my face, I turned away. 'Heavenly Father' The sight was too horrible.

"In the corner of the cellar, we saw bloated bodies piled in heaps, tongues protruded from open mouths, lifeless eyes bulged from faces that had been scratched, contorted in agony.

"'Boy!' The man's voice was low, gruff. 'Help me tie the rope around this body so we can pull it out.' He lifted a little girl from the floor.

"'You'll hurt her,' I cried.

"'She's dead.' His voice was harsh and final.

"Dead. Sweat trickled from my brow as I pulled the rope under the small, twisted body. She was about the size of my little sister. The only dead person I'd ever seen was my grandma lying in an open casket—the old face so peaceful. Eyes closed in sleep.

"We pulled out body after body, and spread them in rows on the ground. Here and there someone recognized a corpse and pinned a note with the name on singed, tattered clothes. The living cried out in agony. Some cursed with anger, shaking their fist at the sky. A few stood and stared, shoulders slouched, before shuffling away in resignation.

"Soldiers were identified by the tags around their necks. The rest were listed by the address where they were found or just the area of the city. In front of one house a washtub held bones and pieces of clothing marked, 'Remains of Monkstreet Community.'

"People stumbled about, trying to claim their dead. Most corpses could not be identified. No hands, no legs, sometimes no heads. Many were burned black and shrunken to the size of little wooden dolls—like mummies. For days, the city resembled a morgue.

"Sonja and her mother walked up and down the rows of bodies. None resembled Heinz—or Dieter.

"Early that evening, we lifted the corpses onto trailers. A farm truck pulled the load up a hill, where an earth mover with a strong blade had already dug a hole—a cavity large enough to hold a thousand bodies. We took another swig from the bottle our boss passed around and unloaded the trailer. One by one, we lowered the dead into the mass grave.

"The first time I watched white powder being spread over the bodies, I cried.

"'The lime accelerates decomposition, preventing rot and stink,' explained the man.

"Very soon, the task of uncovering and burying bodies became as impersonal as the wanton killings by the bombs.

"Day by day, the process was repeated. More mass graves were dug, more bodies dumped, more lime spread. Men with the letters KZ stenciled on their prison garb helped carry the dead. By the end of the third week, the pungent stench of death became unbearable. Steel teeth crunched into the rubble, dumping bodies and dirt into the cavities called graves."

Wally faced the window where the moon that had hung in the starless sky as though waiting for the end of the tale of horror was now covered by a sinister cloud. Tears streamed down my cheeks. King of night, have you deserted us too?

A soft knock on the bedroom door pulled us back from hell. "Time to leave," called Lina.

My feet felt like bags of sand as I walked my family to the train station.

"You're better off spending Christmas in Brackenheim," said Auntie. "Heilbronn is doomed." Hunting for change to buy a ticket, she lifted a ring of keys from her purse; they clanged together, mournful as temple bells. Lina paused as if searching for words. "Study your catechism," she said, her eyes clouding with tears.

I nodded. Are the teachings of Jesus the answer?

Wally shook my hand. Sonja wept. Auntie's hug seemed to last forever. They boarded the train.

"See you for confirmation at Easter." I waved until the train disappeared from sight.

Twilight faded into night, and it had grown dark by the time I climbed the stone steps to the big house on the hill. A cold wind blew and snowflakes began to fall.

I tiptoed to my room upstairs and stood by the window where I could watch the white crystals dance in the dark. I thought of Wally's ordeal, Sonja's terror. Lieber Gott, warum? Dear God, why?

Long ago, I had learned to safely cage all emotions. I felt no anger, no joy of being alive; only resignation. I was convinced that for whatever reason, the bombs eventually would destroy us all.

When I was a child, Mamma told me that God is all knowing. He sees and hears everything. Even when you stick your wet finger in the sugar bowl and then lick it. Or kick the cat.

God must be mad. Or perhaps, I reasoned, perhaps God knows something about us Germans to justify why they must perish from the earth.

The window shutter tore from its latch and rattled in the wind. Wiping the delicately draped patterns of white fern from the window, I looked outside again. Through the raging snowflakes, I could see, far, far below the steps leading to the gazebo and the stone urns, tiny now and mounded high with snow—like ice cream cones.

I closed my eyes. Instead of the cold beauty of nature, I saw the synagogue ablaze in Frankfurt and heard the woman say, "Some day God is going to punish us for burning His house."

It seemed so long ago.

CHAPTER TWENTY-EIGHT—Beginning of 1945

It was the sixth year the midnight bells did not ring in peace. From all directions Allied forces now pushed across German soil toward Berlin.

Early dawn revealed a radiant sky that prompted Frau Hofmann to exclaim, "I hope the auroral brilliance of the first day of the new year is an omen that better days lie ahead." Even as a twelve-year-old, I could appreciate the poetry of the words uttered by my usually formal and reserved employer.

After breakfast, Frau Hofmann suggested that I take the afternoon off and go sledding with the children. It sounded delightful. Yet I was afraid, for I'd never ridden on a sled before. I remembered slipping and sliding in my new boots on ice-covered sidewalks in Frankfurt. At the school yard, we'd compete for the longest, fastest ice slide. But once I fell and everyone laughed—even Hannelore. It seemed so long ago.

Looking at the stack of dirty dishes, I asked, "What about the kitchen?" Preparation of the roasted duck had left grease all over the stove, and pots and pans were stacked high in the sink.

"Don't worry about the cleanup," said Frau Hofmann's mother in a matter-of-fact tone of voice. "I'll take care of the kitchen. You go and have fun playing."

Playing! I'd forgotten what it was like.

Wearing warm sweaters and mittens, Anton and Guthrun noisily entered the kitchen to get to the back porch where the sled was stored. "We're going to the slope on the other side of the village," said Anton.

"Oh," I said, "that hill is steep." My heart raced.

Anton, who had turned nine a month ago, laughed. "It's just a little bump, Anneliese. Hurry up! The snow is packed tight for sledding. You'll love it!"

Holding onto Granny's hand, little Rolfi stood in the doorway, his face barely visible under the woolen cap and scarf. "Please come," he begged, tugging me toward the back door. His sad, brown eyes and sweet smile always did make my heart melt.

The sun was warm and its reflection made me squint. Heading for the hill, we took turns pulling Rolfi on the sled. Squeals and laughter got louder as we approached the slope. Suddenly, we were bombarded with snowballs by boys and girls. It didn't take us long to retaliate, and soon a friendly fight with the wet white powder was in progress.

The slope was steeper than I'd imagined. Holding onto Rolfi's hand, I told Anton and Guthrun, "You two go first. I'll give your sled a push."

Down the hill they went, shrieking with joy, maneuvering their sled over humps and bumps, racing toward the bottom where they skidded into a pile of snow.

Rolfie jumped up and down in excitement, yelling, "Schneller ! Faster!" while I shouted, "Langsam ! Slow down!"

Anton jumped off. "Your turn, Anneliese!"

"Me next! Me next!" cried Rolfie.

I sat on the back of the sled, put the little one between his brother and me, and down the hill we sped: squealing, laughing, shouting. Braking near the bottom, we, too, tumbled into a snow bank.

"Go again!" cried Rolfie as his sister took my place.

It was the most exuberant New Year's day I had ever experienced. Happy and gay, I felt like a child. From the high hill, I looked down at the peaceful countryside. War? That's a game grownups play.

My mind changed quickly when a boy in uniform pushed a leaflet into my hand.

Startled, I said, "What's that?"

"It's an invitation to view a movie at the school auditorium," said the soldier puppet. Clicking his heels, he turned and left me staring at the paper.

Anton came up the slope. "I got one, also," he said, pulling a crumpled piece of paper out of his pocket.

"Me too." Guthrun's paper was neatly folded. "When is it?"

"Next Saturday," shouted the boy over his shoulder. His voice turned officious. "Attendance is mandatory. It's all about the youth of Amerika!"

The children became excited. "Amerika!" shouted some. "A movie!" exclaimed others. Since there was no cinema in the village, rarely did any of us have the opportunity to see a film.

After we returned home, I asked Frau Hofmann about the movie. What shall I do? It conflicts with my catechism lesson.

"You must forfeit your class," said Herr Hofmann and sighed his disapproval. "I saw the documentary at the plant in Wilhelmsburg. It's a behind-the-scene look at life in America—propaganda kitsch, and we are all compelled to see it. Or no ration cards."

The following Saturday, we sat with the farm folks shivering on the benches inside the gymnasium, waiting for the movie to begin. While the operator behind the projector fidgeted with the knobs to center the picture on the portable screen, cold feet scuffed and scraped the ground.

"Ruhe!" commanded a voice from the crowd. All eyes concentrated on the white background of the screen. Someone had demanded silence and we obeyed.

An image of Hitler Youth marched across the screen. "Discipline!" The commentator didn't have to explain the goose step.

"Heil Hitler!" shouted some of the spectators.

The picture changed. "American Youth," said the caption. Sitting on top of bar stools and slouched into armchairs with feet propped on coffee tables, they looked like wimps and streetwalkers in their frilly clothes and exaggerated hair-do's. Cigarettes dangled from brightly painted lips, a haze of smoke veiled seductive eyes—and jazz blared.

Disapproving whistles, heckling, and laughter darted through the audience.

I felt confused. How did these limp youths ever learn to fly airplanes? Fight wars? Make bombs? Why were we worried about the Americans?

Switching to German youth, the screen showed them apprenticing in crafts and trades, toiling the earth, training to become soldiers, to handle weapons and man tanks and cannons.

"Jawohl." A few in the gym nodded self-righteously to each other.

Granny, sitting next to me, grumbled, "Kanonenfutter! Cannonfodder!"

"Chicago." The camera focused on dilapidated neighborhoods. "Ghettos," shouted the announcer. "Nothing but fights and brawls." On screen, drunks staggered.

Evil-looking men beat workers. "Breeding ground of hoodlums," said the commentator, his scowl evident. Police, armed with guns, pistol-whipped a citizen. There was shooting in the streets. "Brutality," interjected the perfectionist. We saw people knifed and shot in alleys. "Gangsters do this," was what the man said.

"Pfui!" jeered the crowd watching the film.

Looking around me, I thought, these farm people haven't heard of the misery and violence in our cities. Nothing much had changed here. They were so lucky. All they know is how to deal with the elements that adversely affect their crops: floods, drought, lightning, hail.

Before the war, I dodged drunks on Saturday night; stepped across puke and used condoms on sidewalks Sunday mornings; avoided boys carrying sticks and clubs during the week.

After the war started, the street gangs disappeared, but a new type of violence erupted. I'll never forget Crystal Night: the synagogue burning, food trampled in shops, display windows of stores smashed, the storm trooper's boots kicking David. I wondered. David…Where was he?

The black and white film switched to portraying typical German youths. Superior. Girls in glowing blond braids, boys with broad shoulders and fair skin. Aryan.

"Ja, Ja,." The girls pulled at their tresses, the boys sat straight and proud, as I hid a wisp of straggly brown hair under my scarf.

"Look!" The room turned silent. On the screen appeared people of different shades of brown and black. Their lips were thick, and dark curls covered their heads.

Mulattoes. "Rassenschande!" White people joined the crowd of non-whites. A fight started. Fists, clubs, knives, and guns. Who was killing whom? It was hard to tell. The violence was terrifying.

Voicing disapproval of what was happening on the screen, a boy put two fingers in his mouth, making a harsh whistling sound.

I had never seen a black or brown person, except in paintings. Once I had a little black doll about a foot tall who had an innocent smile on her sweet face. She used to live in Afrika, I was told.

But the dark people on the screen did not smile. Were they the ones doing the fighting from the planes? They look scary enough, I thought.

The movie ended the way it had begun. Hitler Youth marching to the sound of drums. The Master Race!

Disappointed, I sat, waiting for the auditorium to clear. What did I expect? A love story? Yes. Even a good patriotic war story had a plot I could understand. I felt cheated.

Someone tapped me on the shoulder. "Frau Hofmann gave permission to make up the Catechism lesson this afternoon."

Startled, I confessed to the man dressed in dark clothes, "I have no book, Herr Pastor."

Handing me a copy of The New Testament, he said, "Its pages are tattered, the teachings are nearly two thousand years old, but the message holds true!" Patiently, he waited for the crowd to clear the auditorium until only a small flock was left behind. Lowering his serious eyes, he opened the Bible and began to read.

What was the message? I tried to comprehend.

The epistle from the New Testament was as clear and terrible as the trumpet of the Judgment Day. "Gerechter Gott, vor Dein Gericht, Muss alle Welt sich stellen."

I repeated the words often. "Great and just God, the whole world must be judged by You."

Time passed quickly now. Spring thaws replaced the icy winter that had settled on the landscape, but the war continued. After more than five years of fighting in foreign countries, German soldiers fought on German soil. Here and there, while dusting upstairs, I caught bits of news from the radio— American troops had crossed the Rhine at Remagen, and also somewhere near Mainz. That's getting close to Frankfurt, I thought. Anxiously I quizzed Herr Hofmann. "Did I get a letter? A telephone call?

He shook his head and mumbled something about the communication network falling apart.

Once, I glimpsed a headline from the newspaper uncle was reading. The Soviet army thrust into Silesia and East Prussia.

"Germany is beginning to feel the dreaded bear-hug of the Russian Armies," said Herr Hofmann. "It's crushing all resistance."

In February, I overheard Herr Hofmann tell his wife of the fire bombing in Dresden. "More than a hundred times as many dead as Heilbronn," he said. "The city was overflowing with civilian refugees fleeing from the Russians. It must've been a slaughterhouse!"

"When will it all end?" I sighed, weary and discouraged.

Early in March, Allied bombers began four days of raids over Germany. In mid-March British bombers staged a heavy attack on Stuttgart, a short distance from our village.

"Hitler promises the miracle bomb will be ready to retaliate any day now." Herr Hofmann didn't sound convincing.

"I don't believe in the Fuehrer's infamous propaganda campaign any more," said his wife.

"Me, either," her husband replied. Herr Hofmann paced the floor. "At the factory, the Russian laborers are getting restless. They talked about going home. Tatiana is the instigator of the unrest. I don't trust her."

"Neither do I. When she cleans, she looks haughty and hateful." Frau Hofmann poured her husband another cup of ersatz coffee. "She's a good worker, but I preferred Olga."

"Olga became too friendly with Anneliese. Uncle reported it to the authorities. They want to transfer the Russian laborer to a concentration camp." He finished his coffee with a slurp. "I'm doing all I can to keep her on at the factory."

I had wondered why Olga stayed away. I missed her voice and especially liked hearing her call me Sistra. Tatiana never talked. Just stared with hate and vengeance.

It was late March. The snow had melted, farmers started to plow the fields, and birds began to build nests. One day, Frau Hofmann and I walked along the road to the next village to buy fresh meat for Sunday dinner.

Suddenly, she stopped. "Listen!"

I did. "Chop, chop, chop," is all I heard. It's too loud for a woodpecker, I thought, and listened again. Voices! Men's voices. Commands! Soldiers!

We stepped over the rail on the side of the road and ventured into the woods. "Crash!" A tree fell five meters from where we were standing. Then another.

Frau Hofmann let out a scream.

I froze.

"Was ist los?" A corporal, short and stocky, emerged from the forest.

"What's going on? Why are you doing this?" Frau Hofmann appeared shocked by what she saw.

"We must erect barricades on the roads," was the answer.

"For what?"

"Tanks."

"Whose tanks?"

"Americans!"

Another tree fell. The corporal called to his men. "Aufladen!" They loaded their army truck with the felled tree trunks and sped away.

"Let's hurry home," said Frau Hofmann, "I must talk with my husband. The Allies must be closer than the war news tell us." She rushed as though battalions were after her.

When we passed the farm house just below the Hofmann residence, the French prisoner-of-war stood in front. "Bon jour, Madame. Bon jour, Mademoiselle." He lifted his cap and bowed. In the sky, planes approached.

We looked up.

Pointing to the dive bombers, the Frenchman said, "Freunde, American friends!" He winked at me, then grinned forebodingly at Frau Hofmann.

"Let's go," she said, looking straight ahead. "I don't trust him." A gust of wind tore at her skirt.

"Bon Ami," he chanted after us. I shuddered, as we hurried along. God help us all, I thought, not knowing what to expect.

On Good Friday, I was to take the train to my grandmother's house in Heilbronn-Boeckingen and make my confirmation Easter Sunday.

When we reached home, Frau Hofmann led me to the front room where her husband was already seated. "Anneliese, please sit down," she said. "Let's have a talk."

My heart started to pound. They won't let me go home, I thought. Suddenly, I wanted to be with my family, no matter what. I sat on the edge of the chair.

She smiled and handed me a piece of paper. "Relax. The pastor sent this certificate of completion to give to you. You passed the examination and are ready to confirm your belief in Christianity."

A sigh of relief swept through me. "Thank you. I can hardly wait to see my family again. My Mamma wrote that she and Walter would try to get a train out of Frankfurt to attend the Confirmation."

Frau Hofmann clasped one of my hands between hers. "The Americans have occupied Frankfurt. There was no fighting." Looking at her husband, she hesitated before continuing. "Your mother and brother may not have been able to get out of the city in time."

Fear gripped me. "How close are the enemy troops to Brackenheim?"

"Too close." Herr Hofmann's voice was curt. "We're still waiting for the wonder weapon."

I nodded. Whatever that was, I thought.

Frau Hofmann said, "We talked it over with the Pastor. We all feel it's safer for you to walk to Heilbronn instead of taking the train. The Bummelzug moves too slowly and is a sure target. Only yesterday, dive bombers disabled one of their engines."

I want to be with my family, I thought. But what if I get lost?

"It's about a fifteen kilometer hike from here to Heilbronn on the main road," said Herr Hofmann.

The need to go home overrode my anxieties. I must trust the grownups judgment, must not disappoint their belief that I will succeed. It will be an adventure, I thought. Again, I nodded. "I'll leave early."

"Yes," he agreed. "Start right after dawn breaks. It will be before sunrise and cold, but if you walk fast…"

CHAPTER TWENTY-NINE—Good Friday

I took my red coat from the rack in the hallway, but Frau Hofmann stopped me. "You better leave that here until you return next week," she advised. "That bright color will make you a sure target for the JABOs. Those savage dive bombers are everywhere."

Reluctantly, I draped my most prized possession across the chair. The thought of being shot at by JABOs while walking on the highway filled me with terror.

Frau Hofmann untied my Rucksack and placed a tin container on top of sandwiches, hard-boiled eggs and apples. "I baked this Bundt cake last night for your family to enjoy on Easter after your confirmation."

"Thank you," I said, and anxiously hurried outside.

She accompanied me to the bottom of the steep flight of stone steps. "Walk fast and steady," she said. "Recite your favorite poems or sing a song. Singing out loud makes the legs step faster and scares the ghosts away." Slipping a copy of The New Testament in the outside pocket of the Rucksack, she gave me a hug and whispered, "God is with you, child."

"Thanks," I said again and, with feelings of confidence and exhilaration, started the ten-mile trip to the house of my grandparents outside Heilbronn.

It was long before sunrise—even the rooster had not yet announced the day. Walking briskly, I watched the stars fade into the pink light of early morning. Dawn broke over the countryside, and here and there, I could see the outline of a farm house. Slowly, the new day emerged. Good Friday.

My thoughts wandered to my grandparents' home. Who all was living there now? Where would I sleep: Upstairs? Downstairs? Would I have to share a bed with Aunt Erika again. She's so small. Last time we compared our heights, I was a head taller than she.

Chilled by the brisk March breeze, I tried buttoning my cardigan, but it wouldn't stretch across my chest. All of my clothes seemed to have shrunk— or was I budding out and becoming a woman?

What would I wear to the church services on my confirmation? It was customary to attend the ceremony in a solemn-colored dress, black or navy blue. I had none. Even if we had time to shop, the stores in Heilbronn, according to my aunt, were all burned to the ground. Perhaps I can borrow a dark dress from one of my aunts?

Passing a row of trees, I heard a multitude of birds chirp and twitter. Were they protecting their nests or greeting the new day?

In the distance a church steeple appeared. I wondered where the confirmation ceremony would be held and if Frau Burkhardt would be the pastor. I'd love seeing her again.

Treading along the well-worn furrows of the country road, I passed a farmer on his ox-drawn wagon.

"Gruess Gott! How far to the asphalt road?"

"Gruess Gott!" *It was a woman's voice that answered. "Half an hour, Kind, if you walk fast. It's straight ahead. You can't miss it."

"Thanks a lot," I said and gave her a quick smile. She must not have a farm hand, I thought, watching her prod the beast with a stick.

In the dim, early morning light, I looked down the bumpy dirt road, trying to see the highway. All I saw were trees with fields behind them. Quickening the pace, my thoughts returned to my family.

Had my mother and brother gotten out of Frankfurt in time? I could not comprehend Frankfurt being occupied by the enemy. Only a month ago, Mamma wrote their home in the basement under their former residence was bombed again, this time in the middle of the day. A direct hit on the cellar left nothing but a big hole in the ground, destroying their make-shift shelter and the meager belongings they had accumulated. Luckily, Mamma and Pappa were away working, Walter scavenging fire wood, and Paula clearing rubble from the streets.

"The housing authorities assigned us a furnished apartment," Mamma wrote. "It's at the north end of the city in a nice neighborhood with little war damage. I was told that to escape the bombing, the owners had vacated the flat and gone to live with relatives in the country."

I wanted to believe Mamma and Walter had left Frankfurt before the American troops arrived, but if there had been shooting, how would they have gotten away? Trains? Too dangerous! Perhaps they walked, like me. I calculated the distance and hours from Frankfurt to Heilbronn and wondered if they could have hiked a hundred miles in five days.

The sky was getting lighter. Was that the end of the dirt road? I climbed atop a boulder. Yes! The wide, paved street was clearly visible.

As I turned east onto the Landstrasse, the countryside around me blazed with the brilliance of the sun rising over the horizon. It reminded me of a song we sang while hiking in the Alps, and I started to sing. The lyrics described the early morning hour—the sun and wind tearing down the worries of night, larks praising the newborn day.

Over and over I repeated the verses. Happy to be going home, I stepped out to the beat of the melody, the knapsack bouncing on my back. Suddenly, I heard a piercing sound from above. I stopped.

Howling like Valkyries on a rampage, silver dots came screaming from the sky. One of them came closer, closer, closer—until I could see a man behind the plexiglass of the plane's cockpit.

JABOs!

I jumped toward a clump of bushes to hide.

Sprawled face down in the shrubs, hardly breathing, I heard the yak-yak of machine guns and felt a sharp pain in the back of my head. I knew I'd been hit by a bullet. I couldn't move. I could hardly breathe. In front of my face lay a dead mouse.

I'm dead. Mausetot. Just like you. Did I see it twitch?

More noise from above. Was it more JABOs? Again? Trembling, I listened to the warble and twitter. Angels! No. It's birds chirping! I squeezed one hand—it moved. I tried the other—the same. I wiggled my toes—and sat up. I'm alive! In astonishment, I rubbed the sand out of my eyes, spit out the dirt, and wiped my nose. Touching my head in the back, I felt a lump. The pelt must have been from a bouncing stone hit by a bullet.

"I'm not dead!" First, I whispered the words in disbelief, then shouted with joy, and finally, I screamed in defiance to the silver dots now high in the sky, "You missed me! You damn JABOs! I'm alive. Alive!"

I struggled to my feet and almost stepped on a small flower. Seeing the beauty of its delicate petals quivering helplessly on its short stem evoked a gush of tears. Sobbing, I packed damp earth around the little Crocus until it stood secure, its face fearlessly reaching for the sky. It will survive, I thought.

With my handkerchief, I brushed the dirt off my dress and stockings. Checking for JABOs, I continued on down the Landstrasse.

That face in the cockpit—I couldn't erase its image from my mind. It looked fierce and determined—much like the pilot in the movie STUKAs I had seen several years ago. Karl Raddatz was the handsome hero whose plane streaked and plummeted through the skies after American bombers—like a falcon after field mice.

221

I'm not a mouse, I thought. I'm a girl. And that JABO was more than a machine. The pilot didn't know me and I didn't know him. I'd never done anything to him. Why was he after me? Because I was German? Angry thoughts made me walk faster. He was not going to get me!

By the time the sun stood high, I had been chased twice more by the tyrants from the sky. Tired and hungry, I decided to stop for lunch under the next tree.

To my surprise, two young boys in uniform greeted me. It was not the standard gray army issue, but the brown one worn by Hitler Youth. They leaned against a tree trunk. Neither had a gun or rifle, but both carried metal projectiles. Huge ones!

"It's a Panzerfaustkanone, said one of the boys.

"The newest weapon to destroy tanks," explained the other. "It's called an Iron Fist and you hurl it against the tank. BANG!"

Curious, yet cautious, I stepped closer. "I saw one of those on a newsreel. They were using it on the Russian front—or was it Africa? BANG! In the film, the enemy tank exploded into a thousand pieces!" Will it do that just like in the movie?

I looked toward the street. "Where are the tanks?"

"Not far," said the shorter boy. Bright blue eyes barely showed under his too large steel helmet. His uniform was rumpled and dirty, but he did have a nice smile.

The other lad looked worried. He was tall and thin, with unkempt hair. His dark eyes darted to the sky, then up the street. "We think the Americans are about twenty-five kilometers in that direction." He pointed to where I came from.

An open truck, loaded with somber-faced soldiers, rumbled past, heading west, opposite from my direction.

The shorter boy shifted the weapon to his other shoulder. "Where're you heading?" he asked me.

"Heilbronn." I slipped the Rucksack off my back. "I'm tired." I sat down and untied my shoes. "I've walked for hours." Lifting the tin container out of the backpack, I mumbled, "Hope the sandwiches didn't get smashed. I'm hungry."

"Me, too," said the lad with the smile.

"We haven't eaten since noon yesterday," said the tall, lanky one. "All the field kitchen had to offer was a slice of black bread and a helmet of watery pea soup." With the tip of his toe, he lifted his steel helmet from the ground. His civilian shoes were laced with knotted twine.

I could almost hear their stomachs growl. "Here." I handed each one half of a sandwich and kept the other for myself.

"Thanks." They placed their weapons on the ground.

"My name's Wolfgang." The short one extended his hand.

"Alfred," said the other, wolfing down the sandwich.

"Anneliese." I shook hands, then looked at the eggs in the open Rucksack. "One for each," I said.

"Where is yours?" Alfred was already peeling his.

"I have an apple."

Silently, we munched, watching another military truck pass by.

"When will you get your army uniforms?" I asked.

Alfred shrugged. "Who knows? They don't have any our size, I guess."

"We've only been soldiers for two weeks," added Wolfgang. "Ja,. I was drafted on my sixteenth birthday."

"Me, too." Alfred kicked his heel into the ground. "I had an apprenticeship contract with a woodshop. The draft official waited at the shop and marched me directly to the barracks."

"Is that where you got your training?" I looked at the Iron Fist on the ground that was to destroy tanks.

"Some training!" He laughed. Alfred lifted the weapon with two hands and groaned. "Tell her, Wolf!"

"The sergeant must have read our minds. 'Anyone planning to desert will be executed. You understand?'"

The two boys clicked their heels and mocked, "Jawohl, Herr Feldwebel!"

"He took us to the woods." Wolfgang snapped a dead twig off a tree branch. "Three of our buddies dangled from ropes."

Alfred mocked the words of the sergeant. "We don't waste bullets on deserters!"

I shuddered. Wally's brother, Kurt will be sixteen in April. Slowly, I picked up the Rucksack and strapped it on my back. "What are you going to do when the tanks come?"

Wolfgang raised his hands above his head. "Haende hoch!"

"Surrender?"

He grinned. "I hear the Americans feed their prisoners well." His facial expression turned into a frown. "I don't know about the French or English."

The reality that the ground war was not far from where we stood began to sink in. I felt scared! Looking East, I asked, "How much farther to Heilbronn?"

"A few more hours," said Alfred. "If you walk fast, you'll make it by nightfall."

I looked at the sky. "The JABOs slow me down."

Hoisting the sizable weapon on his shoulders, Wolfgang sneered, "I hate those devils."

We shook hands and said "Auf Wiedersehen," and "Alles Gute," fully aware that "all might not be good" and in all likelihood, we'd never see each other again. Their bodies bent under the load of their weapons, they trudged west to destroy the enemy, while I headed east to meet friends and family— I hoped.

"Anneliese!"

I turned.

Wolfgang shouted, "What day is it?"

Cupping both hands around my mouth, I yelled, "Karfreitag."

Good Friday. I visualized Christ carrying the wooden cross up the hill, struggling, stumbling, falling. He was despised and rejected by men. How He must have suffered! But He picked up his cross and carried it to the Mount of Calvary.

Suddenly, my backpack felt lighter and I quickened my pace with renewed energy.

I thought of the many miracles Jesus performed during His life on earth: The blind received their sight, the lame walked, lepers were cleansed, the deaf heard, dead rose up, and the poor had the gospel preached to them.

I tried to understand the message. Believe in the resurrection of Christ. I wanted to see and hear the truth, to keep mind and body clean of dirt and disease. Grow. Stay alive.

My thoughts were interrupted by fast approaching trucks. Why did our soldiers look so grim? What happened to the victorious army I'd seen on newsreels just a few weeks ago? Where were the heroes?

War. It was all around me. I must hurry home! Walk faster. Get away! Not yet, but soon—any minute—the countryside would be swarming with trillions of soldiers—Americans, British, French—all carrying rifles and bayonets. Roads would be covered with tanks, artillery, cannons.

Whipped by fear, I hooked my thumbs under the backpack straps to keep it from bouncing, and started to run—I don't know how far or for how long, sweating and breathless, I slowed, then collapsed under a tree. Except for the twitter of birds in the leaf-budding branches above me, all was quiet. "Sing with us!" the sparrows seemed to say. "Don't be afraid."

Leaning against the trunk, I recalled a verse of Martin Luther's hymn, "A Mighty Fortress Is Our God." Still trembling, I started to sing—softly at first, then shouting the words:

"Though devils all the world should fill,
All eager to devour us,
We tremble not, we fear no ill,
They shall not overpower us."

I felt better and took the last apple out of my Rucksack. I wondered what time it was? Since I had no watch, I tried estimating how much longer until dark.

Shielding my eyes from the sun, I looked west—and saw the column of vehicles. I shuddered. Freund oder Feind? Friend or foe? They came closer. Trucks, cars, motorcycles, bicycles…. Thank God! They were German.

A gray-colored Volkswagen slowed to where I stood.

"Where are you heading, Kleine?

"Home," I stuttered. "Boeckingen. It's outside Heilbronn."

The sergeant exchanged a few words with the driver. "That's where we're going. Heilbronn." He opened the door. "Hop in. We'll let you off at the Boeckingen crossroad."

I was so excited, I almost dropped my apple. Except for the ride in the ambulance to Salzburg, I had never ridden in an automobile before.

Squeezing between the two soldiers in the back, I noticed their dirty uniforms, unshaven faces, tired eyes. The younger one stared at the fruit I held in my lap. It was the same hungry look I had seen on the faces of Alfred and Wolfgang.

"Do you want it?"

He grabbed the apple from my hand, took a bite, and between crunches mumbled something that sounded like, "Danke!"

"You're quite welcome," I said, watching him chew and swallow the core.

I remembered the Kuchen in the Rucksack. Should I offer it to the others in the car? They looked so hungry. I debated. The small Bundtcake was hardly enough for everyone in my family. No doubt, grandma baked raisin bread—my favorite—for Easter. I had helped her many times roll the dough, twist it into a braid, and then brush the top with egg white before sprinkling on the thin-sliced almonds.

"Why don't you put your backpack on your lap to be more comfortable," suggested the older soldier. He helped me with the straps. "We have another hour or so to go."

I held onto the backpack thinking of the cake inside. Frau Hofmann went to a lot of trouble to make it, I argued. It's to celebrate my confirmation.

"We'll hold the line at Heilbronn," said the sergeant sitting in the front. "The town is but a pile of rubble."

This may be their last meal, I thought.

A motorcycle pulled up and the driver shouted something. "Verflucht," cursed the man on the wheel. "Barricades ahead!"

Jumping out of the car, the sergeant strode to the pile of tree trunks sprawled across the road, tapped his temple, and yelled words like, "Wahnsinn! Idiots!"

The older soldier crawled out of the car, scratched his head, and added a few more curses I'd never heard before.

Through the open door, he shouted to me, "You wait there."

I obeyed the order and watched as soldiers checked for mines, then opened a path wide enough for the vehicles to get through.

Surprised at how quickly the barricade was removed, I wondered in silence how long would it take the enemy to do the same? Better not think about that, I decided.

Returning to the car, the sergeant looked at the vehicles lined up behind us. He waved a Red Cross truck to the front of the caravan. "Poor devils," he mumbled before slamming the door. "Don't know where they'll find a hospital."

Ominously, dusk spread its cloak. I knew that before the hour was over, it would be dark and I started to fidget with fear.

The older soldier put his hand over mine. "Don't worry. We'll be there, soon." The driver turned on the headlights.

I saw the sign first. BOECKINGEN.

He stopped to let me out. "Thanks for the ride," I said, then handed the tin containing my confirmation cake to the sergeant.

In the dark, I watched the vehicles retreat toward Heilbronn. To the right was a bed of tracks—the railroad. Next to it, I could see a faint outline of steepled houses, all alike. It must be Haselter Road, the street my grandparents live on. The railroad crossing couldn't be far. It's the sixth house on the right. Should I knock—or just step inside?

CHAPTER THIRTY—Confirmation—Easter Sunday 1945

No one heard me enter. My heart was pounding with joy and my eyes filled with tears as I heard the voices of my loved ones.

The family kitchen was buzzing with conversation and activities. Cousins Sonja and Ellen were arguing over washing and drying dishes; Aunt Hedwig was busy pedaling the old Singer sewing machine; Aunts Lina and Erika were sorting socks to be darned; grandmother was listening to Roland read; and grandfather had his ear pressed to the speaker of the radio that crackled out bleeps and beeps.

"Ruhe!" Grandpa's request for silence quieted the room.

"The enemy is retreating to…" The newscaster's voice faded.

Grandpa slowly turned the dials to get rid of static and increase the volume. It worked.

In the tone of an angry field marshall, the little black box blasted. "Citizens! Women and children! Stand next to our courageous soldiers and defend the honor of Germany against the enemy. Man your pitch forks, if you must, but fight to the bitter end."

The radio went silent as overhead lights blinked on and off. Another power failure.

While Erika fetched the box of matches and lit a candle, Grandpa grumbled, "Great God in Heaven! I believe they have gone mad!"

What is he talking about, I wondered.

From the bottom of the staircase, the shadow of a figure emerged. "I'm worried about Anneliese."

I couldn't make out the face in the dim light, but I knew the voice. "Mamma," I called, "I'm here!"

Amid shouts, laughter, hugs and kisses, there were questions from everyone. "Did you take the train? No? Walk? Indeed! How long? JABOs shot at you? The monsters! Are you hurt? Did you see troops? Where? How many? Let her sit down. She must be tired!"

"I'm hungry!" I glanced at the pot sitting on the stove top. Something smelled good.

"We saved some lentil soup for you," said Mamma, filling a bowl to the brim and setting it before me.

Stirring the soup with a spoon to cool it, I realized I hadn't heard or seen my brother. "Where's Walter?"

"Upstairs, asleep," Mamma answered, sitting next to me. She sounded tired.

"Frau Hofmann told me that Frankfurt was captured by the Americans. How did you escape?" I asked.

Mamma took a deep breath and let it out in the direction of the candle. The light flickered. "We didn't run from the Allies—whoever they are. We had to flee from the Nazis."

My spoon dropped into the bowl. "Why?"

"Finish your soup," said Mamma. "It's a long story. Perhaps Walter will tell you all about it tomorrow.

The next day, Aunt Hedwig and Mamma were busy sewing our confirmation dresses. Since they had to be black, Sonja's mother altered the high-necked wool dress she had been wearing since Heinz perished in December during the Heilbronn bombing. "Mourning won't bring him back," she said, putting another gather in the skirt to accommodate Sonja's slim hips.

Aunt Lina let me have a dress she had bought when she became a war widow. It was of black silk with long, narrow sleeves, a blowsy bodice, and a slim skirt. I thought it looked very elegant.

All day Saturday, I climbed up and down a stool, turning this way and that, while Mamma measured and pinned, basted and sewed, then fitted again. My body seemed to have developed in the wrong directions: my bottom stuck out too much, my chest was too flat, and my waist was too long. But Mamma was a magician when it came to alterations. She snipped a little here, let out a seam there, added a tuck, and had me try on the dress again.

Between fittings, I had time to visit with Walter—and that's how I learned about my family's fearful flight from Frankfurt.

"I was scared to death," Walter began. "It all started when a young Hitler Youth leader showed up at our new quarters on Gleimstrasse. He demanded that I join the organization.

"'My son is only twelve years old,' Mamma protested. 'And he doesn't own a decent pair of shoes.'

"The man threatened to take me by force.

"'You come one step closer,' yelled Mamma, 'I'll throw you down the stairs.'" She slammed the door in his face.

"A day later, Mamma was summoned to appear at Kleistschule. The makeshift district court was at a partially bombed-out school around the corner from where we lived.

"When Mamma and I stood in front of the low partition that separated us from the three men and two women, we were told I must become a member of the Hitler Youth immediately—or else!"

Outside it was pouring rain.

"Mamma pleaded. 'Look at his shoes. His toes are gaping through the holes, the strings are knotted in several places, and the worn soles are covered with cardboard.'

"An argument followed. One man accused her of sabotage, another called her a traitor. 'Konzentrationslager,' shouted a woman. 'We need workers in concentration camps.'"

Walter brushed away a fly that buzzed around his head before continuing. "Anneliese," he said, "I wanted to run away, but instead I stood as though glued in place. I don't know if I shook more from the cold or trembled with fear.

"Mamma stared at the assembly and began screaming. 'What did you call me? Verraeter! A traitor? How dare you!' Swiftly, she stepped over the short wall, slapped the man's face twice, turned, and climbed back."

Facing my brother, I said, "Mamma hit him? A big official? I don't believe it!" I was stunned.

Walter nodded. "You should have seen it! Open-mouthed, everyone watched. 'Clap-clap,' it echoed through the room.

"Shocked, I stood paralyzed," said Walter. "It all happened so fast!"

From the kitchen, Mamma interrupted Walter's story. "My hand reacted faster than my brain. But I realized in an instant that we were in grave danger and had to run for our lives!"

Walter continued the story. "Grabbing my hand, Mamma dragged me out of the room, and together we ran through the rain to the apartment. 'We must leave the city at once,' she said. We had been prepared and ready to flee the approaching enemy for more than a week and strapped the blanket-wrapped suitcases to our backs with belts and suspenders."

Again, Mamma's voice broke into Walter's story. "Never had I dreamed we'd be fleeing from our own countrymen!"

Walter continued. "On our way out, Mamma asked a neighbor to inform

Pappa of our sudden departure. 'Tell him the GESTAPO is after us,' she told the woman.

"Avoiding the passenger train station because of GESTAPO checks, we took a detour away from the main drag. We weaved our way around piles of rubble and past ruins of bombed-out homes until we finally reached the freight station and caught a train out of the city.

"A major bomb attack struck at the Friedberg railroad station. All trains halted while the passengers waited in terror. When it was over, we hopped another train. Back and forth we shuttled, through Fulda, Aschaffenburg, Wuerzburg, Heidelberg, Jagsfeld, always heading in the direction of Heilbronn.

"We walked the roads and highways, hitchhiked on military vehicles, and at night sought shelter in barns. With the enemy approaching, people began to argue, steal, and kill. Some nights, we slept alone at the side of the road." Walter momentarily covered his face with his hands. "It was safer," he added, "to avoid others." His words sounded wise, like those of an old man.

"Everywhere German troops were retreating on foot, bicycles, and trucks. Their garments were lamentable affairs—a combination of tattered uniforms and ragged civilian clothes. Sometimes, the soldiers took pity and shared their soup ration with the civilians. Refugees fleeing from the advancing Russian armies told horror stories of looting and rape.

"The eighth day, we were lucky to catch another ride on a train. Approaching a city, it slowed, and we were able to jump onto the rung below the platform. Suddenly, the train stopped, and the conductor told everyone to leave and head in the opposite direction. 'Americans are advancing from the other side,' he yelled.

"Mamma didn't believe him, so we stayed. When the JABOs attacked from above, everyone panicked. Pushing and shoving, they scattered into the forest to take refuge from the chasing bombers."

"No one was hit, but the engine suffered some damage. It was quickly repaired by the crew and the train continued on in the opposite direction. More JABOs. 'Take cover!' Screaming in panic, everyone jumped into the ditch next to the tracks."

"I was scared to death all eight days," said Walter.

"I believe it," I said, recalling my ordeal from Brackenheim to Heilbronn. Angst had become our steady companion.

In the kitchen, I watched as Mamma carefully pressed the seams of my dress with a flat iron she heated on the gas stove. Electric power had not been restored.

She deserved a medal, I thought. Some suffer in silence—Mamma reacted with anger. I wondered if anybody else ever had the courage to slap the face of a Nazi official. They could have stood her against a wall and shot her on the spot—but for an instant, that evil man in the courtroom shrank as the devil does from the cross.

On Easter, we assembled in a beer hall that had been converted into a place of worship. A simple wooden cross decorated the counter. The minister stood in front of the boys and girls ready to confirm their belief in Jesus Christ. Family members, mostly women, sat in rows of straight chairs behind the confirmants—all dressed in their Sunday finest.

It had rained the night before, but we hoped the pink morning glow of this important day was an omen that peaceful days lay ahead.

Fresh violets from grandfather's garden were tied into small bouquets and pinned to our dresses—symbols of innocence. Sonja and I tried not to wobble in shoes that had two-inch heels as we tugged at our silk stockings to keep the seams straight. We didn't know where our mothers could have possibly obtained these fancy items, but wearing them made us feel grownup.

There were no song books, nor organ music, but a short, chubby woman began singing a hymn by Martin Luther; others joined her. Behind me, I could clearly hear Aunt Hedwig's high soprano and Aunt Else's deep alto. Mamma, as always, sang harmony.

Opening the book, Die Heilige Schrift, the minister read from The Holy Scripture, then held a short examination about The New Testament with the candidates.

I thought I heard the distant sound of airplanes. Surely, I must be wrong. This was Easter.

The minister looked up and closed the Bible. "In the interest of safety," he said "I'll make the ceremony brief."

We bowed and silently confessed our sins.

"God forgives those who will sin no more," said the man of the cloth and administered the Sacrament of Holy Communion.

"This is my body…" I let the wafer melt on my tongue, "and this is my blood…" I sipped the wine from the chalice.

In unison, we recited The Apostle's Creed. "I believe in God, the Father Almighty…"

We finished the service with the Lord's Prayer, but the minister did not ask for protection and wisdom from our leaders. Instead he said, "Let there be peace soon. Go home and read Psalm 37, The Heritage of the Righteous and the Calamity of the Wicked. Memorize verse 37.5. Commit your way to the Lord, Trust also in Him, and He shall bring it to pass. Amen."

Feeling a sense of elation and accomplishment, I walked out into the bright day. Mamma congratulated me first.

"You're a big girl now, Anneliese," she said, catching a tear that ran down her cheek.

Aunt Lina told me for the third time how grown-up I looked and complimented Mamma on the good job she did altering the dress. "I'm so proud of you all," she beamed.

Five-year old Roland held hands with little Ursula, whose golden curls shimmered in the sunlight.

"The world is still beautiful," said Aunt Hedwig. Trees were bending in the wind and the white blossoms on the linden trees smelled so fresh after the rain. She tried looking at the sky, but the sun rays were too bright.

Linking arms in two's and three's, we walked down the country road, careful not to step into rain puddles.

"JABOs!"

"Down!" I yelled, then hit the muddy ground with the others.

The barrage of shouted curses were drowned by the diving bombers emptying their bullets across the field.

Out-screaming the howl of bombers' engines, the little ones sat in front of me and cried, "Mutterle, Mutterle," until their mothers came crawling from behind.

"Fear not!" said Aunt Else, trying to comfort her little girl. "God is with you!"

"Zum Teufel!" Shaking her fist after the bombers, Aunt Hedwig yelled again, "The devil will get you!"

I didn't care anymore about heaven or hell. When the planes had passed, I looked at my mud-caked dress, pulled up torn silk stockings, and sobbed in anger and defeat. My spirit was as broken as the heel of my shoe, and I limped home, waiting for the next assault.

CHAPTER THIRTY-ONE—Looting—Easter Monday 1945

Early in the day, the distant thunder of guns told of the approaching maelstrom. "It sounds like artillery," said grandfather and pulled on the ends of his bushy mustache. Unperturbed, he picked up his spade, walked to a strip of land in front of the house near the roadway, and started digging holes, a foot apart, to plant potatoes.

Food was scarce, and so many people lived with my grandparents now. Not counting Aunt Lina, who was childless, there were four families. Hedwig and my Mamma's family were without a home. Lina's had been destroyed early in the war by some stray bombs dumped on Heilbronn. She escaped the fire, wearing nothing but a sheer nightgown.

The women outnumbered the men: eight females and three males. The youngest child, Roland, was six, Ellen eleven, my brother twelve, me thirteen, Sonja fourteen.

Erika followed Grandpa outside with a hoe, spreading the earth until it was packed firmly around each bud. "Hope it'll rain tonight," she said, ignoring the threat of the returning fighter bombers that swept down the valley below tree level.

I watched the two in wonder as they carried on their tasks, the only sane element in an insane world.

Erika didn't stop hoeing when Herr Schroeder's two grown daughters approached from down the road.

"What are we going to do when the enemy attacks?" one of them whispered to Grandpa behind cupped hands.

"Father took Hitler's picture off the wall by the front entrance and hid it in the attic," said the other.

Grandpa chuckled. "We have nothing to hide." Straightening his back, he leaned on the spade and watched as his youngest daughter raked dirt over the last row.

233

One of the girls, about my aunt's age, stood close to grandfather and asked, "Herr Eisenkraemer, are you going to fight with pitchforks, like they tell us to do?"

Grandpa looked toward Herr Schroeder's home. "What did your father advise you to do?"

"Regardless of what he says, we're not going to fight," said the younger of the two.

"But if we surrender," argued her sister, "the party officials will call us saboteurs and shoot us once the enemies are driven back again."

Erika brushed the dirt off her hands. "Who says?"

"My father," replied the older girl as she looked down the street. "He's a Hitler fanatic, you know."

Grandpa nodded and picked up his tools.

"I have an idea," said the younger girl. "We'll wave our white bed linen out the window when they come. The enemy will take it as a sign of surrender."

"Sounds like a good scheme," said Aunt Erika. "But how will your father react to that?"

A sly smile crept over the girls' faces. "We'll tell him we were only airing out the sheets before making the beds."

Everyone laughed while I tried to figure out what was so funny. Surrender to whom? I wondered. I was about to ask my grandfather for the answer—he knows everything—when I saw Aunt Hedwig running up the road. She had been at the corner dairy where one always hears the latest gossip.

Out of breath, she called, "Schnell! Fetch a couple of empty bags or something. Quick! A whole train of supplies, including a carload of sugar has been abandoned at the freight depot."

"That's a long way," said Erika, "and dangerous. The JABOs are very active today. Besides, it's stealing!"

"I know what I'm doing," said Hedwig and ran inside. In a minute or two she returned with two pillow cases. Turning to Grandpa, she said, "They say the enemy is on the other side of the hill. Some boys stood at the top of it and saw tanks lined up on one side and artillery on the other." Her voice quavered with fear as she cried, "We may be holed up in our houses for days! What are we going to eat while waiting?" Determined to procure food whatever and whichever way she could, she rushed off.

"She's right," said Grandpa in his firm but calm voice. "The number of people in this household has doubled. Shelves in the cellar are bare of canned goods and jam, and the potato pile is shrinking fast."

The flour bin is almost empty," added Aunt Erika. "We must let her go." She walked inside with Grandpa to join her sisters. "Do you think those are French troops battling our soldiers on the other side of the hill?" she blurted out, her voice projecting anxiety. Her husband had lost his life in France in 1940 while fighting in the infantry.

"I hope not!" Aunt Lina's voice rang with alarm. "How they must hate us for occupying their country!" She loved anything French: dress style, Impressionist paintings, wine. Even her honeymoon had been spent in Paris. Yet she knew French soldiers wouldn't understand.

Mamma wondered out loud, "Will the British make it this far south?"

"I've read in old books the English are perfect gentlemen with good manners," said Erika.

"They hate our guts," snapped Lina. "Because of our V2 missiles."

Walter said excitedly, "Remember when one of them backfired and crashed in downtown Frankfurt, destroying a whole office complex?"

Mamma's voice rose above the others. "The English did their share of bombing us. I lost everything I worked for all my life. Twice my home was destroyed by the Tommys."

Walter corrected her. "The second time it was Americans."

"Ruhe!" Grandpa wanted us to be quiet. He'd tried to tune in the radio for a news update, although it was next to impossible to get accurate bulletins from the front. When we had power to turn on the radio, static interference distorted most of the sound.

"What they're saying doesn't make sense," he said, pointing to the radio. Agitated, he walked outside.

Through the open door we heard the faint rumble of thunder.

"It's artillery!" said Grandpa, coming back into the kitchen. "It sounds the same as it did thirty years ago when I was fighting in the first war in Russia." He sat down and twirled his long mustache. "They can't be more than ten kilometers away—at the most!"

The door burst open. Everyone froze.

Aunt Hedwig stumbled in, huffing under the weight of two pillow cases filled with sugar. "I hope I never have to do that again," she moaned and sat down. When she raised her arms to fasten the disheveled bun at the back of her nape, we all saw the torn sleeves of her dress.

Erika brought a brush and some hairpins. "You look like you've been in a fight, Sis."

"It was awful," said Hedwig. "Everyone elbowed, pushed and shoved to get into the freight cars. They ripped open the sacks—it was a stampede. The contents spilled onto the ground. Knee-deep, I stood in sugar, trying to fill the cases with my hands. One woman kicked me. I punched her in the nose. Another one pulled my hair. People turned into animals. Like scraggly scavengers they bared their teeth and hissed and growled and snarled to get the loot."

A scene from Schiller's poem, Die Glocke, flashed through my mind—women turning into hyenas. Silently I recalled the words from The Bell. "Da werden Weiber zu Hyaenen…"

A voice out of the corner of the kitchen recited more lines. "How terrible to wake the lion, how poisonous his bite; but man in his madness, is the worst terror of fright."

The words hung in the air, like the toll of a bell.

Grandpa broke the moment. As though thinking out loud, he said in his quiet, slow voice, "I believe our manifest destiny is Germany's ultimate defeat." He placed his hands flat on the table and raised himself from the chair. His voice was no longer quiet. I didn't have to strain to hear.

"Contrary to what our government says, we want to survive, not fight until death." He walked to the door. "I'll go to the freight depot to find more food."

"I'll go with you," called Walter, then Roland.

Shouts of a firm "Nix!" flew through the air. The young boys were not to go.

Aunt Hedwig stepped next to her father and said, "May I suggest, Vater, that you take along an axe to break open the box cars, and take the rackwagon so you can carry more home."

Amid the talking and shouting, Grandma entered the kitchen from the small front room. I had wondered where she was.

Her face ashen, she looked at her husband. "Franz," she pleaded, "I want you to stay. We need a man in the house."

Mamma and Aunt Lina agreed. "Mutter is right. You are needed here. We'll go."

"Your mother may have a point," said grandpa. "However, you two are needed to fetch water from the fire hydrant up the hill—we may be under siege a long time."

Sonja and I looked at each other and nodded in silent agreement. "We're swift and strong," said Sonja. "We'll take the wagon and run to the trains and back."

Wringing their hands, the women objected. "Ach Du Lieber! Too dangerous. Die Maedele, die Kinder, nein!"

236

"It's looting! Um Himmelswillen! Plundering! Nix! Stealing! No!" shouted Grandma.

I don't know how we convinced everyone, but eventually we did.

Before we left, Grandfather took the axe from the wagon. "It may harm you more than help," he said. "And remember, scramble for food only."

On the way to the depot, we passed some of our neighbors returning, their wagons laden with boxes and cartons of various contraband: dishes, linen, and sacks of flour.

Hoping there was something left, we hurried along, determined to find the treasures.

When we arrived at the depot, we bumped into an old man carrying a rifle. Although in civilian clothes, he wore the familiar swastika band on his arm. Volkssturm: The older folkes storm.

In a quavery voice, he stammered, "I'm guarding this compound—so don't let me see you." Shifting the rifle to his other shoulder, he whispered, "Go toward the back, Maedele. There may be some unlocked wagons." He turned and walked away.

Behind him loomed dozens of box cars lined up in rows. People milled around, trying to pry open doors with bare hands.

We moved away from the crowd, hoping to find an open car farther back. No luck. Sonja attempted to push open one of the doors. It wouldn't budge.

"Psst."

I glanced at my cousin. "Did you hear that?"

"Over here." The male voice came from an open car nearby.

"Pull up your cart," he said, motioning us over. With the aid of a wooden crutch, he hobbled toward the car and pointed to the boxes inside. CAMELIA was stenciled on every one. Sanitary napkins!

Sonja's face fell. "We're looking for food," she said.

"Me, too," he groaned, manipulating one of the cartons to the front of the car. "But I know the women will appreciate these."

Sonja grumbled, "I don't need them."

Starting to load our wagon, I assured her, "You will, soon. Every month."

Suddenly, the man lifted his head to the sky. Shading his eyes from the sun, he said, "Fighter bombers circling above."

I squinted up and realized they had formed a line, heading in our direction.

"Hide!" he yelled.

Dropping our cartons, we crawled under the nearest car and waited, while the planes whined down toward us in one attack after another. Bullets zinged by our heads, splattered to the ground on either side of the box car, and crashed through others. Too terrified to scream, we hovered under the car, rigid with fear.

When the shooting stopped, we crept forward slowly, peeking right and left around the wheels, searching for our benefactor.

"Where is he?" whispered Sonja.

A splintering crash told us. Bullets had ripped holes in one of the box car panels.

"Soup," he yelled. "Knorr's dried pea soup! One gross to a carton."

I crinkled my nose. "Wonder what it tastes like?"

"When you're hungry, it tastes delicious," he said. The man scrutinized the labels on the boxes. "Hey, how about some Fruehlingssuppe? Soup of Spring—made from vegetables."

That's even worse, I thought, but dutifully piled two boxes of each into our little wagon.

"Mach' schnell!" urged the man. "Hurry up, before the plunderers up front discover the loot and stampede you to death." He helped rearrange the boxes and then described the shortest way back to the road. "Don't worry about George, who wields the rifle," he said. "He doesn't even know how to shoot."

As we hastened west, the rumble of artillery fire grew louder. Surprisingly, there were no more attacks by JABOs. Scanning the skies, I said, "The dive bombers must've run out of ammunition."

Sonja seemed less concerned about the planes; she worried about how our "loot" would be received at home.

No need. Accolades, hugs, and praise gushed on us when the "goods" were unloaded. "Heilig' Sakrament!" exclaimed Grandpa.

"Holy Sacrament!" screeched Erika. "CAMELIAs!"

"Auch Du Lieber!" sang Lina, waltzing away with a box.

Hedwig and Mamma greeted us with kisses. "I'm so glad to see you Maedele back in one piece," cried Hedwig, while Mamma said with self-satisfaction, "We've certainly raised smart little girls!"

The boys inspected the boxes of soup with contempt. "We better learn to like peas and vegetables," said Walter.

Grandpa called the family together. "We must all sleep in the cellar tonight," he stated. "The JABOs have been inactive for some hours, which means they're afraid they'll hit their own troops. The enemy must be closer than the propaganda apparatus tells us." Disdainfully, he glanced at the radio.

Everyone sat quiet. Dull booming in the distance was the only sound. "Artillery," said Grandpa. "It will get louder once the battle begins." This is it, I thought.

Grandpa continued. "I've cleared the pallets in the cellar and covered them with straw and blankets." He faced Sonja and me. "You two will sleep on the board I put against the wall across two cider barrels. It's only half a meter wide, but if you lie on your side spoon-fashion..."

Her voice shaky, Aunt Hedwig interrupted her father. "Vater, I'm worried about the safety of the girls—not the sleeping arrangements."

"Me, too," said Mamma.

All eyes were on Sonja and me.

What is the problem? I wondered. I didn't understand why the adults talked this way, but sensed I dare not ask.

"Perhaps they should dress to look like old women," suggested Lina. "I have some makeup left to put wrinkles on their faces..."

Erika piped up with the question, "What about the hair? There's not enough time to die it gray."

Lina found the solution to the problem. "Cover it with a dark wool scarf."

"Ruhe!" Grandpa's voice silenced all. "There's only one way you can save those young girls from assault by the invading conquerors." He stared at his four daughters. "We distract the soldiers by being cooperative."

"You mean..."

"You know what I mean," said Grandpa. "Cooperate! Do anything they want you to do. Anything!"

I trembled. Anything? I looked from one to the other for an answer. Where was Oma?

Grandpa clearly wondered the same thing. "Luise," he called. "Where are you?"

From the dark parlor adjacent to the kitchen a quaking voice replied. "I'm not going down into the cellar."

Glancing toward the room, then back at his daughters, Grandpa raised his hand. "I'll take care of it. You go downstairs with your children." Slowly he shuffled into the dark room.

Lingering in the kitchen near the parlor door, I watched him place a fresh candle in the ceramic holder on the table. He struck a match, lit the taper, and sat on a chair across from grandmother.

What I saw was a tired old woman with matted grey hair. Hollow eyes in a haggard face. Open mouth quivering. Dry lips trying to form words. This grandmother I didn't know. A ghost from another world.

Where was the woman whose sparkling eyes had read romance novels with me?...Who chased flies with a folded newspaper and once killed three with one stroke!...Who, when grandpa wasn't around, held a contest to determine who could slurp the soup the loudest—and usually won?

Grandfather's soft and gentle words pierced the silence of the room. "Put it down, Luise."

Her raspy voice answered. "They've taken my only son. Killed two sons-in-law. Murdered my oldest grandson. Burned down my daughters' homes." Tired eyes, ragged with pain, flared from a decrepit face. "No enemy soldier is going to set foot in my house. I'll kill myself first!" She breathed hard.

Paralyzed with fear, I held my breath.

In the flickering light, the blade of the butcher knife flashed as she held its handle in her clenched fist.

CHAPTER THIRTY-TWO—Angst—Wednesday after Easter

Daybreak.

It began as a distant rumble, like rolling thunder from somewhere over the hills. The din grew to a threatening, deep-throated, walls-come-tumbling-down roar, making the earth vibrate and tremble under our feet.

The invading horde!

Six-year-old Roland's eyes widened. "There're giants with big feet up above us." His lips quivered. "Monsters!" He hid his face in a fold of his mother's apron.

At times the explosions reminded me of the bomb attacks I had experienced in Frankfurt—but those never lasted much longer than thirty minutes. After the planes unloaded their deadly cargo over the target, they went back to England, and we stayed in the cellar and slept.

This was different.

All night, bombardment from artillery fire and mortar batteries rocked the countryside. No one slept. For hours, the big guns crashed and thundered all around us. Later I learned that when a direct hit leveled the detached storage building and blew a two-meter hole in the ground, Grandfather was finally able to persuade Grandma to take shelter with us in the basement.

After providing her a place to sit in the far corner, Mamma moved to Grandpa's side and whispered, "How'd you get the butcher knife away from her?"

He smiled and cupped his hand over his lips, "She dropped it when the bomb shook the house."

Relieved, I closed my eyes. I couldn't imagine my Grandma plunging that sharp knife into her own chest. Why would she want to kill herself?

The seemingly endless shelling stopped in the early morning hours. Impaled by our fears, we waited. Was it over? Was the enemy driven back? Had the siege ended; or was it just a lull between assaults?

A new sound brought Grandpa to his feet. The earth trembled. "Tanks," he said. He walked toward the cellar stairs and stopped.

Above, iron-sided fortresses rolled over the gravel-packed road, then slowed to a halt.

Holding onto the staircase rail, Grandpa spoke. "Whoever they are, remember they're as scared as you and I."

Grandpa scared? Just like me? He must have read my mind.

"In the last war," Grandpa continued, "the first time I stepped inside a house in Russia I was so afraid, I shit in my pants." He paused before continuing. "I would have shot anyone at the slightest provocation—and so will they." He pointed to the ceiling, cocked his head slightly, and listened.

I was afraid to breathe.

Footsteps? A crash. Voices. The cellar door slammed against the wall.

"Sol-dat!" Two pairs of eyes narrowed to slits from under strange-looking steel helmets. With guns pointed, the soldiers repeated, "Sol-dat!"

I didn't understand what they said—the accent was on the second syllable, but whatever it meant, it sounded fierce. Yet I wondered. Was there a tinge of fear in their voices? I tried looking past the stead hands that held the gun. The faces were young and set with determination.

"Nix Soldat," Grandpa shook his head, raised his hands to the level of his face, and slowly ascended the stairs. "Nix Soldat," he said once more in a calm, steady voice as he met them on the top landing that led into the kitchen.

Now I understood. These men, whatever their nationality, were looking for German soldiers.

No one in the cellar said a word. In silence I waited, and listened, and feared. What will happen to my Opa? I could hear his voice above as he moved upstairs, downstairs, from room to room repeating over and over, "Nix Soldat." No soldiers.

Finally, he returned to the kitchen and called to us. "Everyone upstairs."

Hedwig whispered to Grandpa loud enough for us to hear. "The girls better remain in the cellar."

Sonja and I looked at each other. "Why not us, too?"

"Safe is safe," said Mamma. "Keep quiet and stay out of sight!"

Begrudgingly, we obeyed and hid near the pantry shelves.

It wasn't long before two soldiers, one carrying a gun, the other a flashlight, came downstairs. they looked around, lifted up a blanket, kicked a chair, and finally picked up a glass of jam and loaf of bread from the side board. That's when one of them saw me.

Pressed against the wall, staring at the barrel of the gun, I stood still as a statue. He'll shoot me dead, I thought.

They shouted something upstairs and two more soldiers appeared, shining lights around the cellar. But whatever was decided, the one with the weapon shrugged and backed away.

Alone again in the dark, Sonja and I didn't move.

"We'll hide when they come again," Sonja whispered.

"What will they do to us?" I whispered back.

"Torture!"

"How?"

"They'll stick a knife in us—or something."

I scooted back a little more and pulled the blanket up to my chin. Why would they want to hurt us? I remembered stories I'd read about medieval times. Castles with dungeons and chains. I wondered what was going on in our house. Was anyone getting killed? Yet I heard no screams. "Listen!" I elbowed Sonja. What was all that shouting upstairs! What are they talking about?

"Brot? Duenn oder dick?" That was my mother asking how thin or thick to slice the bread. I visualized her holding the knife in one hand and pressing the loaf against her ample bosom, ready to cut.

"Eier? Wieviel?" Erika wanted to know how many eggs.

Sonja sniffed the air. "I smell food frying."

"Me, too," I grumbled. "It makes me hungry."

The talk upstairs continued. Ja! O.K. So? O.K. Gut? O.K." There was even some laughter.

Where had I heard that expression, "O.K." before? I searched through the memory files of my brain. K.O. No. That was a song we girls clapped to about boxing. Max Schmeling knocked out Joe Lewis. That's it! Amerikaner! The soldiers are Americans. And they are laughing in our kitchen.

"They're having a party up there." I said, suddenly resentful. "Why can't we join the fun, too?"

"You heard Grossvater's orders!" Sonja always called him grandfather, never Opa.

I was really peeved now. "I've got to go to the toilet," I said, crossing my legs. "Badly!"

"I' auch!" Sonja said she had to go, too. "You go first!"

I uncrossed my legs, but hesitated. Did I really have to go that badly? I hated to be disobedient. What if Grandpa got mad? No. I'd never seen my Opa angry. Though I'd heard him shout a string of swear words in the tool shed once. And sometimes he and Grandma had a disagreement; she usually won. But he never yelled at me, or Roland, much less beat either one of us. He was no child-beater, not like my stepfather.

I heard laughter again. Sonja wiggled back and forth. "I'm going to pee my pants!"

Scrambling to our feet, we groped our way to the staircase and quietly crept upstairs.

What if the door squeaks? It won't. Grandpa greased it last week. Knees shaking, I clicked down the handle and slowly pushed back. Ach Du Lieber! Oh my goodness! I covered my eyes and backed away, but Sonja pressed forward. Adjusting to the bright light of the kitchen, all I saw was the barrel of a gun. In disbelief, I squinted at the horrible monstrosity facing us. Never had I imagined I'd see a weapon so close, so big, so fierce.

Quivering, I looked at the soldier holding the shooting iron. Never had I seen a man so mean-looking. Sitting on a chair in the middle of the kitchen, his eyes were as black as the hair matted on his head.

I didn't dare take another step—just stared at the weapon, sure now that he was going to pull the trigger. The kitchen was so quiet, you could have heard a mouse scurry across the floor. Mausestill! Where's Grandpa? I thought.

"Ah, Frauleins!"

Startled by the voice from the table, I looked away from the gun-wielding soldier to the towering figure who called us not "girls," but "Miss!" What I saw was a wide smile, gleaming white teeth, sparkling blue eyes, blond hair. Never had I laid eyes on such a good-looking man—except in dreams when I'd pretend a knight in shining armor would sweep me up on his horse and carry me to his castle. Even my favorite film star, the handsome Karl Raddatz, piloting his STUKA bomber like a hero on screen—even he could not compare with this prince standing in our kitchen, smiling. My knees felt weak—I thought I was going to faint!

Sonja poked me in the ribs. "We have to go to the toilet," she said.

"I thought as much!" Grandpa stood next to the radio. "Go ahead!" he said without a trace of anger in his voice.

Pushing me aside, Sonja hurried to the toilet while I waited for my turn.

It gave me a chance to look around the kitchen. Mamma and Aunt Hedwig had disapproving frowns on their faces, but Grandma winked at me. Aunt Erika carried steaming water from the stove and poured it into an enamel bowl in the sink. At first I thought she was about to wash all those dirty plates and silverware sitting on the drain board. But when Aunt Lina handed a washcloth and towel to a young man stripped to the waist, I realized the water was for the soldiers, not the dishes.

When I returned from the toilet, the blond giant who looked like a movie star, walked toward me with big steps. He didn't look like a prince any more in his camouflage-green, baggy trousers. And where were his medals? But he still smiled in a way that made my heart flutter.

"Wie heisst Du?" he asked. His German had but a trace of an accent.

"Anneliese." I stuttered, looking at my feet.

He lifted up my chin, brushed strands of hair from my forehead, and looked into eyes that surely must have reflected terror.

What was he going to do to me?

In that strange language, he said something to his comrades that made them laugh. Then he reached in his pocket and pulled out a small package. He took off the silver wrapper, put something in his mouth—and began chewing.

In an instant, I remembered what it was. "Kaugummi!" I said, but shook my head when he offered me a piece.

The soldier searched the big pockets in his uniform and found candy bars. "Schokolade!" He tried giving me the chocolate.

But recalling Mamma's many warnings, I clasped both hands behind my back and looked to the floor. "Don't take anything from strangers—especially men," she'd say. "They'll make you pay for it one way or another!"

With one finger, the man in front of me lifted my chin again. I watched him unwrap one end of the chocolate bar, break off a small piece, put it in his mouth and handed me the remainder.

I knew better than to take it! After all, hadn't the witch bit into the good half of the apple and given Snow White the poisoned part?

He must've read the story, too. With a smile, he ate a piece at the other end. "Gut, he said with a grin. "Good!"

My mouth started to water. Eat it, growled my stomach. But what about the story in the Bible about the wolf in sheep's clothing?

Behind me, Mamma's voice said the magic words. "It's all right, Kind." She reached over my shoulder, broke off a small morsel, and put it into her mouth. It won't hurt you!"

Quickly, I grabbed the bar, broke off small pieces for Walter, Roland, and Sonja, and put the remainder in my mouth. Delicious!

All this time, with four daughters bustling around her, Grandma sat quietly in her chair near the front room, hands folded idly over her big belly. Her eyes seemed to observe the people around, but showed no expression. She didn't say a word. Occasionally, she'd nod her head.

When one of the soldiers stepped into the parlor and stretched out on the sofa, she propelled her less than five-foot frame out of the chair and into the adjacent room. Standing in front of the soldier, she pointed to his boots and glared. Words were unnecessary—her eyes conveyed the message. Not even Grandpa would dare step into that room in his work clothes and certainly not without first removing his shoes, much less lie on the couch! That was the unwritten law of the house.

Grandpa stopped fiddling with the knobs on the radio. "Luise," he called, "fighting men cannot take off their boots while in combat."

The German-speaking soldier put down the towel he had been using to dry his face, found a newspaper, and handed it to the man on the sofa. There was a brief exchange of words, but the paper was placed under the boots. Before returning to the wash basin, he looked down on Grandma and said, "Mamma, O.K.?"

She nodded. With a satisfied look on her face, she walked back to the kitchen and told one of her daughters, "Pour the boy some fresh water." Turning to her husband, she said, "He comes from a good Kinderstube!"

I watched in wonder and tried to understand. It all seemed so incredible. Was this the same Grandma who would have thrust a knife into her chest less than a day ago? These young soldiers, who probably fought all night against our army, did they have brothers who shot at me only yesterday from their dive bombers? I looked at the one sitting in the center of the kitchen. His hands were still holding that mighty gun, ready to kill.

Garbled words and static from the radio attracted everyone's attention. Gathering near the little box, we listened to the faint broadcast. "Our courageous army, with artillery drawn by horses and oxen, is holding back a battalion of American tanks. Infantrymen, armed with Panzerfausts, are busting up enemy tanks ten kilometers west of Heilbronn," announced the newscaster.

"Idioten!" Mamma pointed to her temple and screamed at the invisible man talking from the radio. "Idiots! We have a tank sitting right outside our house!"

From the radio, the fanatic voice rose to a high pitch. "Women and children, don't surrender! Fight! Defend your Fuehrer und Vaterland to the end!"

"Turn off that lying noise machine," said Grandma. "These soldier boys need some sleep."

Aunt Lina picked up a broom. Starting to sweep, she called, "Outside, children."

"Let's go see the tank out front," said Walter, grabbing my hand.

"There's a big hole in the backyard," added Roland.

He dashed ahead of us and started singing at the top of his lungs.

"Grosser Gott im Himmel!" His mother came running from the kitchen, calling to the Great God in heaven. "Stop that noise!" she yelled.

Roland protested. "You praised me last week when I got a gold star in kindergarten for knowing all the words and singing the loudest." He hung his head. "You were so proud then."

She hugged him. "You'll learn new songs, soon. But right now, we just need some quiet."

"Let's go look at the tank," I suggested and ran to the front.

It was gigantic! Encased in heavy steel plates, equipped with machine guns and mounted on a caterpillar tractor, the war machine spread across the entire plot where the potatoes had been planted the day before. I'd seen German tanks in parades—and had watched them in newsreels traversing rough ground and crashing over heavy obstacles—but never had I seen a tank this close. Its enormous size dwarfed our two-story duplex. No wonder the earth trembled this morning when they rolled in.

"Aren't they huge?" asked Roland. "There's one parked in front of every house."

I looked up and down the road. On top of each tank sat a soldier holding a machine gun. Ours smiled, and when Roland waved to him, he was rewarded with a Hershey candy bar. My cousin was about to sing again, so I put my hand over his mouth. "Let's take a look at the big hole you told me about," I insisted.

We ran to the rear of the yard. Puzzled, I looked at the huge void. "Where are the chickens? The tool house? The storage shed?"

"Artillery," said Walter. "A direct hit!" He kicked at something that looked like a hammer. "Remember the big bang during the night? Just before Grandpa and Grandma came down into the cellar?"

"Yes," I said. "I thought the house had collapsed over our heads, the blast was so fierce." I walked to the rim of the cavity and peered into the crater. "It looks like a meteor crashed. What if the mortar had hit the house?"

Roland picked up a crimson feather. "No more roosters chasing chickens!" he teased.

His words reminded me of that rooster who chased me when I invaded his territory.

"And no more hens to lay eggs," added Ellen, who had been visiting the rabbits in their hutches. "You should've seen the soldiers this morning! They came from the neighbors, helmets filled with eggs. Dozens!" She joined the boys sprinting around the edge of the big hole in the ground.

"Let's go back to the kitchen," suggested Sonja.

The soldiers were bent over a map spread on the table, pointing and talking. One was buttoning his shirt, another combing his hair. Next to the small mirror on the wall were pictures of my uncles. A black ribbon was tied to the frame of those who had died.

Were these the men that killed them?

"Nazi!" exclaimed the soldier, sliding the comb into his pocket. He stared intently at the swastika on the shirt collar in the photo of Uncle Franz.

The chatter in the kitchen ceased. "Nix Nazi!" Grandma's face turned red with anger, then white. "Tot." A tear rolled down her ashen face. "Dead in Russia."

Grandpa pointed to the uniforms on the other pictures. All had pins of the crooked cross. "German symbol," he shrugged. Seeing a stars and stripes flag on the map, he said, "American symbol. Ja?"

One by one, my aunts took down the pictures of their husbands.

"France," Erika said. "He was a sergeant!"

"Medic in Russia." Lina straightened the ribbon and returned it to the wall.

Hedwig produced a letter from her husband and showed the address. "Gefangenschaft," she said, crossing her wrists to indicate that he was a prisoner-of-war. "Are they treating him well?" she asked in German. "Alles O.K.?"

My, I thought, she's speaking English.

The tall soldier nodded. "Ja," he said, "Gut essen!" He lifted a spoon to his mouth. "Viel trinken!" He pretended to drink out of a glass.

The mean-looking fellow with the machine gun said, "Ja. Much whiskey!"

Anxiously, Auntie asked, "What is whiskey?"

"Schnapps," interpreted the tall one.

"Really?" Auntie thought for a moment. "I guess it's O.K.," she said. "I could've used one or two myself last night. With all the boom, boom, I couldn't sleep."

248

"And sleeping with the Fraeulein!" The face of the soldier holding the machine gun broke out in a mischievous grin. "Translate that," he told the tall one.

"What Fraeulein?" Aunt Hedwig's eyes spit fire.

"The British Fraeulein!"

"Ja, ja," agreed the other soldiers. "Drinking schnapps and sleeping with an English Fraeulein."

Shaking a finger, Auntie jumped up. Her big bosom heaved in anger. "When he comes back, I'm going to give it to him!" she scolded.

The soldiers rocked with laughter, especially the one with the gun.

"They're just teasing you," said Grandpa, trying to calm his daughter.

Hedwig scrutinized her letter. "I don't trust those English Fraeuleins with my husband," were her final words.

Returning their attention to the map, the soldiers marked it with a thick pen near the area where my Aunt Else lived.

Suddenly, Grandma approached them with a photo of Aunt Else and her babies. "Nix shoot," she begged. Her voice trembling, she pointed to Uncle Eugen's picture on the wall. Nix Nazi!"

We all looked in disbelief at Grandma standing there pleading with the enemy for the safety of her daughter and grandchildren. The request seemed outrageous, the promise vague. But for a magic second, we believed.

"Nix shoot Mamma and babies," the tall one assured her. "Nix boom, boom." He circled the hill where they lived with a pen, then produced a Hershey bar. "For babies!" He shoved the candy back into one of his many pockets and rolled up the map.

Outside, I watched the team climb into the tank, one by one. The last waved as engines roared. Be safe, I thought, my handkerchief fluttering in the wind.

"They all have mothers, or wives, or sweethearts, waiting for them in America." Aunt Lina sighed. "How many will return?"

The tank dug out easily from the soft earth of the potato patch, leaving only broad prints of tracks behind. As the column started to move, the ground again trembled under my feet.

Watching tank after tank roll by, I stopped waving when I saw figures crouching on one of them. Grey uniforms. Dirty faces. Eyes cast down in shame. The kerchief fell out of my hand.

"Ours!" said Grandpa. "They must have hidden in one of the houses."

Down the street, Herr Schroeder passed a bottle to American soldiers. "Come have a drink with me," the neighbor shouted to my grandfather.

"I only drink with friends," Grandpa said.

CHAPTER THIRTY-THREE—Defeat—April 1945

What was all the shouting? Cautiously, I stepped outside. Like a messenger, Roland ran up and down the street. "The soldiers! Come out and see the soldiers!"

I stopped him at the garden gate. "What soldiers? Where?"

He was out of breath. "Germans!" he gasped. "Hundreds! Thousands! They're marching on the other side of the railroad track."

Goodness, I thought, the last time I saw a German soldier, he was a prisoner on top of an American tank.

For two weeks now, we'd been under martial law. Everyone had to stay inside their homes except at posted times—two hours in the morning, another two in the afternoon. No more than three people could gather at one time in public places. The rules were enforced by American military police patrolling in jeeps. Only an hour earlier, when I was pulling the shutters, an MP had aimed a machine gun at the house and commanded me to move away from the window.

Dare we go out now? Without taking off my apron, I joined the women and children who streamed out of their homes, and hastened down the street.

"Perhaps I'll see my husband," cried Frau Schmidt.

"I'm looking for my son," said Frau Bauer. "They drafted him a month ago, the day he turned sixteen." With determination, she pushed her baby carriage over the rough graveled street.

"I hear that thousands are marching back," called Mamma, walking faster with each step.

I turned to Aunt Hedwig, who was trying to catch up with us. "Is the war over?" Since there hadn't been any shooting for several days—maybe it was. But neither had I heard any bells ringing for peace.

"No," huffed my aunt. "They won't quit fighting until the whole world is smashed to bits."

As we approached the road, we saw our people—the parade of defeat. A hush fell over the crowd. I stared in disbelief at the shuffling corpses dressed in ragged grey uniforms trudging west. By comparison, scarecrows would have looked elegant. Mud-caked beards on haggard faces did not hide the fear, the look of despair, The dull eyes downcast, like whipped dogs.

Slow and silent, the mass of figures limped forward. Some in boots held together with twine, others dragged their feet; but most just shuffled along, shoulders hunched, arms dangling, gaunt faces void of expression. When a man stumbled, the one behind fell over him, and the column slowed until both were back on their feet.

I could see their humiliation, their disgrace, their dishonor—and felt overwhelming sadness. Were these the same men who once marched triumphantly in rows of sixteen down the main streets of Frankfurt in torchlight parades, heads held high to the beat of drums?

Covering my face with both hands, I wept.

Through spread fingers, I watched yet another soldier fall. Gasps and cries came from bystanders. Some lurched forward to help, but retreated when grim guards pointed guns. The American shouts sounded more like curses than commands.

The column slowed long enough for two prisoners to pick up their comrade and drag him to a waiting jeep.

"Poor devils," said Aunt Lina, watching the departure of the vehicle packed with captives too weak to walk.

We stood there in the street for two hours, hoping to recognize a relative, a friend, a neighbor, a familiar face.

The ugly parade continued. Trying to get their attention, I waved. They plodded on, never glancing right or left.

"Why don't they look at us?" I whispered.

Aunt Hedwig let out a deep sigh. "They feel ashamed," she said. "They thought they were going to whip the world!"

Once more, unable to hold back the tears, I wiped my eyes with the edge of my apron.

Aunt Lina pulled a handkerchief from her pocket. "This is the saddest sight of my life," she sobbed.

Women cried for the men without shame. Even the children forgot their playful prattle and stood stone-faced.

To comply with the two-hour curfew, we turned our backs to the victory parade in reverse—almost thankful to return to our homes. Sinister clouds loomed in the west. Having changed from steel blue to blood red in the setting sun, the whole sky came alive to meet with the ever-changing shapes of looming monsters.

Many asked, "Where will the prisoners be taken? In the open country?" The shelters in town had been reduced to pulverized piles by Allied bombers. Rubble.

That night it poured. Sharing a bed with Sonja, I snuggled close to her to keep warm. "They'll be drenched," I whispered.

"Perhaps the Americans put up tents for them," she said. "They have everything!"

"Soldiers are used to sleeping in the open," Walter mumbled from his mattress on the floor.

As we listened to the rain pound against the shutters, I worried aloud, "What if they get sick?"

"The Americans have great medicines," said Sonja. "Wally told me this afternoon they took good care of his brother, Kurt."

"I thought young Kurt was drafted a week ago," Aunt Hedwig said, sitting up in the bed she shared with Mamma.

"He deserted," said Sonja. "Our leaders gave those young recruits no weapons, no training, no uniforms—hardly any food. According to Wally, Kurt's sergeant told the boys who lived here to leave and find their way home."

"Is it possible?" Aunt Hedwig clapped her hands together.

"It's true," Sonja replied. The sergeant himself stripped the Swastikas from their arms and advised them to hide from the Germans. He warned the boys that if the SS caught them, they would string them up to the nearest tree."

"The swine!" The words came from our grandparents' bedroom. They wanted to hear the story, too, so we all moved into their bed, huddling under their fluffy featherbed. "Schweinehunde," Grandpa said again.

By the tone of his voice, I knew he was pulling and twisting his mustache.

"Do you know what happened to Kurt?" asked Grandma.

"He got caught in machine gun fire. Americans picked him up in a jeep and drove him to a field hospital. There, they removed the bullets, bandaged his wounds, and sent him on his way with pockets full of candy bars."

"Hit me! Hit me!" yelled Roland, bouncing up and down on the bed, making

rat-tat-tat-tat machine gun noises.

"Get under the covers and be quiet, boy!" Grandpa admonished. "Where did Kurt get shot?"

Sonja giggled. "In his behind."

A few days later, a posted proclamation at the dairy announced that civilians could obtain permits to visit the prisoners. The word spread faster than fire.

Clutching a picture of Uncle Eugen, we walked less than a kilometer up the slope to Frankenbacher Hoehe, and talked to those standing behind the barbed wire. Pieces of paper passed through tightly woven mesh in hopes of locating loved ones.

A steady drizzle began again, turning the ground around the fence into a slippery muck. Deadpan, the military police patrolled the perimeter of the camp that had neither toilet facilities, nor shelter for the captives, only a few tents for the guards.

Anxious, Aunt Hedwig put her face close to the wire and asked one of the prisoners, "How are they treating you?"

Silly wide grins beamed from dirty, unshaven faces. "Good."

"Even the food is plenty," one added, "considering they're sharing their rations with us."

We were astounded. "The Americans are giving you some of their own food?"

"Jawohl! And it's more and it's better than we've had from our own supply for the last two years," said another.

"When the Russians surrendered by the thousands," recalled a third, "our supplies sat in the mud behind the lines. For weeks we had nothing to share with them but watery peasoup!"

"How many soldiers are in this camp?"

"Several thousand. More coming each day."

Except for an occasional hint of anger or despair, most soldiers stood quiet, faces expressionless; some talked with animation about their hometowns and families. They asked us to bring pencils and paper so they could jot down addresses of their families.

Rummaging through dresser drawers at home, we found other items we could spare: a pocket mirror and comb, a shaving brush and razor. No soap, but a washcloth—and playing cards. There was nothing edible to share.

Sonja and I were the food gatherers. Still we had only those split four hours in the morning and afternoon to fetch water, tend the garden, and stand in line at a butchershop, bakery, or dairy. One second past ten, we would race out of the house to be first in line. But all too often, the last loaf of bread went to a person waiting just in front of us.

Milk was carried by the farmers directly from teat-to-dairy. There was no time to churn, much less to pasteurize. The rich white liquid tasted like pure cream. When fodder ran low, the cows were slaughtered.

Carefully, we rationed our dried cubes of soup. Pea one day, vegetable the next. Once in awhile, Aunt Hedwig made candy from the sugar she had looted at the freight train depot. It smelled like burnt caramel and gave us children an abundance of energy for a short time.

One day, Herr Schroeder's two daughters staggered up the street, carrying a bottle in each hand. Laughing and giggling, they shouted, "Free wine for all! At the basement of the Ratskeller. We found a secret supply. Come and get it!"

"They're drunk!" Mamma and Aunt Hedwig turned away in disgust.

Grandpa looked at the bottles with longing. "Let me have a little sip," he asked one of the girls. "It's been a long time since I had a glass of wine before supper."

I elbowed Sonja. "Let's go and get some."

"I heard that," cried Mamma. "You girls stay here!" She called Hedwig for reinforcement.

"All you need are empty bottles, Herr Eisenkraemer," one of the Schroeder's girls tempted.

Grandpa pulled the rackwagon to the back door while Sonja and I carried an armful of dusty bottles from the cellar.

Hands on hips, Aunt Hedwig shouted, "What do you think you're doing?" Turning to her father, she demanded, "The girls are not going!"

"There's no harm in getting a little wine," argued Lina.

While everyone yelled and shouted and argued, Sonja and I took off with bottles clinking and rattling in the wagon.

The Rathskeller, once a place where the Buergermeister and city council members debated, was now reeking with the pungent smell of pear cider and overflowing with laughter of soldiers. Pinching my nose, I followed the ungodly sounds to the cellar and looked in shock at the sight before me.

Gleaming white teeth and eyes as black as coal glowed in faces the color of ebony. The heads wobbled on top of bodies in uniforms and the legs slushed in ankle-deep liquid that glowed like the Red Sea. Those are the black night fighters, I thought as I watched them wallow in the wine.

"Let's get out of here," I whispered to Sonja, who stood like a transfixed fountain statue staring at the drunken conquerors.

One of the soldiers poured wine over his head covered with tight curly hair. It looked as if it had too much of a permanent. He stumbled toward us, slipped, and fell forward.

People pushed and shoved from behind. Terrified, I was backing away when a hand grabbed both empty bottles from me.

"Let me fill those for your grandfather."

I knew that voice! Schroeder!

He pulled the corks off the bottles and told me not to lose them. Then, elbowing his way down the wide stairs of stone to the barrels, he found the open spigots.

Some people dipped their vessels into the liquid sideways until the gurgling ceased.

Herr Schroeder returned and handed me the full bottles. "Push the corks in tightly," he said, taking the empty containers from Sonja.

It worked like a production. Schroeder filled the bottles, Sonja corked them, and I loaded the wagon. Our neighbor took a swig from the last one before sealing it and bellowed, "Tell Herr Eisenkraemer, 'Prost!'"

The fighting may have been over for us in the Spring of 1945, but it still raged in many other places throughout Germany. When would it end? On April 20th, the radio news broadcast hailed the celebration of Hitler's sixty-third birthday. It also announced that the US 7th Army had captured Nuremberg. The announcers staccato voice predicted, "We will fight to the bitter end!"

Our meager supplies continued to dwindle even more. Hunger, not fear, became our steady companion. We sat around in a stupor, existing without a goal, unable to project the future. Sometimes I closed my eyes, remembering the past. I could smell bread baking in the village oven in Brackenheim, taste the sticky rice with caraway seeds at the hospital in Salzburg, see dozens of salami sausages dangle from ceiling to floor in the Frankfurt butchershop. But the smooth texture of a leather button I found in an old jacket evoked pangs of sadness. It all seemed so long ago.

April's weather, as always, carried on in its fickle way, sometimes sunny, other times stormy. We're luckier than most," remarked Grandma, shutting the windows to protect against the rain. "At least we have a roof over our heads."

"I heard rumors that the occupation forces need housing," said Aunt Erika. "The Americans have been driving up and down our streets in their jeeps, inspecting properties."

"One house is identical to all others, except for their colors," mumbled Aunt Lina.

"Exactly," said Erika. "Ideal for barracks!"

Silently, Grandpa twirled his mustache, took another sip of wine, and tapped the tobacco from his pipe. "Bismarck once said, 'Life is like being at the dentist. You always think that the worst is still to come, and yet it is already over.'"

At ten in the morning, on May 8th, two American Military Police entered the kitchen. Grandpa read aloud from the piece of paper handed him. 'YOU ARE ORDERED TO VACATE THE PREMISES BY TWELVE NOON. YOU ARE ALLOWED TO TAKE WHATEVER YOU CAN CARRY! Signed: Commandant of the American Occupational Forces."

We looked at each other in shock. We had only two hours to vacate our home! Where would we go?

CHAPTER THIRTY-FOUR—Capitulation— May 1945

Homeless.

This is how Adam and Eve must have felt, I thought. Driven from paradise—except there was no enticing fruit, no Tree of Knowledge, no slithering serpent, no finger-pointing God. Only exile.

Heads hung low, five of us walked a kilometer down the road, hoping to find shelter for a night with my Russian aunt. Hedwig and her daughters stayed with Grandpa and the two boys in an empty warehouse across the railroad track, where our meager belongings were stored.

Leaning out the window of Aunt Musja's second floor apartment, I watched soldiers mill around the street. "Look," I called to Aunt Lina who was standing with Mamma and Aunt Erika in the tiny kitchen, "they're wearing different uniforms."

"French," said Lina. She listened awhile, then shook her head. "I can't make out much of what they're saying, but it seems they're celebrating something."

Cousin Tamara joined me at the wide, oak windowsill. At fifteen, she was two years older than I. Round, light blue eyes accentuated the slavic features of her moon-shaped face. Unlike her mother, Musja, she spoke German fluently, but was shy and seldom articulated.

Below, Aunt Musja argued with the owner of the dairy. "You give me more milk," she shouted, shaking the two-liter vessel in front of his eyes.

"She hates that man," said Tamara. "As long as I can remember, he's made fun of her Russian accent."

The milkman gave Musja a shove. "I gave you half a liter this morning," he retorted. "The American and French soldiers took the rest."

Musja pushed back. "You bastard, lie," she screamed, swinging the milk can wide to hit him.

BANG!

Wincing, he twisted her free arm as the enamel container bounced off his head. "Dirty Russian witch!"

"Let go, you Schweinehund!"

Without the slightest trace of emotion, Tamara said, "She wants to kill that pig."

A tall Frenchman in uniform intervened. "Was ist los?" His German had but a slight French accent and was distinctly different from Musja's guttural Russian. "What's the matter?" The dark-haired soldier asked again.

"Him Nazi," said Musja. "Big Nazi!" She pounded a fist against her chest. "Me Rusky! Friend!" She smiled, her full lips revealing pearly teeth.

"Russian? You're Russian?" Towering a head over my petite aunt, the soldier fired several questions at her. "Nationality? Birth place? Name? His German now was flawless.

"My identification card say me German." Musja's voice sounded hard, but changed to pride when she thumbed her chest and said, "But my heart beat Russian!"

"Bon Ami!" A wide smile covered the Frenchman's face. "Freund!" Pointing to my aunt, he told the crowd of civilians and soldiers that had gathered, "Russian friend!"

Musja tapped the side of the can. "Please. Milk," she reminded her new ally—and waited until the dairyman returned with the two-liter container filled to the brim. Auntie smiled sweetly at the Frenchman and said, "Merci." Turning to the milkman, she hissed, "Nazi swine!" and spit on the ground—barely missing his shoes.

In Musja's tiny kitchen—only she and Grandma could sit—the other six leaned against the walls and hungrily drank warm milk while talking about the day's events.

Grandma worried. "Did I turn off the gas burner under the boiling potatoes?"

I remembered the clothesline. Grandpa threw it on top of the pile of things to take and Grandma pretended to tie the rope around her neck. Watching, the man with the MP initials on his helmet and armband shrugged, and turned away.

"It was decent of the rich ragman to let the homeless use his storage barn across the road," said Aunt Lina. "Herr Schrewele made room for a hundred people or more."

I remembered Grandpa carrying his prize-winning rabbit to the barn—the only one surviving the butcher knife.

"I hope Hedwig has a way to dry the underwear we put into the wash basin," said Mamma.

I remembered her fishing for the garments in the hot laundry tub and scalding her hand.

"Who will water and hoe the garden?" Aunt Erika lamented.

I remembered her cutting the first Maybelles. She put them in water and carried the vase to the shelter. Roland and Walter pulled the rackwagon with whatever it could carry—a few pillows and blankets, a pot, a pan, some silverware. Amid the noise and confusion, I wondered where they would sleep. Hedwig insisted that Sonja and Ellen stay with her, and Grandpa wanted the boys to be with him.

"You safe here today," said Musja. "But tomorrow you get other place. No room here."

I could feel the atmosphere turn brittle, as if the kitchen were made of glued eggshells. There never was much love between Grandma and "that foreign woman with child" her son had brought into the Eisenkraemer family.

"You're right," said Erika. She was close to her sister-in-law. "The dressing room is already crammed with furniture odds and ends—it will be crowded with the five of us."

Musja glanced at her mother-in-law. "You can sleep with Tamara in our bedroom. Me stay awake. Watch!"

Grandma's face hardened. Her eyes grew cold. In a breathless whisper, she mumbled, "I feel like a beggar eating crumbs at a banquet." Gathering her thin, steel-grey hair in a sparse wispy knot at the back of her head, she said as if to herself, "I've never been ordered out of my house. Never been behind in the mortgage. Never had my family camp out in the road. Never, never..."

"Listen!" Lina held up her hand. "Someone's unlocking the door to the entrance hall."

"It must be the landlord," said Musja and opened the kitchen door a crack.

It was. But he was not alone. Looming behind him stood the tall Frenchman, the same who had helped Musja procure the milk earlier, carrying a radio under his arm.

"This officer will occupy the vacant room across the hall," said Herr Froehlich in a voice that squeaked like a meek mouse caught in a trap. "His staff will celebrate victory..."

He drew out a deep sigh before continuing. "We have surrendered...to the Allied Forces.

Stunned by the news, we watched the sad little man hand the door keys to the Frenchman and disappear down the stairs.

All eyes stared at the officer still standing in the hallway.

Lina was the first to break the silence. "Thank God it's over!"

I was afraid to think beyond surrender.

"It will be noisy in the streets tonight," the soldier commented in his perfect German. "I advise you to lock the doors, leave the lights turned off, and stay inside." Turning to Musja, he suggested, "Why don't you come to the party downstairs and celebrate with us?" He didn't have to wait long for an answer.

Musja opened the door to the wardrobe closet. From behind bright-colored dresses she hadn't worn in years, she retrieved a round-shaped instrument popular with Russian peasants. Cradling it on her lap, she strummed the strings and said, "I'll play and sing for my new friends all night."

The Frenchman pointed to a large photograph on the wall. "Husband?"

Musja's facial expression changed in an instant from joy to torment. "Partisans kill him!" She cried, almost dropping the instrument. "My own people!" Shedding copious tears, she stroked her husband's face on the picture. "My Franz." Her voice softened to a hush. "Him good German!" She paused and quiet filled the room.

I'd heard her say that last sentence before and wondered if she considered everyone else a bad German. Glancing at the unsmiling French soldier, I felt certain that he hated all of us—except my weeping aunt.

To my astonishment, he looked straight at me and said, "I don't hate any of you." His low voice barely audible, he continued to speak. "True, when I joined the French Resistance, I wanted to kill all Germans. I still despise many for what they have done." His eyes moved to Grandma who stood staring with dry eyes at her son's picture. "My Mamma sang German lullabies to my little sister. How could I not like you?"

Dramatically, Musja lifted her balaleika. "I sing and play for you…songs of Russia…of people…of lust and pain." In a melancholy voice, she began the ballad of "Dubinuschka," the song of the little stick that prods the farmer and worker.

I liked the melody of the folk song—it conveyed a feeling of hope along with the suffering.

The Frenchman clapped "Bravo!" after the song ended, then walked to the open wardrobe and pulled out a dress with bright colors.

Musja grabbed it away from him and hugged it to her body. "My Franz bought it for me. It was his favorite!"

"Exchange it for the black wool you're wearing," coaxed the officer. "It's a celebration, not a funeral." He turned, carrying the radio to his room.

At first, the dress wouldn't glide over auntie's hips. But with Mamma and Lina's help, they pulled and tugged on the laces of the stiff girdle until the garment slid with ease and fit.

"You need a dab of powder on your nose," suggested Erika.

"And a touch of gloss on your lips," added Lina.

How beautiful she looks! Watching my aunts transform the sad-eyed black-clothed widow into a sparkling, attractive woman reminded me of the fairies turning Cinderella into a dream of loveliness.

My thoughts were interrupted by noises from the street: guns barking, soldiers shouting, and women shrieking.

"Close the window and pull the shades," ordered Grandma. "Remember what the French fellow told us!"

A frightened look crept over Tamara's face, as she begged her mother, "Please don't leave, Mutter! What if they do bad things to you?"

"I must go," said Musja and picked up the string instrument. Switching off the lights, she turned before leaving. "It's for you, to protect you—all of you."

Just then the soldier also stepped out of his room and locked the door behind him. From the inside, I could hear sounds from his radio. "I didn't shut it off on purpose," he said. "You might want to listen to the terms and conditions of Germany's surrender and capitulation—but don't under any circumstances unlock the entrance hall."

They left together for the celebration below.

I turned the large key in the lock of the door that led to the stairway until it clicked shut. With outstretched arms I groped my way through the complete darkness of the apartment toward the sound of the radio. An announcement from the locked bedroom penetrated the silence.

Surrender?

"Anneliese," Aunt Lina called softly from the dressing room. "What are they saying?"

"The sound is too low to make out the words," I whispered, hoping they could hear me.

"Put your ear against the door!"

My heart pounding with a mixture of importance and fear, I shuffled toward the sound.

"Achtung! Achtung!" The familiar phrase called for immediate attention. "Kapitulation!" This word I had heard before...many years ago...only the countries that went with it were Poland, Norway, Denmark, Holland, Belgium, France.

"What are they saying?" Mamma repeated her sister's question.

My eyes and ears had adjusted to the darkness. Following the sound of voices, I moved to our bedroom door. "They say—we've capitulated," I stammered. "Germany signed an unconditional surrender at General Eisenhower's headquarters in Rheims, France.

"I don't believe it!" Erika said. "What's the German general's name?"

I returned to the wall to hear some more and relayed the messages to the dark bedroom. "Surrender! Stop fighting! Surrender! Put down your arms! Surrender! Give up! Surrender! The war is over! Surrender!" The order was repeated over and over. "Achtung! Achtung! Kapitulation!"

It was May 7, 1945. The end of the European stage of World War II.

Quietly, I crept back to my place by the window in the small bedroom. The room felt cold like a morgue and its occupants were silent—except I knew the bodies were alive.

Grandma broke the stillness. "At last," she sighed, "there will be peace!" Peace?

I didn't have to peek outside to see the tumult—but I did anyway. Carefully, I lifted an edge of the blackout shade. It was hard to tell what was laughter, what was fear. Were the women willing, or frantic? Every soldier had one on his arm and a bottle in his hand. There seemed to be some kind of contest as to who could uncork bottles the fastest and pepper windows the quickest with rifle bullets. I couldn't tell which uniform was American, which French. All the soldiers rampaged like drunken savages. Was this peace.

I dropped the curtain and crouched into my corner—strangling a scream of terror.

Frieden! The word fluttered through the darkness like a moth near a flame.

"Peace!" said Erika, sitting opposite me. "How I dreamed about tearing down those black shrouds from the windows!"

Lina mumbled, "Yes, light. I hoped to turn on every lamp in the city to celebrate."

"I wanted the bells to peal across the land," said Mamma. "Harmonize with the deep toll of the cathedral to the tiniest chime from a mountain chapel."

"Angels!" I whispered. "I prayed for angels to sing Hallelujah." Instead, I covered my ears to drown out the devilish noises from the marauding conquerors in the street.

"We've been deceived by Adolf!" Grandma said, now freely showing her contempt by calling him by his first name. "I always said that madman was a destroyer with a diabolic streak, not a creator, like Bismarck."

"Quiet," called Tamara from the other room. "I hear something."

For a minute, we sat in silence, straining to hear a sound from the hallway.

"It's the radio in the room across the hall," said Mamma. "Wonder what more they're broadcasting?"

Offering to find out, I carefully crept through the blackness and pressed my ear against the wall of the hall bedroom. At first, all I heard was static interfering with what was said. Then I discerned the words. Shocked by what I heard, I ran back and stuck my head inside our bedroom.

"Hitler shot himself!"

For awhile, no one spoke.

"The damned coward!" The voice came from Grandma's bed. "What else?" she asked.

I went back to listen, then returned to report. "He married Eva Braun. Ordered their bodies be doused with gasoline and set on fire in the gardens of the Reichskanzlei in Berlin."

"Bastard!" It was Mamma's worst word.

From the other room, Lina's voice droned. "I envy the Italians! They had the satisfaction of dragging their Fascist pig by the feet through the streets, and stringing him up like a slaughtered hog for all to see!"

"And to spit on him," hissed Erika.

Listening to the women inside vent their wrath, I decided to rejoin them.

Suddenly, the entrance door handle clicked.

Terrified, I fled inside and slammed the bedroom door behind me. "Somebody is trying to get in," I pressed out. As I groped through the darkness I stumbled over a stool and fell against Erika who was bedding on the floor. She started to scream.

What is going on? I thought. One of the soldiers must've climbed through the window! Frightened and disoriented, I backed away on all fours—bumping into another body.

Now Lina let out a piercing screech, while Erika continued to whimper, "No, no."

Rape! The street scene flashed through my mind. Dishonor. Yells from Grandma and Tamara in the adjacent room increased the mad furor.

Dear God, there are soldiers all over the place. I pushed my back against the wall, hoping to be missed.

Then Mamma yelled, "Pound on the floor! Musja! Musja! Help! Help! Help!"

I grabbed a chair and pounded; Mamma stomped; and Grandma yelled from the next room. "Hilfe! Hilfe! Hilfe!" In panic, crazy with fear—or was it pent-up anger—we continued to cry and scream, stomp and kick, each thinking the other was being assaulted—until the door crashed open and the room was flooded with light.

In silence, we stared at each other.

"Was ist los?" he asked again. Behind him, weaving on unsteady legs, stood half a dozen leering Frenchmen. The one closest wobbled toward me, mumbling something about protecting the Fraulein.

I pulled down my short dress, a size too small. And I wasn't wearing underwear! The only pair I owned was to be laundered.

Mamma quickly moved in front of me. "Someone was trying to break in!" Her voice was hoarse.

"Somebody jumped on top of me," Erika quavered.

"On me, too," said Lina. "The hand tore my slip."

"I heard the noise in the hall!" Tamara crept from under the bed where she had been hiding.

Wailing in Russian, Musja rushed to her daughter's side.

"On our way up, we met two soldiers running down the stairs," said the officer, "but the entrance door was locked!"

Suddenly, I wondered if it was I who had been perceived as the intruder. Confused, I stayed behind Mamma and kept my mouth shut.

The commotion subsided. Now we had a real problem, not an imagined one—how to convince our rescuers that we didn't need their protection. They insisted we come with them and drink some wine to steady our nerves.

Musja, again, came to our rescue. Shouting, "Viva La France!" she led the soldiers down the stairs.

After they left, I locked the door behind them, then joined Grandma, Mamma, cousin Tamara, and my two aunts. I explained what I thought had happened. Everyone sighed with relief. We even laughed a little.

We wondered about the rest of the family—the ones who had found shelter in the junkman's warehouse? Were they safe?

Huddling in a heap on the floor, we fell asleep.

Exhausted.

CHAPTER THIRTY-FIVE—Shelters— Summer 1945

As we walked up the road toward the warehouses that sheltered most of the community, I was the first to see him. An old man, his back bent and shoulders hunched, dragged his mud-caked shoes along the rain-spattered sidewalk. Stubble covered his chin. The edges of his mustache drooped. He stopped to stretch, and when he brushed his dirty grey hair from his brow, I recognized him.

"Opa!" I shouted. "What happened?"

A hacking cough interfered with his breathing, but he finally managed to sputter,

"Fire…just before dawn. The barn burned to the ground."

Erika squealed like an animal being slaughtered. "My boy! Roland!"

Grandpa reached to calm her. "Hush now! Everyone's safe! They'll be along soon." His face took on lines of determination. He was in charge again.

Fumbling in his pants pockets, Grandpa pulled out his reading glasses and a slip of paper and studied it with care. "We were assigned shelter at Karle's Weinstube."

"That's where Eugen's handball club went for wine after the game on Sunday afternoons," said Lina. "Our sister, Else, used to join him, along with some of the other wives." She let out a sigh. "So long ago."

"Ja, ja. I remember." Erika nodded. "It's gemuetlich! Comfortable and friendly."

In the distance, I saw Walter, Roland, and Ellen running up the road. Ellen liked being with the boys. Not far behind came Aunt Hedwig and Cousin Sonja.

"Will there be room for all us?" Lina asked

Grandpa shrugged. A puzzled look came into his eyes. "What happened at Musja's apartment? Why aren't you there now?

"She's still asleep," said Grandma, a shadow falling across her face.

"Too much celebrating last night," said Erika.

"With her new friends, the French and Americans, no doubt," added Mamma.

Lina interrupted. "It's her business who she associates with. Musja told us from the beginning she can ony give us temporary shelter."

"You're right," Grandpa agreed. "We don't want to wear out our welcome."

When the rest of the family members caught up with us, they related their experiences in escaping the fire. Every story was followed with exclamations of "Ach Du Lieber!" and "Oh, my goodness!" mingled with shock, surprise, joy and fear. They were safe.

Finally, Grandpa prodded the group to get going. "Let's find out how much room there is at the inn," he said and led the way.

By the time we arrived, Karle's two-room inn was overflowing with members of many families. Boys and girls played hide-and-seek under large oak tables and around matching chairs. Someone had lit the potbellied stove in the corner. A baby kicked and wailed while its soiled diaper was being changed. I looked at the scene with dismay. Our new home. A far cry from Gemuetlichkeit !

"Who's in charge of the housing committee?" Grandpa asked, looking around the room.

From behind the counter, a tough, wiry woman emerged. "I am the innkeeper," she snapped. Her quick eyes, small as raisins and black as the night sky, darted from person to person before resting on Grandpa.

He walked slowly to where she stood, extended his hand and said, "Gruess Gott, Frau Knoepfle. I'm Franz Eisenkraemer, Eugen Rau's father-in-law. He praised your Weinstube highly."

The wrinkles in her face deepened as she smiled. "You don't say. Eugen, the handsome handball player of the VFH Heilbronn." She shook Grandpa's hand with vigor. "A good team, those guys from Heilbronn. Never rowdy. Win or lose, they always discussed the game over a glass of wine—or two," she winked, "right here in my Weinstube."

In the back of the room, chairs toppled over with a crash. A child screamed. One mother scolded, another soothed.

Frau Knoepfle's smile turned into a frown. "Starting right now, Herr Eisenkraemer is in charge of this…this…bedlam."

No one protested. For the first time, I realized how much respect people held for my grandfather. And I felt proud.

Keeping reasonable order in the crowded, make-shift accommodation was easier than finding food. A bartering system had replaced the worthless currency engraved with an image of Hitler's face, but we had nothing to exchange with the farmers for food. So the children learned to steal and scavenge what the American occupation forces dumped. The shortening left in an empty can labelled CRISCO was enough to fry a stolen egg.

Walter became the king of young beggars who haunted military headquarters—especially the place where black soldiers lived in segregated quarters from the whites. He let them count his protruding ribs on his lean frame.

Mamma warned him. "Don't loiter around the school. It's filled with those night fighters."

Walter pouted. "But the black-faced soldiers give us the most chocolate," he said. "Sometimes they call me Max Schmeling."

"Some shout, 'Hey, boy,' and then throw a Hershey bar," cousin Roland said. "One likes to rub my head with his black hand. Sometimes I wonder if the color comes off."

"Your hair turned dark from dirt, son," laughed Erika. "A good scrubbing of the scalp will make it blond again—if we only had soap."

"When I collect cigarette butts," said Walter, the white soldiers in the other camp shout 'Kraut' before throwing them away.

Mamma and Lina carefully removed the old paper and rolled their own cigarettes from what was left. They arranged the tobacco, sealed the paper, lit up, and inhaled with profound pleasure.

I hated the smoke. It made my eyes water, my hair smell; sometimes it even made me choke.

Disgusting!

I'd always detested the stale tobacco odor and refused to pick up, much less help, re-wrap the foul-smelling cigarettes. "Wonder why they call us Krauts," mused Mamma. "Do we look like cabbages?"

"I planted enough seedlings of the red and white kind last spring to last through the year," said Grandpa, stuffing tobacco from discarded cigarette butts in his pipe. "Rumor has it, we'll get permission to harvest the crop."

"Let's pray they keep their word," said Grandma.

By mid-summer, we got a two-hour permit to go to the garden around our homes and fill baskets and aprons with as much fruit and vegetables as we could carry. Despite the thorns on the bushes, I had a feast plucking gooseberries and putting as many into my mouth as in the basket.

"You'll have a stomach ache tonight," warned Mamma, who was trying to pick shelling beans. When her short arms couldn't reach the six-foot stalks, a soldier brought a ladder and helped her. Soon his buddies joined in the task.

Grandpa grumbled about his radishes, especially the sharp-tasting white ones—his favorite. It seemed the occupants of our home liked them as much as he did.

Although we were not allowed to step into the interior of the house, one soldier took Grandma's hand and led her inside. He looked like the one who had observed her putting the rope around her neck the day we had to vacate our homes.

When Oma returned, she beamed. "The house is spotless. Clean floors. Polished furniture. Even the windows sparkle." Patting the young soldier's cheek, she praised, "Gute Kinderstube!"

He seemed to know the phrase. "I'll tell my mother in a letter," he said, and helped us load the wagon with the harvest.

Once or twice a week, some of us took the long walk to the street across the railroad track to look at our homes. We'd wave, and often the greeting was returned. One day, when somebody let me use a pair of binoculars, I observed the soldiers in the upstairs bedroom window trying on Tante Lina's hats and handed the glasses to my aunt.

"Those rascals," laughed Lina. "Let them have fun."

We made the fresh fruit and vegetables last as long as possible, but with our extended family, they were consumed within a week. We had no refrigeration, no storage place, no access to a kitchen, no privacy. Since several families shared the dining room of the former restaurant, the floor space at night was covered with make-shift mattresses and blankets.

There were few rules. Cleanliness was a must. Bad language was not tolerated. In case of conflict, Grandpa acted as an arbitrator, but Grandma was the boss concerning morals. Before retiring, and after rising, the males had to face the opposite wall while the girls and women undressed—and vice versa. "No peeking!" ordered Grandma.

Eighteen people shared the one small sink with cold running water for sponge-bathing, washing dishes, and doing laundry. A single flush toilet always had a line.

One by one, the wooden chairs and tables were reduced to kindling in the small potbelly stove—our only source for cooking. Every day, Walter, Roland and Adolf scoured the ruins in Heilbronn for anything that could be used for firewood. I soon learned to pull and push a saw with Mamma or one of my aunts, and wield an axe as well as the fifteen-year old son of Frau Bauer.

Adolf was shy around grownups, but outgoing with the younger children. They looked up to the lanky lad. I thought he was handsome, but I pretended not to notice him. "I don't care about him one bit," I'd retort when my aunts teased me about stealing glances at him—all the while wondering how much he noticed me.

One time, after the boys had been gone most all day, an army jeep with a red cross on the side stopped in front of the inn. Roland and Walter jumped out first, followed by two American soldiers dressed in khaki-colored uniforms.

Where's Adolf? I wondered.

"A mine exploded," yelled Roland. "This morning."

"Inside the cellar near the train station," added Walter. "We were trying to break free a piece of lumber."

I covered my mouth to stifle a cry. Adolf's head and one eye were completely swathed in white gauze, his shirt covered with blood.

As the medics carried him inside, Frau Bauer let out an agonized scream.

"His left eye's gone," whispered Walter, pale and shaken.

"My Adolf, my Adolf," sobbed Frau Bauer while stroking his cheek. Lifting his wrist, she checked the pulse rate. "I'll take care of my boy," she told the soldiers who handed her pills and sterile bandages. "Me nurse. Army nurse. I make him well!"

I wanted to comfort my friend, be at his side, hold his hand, tell him how I suffered with him, but I couldn't get near him. Silently I crawled into a corner, closed my eyes, and wondered if it was normal to feel this lonely inside a room crowded with people.

In the days that followed, Frau Bauer, like a lioness licking the wounds of her young, protectively hovered over her injured son, changing the dressing that covered the opening once filled with an eyeball.

Frau Knoepfle, the innkeeper, occasionally brought a bowl of potato salad mixed with salt, pepper, and vinegar to us and freely offered a broom and mop to maintain a reasonable standard of housekeeping. But as time passed, she complained about too much noise, too many plumbing repairs, and constantly grumbled.

In late summer, we were told to move. Eleven of us jammed into Aunt Else's tiny two-room flat. Auntie's youngest, Gertraude, was almost a year old, Ingrid was three, and Ursula five.

There was little food. Some days we lived on leftover coffee sweetened with cream and sugar that my brother begged from the American soldiers.

Even the baby sucked the warm liquid when her mother's breasts ran dry.

All modes of communication were shut off: no radio, no newspaper, no telephone. Public offices, postal services, and schools remained closed. The Allied High Command posted bulletins near the dairy and bakery as to the changes in curfew hours. Eventually the curfew was lifted all together.

At autumn's end, the lack of shoes and warm clothing prompted Mamma and me to fetch my belongings from my former employer, the Hofmann family. While dawn was still yawning over the countryside, we started out. Walking in the brisk morning air, I wondered if my red coat would still fit.

When a lone motorcyclist roared up behind us, Mamma flagged him down.

He stopped. "Brackenheim? It's a little out of my way, but I can take you to the edge of the village," the civilian drawled in the local Swabian dialect.

"Probably one of those rich farmers," Mamma whispered and climbed into the sidecar, and I sat behind him.

The wind whipping around my head was great fun at first. But when a light rain turned into a face-slapping downpour, I held onto the rider for dear life. By the time we arrived at the big house on the hill, we were soaked.

"I hoped you'd come back," said Frau Hofmann. She ushered us into the cold kitchen and heated some ersatz coffee on the gas stove.

"Anneliese isn't staying." Mamma's voice was firm.

"Can I visit with the children?" I wondered if they'd remember me.

Frau Hofmann nodded. "They're upstairs."

As I left the kitchen, I heard Frau Hofmann's voice through the crack of the open door. "Thank God, Anneliese wasn't here when all hell broke loose."

Mamma gasped. "What happened?"

"We were shelled by artillery. So all of us, the children, the grandmothers, Mr. Hofmann, and my uncle bedded down in the cellar for safety. When the shooting stopped, we heard a noise outside. My husband and uncle went to check."

"I bet someone tried to steal the chickens," Mamma said.

"No. We heard footsteps coming down the stairs. Frau Hofmann's voice turned into a whisper. "The first intruder to appear was that French prisoner-of-war who'd worked as a farmhand down the road. He had brought one of his buddies and two

dark-skinned soldiers—Moroccans.

"Scared to death, I couldn't utter a word.

'Fraulein,' the Frenchman demanded, grabbing my arm.

"Not here," I said.

"He gave me a hard shake. "Fraulein," he said again.

"Not here," I repeated.

Cursing, he shoved me down onto the pile of potatoes.

Mamma stifled a cry. "They didn't...?"

"They did. All four of them." She began to sob quietly. "The assault was humiliating enough, but..." The sob became a whimper. "They did it in front of my mother, my mother-in-law." She paused. "And my children."

In the hallway, I felt sick to my stomach. Quickly, I ascended the stairs to the bathroom. I remembered that Frenchman. How he beckoned to me when I passed on the way to the dairy. How his leers had always made me shudder. My stomach heaved.

Exhausted, I slumped to the floor. Guilt swept my soul. They wanted me. I should be glad I wasn't there. But why did it have to happen to her? Again, I retched, the pain tearing the stomach out of my body.

Rape! The worst thing that could happen to a woman.

Taking turns lugging my suitcase, Mamma and I trudged the long road back to Heilbronn-Boeckingen. "Horrible," Mamma mumbled intermittently, shaking her head. "Dreadful." After a couple hours, she slowed to rest. "I guess that's what happens when you're on the losing side of the war."

Did she know I knew?

Mamma took two apples out of the brown bag Frau Hofmann packed for us. "They arrested Herr Hofmann because he belonged to the party. The old uncle was dragged away, too. He's serving a prison sentence for being an honorary member."

"Did Frau Hofmann report the assault?" I had seen American Military Police bulletins broadcast that rape and looting is forbidden.

Mamma glanced at me sideways. "She saw a midwife in the village. The farmers had little pity for the director's wife."

The road ahead, once cluttered with war machinery, lay as deserted as the barren wheat fields to the right and left. Last rays of sunshine painted the countryside in hues of yellow and gold. Raindrops glittered like diamonds in tree branches. In the distance, an ox-driven cart slowly moved over the rutted dirt road to a lone farm house.

With wonder I absorbed the serenity. How can a world filled with pastoral landscapes and peace be fraught with assault, deceit and death?

Back in Aunt Else's tiny apartment, I saw the same things over and over—the same walls, the same chair. Everyone sleeping in the same room. I had my little corner, my little space of air, but I felt myself slowly shriveling into a void.

When Else's husband, Eugen, was released from an American prison camp, Mamma decided it was time to move out. She wanted to go home to Frankfurt. Walter did, too. Even Aunt Lina decided to join her.

I hesitated. Where was home for me?

CHAPTER THIRTY-SIX—Return—October 1945

Mamma, Aunt Lina, Walter and I had been waiting at the station in Heilbronn to catch a train going north, toward Frankfurt. Anxiously, we wound our way through the small clusters of people, all watching like us up and down next to the railroad tracks, ears alert to detect the rumble of an approaching train, ready to be the first to board a car. One small piece of luggage contained all our belongings, including two pounds of coarse unrefined salt, bartered for my red coat. We hoped to trade the treasure for food.

There were no time schedules to check, no clocks to read, no tickets to buy, and no stationmasters to answer questions. Waiting for the train…well, it took as long as it took.

Tante Lina was the first to detect a scent. She sniffed the air, disbelieving the smell of coffee. "I'm chilled to the bone," she said, teeth chattering. "A cup of hot ersatz, anything, would warm me up."

It didn't take Walter long to learn the source of the aroma. "An American Red Cross truck is parked on the other side of the station house," he yelled excitedly. "They have hot chocolate, too, but we need something to drink out of."

"We don't have any cups," said Mamma. "You better stay here. We might miss the train if we leave."

"They have doughnuts," Walter whined, "and I'm hungry."

Food! My stomach knotted. The last time I'd eaten was yesterday, when I had some pieces of dried apple. Listening for the sound of an engine that I could not hear, I looked up and down the iron rails. People carrying tumblers, bowls, and thermos bottles rushed toward the vehicle where food was being dispensed. "We'll run, Mamma," I said, trying to convince her we'd make it back in time.

"You stay!"

I knew from her tone that obedience was mandatory. Even Lina didn't challenge her.

Dejected, hungry, and cold, I sat on my dilapidated suitcase. The strings holding it together threatened to break, but I didn't care. Lately, Mamma and I didn't seem to agree on anything. I was too young to talk to boys; too old to play with children; too tough to cry. So what, if we miss the train, I thought. I wanted to stay with Grandma and Grandpa, anyway, not return to Pappa.

First I heard a whistle, then shouts. "The train! The train! It's coming!" The message moved from mouth to mouth like an echo bouncing off mountain walls. I picked up my suitcase and ran. The train never stopped, only slowed as it moved past the jam-packed station platform.

But Mamma jogged alongside. She elbowed and shoved through the rushing crowd and reached for a handle on the outside of one of the freight cars. In a single movement, she pulled herself on to the first rung of the ladder leading to the back platform.

Walter lifted himself up behind her. "Throw the bag, Anneliese," he yelled.

While running, I lifted it high over my head until he grabbed it, then tried to catch hold of Mamma's outstretched hand.

I missed.

"Run," screamed Mamma, kicking at a man who tried to get in front of me.

The stranger slowed and cursed, while Lina pushed ahead of him, got hold of the handle and hoisted herself up on the rung.

Run, Anneliese," they both screamed. "Reach."

Heaven help me, I prayed. Pain pierced my lungs as I sprinted toward outstretched hands. I stumbled, but somehow a strong hand grasped mine and pulled me up.

"Gerettet!" said Mamma. Her rough-skinned hand held me tightly. I knew she wouldn't drop me.

Lina grabbed my dress. "Safe!" she puffed, as she helped me get my foot on the bottom step.

Moving up the ladder, I was convinced my guardian angel had returned.

As the train increased speed, the cars lurched. Empty freight cars echoed like broken drums. The Red Cross truck and dozens of people disappeared from view.

Bracing against an iron guard, I peered at the others. A skinny woman with stringy hair and steel-rimmed glasses and an old lady wearing a black scarf tied under her chin, clung together. The short man scowling in the corner spread his arms and legs to gain more space and grumbled, "There's not enough room."

When I tried to edge away, Aunt Lina suggested we go inside.

"You don't want to go in there." The lean woman's spectacles had slid down her nose. "Men are sprawled all over the floor."

As Mamma stuck her head through the door opening, I stretched to peek above her shoulder. Brown eyes in olive-colored faces looked back at us. Black hair glistened in the dark.

"Buon Giorno, Signora," a male voice called from the back.

I turned and whispered to my aunt, "I think they're Italians."

"Italians!" Lina exclaimed. "What are they doing on this train?"

The man squatting closest to the door winked at me. Bright blue eyes and blond hair with a Nordic-like appearance made me wonder if he was a German officer dressed in civilian clothing. "Go back to my homeland," he explained in broken German. "My name Antonio. Captured by Germans— end of war. Me from Alpine Italy."

Lina moved forward. "Italy is south," she gasped. "We're going in the wrong direction."

Without a word, Mamma slumped against the wall. She seemed to shrivel a little.

I looked to my aunt for reassurance. Lina merely shrugged. "Don't worry," she mumbled. "We can get off at the first stop."

Now I realized that in our eagerness to catch a train, any train, none of us had paid attention as to the direction we were going. I felt wretched.

Inside the car, Antonio lifted himself from the floor, stepped outside, and put his arm around my waist. "Come with me to Italy!" he said, squeezing me toward him. "Nice country!"

Scared, I tried to pull away.

He held me closer. "Pretty girl."

I'd never been called pretty before and felt embarrassed.

"Hands off!" Mamma slammed down his arm and pulled me toward her. "Nix. She is still a Kind."

I am thirteen, I thought, not an adult yet, but no longer a child. Why do I feel embarrassed?

Suddenly, the train screeched to a halt. When the rumbling of freight cars ceased, many ventured off to the platform to determine what was going on. All around, the countryside was flat with empty fields. There were no crops to steal. Not even a house in sight.

Moving up and down the long string of covered cattle cars, Walter asked questions of the others. No one knew why or where we'd stopped. Some thought the track had to be cleared of mines; others speculated they had to be repaired.

An hour passed. Another. And another. Anxiously, we sat deceptively hiding, and waited. The train didn't move.

As dusk signaled the end of day, the sky darkened with huge cumulus clouds.

The Italians found some onions buried in one of the fields and started a campfire. Cooking smells teased my nostrils and my stomach cramped with pangs of hunger. The dried apples of yesterday were just a memory. And I was so thirsty. As a light rain began to fall, I stood on the uncovered platform, tilted back my head and tried to catch raindrops with my tongue.

Mamma asked impatiently, "When will the train start again?"

"Perhaps the engine broke down," Lina conjectured.

"Maybe they ran out of coal," guessed Walter.

The rain turned into a downpour and the Italians ran to the cars for shelter and sleep.

Antonio brought some fried onions and insisted we step inside. Hungry, soaked to the skin, we followed with gratitude and gulped down the morsels like starving animals.

The odor of wet bodies permeated the dark compartment. At least, the roof didn't leak. Pounding rain drowned out the snoring of men stretched out along the walls. I, too, wanted to crouch down somewhere in a corner and sleep, but there was hardly room to stand. I stood amid a tight cluster of bodies, occasionally leaning forward, then swaying back, not sleeping, but intermittently dozing.

In the darkness, some of us had become separated, so once in awhile, we called each other's name.

"Are you awake, Anneliese?"

"Yes, Mamma."

"Where are you, Walter?"

"Here, Auntie."

Jolted by a sharp poke in the back, I edged sideways, only to feel something stabbing me in the front. What was this moving up between my legs? A hand? I squeezed my legs together. Suddenly, my body seemed to crawl with hands from every direction. Someone pulled my dress, pinched a nipple, bit my neck. I shoved with knees and elbows, but probing fingers

276

found my buttocks. A hand jerked mine to an open crotch. Shame and fear throttled the cry in my throat. Foul breath clogged my nostrils. Memories of another time flashed to my consciousness. Pappa! I felt my panties being pulled down—and bolted, screaming, "Tante Lina! Tante Lina!"

She seemed to know exactly what was happening.

"Dreckschweine!" she yelled. "Dirty pigs!"

From the corner of the wagon Antonio shot a barrage of Italian words. His voice was sharp with anger. He then took me to where he sat so I could lean against him.

With Auntie and Mamma towering over me like angels with spread wings, my head rested on Antonio's shoulder. Exhausted, I slept.

The next morning, the four of us hopped on another train. Mamma made sure this time that it went in the direction we wanted to go. "North to Frankfurt?" she inquired.

"Don't know about Frankfurt," said the man and hoisted himself up one of the topless box cars. "I'm hoping to make it to Mannheim."

"That's the right direction!" Mamma shouted and led the way to reach a car. Experts now, we ran, jumped, grasped handles, pulled, and scrambled until we sat safely on top of empty American gasoline cans.

I watched as a man patiently moved from can to can and drained the last drops of petro from each one into the container he held between his knees. He caught me watching him.

"To sell on the black market." He explained. To trade for cigarettes, maybe barter for a winter coat." He stretched and arched his back, then scratched the stubble on his chin. "They say we're going to have a very cold winter this year."

At the far end of the car, some children played hopscotch games on the olive-colored metal cans. Others drummed them with their fists and sang.

Mamma and Aunt Lina talked about a better life in the city. They built castles into a future I could not perceive. "I have friends in Frankfurt," said Mamma. "Franzi, the woman I worked with at the post office, is resourceful. She'll help us get food for our salt. I'll find work knitting and mending."

Walter chimed in. "I hear there are lots of Americans in the city. That means lots of cigarette butts!"

"What about housing? What if the former tenants return to their flat? Where will we go?"

Walter interrupted again. "Don't worry. Pappa will be waiting. He'll know everything! He even knew how to find us under the rubble after the house had burned."

Walter remembered the past differently, I thought. He remembers all the good things Papa did.

I wanted to forget the past. It's history. It is the present that I must remember: The rudderless drift into nowhere; human beings fighting for a space in a cattle car; survivors without hope. If I had pencil and paper, I'd write about it. Someday I will!

CHAPTER THIRTY-SEVEN—Frankfurt—Fall 1945

Late in the afternoon, the train pulled into the station at Frankfurt. Hungry and tired, and wondering how much my hometown had changed, I followed Mamma, Aunt Lina, and Walter through the bombed-out railroad yard. "How far do we have to walk?" I asked.

"About an hour," answered Mamma. "The apartment is at the other end of town, across the bridge and past the railway station."

"Maybe we'll meet Pappa at his favorite place, the main depot," said Walter. "Black market dealers always hang around the station. We can start bartering our salt for food."

"First we must find a place to cross the river," said Mamma. "I hear all the bridges are gone now."

We hurried along the river bank looking for a crossing. Each of the bridges that once spanned the eighty-foot wide Main was destroyed. Die Eisenbahnbruecke, the one with the wide railroad tracks, was a tangled mass of iron and steel jutting grotesquely into the air. Water gurgled around huge blocks of cement partially submerged in the river bed.

Two young boys balanced on top of the railings like high-wire artists, then leapt like monkeys to beams and boulders, sometimes swinging from one obstruction to another.

Although, Walter and I were astounded by their bravery, neither of us decided to copy such acrobatics.

"Sheer suicide," mumbled Aunt Lina, shaking her head in disapproval.

Hurrying toward the next bridge, Der Eiserner Steg, once a graceful span of similar construction, we could see from far away the gap between twisted rods.

The historic Alte Bruecke made famous in Goethe's "Faust," didn't fare any better. "The devil himself must have blown it to bits," said Mamma.

"Isn't there one bridge left?" Mamma asked an old lady sitting on a bench.

"Nah, none that I know," the woman answered in the Frankfurt dialect. She had taken off her black boots, revealing ugly woolen stockings that were thin and holed. The leather of the shoes was cracked and the laces knotted and frayed. "No," she said again. "Our own troops dynamited every bridge not shattered by enemy artillery or planes." Short jerky cackles of laughter escaped her thin lips. "The conquerors fooled them. They built a floating bridge of pontoons and ran their tanks across in no time." She pointed down the stream. "It's less than half a kilometer from here."

Teeth chattering, I pulled my thin jacket across my chest to keep out the biting cold wind and trudged on down the river bank in search of the marvelous new crossing. As we approached the floating span, Aunt Lina, despite her recent courage hopping trains, took one look at it and refused to set foot on the contraption. "What? No sides?" Her voice quavered with fright. "I get dizzy just looking at those wobbly things on top of the water."

Carefully, suitcase in hand, I stepped onto the bridge. Under my feet, it swayed and cracked, while to the left and right the water washed across.

Aunt Lina tightened the headscarf under her chin to keep a sudden gust from blowing it away. "I can't even swim."

Neither could I. But her fear gave me courage. Besides, I saw my younger brother bolt with joy onto the span.

"Stop bouncing," I yelled at him, trying to keep my balance.

"You take Lina's hand and lead the way," Mamma ordered me.

I hesitated.

"Don't worry! I'll be close behind." Looking straight ahead, I braced myself against the wind, took a deep breath, and started walking.

Waving at us, Walter stood waiting on the other side of the river.

"Hurry!" He shouted. "We want to get to the train station before dark."

As the rest of us reached him, he said with importance, "I know Pappa will be at the Bahnhof trading."

"What kind of business is that?" Needless to say, I was suspicious of anything my stepfather did.

"Schwarzmarkt!" Walter said with authority. "He can get anything on the Black Market: food, clothing, cigarettes, coal. He never gets caught!"

The gaunt, grey ruins of the city started to close in around us. House after house was an empty shell with heaps of ruble stacked to gaping windows. Walls of the upper floors were blown in, blown out, blown away, like open-fronted dolls' houses. What was left of the cathedral rose to the sky like an accusing finger.

Olive-colored jeeps and trucks, flying small flags with stars and stripes rumbled by, dominating the fast-moving traffic of bicycles and taxis. But the long, sleek American cars with shiny bumpers and loud horns were the prime objects of admiration.

"Some day I'm going to drive one of those cars," I whispered to Walter. I didn't want Mamma to hear of my dream—she'd call it foolish.

"Look!' Mamma pointed to a streetcar moving up the main thoroughfare. "Let's find out how far it goes."

A familiar voice behind us said, "I can tell you that. It travels up the old Kaiser Strasse to Hauptwache."

"Pappa!" Walter yelled as he ran to greet our stepfather. "We're back home." He jumped up and down until Pappa calmed him by ruffling his hair and patting his cheek.

Mamma just stood and looked at Pappa, beaming with pride and satisfaction. "We made it."

He walked toward her slowly. "I'm so glad you're safe." His voice quivered—he blinked, swallowed, then continued. "How I worried when you fled with Walter just before the American tanks arrived in town!" He took off his glasses, blinked again, and said, "I'm glad you're back."

Briefly, they embraced. I never had seen much affection between them.

"You remember my sister?" Mamma put her arm around Lina.

Pappa nodded and proffered his hand. "Guten Abend, Frau Lina," he said, in a friendly but formal voice.

He didn't look as tall as I remembered—and he was much thinner. Despite the deepening dusk, his bristled chin showed the grime of the city. A rumpled shirt, tucked into baggy pants that flopped around bare ankles, underscored his raunchy appearance.

Avoiding his eyes, I stood in sullen silence. Must I fake affection to please Mamma?

"Anneliese, aren't you going to greet your Pappa proper?" Mamma's question sounded more like a command.

Obediently, I managed a half-hearted smile and stepped toward him, saying something that approximated the words, "Good Evening."

"You've grown up, Anneliese," he said, his eyes lingering on my budding curves.

Bending forward slightly, he lifted my chin with his forefinger. "Don't I deserve a little welcome kiss?"

The thought of it caused the bile to churn in my stomach. Just the touch of his finger made me cringe.

He must have sensed my rejection for a fraction of a second. Later, his steel-grey eyes turned angry before clouding with charm. "Let's all try and get a spot on the next streetcar before it stops running for the night."

Despite pulling two wagons, the closed-in tram filled to capacity in seconds. "Langsam, langsam," yelled Mamma, "please make room for the Kinder."

Everyone ignored her plea to slow down, but continued shoving until the only room left were the two steps leading to the open platform. A quick glance to the rear showed people clinging to the outside of cars, with one foot on a step, the other in the air.

Will I be able to do that without falling off? Should I chance it? Bells clanging, the car slowly started down its tracks. Determined not to be left behind, I grasped the side handle, jumped with one foot onto the lower step, and held on for dear life. I was not the only brave one. Behind me, an American soldier raced along the car, leaped past me onto the upper step, shouting and waving, "Yippee," to the pedestrians walking down Kaiserstrasse.

We got off at Eschenheimer Tower and walked the rest of the way. Walter could hardly contain himself. How he wanted to show me the new part of town, one I had never seen, never visited. "It's a nice neighborhood," he said. "And our flat is fully furnished."

"I'll settle for a safe corner where I can crouch down and sleep," I said. Weak and tired, I trudged past the bombed-out library where I used to check out books, and hardly recognized the park to the left. Once encircling the city like a green belt embroidered with seasonal flowers and walks shaded by chestnut trees, it now choked with overgrown weeds and ugly debris.

Prestigious-looking apartment houses that had suffered little bombing came in view, when we turned the corner. "Two more blocks," said Walter, past Kleistschule.

I whispered to him. "Is that the school where Mamma slapped the Nazi official?" It still seemed incredible she did that and was able to flee the scene. Most of the building showed extensive fire damage and the yard was littered with chunks of collapsed walls.

Mamma unlocked the door to the main entrance, walked up a few steps and put the key into the door of what was to be our home for now. I learned the original renters had not returned from the country where they had taken refuge from the air assaults.

Inside, the hallway ceiling was as high as Mamma had described it. She opened the first door to the left. "This is where the three of you will sleep," she said.

I surveyed the room. Twin beds with night stands, two chairs, a chest of drawers, and a wardrobe. Nice furniture, I reflected. Clean sheets, plump pillows, down covers. Wonder who slept here? A picture on the wall depicted an angel protecting a little boy and girl crossing a narrow footbridge over a brook. The one window faced the street and was covered with heavy pull-back drapes. "This is more space than we've had in a long time," I said. "If we push the beds together, there'll be plenty of room for Walter, Lina and me."

Aunt Lina nodded in agreement. "Where's the sink to wash up?" she asked.

"Right across from your bedroom." Mamma opened the door to the kitchen. It was well equipped with a stove, cupboards, table and chairs. Dingy lace curtains covered the window overlooking the backyard. Lina lifted a panel with two fingers and said, "We'll wash them first thing in the morning."

Suddenly, my need was urgent. "Where is the toilet?"

"Off the hallway, between the kitchen and main bedroom," Mamma said. "There's even a tub to take a bath and a little stove for heating the water."

"We'll live like royalty," exclaimed Auntie.

How long had it been since I'd slept in a real bed? I couldn't remember. At last, I could soak in a tub. Indeed, our new quarters felt like a palace after living with other homeless people and relatives in over-crowded conditions for the past six months.

Mamma opened the room next to ours. A large chandelier suspended over a formal dining set dominated the spacious area, and a locked china closet displayed crystal. "We won't use this room," she said. "The furniture is too fancy and I don't want anything damaged." She closed the door.

News of our salt treasure spread fast. The first customer was a neighbor from the third floor. Carrying a basket filled with carrots, potatoes, and onions from her storage cellar, she pleaded for two teaspoons of salt. Mamma traded for bread, Lina bargained for coffee, and Pappa bartered for cigarettes through his black market channels.

Walter quickly established his territory around the nearby military barracks to pick up the cigarette butts. On the second day of his new job, he came home with a duffel bag loaded with a week's dirty clothes. Handing me a bar of soap, he said, "The soldiers are looking for laundry girls. I told the sergeant I had a sister."

Lina was ecstatic over the soap. "We'll get started right away and do our laundry as well!" She located the wash tub and asked me to help her carry it into the kitchen.

I found a bucket and started to fill it with water from the kitchen tab. "It's my job," I insisted.

"What's the pay?" Mamma asked.

"A pack of cigarettes, and sometimes a couple of candy bars for a tip if the creases on the back of the shirt are lined up properly," said Walter.

"We have no iron," I noted with dismay.

Pappa commandeered a couple of heavy, old cast irons that could be heated on the stove top.

All morning I scrubbed, rinsed, and wrung seven sets of underwear, socks, shirts and trousers. Beads of perspiration trickled down my face and by noon the clothing I wore reeked with sweat. It was hard work. But thinking of the reward made the chore easier. Besides, being productive and helping my family made me feel important.

"Better not hang the laundry on the line outside," said Pappa. "Someone might steal it!"

So we let everything dry overnight above the sink and tub, over chairs, on makeshift clotheslines strung in the bathroom. Mamma spread a blanket over the kitchen table, heated the old-fashioned irons on the stove and showed me how to press and glide the hot iron over the fabric without scorching it. "Anneliese's learning fast," she said as she put a damp linen towel over the back of the shirt to create the first sharp crease.

"Let me do the next one," I said. Handling the clumsy irons wasn't easy. Carefully, I tested the hot plate with a wet middle finger, listened for a sizzle, then manipulated the heavy beast along seams and pockets until every wrinkle lay smooth.

Soon, I took over the job of official laundry girl, contributing to the income of the family. Cigarettes were the unofficial currency; money was meaningless, and the food allowed by ration cards had fallen to twelve-hundred calories per day.

Walter offered to deliver the laundry to the soldiers the following day. "But it's awful heavy," he moaned.

"I'll help you carry the bag to the barracks after Mamma and Aunt Lina leave to register our new residence," I promised him, even though I knew I was disregarding Mamma's strict orders to stay away from the soldier camp.

When I woke up, I was alone. The duffel bag was gone; Walter must have decided to go without me. Perhaps Auntie was making a cup of coffee, I thought. Wearing nothing but a sleep-wrinkled slip, I checked the kitchen, then the toilet, and was about to return to the bedroom, when I saw Pappa standing in his sloppy long johns on the threshold of the master bedroom. "Where's Mamma?" I stammered.

"Gone. For ration cards," he murmured in a breathless whisper. "It's just you and me." As he spoke, I could see his eyes beginning to blaze with lust.

A deep chill struck me as the breath of a passing ghost, and I clasped my arms together to control a shiver. A deathly silence settled over the room. Inside me, a voice screamed, "Stay away from me!"

I felt my body stiffen as I stared at the figure standing but two meters from me. Every muscle in my body became as tense as the steel in a sword. I felt I had become a weapon. Grandma's words came back to me. "Don't ever let him touch you again!"

Hands clenched into fists, my eyes shot piercing daggers in his direction. "You—shall—never—touch me—again!" The words hit him, one by one. I needed one more blow. "You should be ashamed!'

Pappa didn't move.

I did. Pushing against my bedroom door with my behind, I backed inside and slammed the door. What if he follows? I thought of blocking the entrance with the chest of drawers, but knew it was too heavy to budge.

Did I hear the shuffle of feet? In panic, I grabbed a footstool, climbed on a chair, and held it high above my head. Bash his brains out, the voice inside me screamed.

It seemed an eternity until I heard the latch of the hallway door click, then the heavy outside door banged. His bobbing head was visible as he passed the window. My heartbeat was like a drum inside my head.

Silence began to settle over the house again. Like a fog, it filled the corners, slipped behind the curtains, rose from the rug in front of the bed to creep under the covers.

He didn't return that night. Or the night after. Nor the next night. "He must be on a drinking binge again," Mamma said in disgust.

I hoped he'd never come back.

CHAPTER THIRTY-EIGHT—Coping—Early November 1945

The days grew shorter and the wind blew colder. Food remained scarce and we were hungry all the time. No-one, except for the occupation forces, had wood or coal. Occasionally an American army truck heaped with anthracite or briquets would spill some of its precious cargo as it made a quick turn. I'd run and fight with dozens of others to scoop up the black treasure with bare hands.

"Good girl," Mamma would say as I shook the coal from my apron. "It's enough to boil some potatoes and warm the room for a day."

When the original tenants of the apartment returned from the country, the city housing commission assigned the four of us one of the smaller bedrooms. Pappa was still missing. We'd share the toilet and kitchen with Frau Keiling and her two teenage daughters.

The search for shelter had become a nightmare for many families, with forty percent of the city's homes destroyed, and millions of German refugees from the eastern borders seeking to be absorbed somehow. Former air raid shelters and bunkers were turned into housing for the homeless. We considered ourselves lucky to have a furnished room with two twin beds, a wardrobe, and kitchen privileges.

While Mamma displayed a dogged determination to survive by coping with conditions as they were, Aunt Lina kept our spirits alive with humor and hope. Her favorite game was to pretend we were people of noble origin with aristocratic names, living in spacious palaces or medieval castles.

One day, she brought an old friend she had worked with in the military to our crowded quarters. The young woman's family had perished in the bombings. Starving, she had roamed the streets, sleeping with the conquering soldiers for a candy bar, or a cake of soap, or a pack of cigarettes.

"We have a person of nobility with us today. I met her during my stroll on the infamous Kaiserstrasse. The street originally named to honor emperors is populated by pirates and thieves today," Auntie giggled. She haughtily removed her coarse wool gloves as though they were fashioned of soft kid and gracefully flung them on the table.

We all knew that the new people in power consisted of marketers trading Leica cameras and Meissen china for cigarettes, bartering silverware, rugs, furs, and furniture for food.

Her voice now mocking, Auntie held her head high as she spoke—pretending to be an empress introducing royalty.

"Meet Countess Marie Louise Zimmerman," she said, presenting the urchin dressed in an oversized, frayed Luftwaffe jacket that was filthy and missing most of its buttons.

Looking up from her sewing, Mamma growled, "Welcome to the castle of cast-off Krauts." She reluctantly participated in the silly game, as she called it.

Auntie continued the introductions. "My nephew, Walter von Unterberg; my niece, Anneliese von Oberstein."

I curtsied and I tried not to giggle. Lowering my eyes, I said with reverence, "Your Highness."

Lina pointed to a book on the night stand. "The library." Then, straightening the blanket on one of the beds, she said, "Our boudoir." An empty cup magically grew into "Our dining room." A picture became "an exhibit at the art gallery," and a straight chair "the foyer."

The game of make-believe brought momentary relief from the reality of the distressing world and sent a ray of joy into our drab and dull lives. The brief denial fulfilled our need for dignity and esteem. It did not, however, pay the rent or buy what little there was available with ration cards. For that, we needed money.

To obtain it, Mamma did what she knew how to do best—she stitched and knitted. With a borrowed sewing machine, and a sign in the window that read SEWING AND ALTERATIONS, she created something out of nothing. Black, white, and red clothing became popular overnight—not that they were the most fashionable colors of the day, but because cut up Nazi flags made black skirts and white blouses, trimmed with red ruffles.

Sheets were taken off mattresses, curtains and drapes removed from windows, and if anyone had a printed tablecloth, Mama performed her magic and made a little girl's dress.

For me, I tried getting more laundry business to keep the family in soap and barter the cigarettes for food. The older of Frau Keiling's daughters, Ruth, sometimes accompanied me to the American barracks to help with interpreting. She had learned English while attending high school. When I learned how to say, "Me laundry girl," and "Thank you," I was on my own. I once ate an extra candy bar all by myself before going home. I felt selfish, but told myself, I earned it!

Sometimes, a soldier offered to carry his duffel bag full of clothes to my home more than a kilometer from the barracks. But more than once, I lost a laundry customer because I was not allowed to date him. "Nix gibt's," Mamma said, waving an index finger from side to side. "Nothing doing. Fourteen is too young!"

Too young for what? I wondered, but didn't dare ask, for fear of being ridiculed. Instead, I continued lugging the heavy bags to the guard house and showing the military police the name of my customer. "Me laundry girl," I'd say, pointing to the olive-colored canvas cloth.

"Sergeant Frank Parkman," the MP called over the phone.

I watched as soldiers passed by and took small items out of a large box that looked like sticks of gum and put them into their pockets. When one dropped in front of my feet, I picked it up.

"Gummi," laughed the man in uniform. "Keep it."

The word meant elastic. Perhaps it's a rubberband I thought, and shoved it in my apron pocket.

My laundry customer arrived. I recognized him right away. His black hair was neatly combed, and large, dark brown eyes winked from under bushy brows. He was older than most of them, and much more friendly. He even remembered my name. We exchanged bags—one clean, one dirty. The pay was inside the latter: a bar of soap, a package of Pall Mall cigarettes, and two Hershey bars with almonds. Usually he added something extra: chocolate, an orange, or chewing gum.

Today, he grasped my hands and examined them. They were rough and red, fingernails jagged. "I have a daughter your age," he said in broken German. "You should not do such hard work. Makes you old woman too soon. Better to go back to school."

"No school open," I told him. "No other work." I shrugged and left, wanting to hide my ugly hands where no one could see them.

On my way back, I pulled open the small package I'd picked up near the guard house. Disappointed, I stretched the funny-looking piece of latex, then decided it must be a balloon. I blew it up, and proudly presented it to my brother at home.

Lina joined in the innocent fun as we bounced it back and forth inside our room. When the condom burst, she laughed.

Without explanation, Mamma scowled. "What is this world coming to?" she sighed and continued to sew.

What was she talking about, I wondered?

We always divided the chocolate among the four of us, but traded the cigarettes for food and other essentials: a new needle for the sewing machine, matches, thread, an egg, butter, a pair of nylon stockings.

Walter was still collecting discarded cigarette butts. He had a companion now, Frau Keiling's younger daughter, Ingrid. Every day, they marched along the Landstrasse toward the camps, Walter triumphantly singing revised lyrics to a once popular marching song.

"Never again shall we bear weapons;

nevernever again shall there be war;

let the 'big boys' fight their own battles;

without 'the Lords' commanding us."

One day, returning from a laundry delivery, I saw them shuffling along the road ahead of me with heads hung low, never stooping for a burned cigarette butt. Occasionally, Walter would wipe his face with the edge of his sleeve. Neither was singing.

As I came closer, I called, "Walter. Ingrid. Wait for me."

Both stopped and turned.

I gasped.

Blood dripped from Walter's nose onto cracked and cut lips. From an eye not totally swollen shut, a tear rolled down his cheek. He coughed and spat. "I was beaten to a pulp," he choked.

"I saw it all," cried Ingrid.

As a wave of helplessness swept over me, a vague feeling recurred, a distant emotional echo. It was hard to tell whether I was recalling the pain of the past or suffering only from the present. Was Pappa sneaking about? Outraged, I shouted, "Who did this?"

"The MP's. Two of them. I saw it all." Ingrid showed her clenched hands. "With their fists. I was so afraid, I hid behind the guard house—but I watched all of it. They kicked and beat him without mercy!" She started to whimper. "One kept yelling in English, 'I'm gonna kill that Kraut kid!'"

Through bleeding lips, Walter feebly protested, "I didn't beg for their mercy." With a brief flicker of pride, he added, "I was brave!"

Beside myself with anger, I pressed, "Why did they beat you?"

Ingrid blew her nose into a bloody, crumpled handkerchief. "He stole a pack of cigarettes. I saw him do it!"

Walter nodded. "I did it for Mamma," he whispered. "She likes Chesterfields."

I brushed a dirty blond curl from his face. He flinched. The bump on his forehead had grown to the size of a goose egg.

"Let's hurry home and apply some cold compresses," I urged. Glancing at him sideways, I added, "Mamma will be mad, you know. She doesn't tolerate stealing. It's wrong."

"So is a beating," Ingrid hissed.

Looking straight ahead, Walter said in a dull voice, "Mamma will beat me again—for getting caught."

She did.

That moment, I felt hate for what Mamma did.

"Hasn't the boy been punished enough?" Aunt Lina intervened. She wrung out a cloth and wiped Walter's face gently. With disgust in her voice, she grunted, "Military Police! Hoodlums! I thought only GESTAPO had it in them to beat children." She lit a cigarette.

Silently, I swore to never smoke.

School remained closed and existing text books were destroyed. Would I ever finish the eighth grade? No newspapers or magazines were printed, no radios blared—except one station. AFN, the American Forces Network broadcast around the clock to those lucky enough to have a radio.

Old American magazines began to appear. These turned into a treasure of information. Eagerly, we flipped through the pages of LIFE. "All American women look so glamorous," Ruth sighed, pulling on her thick waist length blond braids.

"Like movie stars," I agreed.

"You young girls are nice-looking," Aunt Lina said as she untangled the strips of rags that made my hair curly. Brushing the locks to cascade across my shoulders, she assured me, "Now you're as pretty as all those American girls." She affectionately pinched my nose. "Prettier," she winked.

Mamma glanced up from her knitting. "It makes her look too grown up," she objected. "Maybe we should cut off those curls—then perhaps she would be safe from the leering soldiers." The furious clicking of the needles were accompanied by a sigh. "I don't like those guys who whistle for girls like you do for dogs."

As always, Auntie came to my defense. "Let them. Anneliese knows how to conduct herself." Turning to me, she admonished, "Don't ever step inside one of those soldier's vehicles!"

I knew what she meant. One of the young laundry girls accepted a ride in a jeep and ended up being raped. Horrors! Except for Sergeant Parkman, I didn't know whom to trust anymore around the camps. Rubbing my rough hands, I wondered if I shouldn't stop doing laundry. But how else could I help my family?

One evening, Irmgard and her father came to our apartment. "Who is this man who teaches shorthand?" Lina inquired.

Irmgard's father explained. "I worked as a janitor in the factory where Herr Schuster acted as vice president. In his position, he had to join the Nazi party. Because of his membership, after the peace came he was sentenced to clear rubble from the ruins and his bank account was frozen. It's the denazification process." Irmgard's father paused for a moment. "Herr Schuster has always treated me decent. He needs money to get by."

Auntie talked to Mamma. "It's a good chance for Anneliese to learn something toward making a living, other than doing laundry."

"Stenographers make good money," added Irmgard's father. "He's only asking five marks a lesson per student."

"How many weeks will it take to learn that shorthand?" Furrows appeared on Mamma's forehead. It meant she's counting the pennies.

"Don't worry about the money," said Auntie. "I have small savings. May as well put it to good use."

She's always on my side, I thought, but wasn't so sure about Mamma.

"Don't forget the laundry," Mamma grumbled, and reluctantly conceded.

Thankfully, I hugged them both, happy to learn something new.

Three times a week, Ruth, Ingrid, and myself, met with Herr Schuster at Irmgard's house. He even supplied pencils and paper—items difficult to obtain. With patience, he explained, "Think of it as an abbreviated written language."

Dutifully, I practiced the peculiar-looking shorthand symbols and soon progressed to taking dictation of short sentences. It was fun having friends to study with, to giggle at everything and nothing, and to share successes and failures.

Here and there, signs showed up in windows. "English lessons." Auntie decided I should learn English. "It will be the language of the future," she predicted.

I signed up at a nearby residence. After returning from the first lesson, Mamma quizzed me. "What is your teacher like?"

I had to think about it. "Herr Kreutzer is a tall, melancholy-looking man who smokes a lot," I recalled.

Mamma gave me a quick look.

"He taught us how to pronounce the alphabet in English. Then he wrote one word in big bold letters on the blackboard: It spelled, S U I C I D E."

CHAPTER THIRTY-NINE—Winter—November 1945

Learning to speak and understand English was difficult, but I studied hard. My throat and tongue were not trained to pronounce r's. To produce th's, I pretended to lisp. The consonants "g," and "j" proved another challenge, and the vowels in "neither" or "dance" sounded different when spoken by Americans.

All four of my fellow students were several years older than I and took the lessons to better communicate with their American employers. Two worked as domestics and one as a driver. We sat in a half circle on upholstered straight chairs that matched the shabby decor of the room: a desk heaped with books, papers, an empty coffee cup, a swivel chair that wobbled, a blank blackboard.

"During the war, I lived in England," our teacher told us. "They speak English across the channel, not American." With shoulders stooped, hands folded behind, Herr Kreutzer glumly paced the room and stopped at the window. "I can't get rid of this ongoing feeling of hopelessness when I look around me." In a voice barely audible, he added, "I feel disconnected from my family, my country, my God."

So do I, I thought, clasping my arms to stifle a shiver.

He apologized for the cold room and absent-mindedly buttoned his black wool sweater riddled with holes. "I'm discouraged by what I see in our society," he continued. "Girls coming home to once-chaste beds, now dirty with disease. Children begging." Abruptly, he turned to the blackboard.

What depressing message is it going to be today? Shame?

His hand shaking, he chalked capital letters across the slate. H O P E !

Outside, a gloomy November sky frowned upon endless rubble—heaps of stone, rank with the smell of sewage and filth, grey with the dust of destruction slowly working its way into clothes, skin, and soul.

Hope? For what?

We learned of Grandma's grave illness by word of mouth. The news hit like a hammer. Rather than see my Oma suffer, I wanted to rip my heart from my chest and tear it to shreds.

There were still no telephones for most German civilians, no postal service to send a letter, no telegraph office for a message. Travel was difficult, but a small trucking company across town allowed hitchhikers to ride in the back of their trucks and trailers.

We must go and see Grandma," said Lina.

Torn between conflicting emotions, Mamma made her choice with a heavy heart. "Frau Keiling has threatened to evict us. I must stay here. Someone in the family has to be practical. We have a good chance of moving into that third floor apartment of the building on the corner."

"But there are no walls or windows," said Lina. "It'll be like a barn!"

"Macht nix." Mamma waved away the problem. "Doesn't matter. It has running water, electricity, and we'll have a roof over our heads."

I was only half listening. My concern was for my grandmother. I missed her and longed to see her again. "May I go with Auntie to see my Oma?" I asked.

"Of course," said Mamma. Sometimes she could be so understanding. Slowly I knitted my heart together again.

Before dawn, Lina and I walked to the freight yard and signed up for a ride to Heilbronn. We were in luck. One of the big semi-trailers loaded with goods was headed in that direction.

"Let's go," said Auntie. "Heilbronn is enroute to Stuttgart—perhaps the driver will drop us off on the way."

Several people pushed inside the trailer. As I helped Lina hoist herself over the side, the driver called, "Hey, little girl. Want to sit up front with us?"

"Go ahead," said Lina. "Tell him to let us off in Heilbronn."

High up inside that cab, I felt like a queen between two kings. This is going to be exciting, I thought. Wait until I tell Walter and my girlfriends.

"Call me Otto," said the tall, lean fellow behind the wheel. "I'll call you princess." He pulled the bill of his leather cap farther down his forehead, pushed a button with his thumb and put his right foot on a pedal. The starter whirred and caught, the engine roared.

Wunderbar. This is super. I watched him shift the big stick into low gear. With a shudder, the truck strained across the yard. Away we go!

Gustav, his burly helper, studied a map marked with red and green arrows.

"The road's good for the next fifty kilometers. Then we have to weave our way through the narrow streets of small villages." He folded the map and warned, "Watch for the three-story house when you make that hairpin turn in Seckbach."

A convoy of American trucks passed on the left. Otto waved and gave his horn two short blasts.

"Those guys took a chip out of that corner house twice last week," Gustav scowled.

"The soldiers aren't used to narrow streets," said Otto. "But I understand reparations by the Americans are being made to the homeowners."

"News to me," grumbled Gustav.

"Time for breakfast." Otto pointed to his lunch box beneath the seat and asked me to open it. "Hungry?"

"Always," I nodded.

"Take half of the sandwich," he urged. "It's liverwurst."

"Thanks," I said. "My favorite." Unlike a princess, I took a big bite, chewed, swallowed, and devoured another. It had been a long time since I tasted meat and savored it like manna from heaven.

"Let's take a rest stop after getting off this road," said Otto.

I thought of Aunt Lina sitting in the bumping trailer behind us. "Perhaps my aunt can take a turn up front."

"No way," said Otto, wiping his mouth on the back of his sleeve. "We don't want an old auntie sitting between us. You stay."

I never considered my aunt old at 35—just grown up. But I kept my thoughts to myself and looked straight ahead through the windshield down the ribboning autobahn. I might as well enjoy the comfort of the cab—and I did make an attempt to give up my seat.

After we stopped, Lina came running up front. "Did you ask him to let us off? she whispered.

I nodded.

"What's his name?"

Otto extended his hand to Auntie. "Name's Pflug. Otto Pflug. Little princess here tells me you're going to Heilbronn." He pulled out a pack of Camels. "Cigarette?"

"Danke schoen." Fingers trembling with cold, she let Otto light it and inhaled. "My parents live on the edge of town—in Boeckingen." Auntie looked up at Otto with big puppy-dog, sad eyes. "Name's Duerr. Lina Duerr."

While they puffed and talked, I walked around the truck to stretch my legs.

When I returned, Auntie sat inside the cab.

"My turn," she called.

Pouting, I climbed into the trailer and settled between boxes and barrels for the rest of the journey. Suddenly, I was a princess demoted to the rank of pauper.

Otto dropped us off by the highway next to the railroad bed and promised to pick us up at the same place two days later. Waving, Lina watched until the big semi moved out of sight.

Excitedly, I looked at the rows of houses across the track. "Have the people been allowed to return to their homes?" Where American jeeps and army trucks once parked, children now played.

"According to Otto," Lina said, "the Americans had left six weeks ago. Then the Poles moved in for a month. Not only looted the homes, but left them in shambles. Now the owners are back."

"How does he know all this?"

"Truck drivers get around."

Several months had passed since I last saw Grandma. In the downstairs bedroom that once was mine, she lay quietly in bed, thin wisps of her hair splayed on the pillow, her frail hands curled on the soft feather coverlet. On the night stand lay a copy of the New Testament. Standing next to the bed, I watched her pale face twitch with pain. Her eyes were closed and she sobbed softly, struggling to breathe.

I wanted to open the window to freshen the air, but instead I stroked the gnarled hand that clutched a piece of cloth.

"It's Anneliese," I whispered.

She flinched and opened her eyes. Kind eyes in a wrinkled old face, looked at me with love and care. A flicker of a smile crossed her lips. "Maedele." She still called me a little girl.

I needed to make her feel better, sprinkle her body with comfort, to once more see that sweet toothless smile "I' mag' Die so, Oma,' I said softly, and placed a gentle kiss on her forehead. "I love you so much."

She managed a faint smile.

"Do you remember when we used to read romances?" I said. I swallowed fighting back tears...."And once you killed three flies with one swat, and...when the rooster chased the chickens, after I left open the gate, and they all got out, and..."

A gasp escaped her mouth, then a whimper, a cry. "Pain. Please...close door...leave alone." Eyes open wide, her body became rigid. She screamed...and screamed...and screamed.

My stomach felt as though someone reached in and yanked it out. Unable to help, I fled the room in terror.

Grandpa gently led me to a chair in the kitchen before he entered Grandma's bedroom and closed the door behind him. Inside raged the torment of pending death.

Covering my ears, I asked, "When will she stop?"

Aunt Erika shrugged. "When her voice wears out." She took a wrap from the coat rack on the wall. "Let's go for a walk," she said. "It'll be awhile yet."

Visibly shaken, Lina asked Erika, "What about the doctor? What does he say? Can't he give her a sedative?"

He diagnosed it as colon cancer. Only morphine will help. We don't even have an aspirin." She kicked a large pebble toward the hedge by the railroad. "Mother begs us daily to put her out of her misery. The neighbors have scoured their medicine chests for pain killers. Any kind. Nothing helps. Not even our prayers.

Overwhelmed with a sense of impending loss, I felt weak, drained of all energy. Inside, a cold fire of sadness consumed me. Outside, I watched the world whirl past without a spark of interest.

The dusk deepened. Toward the west, a thin blade of moon was low in the sky. Grandmas should live forever, I prayed.

We walked across the bleak moonscape of Heilbronn the next day. Aunt Hedwig was living with Sonja and Ellen in the cellar of one of the tenement houses.

"It's cool in the summer and warm and cozy in the winter," said Hedwig. "They say winter's going to be a cold one this year." We exchanged the latest news about family, neighbors—our Fatherland. Erika told us about the condition of our house after the Poles left.

"They turned the kitchen into a stable. Even had a horse inside. Unbelievable! Is that how they live in Poland? Ja, ja, such is fate."

"Too bad about Musja. What? She didn't want to live any more. NO! Herzeleid. Her heart broke. She couldn't exist without her Franz. Ja, ja, such is fate."

Else is going to have another baby. Really? Goodness knows, she's skin and bones now. Maybe it'll be a boy this time! One more mouth to feed. Ja, ja, so it is."

"And did you hear about Manfred? He killed a stray cow and butchered it. Received a six-month prison sentence. Ja, ja, such is fate. He was only trying to feed his family."

"They opened the gates of the concentration camps. Let out all the communists and criminals. No! You don't say! I have it from reliable sources. Thieves, murderers and trouble makers traipsing the countryside. Ja, ja, such is fate."

"We heard rumors of terrible things that had been done to people in those prisons. Things we could not believe, done right here in Germany. Things that could only have been done by savages, not our people!"

"Remember those gypsies that camped down the street in house trailers? They were gassed. No! I'm telling you! Who? SS and GESTAPO, who else? Where? Don't know. Buchenwald, Dachau, or Matthausen. Jawohl! Killed them all. Even the children. Jews, too. I can't believe it."

Pictures from the past leaped into my memory. The tramp of marching boots, its hobble nails making horrible noise. The creak and rumble of the departing lorries taking David and his family away into the distance of deserted streets. GESTAPO. They searched my doll house…arrested Mamma…Walter's father, Matthausen. Could it be that he survived?

Two days later, when I bade Grandma goodbye, she whispered in a still small voice, "I love you, Maedele."

Unable to control my sobs, I rushed from the room into my Grandfather's arms and cried like the little girl I used to be.

A horn blasted. Brakes screeched. The big semi-truck stopped. "I told you he'd be here to pick us up," said Auntie.

Otto opened the cab door and let himself out. "Hop in," he called, pointing to Lina. He pulled an old blanket from under the driver's seat. "We'll bundle up the little princess," he said, and helped me climb into the trailer.

It was loaded with cement sacks—the ones on the bottom soft and dusty, the ones on top hard as rock. Wrapped in the musty—smelling wool, I crouched down and leaned against one of the bags that matched the color of the misty morning. I peered over the side of the trailer. Except for a howling dog, the town was still asleep, its houses huddled against a bitter, frigid wind. Splinters of grief stabbed at my heart every time I recalled Grandma's face contorted with pain—the scream of agony that had pierced the air. The helplessness I felt. How long would Grandma have to suffer?

In the midst of the miserable dawn, I saw a light in a distant farmhouse that stood on the horizon as if painted there. New tears rolled down my cheeks, as the truck sped toward home. Would I ever see my Oma again?

CHAPTER FORTY—Shame—November 1945

"Swine!" The word hissed through the tight cluster of people staring at the names and photos of twenty-five Nazi criminals posted on the building across from the school. Body shoved against body, women stood on tiptoes to see over the heads of others, and children were held close to their mothers.

"To call those persons swine," Mamma said, "is an insult to the pigs."

"No." someone else cried. "The pictures must be fake. How can this have happened?"

"It couldn't have," said many.

Some people shook their heads, others covered their faces. "The worst civilian massacre in history done by our leaders? Impossible! Slaughtering millions? The number must be exaggerated."

Lina glared in disgust. "Killing one is too many."

When I tried to push closer to the posters, Auntie pulled me away. "It's too horrible to look at," she said.

She tucked her hand beneath my elbow, in a hurry to leave the scene behind us.

My mind refused to stop. Millions?

"Let's go to the apartment," she insisted. "We'll sort the chunks of plaster. Otto can fit them together and put up a new wall this weekend."

Atrocities! Only the wicked used to be punished. Not little children, not old people. What had they done? My thoughts continued to whirl around and around.

We climbed the two flights to our new home. Rubble and debris lay across the four rooms, hallway and kitchen. Not a single inside wall was standing. Window glass lay shattered on the floor, but most of the doors, including the once elegant wide French louvres connecting two of the rooms were usable.

"I hope Otto can get his hands on a few more bags of cement," said Mamma. "What a wonder he is. Don't know what we'd do without him."

"He's a good man," Lina said, blushing like a bride-to-be. I swept dust and dirt into a heap and thought about the placards I had glimpsed in the street. "How many zeros is a million?" I asked.

"Too many," Mamma said, taking the broom out of my hand. She shoved the broken shards of glass into a corner with a single stroke.

Deep in thought, I went out onto the balcony. People still gathered in the street. They stood peering at the photos of the Nazi leaders that were to go before an international war crimes tribunal in Nuremberg on November 20, 1945, then walked away with lowered heads, their shoulders hunched forward. Silence, no drama, just silence, impenetrable silence. I, too, stood in that stillness, feeling the weight of the offense.

A woman shook her finger at a sullen sky covered with clouds. I closed my eyes. Memories brought forth the smell of smoke, the sight of a synagogue burning, the shout of another woman's voice. "Some day God is going to punish all of us..."

I buried my face in my hands and shuddered.

Each day the knowledge of sin grew more monstrous, more heinous.

On the way to my English lesson, I pondered how I could cope with this legacy of guilt. Who were the perpetrators of such unspeakable crimes? The leaders of a country I loved and respected? Deutschland. Germany. My Fatherland. Germans murdering millions of Germans just because they were different in some way I didn't even understand. I, too, am a German.

A man wearing a tattered coat posted more placards on the wall ahead of me that depicted the odious crimes done in the annihilation camps. Matthausen, Buchenwald, Dachau. During the last weeks, thousands of inmates there died of starvation.

Walking down the street, hunger gnawed at me. My stomach cramped. The pictures on the wall began to spin. Weakly, I clung to a lamp post, wanting to vomit—but couldn't. My belly was empty—why was I still alive?

Mass murder and atrocities.

Outraged, I shook my head in denial, but guilt pierced my soul like tons of bombs once tore out the heart of cities. Explosions deafened, phosphor slithered down cellar stairs, fire sucked up oxygen—everywhere, I saw death juxtapositioned on the posters of shame. A hill to the east of Heilbronn, scarred with eight ugly cavities, each holding a thousand bodies of civilians burnt or poisoned by carbon monoxide in an air raid that lasted ninety minutes.

I recalled the night of rape and looting, the pillage of the land, being kicked out of our home, cattle cars reeking with the sweat and filth of humans, our flat void of furnishings, without walls, except the one covered with black soot.

"Drink some water," suggested a woman passing by. "It helps the dry heaves of hunger pains."

After my dizziness subsided, I hastened past a building now occupied by DP's, Displaced Persons, waiting to return to their homeland, Poland. On the sidewalk, a group of Poles shouted obscene language in my direction. One of the men tried to kick me, then spit. He pointed to a sign at the front of the building. GERMANS AND DOGS STAY OUT, the bold letters said. DEUTSCHE UND HUNDE VERBOTEN ! I ducked the kick, then wiped the spittle off my face.

Years ago, on my way home from school, I remembered dodging street gangs; and the graffiti on walls and park benches had read JEWS NOT DESIRED. JUDEN RAUS! I felt so old now at fourteen.

The bile rose in my throat, clogging it, as I braced against the biting November wind. I imagined my Fatherland displayed on an elevated, revolving platform, crouched like a dying demon. Naked. Covered with warts. The whole world pointed an accusing finger at the shrivelled gnome. "Shame!" the outside voices jeered.

Something died within me. I felt betrayed by the leaders I once trusted. Alone. Once proud of my German heritage, I now felt disgraced.

Shrinking, I prayed to be swallowed by the black earth. How much farther to the English teacher's house. What was the homework for today? I opened my notebook. On the first page, in big bold letters, was printed the word, SUICIDE. Selbstmord.

On billboards, I had seen pictures of Dr. Goebbels, his wife, and their nine children dangling from ropes. "Our big mouth propaganda minister." Aunt Lina had covered dry eyes with clenched fists. "A bully and coward to the end!"

Bombarded with guilt, I remembered images on the billboard showing hollow faces of concentration camp survivors, the piles of dead bodies ravaged by typhus, the thousands killed in the gas chambers of Auschwitz, Belsen, and Buchenwald.

The icy wind blew rain sharp as needles into my face until I was numb with cold. Drifting between the horror of knowing and the anxiety of accepting, I wrestled with my dark side: I couldn't bear to be despised by the world, live with rejection. My Fatherland had lost its honor. There was no future for me. Only shame.

The literal German translation of suicide is self-murder. Selbstmord. I must do it. Drown in the deep abyss of hell.

Guilt drew me to the place where the devil once tempted Faust. Just ahead were the twisted girders jutting from the damaged bridge that once spanned the river. My teeth chattered as I stepped to the edge and looked below into the seething broil.

"Jump," beckoned Satan.

"I can't swim," cried the innocent child inside. As I stepped onto the closest cement boulder my muscles tightened.

"Don't be a coward," Lucifer hissed.

No longer was I aware of the driving rain, only the swollen river below. My head pounded, my feet moved mechanically to the next cement stanchion, perilously close to the edge. Thunder crashed overhead, a bolt of lightning split the sky and zigzagged to the other side of the river. I clutched at the corroded rail beside me. Flakes of rust glittered like dirty crystals in the flash as they fluttered to the yawning pit.

"I can't do it!" A voice inside me screamed, and I clung to a piece of upright rail, trembling with fear. It's dark down there. The wind whipped the water, splashing against mounds of mangled steel and masonry. I was scared. Where was my angel? Please, Lord, hear my prayer. At the count of three, "One...two..."

"Careful!" A hand gripped my wrist like a band of steel. A shard of light flashed across the wrinkled face of a wizened little man.

Is this a messenger of God, I thought? Did I hear the flitter of wings? Could it be that my guardian angel had returned?

Slowly, my body uncoiled.

Led by a firm male hand, never looking, never thinking, I crossed swiftly from rock to pillar and back to shore under the canopy of the dark sky. The rain slackened to a drizzle; the wind died down; for a fleeting moment parting clouds revealed a dazzling light. I caught a glimpse of that waxing moon, just a sliver—then instantly, it was all covered up again by dark clouds. "Never give up hope," the man said and disappeared into the city ruins.

"Danke," I whispered, adding silent words of gratitude. The prayer released the evil thoughts that had invaded my soul. My face softened. I'll find the door to the future, I thought, and shook the clinging drops from my rain-soaked hair.

Above, the lantern of the night still hid behind billowing clouds. Even if I never saw another patch of light for a long time—wouldn't I still be looking up, just in case.

There is something unassailable about the bright paradox that hangs above heavy clouds. Neither fear, nor despair, nor hate can muffle the song in the dark. Hope liberates.

CHAPTER FORTY-ONE—Needs—Mid 1946

"Razzia!" Shouts. Black marketeers, prostitutes, boys, girls, men and women, all scattered at the shrill sound of whistles. Police! Brakes screeched. Jeeps—American MP's. "A raid!"

Mamma, Aunt Lina and I ducked inside the covered entrance of a partially burned-out apartment house on a side street to get away from Friedrich-Ebert Strasse.

"That was a close one!" Auntie gasped. She pulled my hand to her chest. "Feel my heart beat."

From where we stood, we could see people being herded onto trucks. Some looked not much older than myself, but most were grownups dressed in attire ranging from army castoffs to business suits. Terrifying scenes of yesteryear flashed through my mind, like the roundup by the GESTAPO. "Where are they taking them?" I whispered anxiously.

"Police station," Auntie said. "Those caught with contraband and food will get a quick trial and heavy sentences."

Careful not to lean against the push-button bells next to the apartment owners' names, a man joined us on the now crowded porch. He pointed a finger to the military vehicles speeding away. "Serves those black market crooks right." He waited for the sound of sirens to ebb. "Guilty or not, I hear they're going to be checked for social diseases as well."

What about the innocent people, those not infected with diseases or dealing in illegal bartering activities? The thought of being forced to strip for an examination, or worse, put in jail, made me shudder.

Auntie poked me with her elbow. "Let's go."

As fast as the trucks left, the boulevard filled with people who, like us, had taken cover. The surprise police raids of late occurred randomly and often, making black marketing harder to conduct in the open, and exposed those infected with the rampantly spreading syphilis and gonorrhea. But it also humiliated the innocent populace.

From the top of ruined buildings at every street corner, larger-than-life-sized posters loomed, depicting cute blond Frauleins dressed in short skirts. "V D—WATCH OUT!" the caption blared. We knew all too well what the initials meant. I, too, stood in line to see a narrated, forty-five minute movie on "Venereal Disease" in order to get my ration card validated.

After the film, Auntie had exploded. "What a terrible way to introduce young, innocent people to something that should be beautiful and exciting," she had said.

The next day at the neighborhood grocer, the Hausfraus" discussed the documentary. "I never heard of VD before the American soldiers set foot on this land," said Frau Weber.

"These men in uniform are having an orgy with our young women," agreed Mamma. She glanced at me and continued her harangue. "I'm worried day and night about one of those Americans trying to seduce Anneliese!"

She didn't need to be concerned, I thought. After what I had viewed on that screen, I didn't want to have any part of whatever had to be done to get it. Movie close-ups had shown genitals of men and woman eaten up with raw sores, the infection spreading to inner thighs, then buttocks. I couldn't figure out how the ugly, festering boils got to the face and mouth. Fighting the feeling of defilement that crept over my body, I closed my eyes to the hideous sight. Momentarily, a cold fire consumed me.

Exhausted from the turmoil of daily living and the constant entrapments, it seemed all I could do is drag along between Mamma and my aunt as we carried out our routine chores. The outside world didn't interest me. Had I become numb to the continuous horror of a world gone mad and developed a calloused emotional unawareness? Who was I? What happened to my self-esteem? I was beginning to wonder what will happen to my generation.

Luckily, Mamma learned about the "Hoover Food Plan" sponsored by the Americans. (In June 1947, Secretary of State, George C. Marshall, gave a speech at Harvard University in which he outlined an aid program for Europe that came to be known as "The Marshall Plan.) It provided extra rations for the starving, and young children in public school were guaranteed one hot meal a day. Schooling was restored for primary grades to learn the basics of spelling and arithmetic, but no teaching material existed. Textbooks published during the Nazi regime were destroyed and new ones had not been printed. Since all factories were closed, production of goods had ceased, pencils and paper were not available. Machines that were not destroyed by war destruction, stood idle or were dismantled and shipped to England and Russia.

After waiting in line for hours, we each received what amounted to eight ounces of white powder, six ounces of yellow egg powder, and one pound of corn flour. "What is this?" We asked each other.

"The coarse stuff is Mais," someone explained. "On the farm, they use it for pig fodder."

"Perhaps the Americans think we're animals," called a child.

I remembered Grandpa growing stalks of corn to feed the rabbits and chickens.

"You can bake bread with it," said a woman. "I learned how in the American household I work in. Tastes pretty good once you're used to the texture."

But the oven in our kitchen didn't work—and we had no baking soda, so there was no reason to get the recipe from her. And what was Baking Soda? We knew how to use baking powder and yeast, but nothing ever asked for something called "soda."

My girlfriend told me that the fine yellow powder was a substitute for eggs, and the white powder made milk. "You add water and stir," she explained.

Clutching my three packages of "Hoover Food," I hurried upstairs, poured enough cold water over the milk powder to make a paste, and gulped down all of the one-month ration. Never had I tasted anything so good, so delicious, so sweet.

"You selfish girl." When Mamma realized what I had done, she slapped me.

My face stung—but I didn't care. I was only interested in the contented feeling of a full stomach. Like a starving animal, I finished licking the bowl. "It's my ration," I said. I couldn't believe my own words. Me, gentle Anneliese, talking back to my mother.

Mamma grabbed my hair, ready to hit me again.

Aunt Lina stepped between us. "Leave her alone, Johanna. She's hungry."

"Why do you always take her side?" Mamma shouted. "She's my daughter." She stabbed a thumb to her heaving chest. "I give the orders around here."

It wasn't the first time that they argued about me. Only last week they'd disagreed about whether or not I was old enough to use makeup.

"I won't have her wear lipstick. Absolutely not! Makes her look like a harlot. Trading a whole pack of cigarettes for one tube! She's too young. And that hairdo. Only jungle women wear curls frizzing in all directions."

"Don't you remember when we cut our braids into a short bob? We thought it looked chic." Lina vigorously brushed and spun my hair until it glistened, then put a touch of rouge on my lips. "Anneliese's old enough to use a little makeup," she insisted.

I used the opportunity to mention a course in manners and etiquette at a newly opened dancing studio. "My friends are allowed to go," I reasoned. "They also teach about hairstyles, dancing and…"

"I have no money for such nonsense," Mamma interrupted.

"I'll do more laundry."

"You promised not to go to the camps anymore," Mamma said.

Again, Lina came to my rescue. "Anneliese is growing into a young lady and needs to socialize. It will help her self-esteem. Times will soon change." Auntie appeared thoughtful as she watched Mamma's fingers fly furiously with her knitting needles. "I, for one, have not lost faith in the future." She looked from me to Mamma. "Maybe she'll meet a nice German boy in the class. I'll pay for the lessons."

They began the next week. We learned how to set a table. "Never use a knife to cut fish," the instructor taught us. "Always use two forks to pull it apart."

I didn't even know what fish tasted like, except marinated herring, called Rollmops.

"When being seated at a theater, enter the isle fronting the people. Never stick your behind in their faces," she instructed. I must tell Auntie. She was planning to take me to the opera "La Boheme" at a makeshift hall downtown the week after next.

A few days ago, she and I had gone to the ticket office at six in the morning to be the first in line at the opening at ten. We stamped our feet and blew on our cold hands to keep from freezing, but felt the reward was well worth the sacrifice. Food was not the only thing we were hungry for. Our souls were starved for beauty: music, paintings, sculptures, books.

The charm school teacher continued. "A gentleman always opens the door for a lady and lets her enter first. Once inside, he leads the way."

This seemed confusing to some of us. We practiced. My "make-believe" escort opened the door for me, I proceeded to enter, but when he stepped right in front of me, we bumped into each other. How embarrassing.

He scowled.

I flinched.

We tried again.

Then came the exciting part—dance instructions. Someone cranked up the dusty old gramophone and placed a record on the turntable. If the music sounded scratchy, I didn't hear it. I tried paying attention to the instructions ignoring the pinch in too tight pumps that belonged to my aunt.

I had no partner and felt like a wallflower watching my friends practice the steps. Am I not pretty enough, I fretted, forcing myself to stand straight and smile. When I was finally asked, I felt awkward to be held by a boy. The one-step was easy, the slow English waltz stiff and elegant, but suggested once you got used to it, it might be fun. The Strauss waltz made me dizzy. "One-two-three, one-two-three," everyone counted as we twirled around the room stepping on each others toes.

"The boys lead and the girls follow," the instructor reminded us.

No use fighting it, I thought, and moved to the beat.

After we were convinced we had mastered the polka and Spanish tango, we prepared a program to which friends and relatives were invited. Praise and pride abounded from the parents when we demonstrated how well-mannered we could be. Most of us wore dresses borrowed from older relatives, no food or drink was available, but there was music. Someone played on an upright piano that needed tuning as we labored through waltzes, tangos, fox-trots, and polkas. When the player switched to jazz—to the delight of all of us students—it was not met with pleasure by our parents and teachers.

"Zacke!" said my friend Ruth, bouncing to the beat. "Sharp!"

"Abscheulich!" moaned her mother. "Terrible. No harmony!"

Social manners, English, and shorthand lessons provided some new meaning to my life. But hunger still remained my most steady companion.

Mamma cut one piece of bread for each person in the morning. "Chew it slowly," she said. "It will last longer." Sometimes she browned some flour and added water—lots of water, to make a thin soup at noon. If lucky, we ate another slice of bread at bedtime. We chewed on bark, dug out dandelions and ate the greens, even stole food from each other.

Once, Ingrid and I hiked to the countryside and gathered wormy apples that had dropped on the ground. It was forbidden to pick them up, but hunger spoke louder than the law. When the farmer spotted us, we ran. As if for punishment, I lost my identification card. That was as dangerous as driving without a permit. For days I wouldn't leave the house, trembling with fear of the consequences. Then one morning the bell to our apartment buzzed. When I looked out the window to see who was there, I saw the owner of the orchard and his two burly sons standing on the sidewalk, one waving my identification card.

"Anneliese Eisenkraemer," the farmer scowled, "are you the one I saw stealing my apples?"

Not wanting the neighbors to hear, I quickly pushed the button so they could come up.

Mamma met them at the top of the stairs, while I waited by the apartment entrance, trembling with fear. Will I be treated like a criminal and sent to prison? I knew that to steal food was the worst crime one could commit and carried the same sentence as murder: Death. "I'm sorry," I blurted out, lowering my eyes in shame.

Mamma pleaded my case. "She didn't pick the apples from the tree, only gathered up the wormy ones that fell to the ground."

When I swore to never go near his orchards again, he returned my ID card and left without another word. Even as hungry as I was, I kept my promise.

"You got off easy this time," said Auntie's friend, Otto, the truck driver. "Even bartering with the farmers takes finesse," he explained. "I provide a torn bag of cement, a few bricks, some tools. They give me a few eggs, or a bit of bacon."

Otto and his eight-year old daughter, Helga, were steady visitors at our apartment. There was always something to fix: walls to be plastered, doors to be hung, or glass to put into windows. He not only did the work, but "appropriated" the material, called damaged goods.

One night, he surprised us by bringing a slaughtered pig and butchered it in our kitchen. Mamma and Lina ground up the meat, and he supplied the spices and herbs for making sausages. Although the sow was legally his—he had raised it from a piglet—the law demanded half of the animal to be donated to a public slaughterhouse. Otto hadn't reported the existence of the pig. "I don't trust those thieving thugs in authority," he said. "We have less than any one of those new law and order people." Putting a finger on his lips, he said, "Let's keep it a secret."

But someone must have seen him and his buddy carry the pig into the building and ratted on him.

After a feast of pork in the middle of the night, the rest was ground into sausages and hung on a broomstick over the bathtub. In the morning, there was a knock at the entrance door. When I opened it, two German policemen and a member of the American military police barged in.

"I'll get my mother," I said and ran down the hall to the living room.

Otto jumped to his feet. "Johanna, quick! Stall them."

"How?"

"Yell and scream GESTAPO, anything," he said rushing out of the room.

Hands on hips with elbows extended, Mamma blocked their path. "Who do you think you are coming into my house uninvited?" she ranted. "Where are your papers?" Stabbing her finger at one of the Germans, she screamed, "I know the law. Show me your documents that say you are allowed to enter my house!"

One of the men pointed to the American soldier whose helmet bore the initials MP. "He has authority to search the flat for a pig. We..."

Mamma didn't let him finish. "Who are you calling a pig?" She yelled, her mighty voice increasing in volume with every syllable. "GESTAPO methods again. Will we ever be free of them?" Her arms waved in the air as she raved. "We're starving half to death and here comes the GESTAPO again."

The MP tried to calm her. "Nix GESTAPO. Amerikaner," he said in broken German.

When the German police tried to push her aside, she would not budge. "You come one step closer, I kick you in the balls!" she threatened.

His face red, one of the policeman shouted, "I'll report you to my superior!"

"His name must be Hitler." Mamma spit and stepped on the spittle. "And I thought he was dead."

From behind Mamma, Otto approached. "What is all the commotion?" he drawled in his slow Saxonian dialect. "Let them look, Johanna. We have nothing to hide."

"I don't want them in my home," screamed Mamma.

Otto faced the police calmly. "Why are you here?"

"We have orders to search the apartment," said the older of the two.

"To see what else you can steal?" Mamma pointed a finger at the younger one.

"We have nothing worth stealing," Otto stepped in front of Mamma and waved the law enforcement group inside. "See for yourself."

They didn't find a single sausage. Otto had dropped the bunch into the empty bathtub and piled dirty clothing on them.

"You deserve a medal for your performance," Lina said after the police were gone. "I was shaking all over, fearing they would discover the meat and arrest my Otto."

"I told 'em!" Mamma grinned with self-satisfaction. "They couldn't get out of here quick enough!"

Lina suddenly rose from her chair. Her less than five-foot frame stretching another inch, her large brown eyes sparkling like those of a young girl in love, she beamed. "I have a special announcement." She stood next to six-foot Otto and put her arm affectionately around his waist. "We're planning to be married. Soon."

I pictured my cosmopolitan aunt moving into Otto's small two-story home that did have running water, but no bath, and a toilet that was an outhouse next to the storage shed. A vegetable garden and various fruit trees surrounded the house outside the city where a dozen chickens provided fresh eggs. Would she be able to wear makeup and fancy dresses in this rural area?

Auntie provided the answer. "I'll start a new life and cook and clean for my loving husband and little girl." She drew eight-year old Helga into her arms and straightened a ribbon in her hair. "I always wanted my own little girl," Lina said. "We'll bake Christmas cookies together and grow a flower garden."

Helga nodded. "And I'll show you how to milk the goat," she bubbled.

Congratulations abounded, but I had a difficult time seeing my aunt as a Hausfrau. I giggled as I pictured her in one of her outlandish chapeaus while feeding the chickens. I'll miss her, I thought, swallowing hard.

Oh well, I reasoned, the four-room apartment was getting too crowded anyway. Mamma rented one of the bedrooms to Anni, a girl three years my senior, who was apprenticing to become a dental assistant. Paula, Mamma's old-time friend, occupied the second spare bedroom. She came to live with us after Walter found her in an alley. There, huddled in a pile of rubble, sick with fever and a wretched cough, she had a letter clutched in her hand. It was from her husband, Heini. "He's alive," she sobbed. "In a prison camp...somewhere in America."

We nursed Paula back to health by giving her lodging, love and care. Once she recovered, she contributed as best as she could by helping with housekeeping chores and sewing. Finally, Walter had an ally again. Sometimes I thought he loved her more than Mamma.

I enjoyed her company, but stayed away from Mamma's new boyfriend, Fritz, a colleague of Otto's. He was tall, dark-haired, and good-looking, but his sarcasm burned like acid.

Would they get married, too, I wondered? What if Pappa returned? Had Mamma got a divorce? I must ask Lina.

311

CHAPTER FORTY-TWO—Growing Up—Fall 1946

Indian summer. It was one of those hot days in autumn when old women warm their brittle bones before winter blows away the sun. Altweibersommer.

On my way to Aunt Lina's, I transferred to the streetcar going to Schwanheim, a suburb of Frankfurt, where she and Otto lived. Their home reminded me so much of my grandparents' house in Heilbronn.

Poor Grandma. I shut my eyes and thought of her struggle with death. "The night she died," Grandpa wrote, Oma's voice softened to a hush, then paused. A quietness filled the room."

I had another kilometer to walk after the last streetcar stop. The asphalt felt hot under my sandals. I should have worn a sleeveless blouse instead of a handknit sweater. Anxiously I wondered what Auntie fixed for lunch? I'd been without food for more than a day and my stomach made those familiar gurgling noises. "Feed me," it demanded.

My mouth watered in anticipation of salad from new potatoes, a fried egg, goat milk, perhaps fresh plums. She'd fill my shopping net with bruised apples and pears to be cored and sliced. I liked stringing the pieces on strong thread and attaching the ends to hooks on each side of the window. Sun-dried fruit tasted good in the winter.

To my amazement, Auntie wasn't home. Their black Doberman, tied to a long leash, barked fiercely as I walked around the house. I peered into the shed and called Auntie's name many times. Still deathly afraid of dogs, I stayed well out of the animal's reach while scouring the trees and grounds for fruit—but both were picked clean. "Be quiet, Lux!" I commanded in frustration.

A neighbor called from the street. "You looking for the new Frau Pflug?"

"Yes. I'm her niece."

"She left an hour ago to see her sister."

Now I remembered. Auntie had planned to draw money from her meager savings, so that I could enroll in the newly opened commercial school. She was visiting my home today. How could I have confused the days?

Disappointed, I returned to the road. It was going to be a long way home, I thought. Having spent my last Groschen for commuter fare, I'd counted on Auntie to pay my return ticket. And nothing to eat. I tried ignoring the gnawing pain in my gut. Too weak to walk and too tired to think, I just stood there.

A horn tooted behind me. By the sound of it, I knew it was an American army vehicle. "Hey, Fraeulein. Kommen Sie her." The jeep slowed. "Come here, Miss." All GI's seemed to have learned that invitation.

Doggedly I trudged on, ignoring their waves and shouts. My knees felt as though they would buckle with the next step. What if I hitched a ride? The thought was tempting. They might stop at the snackshop near the barracks and buy me something they called a hamburger. Anni had told me about those meat patties, tomatoes and onions between two pieces of bread. Every day, Cliff, her soldier boyfriend, treated her to one. My mouth began to water. Visions of ice cream floated through my mind. Vanilla and chocolate. Donuts with powdered sugar.

Another jeep slowed. "Hey, Fraulein…"

Briefly, I glanced up—then away.

The vehicle moved on.

A sharp cramp in my stomach brought bitter juices to my mouth. I couldn't hold out any longer—the thought of food tempted me. So when another olive-green vehicle approached, I held up my hand to flag it down. "Hamburger," I said to the driver of the jeep.

The three passengers exploded with laughter and shouts.

What were they saying?

"Hamburger," I repeated. "Snack shop."

More laughter. More talk. "Hop in," said the one at the driver's seat.

Jostling between two soldiers on the bench in the back, my heart raced faster than the engine as we sped down the road. I tried to smile, but the ride was bumpy—and I was scared.

The driver stopped near the commissary and jumped off. We all went inside the place that was crowded with American soldiers who ate from metal trays, not dishes. Loud music streamed from a large, shiny machine with many buttons. We sat at a small, square table that slightly wobbled. No waiter took an order or served the food, and the menu appeared in bright, bold letters above a food counter. "Self-service," said a handwritten sign near the cash register.

"Mustard? Ketchup?"

I didn't know what it was, but nodded.

"Drink?"

"Coca Cola." Oh, this was going to be wonderful. I trembled with excitement. Coca Cola. I remembered a picnic in the forest years ago. Uncle Bert bought Walter and me some of that good-tasting brown bubbly beverage. We shared a whole bottle. I couldn't help licking my lips in expectation.

In the corner, the juke box played, "You Are My Sunshine." The aroma of sizzling meat teased my taste buds making me swallow in anticipation. When the hamburger was placed in front of me, I looked for a fork and knife to cut it.

"You pick it up with both hands and bite, like this." The tall soldier with the freckles and red hair grabbed his hamburger and showed me.

It was bad manners to eat with your hands, I thought. I glanced around the room. Here everyone did it. Never mind etiquette, I thought and gingerly picked up the large sandwich that held a thick meat patty garnished with green and red stuff, and took a bite. It tasted like nothing I had ever eaten before. Absolutely heavenly.

I didn't mind the juice dripping down my fingers. Too engrossed in looking around and listening to the music, I didn't pay any attention to what my benefactors were talking about and didn't even notice when one after the other left. I just chewed and swallowed bite after bite until the last morsel had disappeared down my throat. Satisfied, I looked up. Only the tall, freckled-faced jeep driver was left.

"How old are you?" He asked in English.

"Fifteen." I sat up straight to look more grownup because almost everyone took me to be younger.

I wondered how much older than I he could be? Four or five years?

"You want to go to a party?" When he spoke, his deep blue eyes blazed. He was handsome. "More food, and dancing." His white teeth sparkled behind a broad grin.

A party, I thought. Music. It sounded like fun. But was it proper? No. Mamma wouldn't approve. Neither would Lina. Nor Paula. But I wanted to go and what could it hurt? I looked at his freckled face. "OK," I nodded.

He grabbed his army cap, pulled it over his red crew-cut and said, "OK, Babe, let's go!"

Sitting in the front seat next to him, I started wondering where the party was and when I'd get back. Mamma and Lina would be waiting. Worry shadowed my original jubilance.

"What's your name?" When he put his hand on my thigh, an uneasy feeling swept over me.

"Anneliese." Great God, I thought, what am I doing? Mamma's voice boomed in my ears. "Nothing is free. One way or another, you'll have to pay for whatever you receive."

"Mine's Richard," he said, squeezing my thigh again. "Richard Young, from Columbus, Ohio."

I had no idea where Ohio was, and didn't care. All I thought about were his intentions. Pressing my knees together, I pulled on my skirt. Panic tightened my throat. What happens after the party? How would I find my way home? None of the streets looked familiar.

Richard said something, that I didn't understand. Mentally, I had to translate each word, and I was too busy debating within myself what was right or wrong. He'd fed me. It tasted good. I had thanked him. Did I owe him more? Should I offer to do his laundry? Yes, that seemed fair. But the party? Dancing sounded like so much fun. Yet this wasn't like me jumping headlong into something I knew little about.

Slowing the jeep at an intersection, he started whistling and patted my thigh again.

"Stop!" I cried. My heart pounded.

He raised his hand as if I had bitten it.

"Stop the jeep!"

"What the hell..." The brakes squealed.

Without looking back, I opened the door, jumped out, and ran. I don't know how long, how far, or how fast. I just ran for what seemed like hours. Once, I stopped to ask for directions. Luckily, the man knew my street.

Exhausted, I finally arrived at our apartment house and pushed the third bell button to be admitted. Someone depressed the buzzer from the second floor. The door opened and I stumbled up the stairs.

Mamma was waiting. "Where in the world have you been?" She shouted. "We have been worried sick! Do you know what time it is?" No doubt about it, Mamma was upset.

"I lost my way." That's all I confessed. Biting into one of the green apples that Auntie had brought, my mouth puckered. I should never have accepted that ride, nor asked for food. I knew it was a bad decision. What had hunger driven me to do? But I gave myself credit for jumping from the jeep. Wondering how many calories I wasted running, I took another bite out of the sour apple. If I didn't eat it, someone else would.

The next day I took the entrance exam at the commercial school.

"I'm concerned about your age," said the principal, Miss Tierney, a prim and proper English lady who spoke German fluently. "All of the students are at least sixteen. Some are old enough to have finished high school. But you have a lot of gaps in your education..." She paused and studied my application.

"I was hospitalized with typhus," I explained timidly.

"And you didn't finish the first semester of eighth grade." She tapped a finger on the dilapidated wooden desk.

My heart sank. "School closed a year before the end of the war." I hoped it didn't sound like whining. "Because they needed young people to work in households and factories."

"I know." I saw her glancing at my exam, page by page.

Anxiously, I watched her face. The test didn't seem that difficult—except the section on English.

"You'll have a lot of catching up to do, especially in English." Miss Tierney set the papers aside and folded her hands. "You just passed—barely. Even considering your limited educational background..." She smiled. "I'll give you a chance. Be aware, however, that you're up against tough competition."

Eight hours a day I studied—sometimes more. Classes were co-educational, a new experience. One I didn't object to. We were allotted one pencil per person, a little writing paper, but there were no text books, and no typewriters to practice on. From pictures, I learned what the parts of the Schreibmachine were called and how to use them. Keeping my eyes riveted on a chart, I mastered the keyboard by moving fingers across invisible keys. Learning how to write a quality business letter was less of a challenge than economics. Business math was fun.

The principal taught English. I did well in grammar. However, when Miss Tierney returned the results of the first twenty-five-word spelling test, she handed me my paper face down.

Lifting the sheet, I glanced at the numeral twenty-three. Not bad, I thought—until I noticed the minus sign in front of it. Devastated, I hung my head in shame. Spelling had always been my strength in German.

"Don't worry!" whispered Miss Tierney handing me a copy of Reader's Digest. "Join our discussion group after school," she suggested. "We read out loud and converse in Oxford English—not American slang."

I followed her advice. Not only did my command of English improve in leaps, but by copying written words, I mastered spelling.

With pride, Mamma bragged about my good grades to Frau Hild, the woman downstairs. Her husband was the sales manager for a small textile firm in downtown Frankfurt.

"They need help in the office," the neighbor mentioned. "Someone who can type, take dictation, and answer the telephone."

To my surprise, Herr Hild arranged an interview. He even drove me in the company car to the firm.

Outside the office hung a small sign. JAHN & COMPANY, General Manager, Hartwig Bahn, Doctor of Jurisprudence, Doctor of Philosophy. I stopped and stared at his title and degrees.

"Don't worry," said Herr Hild as he opened the heavy front door. "His degrees are in chemistry and law, but all he wants is a good general office worker."

The tall man behind the desk rose and strode toward me. "Please take a seat," he said, after the introduction and handshake had taken place.

He appeared much younger and less studious than I expected for a man with two titles after his name. Shuffling through some papers that cluttered his desk top, he started the interview. "How old are you?"

"Sixteen." I lied, afraid he wouldn't hire me because I wasn't old enough.

"Can you take dictation?"

"Yes. Eighty words a minute." I loved shorthand and hoped to be a newspaper or court stenographer some day.

"What kind of typewriter are you used to?"

I was at a loss for an answer. Adler VII was the only make I could remember. It happened to be an antiquidated model with a keyboard of only three rows.

"Oh—we have more modern equipment than that." Dr. Bahn ushered me to the desk on which sat a shiny Olympia.

"It certainly is different from what I've seen," I stuttered.

"Try it," he said and turned to answer the phone.

Nervously, I looked at the metal monstrosity. Where do you insert the paper. Bending over the machine, I fiddled with the knobs.

From a far corner of the room, a white-haired man came to my rescue.

"Name's Braun," he mumbled without shaking my hand. "I'm the bookkeeper." He peered from behind thick lenses. "Let me show you," he offered and inserted the paper behind the roller.

Fingers resting in the right position, I attempted to push a key.

"Harder," he whispered.

Perspiration began to trickle down my forehead. Determined, I hit another key, and another, until I filled the first line fairly quickly. What next? There must be something you push, pull or turn to advance the paper.

"Try this." Herr Braun moved the carriage return. "Have you ever operated a typewriter?" he asked.

"I've never even seen one," I admitted.

He waited for the boss to get off the phone before approaching him. "Dr. Bahn, I suggest we let Miss Eisenkraemer take the machine home to practice over the weekend so she can get used to the more sophisticated model."

Herr Hild, who was introduced as the sales manager, quickly solved the problem. "I'll be glad to transport the instrument in my car." He even carried it up the stairs and placed it on the kitchen table. "She must practice all weekend," he told Mamma.

"I've got the job!" I exclaimed happily.

"How much?"

I told her.

Mamma frowned. "A hundred Marks a month? That's the price of a package of cigarettes on the black market."

"Better than washing and ironing a duffel bag full of uniforms." Aunt Lina was visiting and fed a few sticks of wood to the feeble flame inside the pot belly stove. "Promise to finish your schooling," she ordered.

I nodded and struck another key.

Paula watched over my shoulder. "If only Haseneier could see her now," she said, and lit a cigarette.

"Her no-good father?" Mamma's voice turned to ice.

My ears perked up. Haseneier, I typed. Funny name. Haseneier. Means rabbit eggs.

Then I heard Mamma's voice again. "I met him downtown the other day—he's a cripple now."

CHAPTER FORTY-THREE—Acceptance— March 1947

The "winter years" continued—leaden month dragging after leaden month. Slowly, almost unnoticeably, things began to change.

I worked hard for the Jahn & Company textile firm. The telephone rang often, dictation was heavy, and my fingers pounded the typewriter keys with fury. Once a week, I made money deposits in a newly opened bank on Friedrich-Ebert-Strasse. Black marketing on this street was on a decline and police raids had diminished. The office work provided new meaning to my existence—a life I'd almost snuffed out when I tried to jump off the Frankfurt bridge.

At the end of the month, I handed my pay envelope to Mamma with pride, and on weekends, I earned spending money by doing laundry for Anni's soldier friend, Cliff. Cigarettes were still currency for anything you couldn't buy in stores: nylons, shoes, textiles, coffee, and food.

When the company offered more hours for better pay, I decided to improve my skills by enrolling in evening courses at the business school my girlfriend, Ingrid, attended.

Before we started our lessons, she shared letters her father wrote to her from a prisoner of war camp in France. She wrote to him daily and hoped he'd be released soon. When I told her of my longing to meet my biological father—even if according to Mamma, he was "no-good"—she helped me plan to find him. It started like an innocent game, but soon my desire to see him became an obsession.

Strolling down the street, we searched the faces of tall, middle-aged men who might bear a resemblance to me. One day, Ingrid whispered excitedly, "That's him!" She pointed to a tall man in a business suit and carrying a cane who got off the streetcar just as we boarded.

I caught but a glimpse of his face—pensive with a touch of melancholy— before he turned and disappeared from view.

"He looked just like you," Ingrid insisted. "Always a little sad."

Every night for the next week, we waited at that same stop for the man who looked as though he could be my father—but he did not appear again.

Determined, I tried wrangling more information from Paula. "I know he lives across the river," she said, "but I don't know his address." She heaved a deep sign. "This is dangerous what you are doing, Anneliese—like playing with fire," she warned. "He may not accept you. Remember, he denied his fatherhood before."

"Just once I want to see him." Then I told her how I used to spin tales about the two of us together. "In my daydreams, I'd pretend he took me to the circus. I'd sit on his lap, and we'd laugh and cry with the clowns, watch the trapeze artists, and see tigers jump through burning hoops."

Paula smiled. "Go on," she said, "tell me more."

"Sometimes, I'd pretend he would let me ride piggy-back while he walked around the zoo, and he'd buy nuts that I could feed to the elephants, and small bags of herring for the sea lions. And on our way home, he'd get a gigantic ice cream for us to share." I stopped talking to take a breath, but I wanted time to enjoy the picture I just painted.

"Go on." Paula poured herself a cup of coffee and seated herself facing me.

"I'd imagine he'd tuck me into bed at night and tell me stories of Snow White, and Red Riding Hood, and Rumpelstilzchen."

Heini, Paula's husband, entered and greeted me with a pinch on the cheek and his wife with a pat on her ample behind. His square face was covered with dust and grime from bricklaying, but he looked content. Often he'd tell what we considered "tall" stories of his life as a POW, picking bushels of oranges in vast groves near a place called Pomona in California. Today, however, he seemed tired.

"At last we finished our project," he said. "Tonight I'll sleep like a stone. But in the morning I'll sing with the larks. Tomorrow we'll start a bigger job near the downtown police station." He turned on the faucet over the sink and scrubbed the cement off his hands and face.

"Aha!' Paula's face lit up like a flash of lightening as she thought of a solution to my dilemma. She leaned closer to me and whispered, "Go to the registrar in the police building. For a small fee, they'll release the address of your father."

I was jubilant! But for a few breaths those feelings turned into apprehension. Would he like me? Of course, he would. What dress was appropriate? Should my hair be styled in curls or worn straight? I must look pretty—my best.

I consulted with Ingrid, and instead of doing homework, we planned into the night what I should wear. Finally, I decided on the pin-striped suit I wore to the job interview several months before.

As always, the streetcar was packed with people as it rattled through downtown Frankfurt, adding people at every stop. But I didn't care that sunny afternoon. "I'm going to meet my father." My heart sang.

Closing my eyes, I pictured his face. Handsome or homely, I'd be happy to see him. Yes, he'd smile and take me into his arms and he'd hug me and say in a low, kind voice, "I'm so proud of you, my daughter."

He should be proud, I thought. I'm earning most of my family's living. I'm a hard worker and a good student.

What if he rejects me? Thorns of grief pierced my fantasy. Silently, I cried out, "Where were you, Vati, when I was a little girl? Why didn't you ever come to see me or remember my birthday with a card while you were a soldier in the war?"

More realistically, I wondered about his military career. Had he fought in the infantry in Russia, or been a hero in a tank battalion in Africa? Perhaps he'd crisscrossed the Atlantic in a submarine—or been a Messerschmitt pilot? Hadn't Mamma once mentioned to Paula that he was an officer?

Cripple. The image of a handicapped person in a wheelchair flashed through my mind. Did Mamma ever utter this painful word? No. I must've imagined it.

The conductor asked for my ticket. "Transfer at the next stop, Fraeulein, and take number eight South." His voice reminded me of the official at the police station who'd renewed my identification card. I could still feel the sting of embarrassment.

"Name of father?"

"I don't have one," I mumbled.

"Everyone has a father, young lady!"

"I don't know his name."

"Unehelich?" I remember seeing the clerk's raised eyebrow, the smirk on his face while he waited for an answer. "Out of wedlock?"

Feeling shame, I wrote the offending word—illegitimate.

Noisy brakes jolted my thoughts. I stepped off the streetcar and waited for another to take me to my final destination. Nice neighborhood, I noticed.

Perhaps my father was rich—not a millionaire, but he could be a prosperous merchant. What if he was a professor with distinguished white hair? What if…?

Nervously, I boarded the next streetcar. Once more, I mentally rehearsed my speech. My name is Anneliese Eisenkraemer. I've come to see my father.

At the next stop, I got off, trying to remember the house number. What if he slammed the door in my face? My legs moved as though weighed down by lumps of lead as I located Sachsenstrasse 45 and stepped up to the apartment house, which was veneered with red sandstone.

I stared at the house number. What if he wasn't home? My heart pounded like a hammer. Palms sweaty, I forced myself to ring the bell and waited for footsteps inside. I heard a dull clunk, then another, a scraping noise…

The door opened wide.

"My name is…" Expecting a tall person, I looked up—then down, down, down at the figure rocking on his rump—a man who had no legs. "…Anneliese Eisenkraemer." I choked out the next words. "I've come to see my father."

In the dimness of the room, I could not make out whether his eyes mirrored gladness or grief, acceptance or denial.

"Come in," he said, moving back, rocking his torso with the help of two block-shaped, padded crutches in his hands. "I knew my daughter would come some day."

Daughter! Had I heard right? Was there a hint of pride in his mellow voice? He called me daughter.

"Lisbeth," he shouted in the direction of another room, and asked me to wait in the spacious but chilly entrance hall. He was gone, faster than seemed possible for someone so handicapped.

I stood in the frigid, musty-smelling room. Waiting. Motionless. Shocked.

Muffled sounds of the city reached me through the window slit. I cried tears of ecstasy and joy. He had acknowledged me.

I have a father. A real father.

Then tears of disbelief and sorrow. He'd lost both legs—completely off. I'm so sorry, Vati…

The woman he called Lisbeth appeared and ushered me inside a formal room. "I'll get some tea," she said.

My father sat propped in an armchair behind the table, a sunny smile on his handsome face, a twinkle in his deep blue eyes. His hair was not white, but black and wavy. I fell in love with him, wanted to throw my arms around him, lay my head on his shoulder, but didn't. Perhaps he'll reach out for me. He didn't.

When the woman returned with a tray, he introduced her. "My wife."

My Mamma is much prettier, I thought.

Frau Haseneier acknowledged the introduction with a nod, then silently poured the tea before leaving the room again.

"How is your mother?"

The question startled me. "She's fine," I said. "She doesn't know I'm here."

He didn't seem surprised. Nodding, he encouraged me to help myself to a cookie. "Sorry I can't offer you more," he said, "but I live on a veteran's pension."

Why did he tell me this? He must have thought I wanted money. Lifting my cup with forefinger and thumb, I sipped daintily and said, "I have a position—stenographer!"

Appearing relieved, he said, "Your mother did a good job raising you."

Why did he give her all the credit? "My salary helps with the rent," I said with pride. "This suit—I bought it with money doing laundry on weekends...."

He continued as though I hadn't spoken. "Johanna was beautiful. So vivacious. So passionate. Always the life of the party." Mechanically, he refilled my cup.

Nibbling a cookie, I thought, who was he talking about? Certainly not my Mamma!

"Sometimes, after she was through with her waitress chores, she'd sing and dance on tables for tips—and she got many."

No! Not Mamma! The thought of Mamma performing in such a scandalous way in front of men was unthinkable.

Frau Haseneier entered with more hot tea. Meekly, she put the pretty pot on the table. "Would you like more cookies?" Like her demeanor, her voice had the timid chime of a mantle clock that needs rewinding.

"No, thank you," I said.

Without saying another word, she left the room.

"How is your mother?" He asked again.

"Fine." I didn't want to talk about Mamma, and kept hoping he'd ask about me. Jealousy engulfed me. Should I tell him she was planning to get married soon? I decided to change the subject. "What did you do in the war?"

His eyes clouded over. The broad smile disappeared. "I was a gunner in a tank," he said. "Got stuck in the frozen earth of Russia during the winter offensive. No gasoline. No ammunition. No food. No roads. Just ice. He pointed to the china cabinet. "There's a box of pictures in that drawer. Would you get it for me, please?"

Seeing him sit so straight behind the table, I'd forgotten he couldn't walk. As he searched through piles of pictures, I was fascinated by his long fingers, strong forearms, and bulging muscles. I fought an urge to touch his hands. Why didn't he grasp mine? I wanted to be touched by my father.

He found a small photograph and handed it to me. "It's me—in uniform. It's the only photo that shows all of me."

Hands shaking, I stared at the picture. At first, all I saw were his legs—two long legs. They supported a lean body that stretched up, up, up, until a smiling face came into focus. Blue eyes, black hair.

Still trembling, I placed the picture on the table and looked at the man sitting in front of me. My father. Without legs.

I saw no self-pity in his bright eyes. No pain. No anger. "Thank you," I said, suppressing a sob.

Why did he glance at the clock on the mantle? Was he tired? I searched his face for signs of fatigue.

"I'm glad you came," he said, quickly rubbing his eyes.

"Can I visit again?"

He shrugged and shook my hand. "Auf Wiedersehn."

Frau Haseneier walked me to the door. It slammed shut.

Riding home on the streetcar, I sat squeezed between a mother bouncing a baby on her knees and an old man reeking of tobacco. My emotions were all mixed up. Joy was jostled by sadness, love pushed by anger. I wrestled with the beast inside that clawed at my heart. "That bum!" it growled. "He ravished Mamma's beauty and passion—and then left her stranded in the streets with a big belly."

Funny, I'd never thought of Mamma as beautiful, nor imagined her dancing. I rarely heard her laugh. Had my real Mamma died? In fact, why did she so often seem bitter? Why was her voice hard with hate? She once told Paula, "I curse that no-good father of Anneliese every day for shirking his responsibility as a parent." Only last week, I heard her say, "God must have answered my prayer and turned him into a cripple. He deserved it!"

Did God punish? I remembered what was taught in catechism. God forgives. Life is so confusing.

Behind closed eyelids, I recalled my father's sunny smile, the sparkling eyes, his dazzling good looks. Suddenly, I felt pain. Anger.

"He's a monster!" I remembered my mother saying. The lion inside me roared. "He insulted my mother in court by insisting he wasn't the only one being roasted by her searing fire."

Envy complicated my thought when I was reminded of how he still yearned for her—my Mamma, yet how little he seemed to appreciate me. He never even said I was pretty. Never said he was proud of my accomplishments.

"They had a few minutes of sexual bliss, all so you, little Anneliese, could live a lifetime of shame," the beast growled.

The streetcar came to a screeching halt. Shivering, I stepped off and walked into the street, bracing against a sudden gust of April wind. No longer did the earth bask in sunshine. I looked around and, as always, the one-legged man on crutches stood at the corner begging. Pity joined the pain piercing my heart. I gritted my teeth to stifle a cry as I imagined my father in uniform standing in front of a tank. He's not a cripple. He's a hero! I protested, trying to deny the feeling of hurt gnawing inside me.

"He's a coward on stumps," argued the beast, "no different than he was with two good legs."

I stumbled over a pile of rubble heaped against burned-out ruins. Suddenly, the need to physically express my feelings caused me to beat my fists against what was left of a crumbling wall. Sweat drenched my brow. Burying my face in bruised hands, I slowly slumped to the ground, sobbing.

Mamma was right. My father was no good. Long ago, he should have faced the responsibility of his passion.

I sat there staring at a weed that had pushed its thorns through the crack of cobblestones and thought of yet another wretched soul—my stepfather. Despite his crippled arm, he had often brutally beaten and abused me and my brother until we cowered in fear. Drunk or sober, sometimes under the cloak of kindness, he'd ruled as a tyrant. How he must have despised himself to commit suicide a week after he disappeared. The image of him dangling from a rope in the dark woods made me shudder.

I remember Mamma returning from the morgue where she'd identified him. She didn't shed a tear. Neither did I.

Standing up to him on that fateful morning in the dim lit hallway took courage, but I had to do it to save my honor.

Only Walter sat in the corner on the small, three-legged stool and sobbed.

I picked up a chunk of rubble and hurled it against the remnants of a distant pillar. As if in slow motion, I watched it crumble. Contemptuous of the present, I angrily continued to tear the past to pieces: My father, my family, my country.

Hitler. He must have been the devil personified. We all had followed our Fuehrer, believed his promises of a greater Fatherland, a better world. All he did was lead us to destruction. He was but a sadistic Satan in the guise of a patriot who exploited a once proud nation. Deceived us—just as my father had deceived my mother. Now our country and its people were beaten to the ground. As crippled as my father.

Is there a tomorrow? If so, what will the future hold?

Guilt. Collective guilt. We must live it the rest of our lives.

Will my children and my grandchildren be carriers of the guilt of their forefathers? Dear God. Not if I can help it.

As if pushed by a higher power, I found myself standing at the threshold of Paula's apartment, rang the doorbell, and raced up the three flights of stairs, two steps at a time. No need to knock. She stood waiting with outstretched arms.

"How did it go?" Pressing my head to her soft, ample bosom, she stroked my tousled hair, then wiped my tear-flooded face with the edge of her wrap-around apron.

"He lost his legs."

"I know." She pulled a handkerchief from her pocket.

After dabbing my eyes and blowing my nose into the crumpled cotton tissue, I said, "He asked about Mamma—twice."

A brief frown creased Paula's brow. "Promise to never tell your Mamma you went to visit him—or that I knew about it. It would mean the end of our long friendship."

I promised, but secretly wished I could confide to my mother as to how I struggled to turn my back on the man who evoked pity and loathing at the same time, my pain to comprehend why he abandoned her and me, and my need to make contact with my biological father. "He' s
handsome," I said.

Paula nodded. "Did he invite you back?"

"He said, 'Auf Wiedersehen' before the door slammed shut." It was my turn to knot my brow. "He might not want me to return."

"What about you? Do you want o see him again?"

I shrugged. Had hope once more turned into despair? "He doesn't deserve to have a daughter," I whispered—and buried my face against her chest again.

"Before drawing a final curtain across the past, let's sit down and talk about the most important person of tomorrow. You."

Reluctantly, I sat. "Me? You mean me?"

"Yes, you. Little Anneliese Eisenkraemer, soon to be a grownup sixteen."

I thought for a long time about some of the people and events that had helped mold me into the person I was today: Family, teachers, friends, foes. The war.

"I'm just simple, plain Anneliese," I said. "But someday, I'm going to be somebody. Have a career. Maybe work for a newspaper. Be an author. Perhaps write stories about the way it was once upon a time."

Paula leaned back in her chair—and listened.

I remembered Miss Thyssen, my first and favorite teacher. In her precise, old-fashioned script she had written in my poetry album. "Child, learn two things in life: First, something to earn a living. Second, to do without that not within your reach."

Paul listened.

"Some day I want to help people regain their dignity with humor and laughter, like my Tante Lina."

I remembered Auntie brightening the darkest sides of life with fantasy and humor. She argued away conflict by singing opera, created a castle for castoffs, and saw the wonder of lightening in even the blackest clouds. "Be good to each other and believe in yourself," was her motto.

Paula listened.

"Caring," I said. "I wish to see the good in people."

I remembered Grandma not only enveloping me with unconditional love, but also being

compassionate to others in an intolerable society. "Wave, children, wave," Oma had cried when a string of freight cars crowded with Jews rumbled past. David.

Paula listened

"Friends. I hope to make new ones."

I remembered Hannelore, sweet innocent Hannelore, who laughed so quickly, died so young.

Paula listened.

"Evil. Like a weed in a flower garden, it spreads and strangles. I want to pull it out by its root."

I remembered how Walter, my half-brother, survived by denying the existence of pain. "It doesn't hurt anymore," he said after another brutal beating.

Paula still listened.

"Courage. It wipes out fear."

I remember standing up to my stepfather, the pervert who derived pleasure and power by intimidation. It had taken courage to face that bully—and it had worked.

Mamma. I remembered her standing up to the young Hitler Youth punk on Crystal Night. And seven years later, just before the collapse of the Third Reich, slapping a Nazi official when he called her a bad name.

She knitted and sewed into the night, and cleaned other people's homes to keep a roof over ours. When the bombs destroyed our meager belongings, she didn't wait for handouts, but rolled up her sleeves and started all over. Never did she clutch long at a thin limb of hope, but instead she reached for a sturdier branch—and kept climbing.

"Some call Mamma stubborn, like an ornery mule that makes it home despite its mean master. Others have called her foolish for fighting for what's right and just."

Paula moved forward in her chair. "How do you see your mother?"

The answer came quick. "She's hard-working, honest and fearless." I wanted to add, "Except for the men she picks to share her life with," but left the words unsaid.

"Johanna's character is complex," said Paula. "One moment, she'll give you the shirt off her back, the next her heart is clad with steel. In style, she swims with the current, in principle, she stands like a rock."

I looked into my confidante's calm eyes—eyes that reflected quiet understanding. "Will I ever learn to be patient like you?"

Ignoring my question, Paula posed a couple of her own. "What if Mr. Wunderbar comes along and you fall in love? Would you want to get married and raise a family?"

"Boys? Marriage? Children?" Emphatically, I shook my head. "Not me!" Besides, few fellows my age or older returned from the war, except..." I thought of the duffel bags of dirty laundry I'd washed and ironed—the men wearing the khaki-colored and olive green uniforms.

"A lot of girls are marrying members of the occupational forces," said Paula. "Isn't your friend, Anni?"

"She's three years older than I."

"Someday you'll be nineteen."

"I want a career."

"You can have both."

I thought about Andy, the Private First Class who'd asked me for a date—but I had declined. He said he'd call again.

What if he does? Has the past prepared me for what lies ahead? Marriage? Emigration? Would my family approve of my marrying a foreigner?

Grandpa had said, "Girl, you got courage."

The phone rang.

"Jahn and Company," I answered.

"Hello? Anneliese?"

It was Andy's voice.

THE END

FAMILY PHOTOGRAPHS

Franz Rester (Opa) & Luise Eisenkramer (Oma)
Wedding Picture
14 July 1906

Lina Pflug
Born 17 September 1910 Heilbronn, Germany
Died 20 November 1981 Frankfurt, Germany

Hedwig Link
Born 11 November 1906 Heilbronn, Germany
Died 27 February 2004 Heilbronn, Germany

Luise Rester (Oma)
Born 26 July 1884 Heilbronn, Germany
Died December 1950 Heilbronn, Germany

Elsa Rau
Born 12 January 1914 Lauffen, Germany
Died 24 December 1991 Mannheim, Germany

Erika Munz
Born 14 January 1920 Heilbronn, Germany
Died late 19th Century Heilbronn, Germany

Photo taken about 1940

Franz born 1908 in Heilbronn, Germany. The only son born to Oma & Opa. He is listed as (MIA) Missing in Action in Russia during WWII. He was drafted into the Army and served as an interpreter for Germany in Russia as he spoke Russian. His body was never found.

Picture taken about 1941.

(Mama) Luise Maria Hoehn
She became a letter carrier in Frankfurt, Germany in 1939.

Albert & Lina Duerr
Albert—Army Medic Private First Class

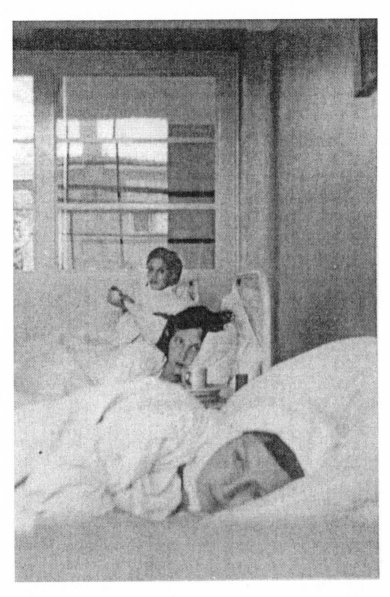

Anneliese
(holding bowl)
Recovering from Typhoid Fever

Left—Summer 1943 Salzburg, Austria Hospital
Right—Mama (middle of photo) visiting Aneliese at hospital

18 June 1960
Tante Paula on left visiting Walter in Halle Germany

Cousin Heinz Weller
Born 10 October 1927 Heilbronn, Germany
Perished 4 December 1944 Heilbronn, Germany in bomb attack.
His body was never found.

Walter Erich Hoehn
Born 8 October 1932 Frankfurt, Germany
Now living in Halle, Germany

"My first Day of School"
(about 1938)

Frankfurt, Germany—A City in Ruins—1945

Left—Cousin Sonja Weller
Born 11 July 1930 Heilbronn, Germany
Immgrated to Anaheim, CA in 1964

Right—Cousin Ursula Rau
Born 18 December 1938 Heilbronn, Germany
Now living in Mannheim, Germany

Oma & Opa's Duplex Home in Heilbronn-Boeckingen, Germany

Anneliese and Mother on Balcony of Apartment on Gleimstreet in Frankfurt. Destroyed buildings in background. About 1946